A complete program for teaching
and self-study

and
GM Lev Alburt,
two-time U.S. Champion

By Roman Pelts

COMPREHENSIVE
CHESS
COURSE

Volumes I & II

(How to teach chess to beginning
and intermediate players)

The Rules of Play
12 Lessons For The Beginning Chessplayer

Level One
of
A Comprehensive Program of Chess Training
From Beginner to Master

by
Roman Pelts
and
GM Lev Alburt, U.S. Champion

Publishing House "Universitetskoye" BSSR
State Press Committee
Masherov avenue 11
Minsk 220048
BSSR

Minsk Order of Red Labour Banner Printing House
MIPE named after Ya. Kolas
Krasnaya 23
Minsk 220005
BSSR

Ordered by the Publishing House "Effect", USA

CONTENTS

ACKNOWLEDGEMENTS

I would like to thank my wife for her help in translating the first volume and for the many hours she spent on the endless small tasks necessary to the production of the books. I would also like to thank Jonathan Berry and Mohan for translating the books and Gordon Howe for proofreading.

Roman Pelts
Toronto
May, 1986

I am very grateful to Faneuil Adams, Dewain Barber, Svetozar Jovanovic, Bruce Pandolfini and all others who helped me in my work on the second edition. The time has come to recognize chess as an excellent tool for education.

Lev Alburt
New York
October 1987

Foreword

This book is primarily intended to serve as a manual for those teaching chess in schools, colleges, universities, and other educational institutions, as well as in chess clubs. However, it can also be used as a textbook for individual study.

Although the lessons can be used by anyone over the age of six who wants to learn chess, they have been particularly designed for children aged 8 to 12. In exceptional cases they can be used to teach 5-year-olds as well. No prior knowledge of the game is presupposed. Children will require three months to complete the beginners' course of twelve lessons, while adults will need only two months. By the end of the first month of study (after five lessons) the student will be acquainted with the moves of all the pieces and will know what is meant by checkmating the opponent.

A chess class should preferably have no more than 10 to 15 students, and lessons should be held once a week. A lesson normally lasts 90 minutes, but since it is difficult for children under ten to concentrate for so long, lessons for them should last only one hour. By the same token, lessons for adults may be extended to two hours. In any case, the total time of a lesson should be split evenly between the theoretical (1–4, below) and practical(5, below) parts.

Recommended Lesson Plan

1. Checking the homework (if necessary)
2. Revision of previously studied material

(Steps 1 and 2 together should not take more than 10-15 minutes.)

3. Introduction of new material
4. Assigning homework for the next lesson

(Steps 3 and 4 together should take 30-35 minutes.)

5. Playing practice (games) — 45 minutes.

Introduction

Chess, one of the oldest games still extant, has been fascinating and challenging people for some 1500 years. At the same time, this game of thought, fantasy and planning remains, in spite of its hoary age, eminently suited to the needs of modern man.

The benefits which children in particular derive from chess can hardly be overestimated. Children who start learning chess between the ages of 8 and 10 show great improvement in mathematics, in physics, and in the ability to do independent research, as regular chess training develops a person's powers of concentration and ability to think logically, as well as strengthening his will-power.

Many people want to learn to play chess but do not know how to go about it in the right way. Some try to learn on their own but often meet with failure. Teaching chess to others is even harder. Even professional chessplayers often lack the teaching ability to teach their own children chess, and instead send them to experienced chess coaches for training.

The majority of parents do not have such an alternative, and therefore try instead to teach their children with the help of chess books. Although many chess books for children are available nowadays, some of them unfortunately do not take into account modern scientific methods of chess instruction.

We have divided the progression from beginner to master into many levels. In order to progress from one level to the next, a player must acquire a certain amount of theoretical knowledge and practice. The exact amount of knowledge that he needs is determined by his level. If he gets too much knowledge for his particular level, he will not benefit by it, and might even be harmed by it.

Thus, at each level the student should study the various aspects of the game in a manner appropriate to that level. For example, the openings are studied in all the levels, but in a progressively more thorough and profound manner.

The lessons and methodological instructions given in this book are self-contained, so that the coach can work through the whole program with his students without any additional literature. At the same time, the coach has plenty of room to exercise his creativity — depending on the age of his students, he can if necessary, add or remove material, providing that he does not contravene the fundamental principles set forth in the methodological instructions. For example, the coach may decide to use in each lesson only two problems out of the many provided. Adults and older children may use these lessons to study chess on their own.

A chess coach has to fulfill two aims: on the one hand, teaching children to play chess correctly and to think logically and self-critically; and on the other hand, instilling in them an appreciation of the beauty of chess ideas and variations, so that they enjoy playing the game. It is very important to kindle a real interest in chess in the very first lessons. Children usually find their first chess lesson the most difficult, and will understand the rules of play faster and more easily if their parents help them at home. By our joint efforts, we can initiate your children into the game of chess, and they will spend many happy hours in the future exploring its mysteries.

For Teachers: Methods of Training

The methodology of teaching chess is based on the rules and principles of teaching methodology in general. It has the same goals — to educate the students, to develop their abilities, and to impart correct habits to them. Its means are also the same — proceeding from the simple to the complex, maintaining a constant unity of theory and practice, and assuring a sound relationship between a teacher and his pupils.

The present chess program is based on a method whereby certain problems are repeatedly presented to the student over some period of time. Each time, however, the problems, while retaining their previous fundamental characteristics, are made more complicated by the addition of something new. For example, the idea of "double attack" is found both in beginners' games and in the games of world champions. It is something that is used by chessplayers of all levels. While, however, intermediate level introduces the student to simple double attacks, expert level shows how the double attack can serve as the basis of multi-move combinations. New themes are thus introduced on the basis of already studied material, thereby not only broadening the student's knowledge but also helping him to better assimilate previously learned material.

Every new item must be explained and demonstrated before the children are given any homework on it. The division of material be-

tween homework and classwork is completely up to the coach. As children are attracted to chess primarily as a game, it is very important to switch over in good time from the theoretical to the practical part of the lesson.

The time taken to complete the twelve lessons of Level I (Beginners) is up to the teacher. The average time for the course ranges from three to four months.

The rules of the game are of course very important, but there should be enough time set aside in each lesson for the students to play games and apply the rules in practice. The coach should make sure that the students have understood well the material that they have been taught before he goes on to the next problem, rule, or item. Not a single lesson should be skipped. Progress can only be made by gradually studying all the lessons, which must be explained to the children. Only when the students have understood a given item will they be able to properly apply it in their games.

A chess lesson can last until the children begin to show signs of weariness. Quality of learning is more important than quantity. Children should not be encouraged to play quick games. They should think over every move thoroughly. It is advisable for beginners to play often and a lot (children can practice with their schoolmates, friends, parents and even with a computer).

By the end of the ninth lesson, the children will know the main rules of chess and will be able to play. They should always follow the rules and never take their moves back. The "touch-move" rule should always be observed.

Formal tournament rules such as the "50-move rule" or the "triple repetition of position" rule are best not introduced at Level I. The Level I program is designed to get a beginner playing chess as soon as possible and to give him the knowledge necessary to proceed to Level II.

It is very important for a chess coach to have a good working style. In particular, he should be efficient and calm, and treat his students evenly and kindly. If some point in a lesson requires him to give a long explanation, he should lighten it by interjecting a joke or some interesting anecdote from the history of chess. It is sometimes useful to distract the children's attention during a lesson, and every chessplayer should know something of the history of chess anyway. The anecdotes should not be irrelevant but should be connected in some way with the theme of the lesson.

In short, every lesson should be interesting and easy to understand, and should not contain more material than the students can absorb in one session. The material should be intelligible to the students, but not too easy, or else it might cause them to lose interest. All material should be presented in such a way as to stimulate the students to try their best to master it.

You will find weak, average and strong players in every group. The coach should plan his lessons for the above-average students, and the weak students will try to catch up. For example, if there are ten students in a group, the coach should aim his explanation of new material at the third-strongest, and enlist the two strongest to assist him in his explanation. The strongest students can be given special Level I tests.

If any students have questions that were not cleared up during the theoretical part of the lesson, the coach can explain them to the students concerned individually during the practical part of the lesson.

On the other hand, it is not advisable to run ahead of the program. Only an individual approach will enable the coach to ascertain each student's chess abilities. If a coach thinks that a player in a group is strong enough to be in Level II, he should give the student a Level I test and transfer him to a Level II group, but only if he passes the test. The Level I tests can also be given to newcomers to find out how they play and to what group or level they should be assigned.

The Chess Board

All beginning chessplayers should start by studying and memorizing the chessboard. Knowing the board by heart has a very great importance. A beginner must learn to see all the squares of the chessboard in his mind. A whole series of exercises has been devised to help the student in this task. Depending on the individual abilities of a given student, three to ten hours should be spent on learning the chessboard. The student's knowledge of the chessboard should be perfect and visualising the board should become an automatic habit. The coach should set aside a few minutes of every lesson at the Level I stage for study of the chessboard. A perfect knowledge of the chessboard is to a chessplayer the same as knowing the multiplication tables is to a mathematician. Gradually, as the lessons progress, the chessboard will contain more and more pawns and pieces, and the player will acquire the very important ability to mentally visualize (during a game) positions that could occur on the board a few moves ahead.

All problems and examples, except the simplest ones, must be demonstrated on a chessboard to the students, especially when the students are in the first stages of studying chess. This will help the students to remember the chessboard better. A chessboard is a visual aid for beginning students. To save space, we usually show only a part (quarter) of the chessboard in the lessons. The edges of the board are shown only when necessary. This helps students to memorize typical chess positions better.

* * *

Level I teaches the beginner the simplest relationships between the various chessmen. As far as the opening is concerned, it is enough in Level I to teach the students the main principles governing the mobilization of the forces, paying special attention to the rapid development of Knights and Bishops, to castling, to the problem of the center and to the disadvantages of bringing the Queen out early or pushing the flank pawns.

Beginners at Level I acquire a mastery of the algebraic system of notation, which is the system used in the succeeding levels of the program. In the future, however, students will also be introduced to the descriptive notation that is prevalent among the majority of players in English-speaking countries, particularly the U.S.A. and the United Kingdom.

The algebraic system has some important advantages over the descriptive. It is more concise, helps to simplify the process of learning, and is internationally understood. In 1980 it became the only system of notation officially recognized by the International Chess Federation (FIDE). Experience has shown that it does not cause any difficulties, and even eight-year-old children can use it by the end of Level I. Using chessboards with the ranks and files marked with the appropriate letters and numbers will help students to master the notation system more rapidly.

Only intensive and correctly planned work by the coach can ensure that the students acquire a sound mastery of the course material. His work with the students should include practical lessons, homework assignments, special control questions, tests, problem solving, and simultaneous exhibitions. The levels that follow include additional means for the review of studied material.

Systematic checking of the student's knowledge is of the utmost importance in teaching chess, since it helps to connect theory with practice. It should always be done promptly, before the students have started to forget the material. The manual provides the coach with enough questions and tests to do this, and he can use them according to his judgement. Good students should be asked difficult questions and poorer students should be asked easier ones. In either case the coach must make sure that the student is able to answer the questions correctly. Questions help to activate the student's learning process. If a student is able to answer questions or solve a problem on the material that he has studied, he acquires confidence, an important asset.

It is also very important to assign children to their proper groups and find them suitable partners. A relatively strong player should not be paired with a weak one because the latter will soon lose interest. This problem is particularly serious in Level I. In higher levels, when the children have acquired a certain understanding and love of the game, they treat their losses differently and do not get discouraged so easily. At the start of Level I, however, it is very important to separate absolute beginners from those who already play a little.

It is impossible to examine in their entirety all the games played during a lesson. The coach must select the most typical mistakes from the games and explain how to avoid them. He can also point out games in which students have skilfully applied material that they have studied. Some time should be devoted to teaching the sudents how to write down the moves of their games. That will enable them to conduct "post-mortems" of a game once it has been finished, i.e., analyze the game in detail with other players.

The coach must encourage and help the students in their study of chess. Many weak player become strong when they study hard and conversely, strong players deteriorate if they do not study. In order to improve, a person must study seriously and every day. The strongest chess players work very hard on chess every day. There are many strong players in the world, and all of them want to win. The ones who succeed are those who systematically work to perfect their knowledge and improve their game.

Tests

The last lesson of Level I is for testing the students. 120 questions covering the entire course have been distributed among 20 tests. These tests are displayed on a table, and each student takes one of them. A student is given 60 minutes to answer the questions in his test. If he fails to answer more than three questions, he can be allowed to try another test. The coach decides who is to be promoted to Level II.

There should be an interval of a few months between Level I and Level II. This interval should be used for practice games, training, and participating in tournaments, simultaneous exhibitions and problem-solving contests (sometimes with prizes in the form of chess books). The contest can be conducted in the following way. A certain chess position is displayed on the demonstration board and students are allowed three to five minutes to give the correct solution. Three points are awarded for a correct answer, and one point is subtracted for a wrong answer. This makes the children think before answering. Such a contest usually consists of three to six problems, and the person who accumulates the greatest number of points is declared the winner.

Each student should have a copy of the textbook. This will make the teacher's task easier and save time. If for some reason this is not possible, the teacher should run off copies of the homework assignment for the next lesson and distribute them to the students at the end of the class. The answers should be included. If in doing the homework a student finds that after spending five to ten minutes on a particular question he is still unable to solve it, he can then look at the answer and try to understand it.

* * *

It is not necessary to go over the homework at the start of the next class unless a student has a question or unless the teacher feels that one of the problems is particularly interesting. In that case the teacher should have one of the students who solved the problem correctly explain the solution to the class on the demonstration board. A student need not do an entire homework assignment in one day. In fact, it is better if he distributes the work over a couple of days. Homework is important since it helps to fix the material learned in the student's mind.

The practical part of the lessons constitutes a major component of the course and it too serves the same purpose as homework. The coach's aim at this level is to eliminate or minimize the occurence of one-move blunders. Beginners react very poorly to their opponent's threats. When their turn to move comes, they quickly make some move that they had planned beforehand, ignoring the fact that the opponent's move has changed the position on the board. As a result, beginners' games abound in one-move losses of pieces and pawns and, furthermore, the numerically superior side sometimes falls into an elementary mate.

Careless play and hasty moves aimed only at capturing the opponent's pieces can allow the opponent to save himself unexpectedly by stalemate or perpetual check. The beginner's tendency toward hasty play must be combatted.

A serious problem is how to teach children not to be afraid of losing. Some children stop playing chess because of this fear. It should be explained to the children that each game lost brings improvement in the future if the mistake (the reason for the loss) is found and understood. All chessplayers always analyze their lost games, and this helps them to play better in the future.

Children who have learned the rules of the game well and have acquired some practical experience should be encouraged to participate in tournaments. All the children should be encouraged to play chess (and, if they have mastered the rules, to participate in tournaments) even during their summer holidays.

The lessons should take place in a hall or large, well-lit room equipped with a large demonstration board and ten to fifteen chess sets and boards laid out on tables. During the theoretical part of the lesson a separate set and board should be available for each student. It is desirable for the pieces to be large, plastic, and of simple design. The boards should be spacious, so that the pieces seem much smaller than the squares.

Level I can be taught by any school teacher, provided that he plays chess better than his pupils and has good teaching skills.

If a coach succeeds in infusing children with a love for chess, they will truly enjoy the game and with it, the beauty of human intellect, the beauty of chess.

Lesson One

Starting Position. How Pawns Move and Capture.

Chess is a very ancient game that first appeared in India around the fourth or fifth century A.D. Although there are many legends about the origin of chess, nobody really knows who invented the game.

Chess is an intellectual competition between two players.

It is played on a square board divided into 64 equal squares that are alternately light and dark. Each player always has a light corner square on his right. Remember: "Light on the Right".

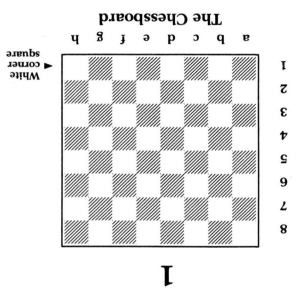

The Chessboard

► White corner square

1

There are 32 chessmen, 16 White and 16 Black. One of the players has the White men and the other the Black men. Diagram 2 shows how the men are set up at the start of a game. In all chess diagrams the White side is shown as moving up the board and the Black side as moving down the board.

Diagram 2 shows the starting position of the men and Diagrams 5–10 show how to set the men up one by one. The player with the White men is called "White," and the player with the Black men is called "Black."

The half of the board on which the White men stand is called the "White Side," and the half with the Black men on it is called the

Name	White	Black	Symbols
King	1	1	K or ♔ ♚
Queen	1	1	Q or ♕ ♛
Rook	2	2	R or ♖ ♜
Bishop	2	2	B or ♗ ♝
Knight	2	2	N or ♘ ♞
pawn	8	8	P or ♙ ♟

A chessman (or man) means either a pawn or a piece. A pawn is never called a piece. Thus each side at the start of a game has eight pawns and eight pieces. The chart below shows how many of each type of piece each player has, and the symbols usually used to represent the pieces in diagrams.

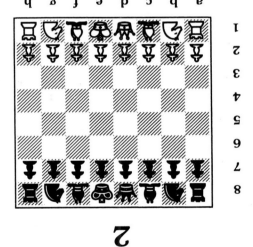

2

"Black Side." This is shown in Diagram 3, where an imaginary horizontal line separates the White Side from the Black Side.

3

If instead a line were drawn vertically down the middle of the board both the Queens would appear on one side of the board while both the Kings would be on the other side. That half of the board containing both Queens is called the "Queenside" and the other half, containing both the Kings, is known as the "Kingside." White's Kingside is always on his right and Black's Kingside is always on his left. This is never changed, no matter where the Kings and Queens move on the board during the game See Diagram 4.

4

Each player moves in turn, with White starting. Two consecutive moves by the same player are prohibited by the rules of play. Nor can a player pass his turn. A move is a transfer of a man from the square on which it is, to another square to which it is permitted by the rules to move.

If an enemy man is on the square to which a move is made, it is captured and removed from the board, and it cannot take part in the game any more. Thus, the number of men in a game of chess can only decrease and never increase. Two men cannot simultaneously occupy the same square, and a player can never capture one of his own men. Each type of chessman has its own way of moving, and all men of the same type move in the same way.

The aim of the game is to capture the opponent's King. The person who succeeds in doing this first is the winner. If neither player succeeds in winning, the game ends in a draw.

Since it is hard to learn the moves of all the different chessmen at one go, we'll take it step by step. Today you will learn the pawn's move and how to play a game using only pawns.

How to Set up Pieces on the Board
Diagrams 5–10

5

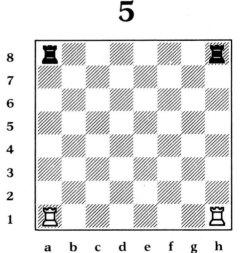

The Rooks start on the corner squares.

6

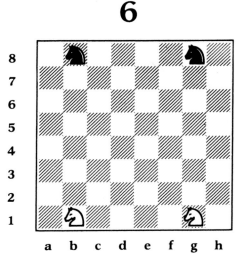

Next to the Rooks go the Knights.

7

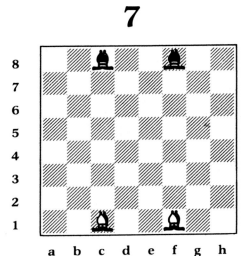

The Bishops go next to the Knights.

8

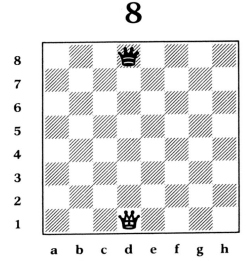

The Queen always starts on a square of her own color.

9

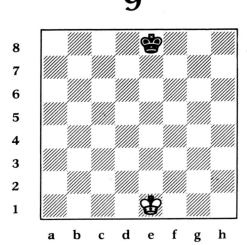

The Kings take the remaining squares White King on dark square, Black King on light.

10

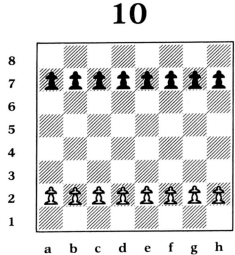

Each side's eight pawns are placed on the row of squares in front of their pieces.

How the Pawn Moves and Captures

Pawns are the smallest of the chessmen. They are valued by experts, but often scorned by beginners. The White pawns start the game on the second rank and move forward, while the Black pawns start the game on the seventh rank and move in the opposite direction, towards the White pawns.

Pawns of the same color all look alike. If we want to identify one of them in particular, we use the name of the piece that it stood in front of in the starting position: the Queen's Rook pawn and the King's Rook pawn, the Queen's

Knight pawn and the King's Knight pawn, the Queen's Bishop pawn and the King's Bishop pawn, the Queen's pawn and the King's pawn.

The pawn is the only chessman that cannot move backwards. Nor can it jump over other men. The pawn moves only forward, one square at a time along the file on which it stands. Every pawn, no matter how far the game has progressed, has a choice on its first move (and only on its first move) of moving forward either one or two squares.

12

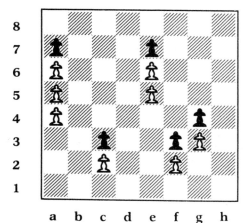

None of the pawns can move.

11

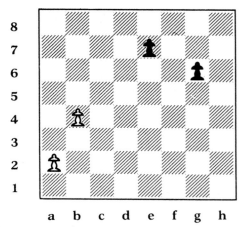

The pawns have moved from White's and Black's sides. The White pawn moved two squares forward, the Black pawn moved one square forward.

In Diagram 11, the White Queen's Knight pawn has moved two squares forward on its first move. This double move is optional. Thus, the Black King's Knight pawn has moved only one square forward on its first move. From now on, these two pawns are allowed to move ahead only one square at a time. On the Queen's Rook file and the King file we can see the move-by-move progress of a pawn from its starting position to the other end of the board.

If a man (either its own or the enemy's) is on the square immediately in front of a pawn, the pawn is blocked and cannot advance. See Diagram 12.

Capturing With the Pawn

The pawn, although it moves straight ahead, captures in a different way. Namely, it captures one square diagonally forward. It cannot capture backwards. Each quarter of Diagram 13 shows an example of a pawn attacking enemy pieces. For example, in 13-I, the White pawn can capture the Black Rook or the Black Knight, but not the Black Bishop. The pawn cannot advance until the Black Bishop gets out of its way. The pawn attacks two squares diagonally ahead of it (one on either side) unless it is a Rook pawn, when it attacks only one square. A capture is carried out in the following way: the pawn moves onto the square occupied by the enemy man, which is removed from the board. Diagrams 13 and 14 show the different ways in which a pawn can capture.

13

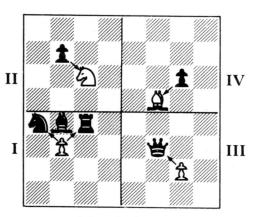

pawn position before capturing

14

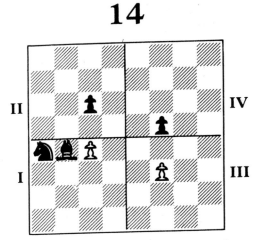

pawn position after capturing

15

I. The White pawn has four possible moves.

II. Each of the four pawns can make a capture, but none of them can advance.

III. Black is threatening to take off White's pawn.

IV. Each pawn can either move forward or capture the opposing pawn.

A pawn which has moved onto a new file by capturing an enemy man advances along this new file even if there is already a pawn of the same color on that file.

In Diagram 12, none of the pawns can move. The middle King pawn could only have got there by capturing. The White King pawns are said to be "doubled." It is quite unusual to have three pawns of the same color on one file, such as the "tripled" pawns on the Rook file in Diagram 12.

Now look at Diagram 16. How many different moves can the White pawns make in all? How many can the Black pawns make in all?

16

How many different moves can the White and Black pawns make?

Answer: The White pawns can make a total of ten different moves. The Black pawns can also make a total of ten moves.

Now you are ready to play!

The Pawn Game

Here are the rules:

1. Choosing for colors. One of the players hides a Black pawn in one fist and a White pawn in the other. He then holds out both fists in front of him and the opponent selects one of them. The opponent will play Black if the fist has a Black pawn, and he will play White if it contains a White pawn. After the first game, the players switch colors every game.

2. The Starting Position. The starting position should be as shown in Diagram 17.

17

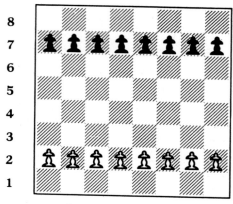

3. You win the game:
a) if your opponent gives up; or
b) if you are the first to capture all your opponent's pawns; or
c) if you are the first to reach the last rank (i.e., your opponent's first rank) with one of your pawns; or
d) if it is your opponent's turn to move but all his pawns are blocked and do not have any moves, while you yourself can make at least one move.

The game is a draw (i.e., a tied game):
a) if the two players agree to call it a draw; or
b) if **both** sides' pawns are blocked up so that **neither** side can make any moves.

Before you start, remember one very important rule: if you touch one of your own men when it is your turn to move, you must move it. If you touch one of your opponent's men, you must capture it if you can. And of course once you make a move, you cannot change it. Get into the habit of playing Touch-Move! First think out your move carefully, and then play it firmly and without hesitation.

HOMEWORK

Write down your answers in the space below.

1. Learn the names and symbols of all the men.

_____

_____

_____

2. Know how to set up the pawns and pieces in the starting position.

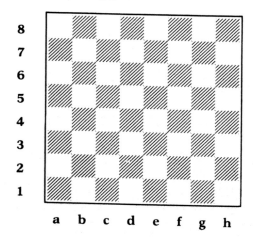

3. Where are the Knights placed in the initial position (between which pieces)?

_____

_____

_____

4. Where are the Bishops placed in the initial position?

_____

_____

_____

5. In the initial position, which men are placed on the corner squares?

_____

_____

_____

6. What color is the right-hand corner square nearest a player?

_____

_____

_____

7. What is the least number of moves in which a pawn starting from its initial position can reach the other end of the board?

_____

_____

_____

8. How many different pawn moves does White have in the starting position?

_____

_____

_____

and a Knight and the other between the King and a Knight (see Diagram 7).

5. The Rooks occupy the corner squares (see Diagram 5).

6. A player's lower right-hand corner square is always a light square. Remember: "light on the right!"

7. A pawn needs five moves from its original square to reach the other end of the board.

8. White has sixteen pawn moves (there are eight pawns, and each can advance either one or two squares.)

HOMEWORK ANSWERS

1. King = K; Queen = Q; Rook = R; Bishop = B; Knight = N; Pawn = P.

2.

a   b   c   d   e   f   g   h

3. Each Knight is placed between a Rook and a Bishop (see Diagram 6).

4. One Bishop stands between the Queen

Lesson Two

Chess Notation

Review Questions:
1. Who moves first in a chess game?
2. What color is the left-hand corner square nearest a player?
3. How many pawns and pieces does White have in the starting position?
4. How many pawns does Black have in the initial position?
5. How many Knights does White have at the beginning of a game?

(Answers below)

Answers to Review Questions
1. White always makes the first move of a game.
2. Dark.
3. White has eight pieces and eight pawns in the starting position.
4. Eight pawns.
5. Two.

Chess Notation

The richness of chess today owes much to the many valuable contributions and ideas of our ancestors. One of the most interesting ideas was that of chess notation. The first chess book was written in Persia in 600 A.D.!

Today, nearly all countries accept the simple and convenient algebraic system of designating squares on the chessboard. In this system, each square on the board has a name which consists of one of the letters from **a** to **h** followed by a number from **1** to **8**. Diagrams 18 and 19 show all the squares and their names. Thus, the corner squares which the White Rooks always occupy in the initial position are **a1** and **h1**, while **a8** and **h8** indicate the location of the Black Rooks.

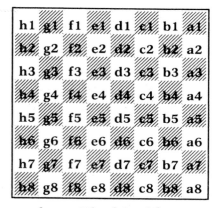

18

8	a8	b8	c8	d8	e8	f8	g8	h8
7	a7	b7	c7	d7	e7	f7	g7	h7
6	a6	b6	c6	d6	e6	f6	g6	h6
5	a5	b5	c5	d5	e5	f5	g5	h5
4	a4	b4	c4	d4	e4	f4	g4	h4
3	a3	b3	c3	d3	e3	f3	g3	h3
2	a2	b2	c2	d2	e2	f2	g2	h2
1	a1	b1	c1	d1	e1	f1	g1	h1

a   b   c   d   e   f   g   h

from White's side

19

h1	g1	f1	e1	d1	c1	b1	a1
h2	g2	f2	e2	d2	c2	b2	a2
h3	g3	f3	e3	d3	c3	b3	a3
h4	g4	f4	e4	d4	c4	b4	a4
h5	g5	f5	e5	d5	c5	b5	a5
h6	g6	f6	e6	d6	c6	b6	a6
h7	g7	f7	e7	d7	c7	b7	a7
h8	g8	f8	e8	d8	c8	b8	a8

from Black's side

Each vertical column of eight squares is called a "file." The files are designated by the first eight letters of the alphabet, a, b, c, d, e, f, g, and h, starting from the left on White's side. They are marked out in Diagram 20.

8

20

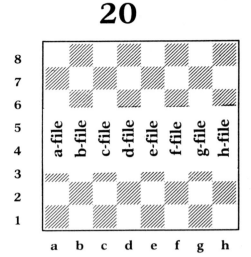

Each row of eight squares running across the board is called a "**rank**." They are designated by the numbers 1, 2, 3, 4, 5, 6, 7, and 8, starting from White's side. The ranks have been marked out in Diagram 21. Thus, in the initial position White's men are placed on the first and second ranks while Black's men are placed on the seventh and eighth ranks.

21

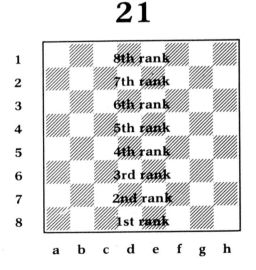

The board can also be divided into twenty-six diagonals varying in length from two to eight squares.

22

While any rank or file contains both light squares and dark squares, the squares making up any given diagonal are all of the same color, either light or dark. This can be seen in Diagram 23.

23

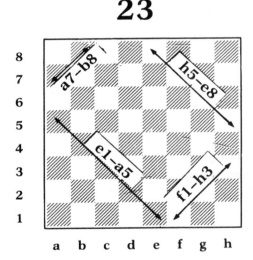

Diagonals are designated by the names of their end squares, for example the a1-h8 and the h1-a8 diagonals. These two diagonals, the only ones consisting of eight squares, are often called the long diagonals. They have been marked in Diagram 22 by the word
DIAGONAL
written across them. Diagonals which consist only of light squares, e.g. h5-e8 and f1-h3, are called light-square diagonals, while diagonals which consist only of dark squares, e.g. a7-b8 and e1-a5, are called dark-square diagonals. These diagonals are marked out in Diagram 23.

How To Write Down A Move

A move is playing a man from one square to another. The following conventional order is used in writing down a move:

1. Piece symbol
2. Square of departure
3. - (moves to) or x (captures on)
4. Square of arrival

You already know the symbols of all the chessmen (see Lesson 1). If there is no prefixing piece symbol, that means that the move is made by a pawn.

Here is an example: If the first move is made by the White pawn in front of the King, the pawn starts its move on e2 and finishes it on e4. The move should therefore be recorded as **1. e2-e4.** If Black replied to this move by pushing the pawn in front of his Queen two squares forward, that move would be written as **1. ... d7-d5** (the three dots mean that the move is made by Black. They are only used when writing Black's move alone, without White's move in front of it). If White on his second move captured the Black pawn on d5 with his pawn on e4, that would be written as **2. e4xd5.**

Pawn Promotion

Because of its limited mobility, a pawn is much weaker than any of the other men. However, it has a compensating quality: when it reaches the other end of the board, it can be changed into any piece of its own color, except the King. No other piece can be changed into anything else, no matter what square it reaches. A pawn moves very slowly, but if it gets to the opposite end of the board it can change into a powerful Queen! Diagram 24 shows how White pawns move towards the eighth rank, and in Diagram 25 you can see the progress of the Black pawns towards the first rank.

24

25

When a player's pawn reaches the last rank (eighth rank for White pawns and first rank for Black pawns), he can promote it to any piece of the same color. That is, he can choose between promoting a pawn to a Queen (the usual choice), a Rook, a Bishop, or a Knight. It doesn't matter if there is a Queen of the same color on the board already: you may have another one. When promoting a pawn to a Queen, chessplayers usually say, "I want a Queen," or just, "Queen!" It is possible for a player to have nine Queens; in practice, however, two should be enough. Similarly, the rules of the game allow a player to have ten Rooks, ten Bishops, or ten Knights, but there is no recorded instance of such cases ever occurring in a game of chess. If you cannot find an extra Queen, Rook, Bishop, or Knight in your set, use an upside-down Rook, spools of white or black thread, or some other suitable objects to represent the extra pieces.

Pawn promotion is compulsory. That is, a pawn reaching the last rank must be exchanged for a piece; it cannot remain a pawn. A pawn is promoted by removing the pawn from the board and placing the chosen piece on the promotion square.

The process of promoting or "Queening" a pawn is illustrated in Diagrams 26 and 27.

26

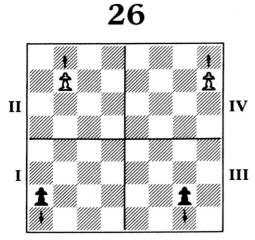

Promotion of a pawn: before the move.

27

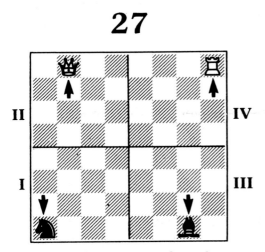

Promotion of a pawn: after the move.

The promotion square is sometimes called the "Queening square."

When a player has exchanged the pawn for a piece, his move is completed. Promotion of a pawn into any piece counts as one move. From his next move, the promoted piece (Queen, Rook, Bishop, or Knight) moves and captures in exactly the same way as a regular piece of that kind.

If a pawn has reached a square on the last rank by capturing an enemy piece on that square, the captured enemy piece is of course also removed from the board. See Diagrams 28 and 29.

28

Promotion by capture: How many different moves does the pawn have in each quarter?

29

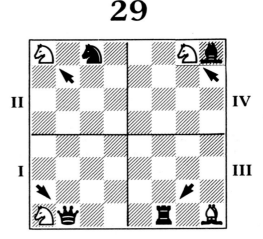

Promotion by capture: after the move.

When a pawn reaches the last rank, we must write down the symbol of the new piece after the usual notation of the move. In Diagrams 26-II and 27-II, we see White advancing his pawn from b7 to b8 and changing it to a Queen. This move is recorded as **b7-b8Q**. A pawn can also be changed into any piece if it reaches a square on the last rank by capturing an enemy piece on that square. The captured enemy piece is of course removed from the board. In Diagrams 28-II and 29-II you can see a White pawn on b7 capturing a Black Queen on a8 and becoming a Knight. This move is recorded as follows: **b7xa8N.**

It is clear that the possibility of promotion greatly increases the value of a pawn.

Now look at Diagram 28 and figure out how many different moves the pawn in each of the quarter diagrams can make.

Answers to Question about Diagram 28
In Quarter I the pawn has four different moves, since it can become four different pieces:

    1. a2 x b1Q
    1. a2 x b1R
    1. a2 x b1B
    1. a2 x b1N

In Quarter II the pawn has twelve different moves, in Quarter III it has twelve different moves, and in Quarter IV it has four different moves.

Recommendations

Do not try to memorize the diagrams, as they are only examples. Try rather to learn the ideas involved. You may never again come across the positions shown in the diagrams, but the ideas that they illustrate will repeat themselves many times in your games.

To understand the rest of the lessons properly, students must have a perfect knowledge of the designation of each square on the chessboard. See Diagrams 18 and 19. In practice, chessboards do not have the designations marked on them and every beginner should become capable as soon as possible of identifying the squares mentally. This is not so easy at first, especially for the Black player, since the squares are always numbered from White's side. In diagrams, White is always shown playing up the board and Black is shown playing down the board.

A useful device to help students memorize the board better is the well-known "Battleship Game," which is played as follows (See Diagrams 30 and 31). Two players each draw two chessboards. On one of them, the player marks the locations of his own ships. One square serves as a torpedo boat, two squares as a

cruiser, and three squares as a liner. This board is kept hidden from the opponent. On the other board, the player tries to search out his opponent's ships by "shooting" or "firing" at them. After each shot, the opponent has to say "hit" or "missed", and the player marks the square that he shot at as being either the location of an enemy ship or a blank spot, to remind him not to shoot at the same spot twice. The battle ends when one of the players has annihilated all his opponent's ships.

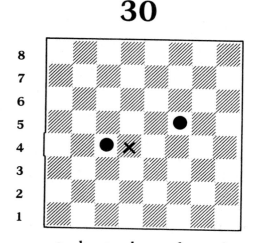

30

Battleship: attacking opponent's ships

31

Battleship: location of own ships

The above game will help students to memorize the board in a very short time. Having a perfect knowledge of the chessboard not only helps a player to memorize positions better, but also improves his game: players who know the chessboard well rarely make mistakes. So, anyone who wants to develop his chessplaying skills should memorize the chessboard as soon as possible.

HOMEWORK
I. Diagrams 32 – 33
(Answers at the end)

32

	a	b	c	d	e	f	g	h
8	7	24	53	36	5	22	51	34
7	54	37	6	23	52	35	4	21
6	25	8	55	38	45	12	33	50
5	58	59	46	13	48	57	20	3
4	9	26	15	56	11	44	49	32
3	60	39	10	47	14	31	2	19
2	27	16	41	62	29	18	43	64
1	40	61	28	17	42	63	30	1

Name the squares in their numeric order. Write your answer:

_____

_____

_____

33

Name the squares on which the various White and Black men stand in the starting position. Write your answer:

Write your answer:

_____

_____

_____

II. Exercises
Write your answers in the spaces below.

1. Place the board as if you are White. Find the following squares: f7, a2, g3, e4, b5, and h6. What color are they? Write L for light or D for dark.

_____

_____

_____

2. Now place the board as if you are Black, and find these squares: g1, d3, c7, b1, h4, and b7. What color are they? Write L for light or D for dark.

_____

_____

_____

3. Which square is the intersection of:
the a1-h8 diagonal and the e-file?
the f1-a6 diagonal and the 5th
rank?

_____

_____

_____

4. Suppose you're playing Black.
Name the square where the second
row of squares (counting from your
side of the board) crosses the second file (counting from your left).

_____

_____

_____

5. Place eight pawns (four of each col-
or) on the board in such a way that
none of them can make a move or a
capture.

_____

_____

_____

6. Place the same eight pawns on the
board in such a way that each side
has six different possible captures.

_____

_____

_____

7. Learn to play the "Battleship
Game" (see Recommendations
and Diagrams 30 and 31).

Homework Answers
I. Diagrams 32-33

D-32 h1, g3, h5, g7, e8, c7, a8, b6, a4, c3,
e4, f6, d5, e3, c4, b2, d1, f2, h3, g5, h7, f8,
d7, b8, a6, b4, a2, c1, e2, g1, f3, h4, g6, h8,
f7, d8, b7, a5, b3, a1, c2, e1, g2, f4, e6, c5,
d3, e5, g4, h6, g8, e7, c8, a7, c6, d4, f5, d6,
b5, a3, b1, d2, f1, h2.

D-33
White: a1, a2, b1, b2, c1, c2, d1, d2, e1, e2,
f1, f2, g1, g2, h1, h2.

Black: a7, a8, b7, b8, c7, c8, d7, d8, e7, e8,
f7, f8, g7, g8, h7, h8.

II. Exercises

1. L, L, D, L, L, D.
2. D, L, D, L, D, L.
3. The a1-h8 diagonal crosses the
   e-file at e5; the f1-a6 diagonal
   crosses the fifth rank at b5.
4. g7.
5. White: a2, c2, e2, h2
   Black: a3, c3, e3, h3.
6. White: b4, c4, d4, e4.
   Black: b5, c5, d5, e5.

Lesson Three

How the Rook and Bishop Move and Capture

Check the homework of Lesson 2 (if necessary).

Review Questions:
1. Name the squares on which the White Bishops, Black Knights, Black Queen, and White King are located in the starting position.
2. How many Queens and Rooks are there on the board in the starting position?
3. Without looking at the board, name:
   (a) the diagonals that intersect at the d3 square;
   (b) the square where the b1-h7 and h5-e8 diagonals intersect;
   (c) the square where the second rank crosses the a1-h8 diagonal.
4. Suppose that you are playing Black. Name the square in the third row from you on the second file from the left.
5. Construct a position where a White pawn has a choice of four different moves.
6. Is it possible for White's a-pawn (the Queen's Rook Pawn) to wind up on the e-file? If so, how?

Answers to Review Questions:
1. At the start of the game, the White Bishops are on **c1** and **f1**, the Black Knights are on **b8** and **g8**, the Black Queen is on the dark square **d8**, and the White King is on **e1**.
2. At the start of the game there are two Queens (one White and one Black) and four Rooks (two White and two Black).
3. (a) **b1-h7** and **f1-a6**.
   (b) **g6**
   (c) **b2**
4. **g6**

5. There are of course many such positions. Here is an example. White pawn on **e2** and Black pawns on **d3** and **f3**. White to play has four different moves with his pawn (the pawn can capture either of the two Black pawns or move one or two squares ahead).
6. The a-pawn can reach the e-file by capturing four times.

The Center

By "center" we mean the four central squares d4, e4, d5, and e5. See Diagram 34. The importance of the center in chess will become clear later on.

34

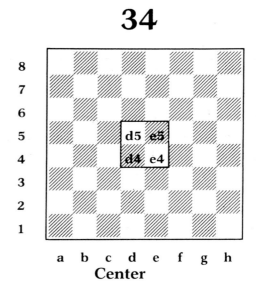

Center

How the Rook Moves and Captures

A Rook can move to any vacant square on the file or rank on which it stands, provided that no men of either color block the path. Diagrams 35 and 36 illustrate how it moves.

35

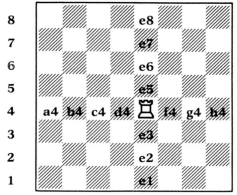

The Rook has 14 moves shown here.

36

The Rook has 6 moves shown here.

It is clear that the Rook enjoys great freedom of action, as it is able to cross the entire board in a single move. However, although it can move in any direction, in any given move it can travel only in one direction, i.e., it cannot change direction in the middle of a move. Thus, on an empty board, a Rook can reach any one of the 14 squares in a single move, see Diagram 35. It can reach any of the other squares in two moves, and can do so in two different ways.

Capturing is optional in chess. However, it is usually good to capture an enemy man since that will make the enemy's forces weaker than yours. As a result, his resistance will be weakened, and it will be much easier for you to win.

If a Rook moves to a square occupied by an enemy man, the latter is captured and re-

moved from the board at once. Diagrams 37–39 show how the Rook captures.

In Diagram 37, the Black Rook is attacking four White men. If it is Black's turn to play, he can capture any one of them.

37

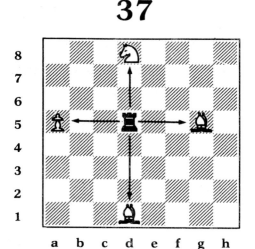

The Rook can capture the Bishop on d1 or g5, or Knight on d8, or pawn on a5.

Diagram 38 shows the resulting position if Black captures the White Bishop on g5, removing it from the board.

38

The Rook has captured the Bishop g5

In Diagram 39, the Black Rook is not attacking the White Bishop on a4, as there is a Black pawn in the way. Don't forget that the Rook cannot jump over men, whether its own or the opponent's. If the Black pawn in Diagram 39 is removed, then the Black Rook would be attacking the White Bishop on a4.

39

a b c d e f g h

The Black Rook can capture only the Bishop h4 or Knight, but not the pawn, Bishop a4, or Rook.

A man that attacks a square occupied by a friendly man (i.e., a man of its own color) is said to defend or protect it, since if an enemy man captures the friendly man, the defending man will in turn be able to capture the enemy man.

In Diagram 39, the Black Rook is attacking the White Knight, which is protected by the White Rook. If Black takes the Knight with his Rook, the White Rook can capture the Black Rook. Black would thus lose a Rook, and White would lose a Knight.

Diagram 40 shows some mini-positions that will help you to better understand the Rook, and also how chessmen move, attack, and defend each other in general.

40

Rooks move, attack, and defend each other.

In 40-I, each Rook defends his partner and attacks an enemy Rook. In this situation, neither side can win a piece for nothing.

In 40-II, each side has a choice of three captures, and the side which moves first can win a Rook by any of those captures. Such situations occur when the four Rooks occupy the same rank or file.

In 40-III, each Rook defends its partner of the same color, and none of the Rooks are attacked.

In 40-IV, none of the Rooks attack or defend any of the other Rooks.

If a man is captured and a similar man has been given up for it (a Bishop for a Bishop, a Rook for a Rook, etc.), there has been no loss to either side. This is known as a trade, or, more exactly, an even trade.

How the Bishop Moves and Captures

The Bishop always moves diagonally, along squares of the same color (Diagrams 41 and 42). It can move in any direction, but in any one move it can move in only one direction: i.e., it cannot change direction during a move. Each player has two Bishops at the start of a game, one standing on a light square and the other on a dark square. The Bishop which stands on a light square at the beginning of the game can never move to a dark square, and similarly, the Bishop on a dark square at the start of the game can never move to a light square. The Bishop that moves only on light squares is called the light-square Bishop and the one that moves only on dark squares is called the dark-square Bishop. A Bishop can move to any vacant square on either of the diagonals (Diagram 41) on which it stands, so long as there are no men of either color blocking the way (Diagram 42).

It is obvious that the Bishop has great mobility when there are no obstructions. It can cross the board in a single move. The Bishop controls 13 squares from a central square and 7 squares from a square on the edge.

41

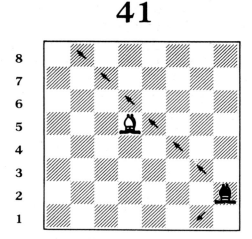

Bishop d5 has 13 moves, and Bishop h2 has 7 moves.

Since the Bishop can only move on squares of one color, enemy men on squares of the other color are immune to attack by it.

42

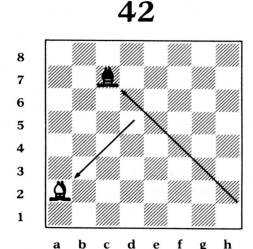

Light-square Bishop moved to a2, dark-square Bishop moved to c7.

If a Bishop moves to a square occupied by an enemy man, the latter is captured and removed from the board at once. See Diagram 43, which shows how the Bishop captures.

43

The Bishop can capture the Rook a1, Knight b4, or pawn d2, but not Knight a5 or Rook h8.

In the position in the diagram, the White Bishop can capture the Ra1, Nb4 or Pd2. Since Bishops cannot jump over enemy men, the White Bishop in the diagram cannot capture the Na5, and it cannot capture the Rh8 since Bishops are not allowed to jump over their own men either.

The Pd2 in Diagram 43 is protected by the Pe3, so if the White Bishop captures the Pd2, Black can take the Bishop with his Pe3! White would lose a Bishop, and Black would lose a pawn.

Diagram 44 shows the resulting position if White captures the Nb4 in Diagram 43.

44

The Bishop had captured the Knight b4

Diagram 45 shows a position where White's light-square Bishop prevents the advance of five Black pawns situated on black squares. If Black moves his pawns, the White Bishop will capture all of them in five moves. We can conclude therefore that a Bishop is stronger than a pawn, but weaker than a Rook, since a Rook can move on squares of both colors.

45

Diagonal d1-h5 is controlled by the Bishop, and all five Black pawns perish.

However, in exceptional cases a pawn can turn out to be stronger than a Bishop. For example, in Diagram 46 the White pawn on a2 can advance to its queening square without being hindered by the Black Bishop, which is blocked in by its own pawns.

46

Black pawns block their Bishop and the Bishop cannot stop the White pawn "a2."

Recommendations

You already know how to play chess with pawns alone. Now that you have learned how the Rook and the Bishop move, you are to play chess using these two pieces as well as pawns!

To begin with, set up the Rooks, Bishops and pawns in the positions they would occupy in an actual full-scale game of chess (see Diagram 47).

47

Now play according to the following rules:

1. A pawn that reaches the other end of the board can and must be promoted into either a Bishop or a Rook, after which the game continues.

2. You win the game:
   (a) if your opponent gives up;
   (b) if you are the first to capture all your opponent's pieces and pawns; or
   (c) if after one of your moves all your opponent's pieces and pawns are blocked and do not have any moves, while at least one of your own pieces or pawns can make at least one move.

3. A game is a draw (tie game):
   (a) if the players agree to call it a draw;
   (b) if both players' pieces and pawns are blocked and neither side can make a move; or
   (c) if fifty (50) consecutive moves go by without either side having moved a pawn or captured a man.

48

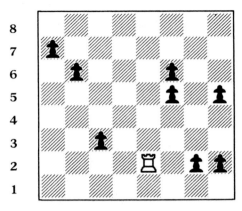

What is the minimum number of moves the White Rook needs to capture all Black pawns, provided the Black pawns do not move?

_____

_____

_____

49

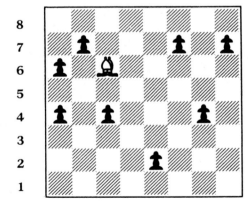

What is the minimum number of moves the White Bishop needs to capture all Black pawns? Assume the Black pawns do not move.

_____

_____

_____

50

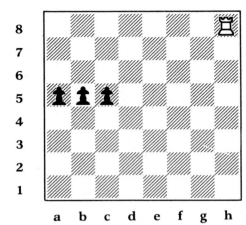

White to move. Who wins?

_____

_____

_____

51

White to move. Who wins?

_____

_____

_____

52

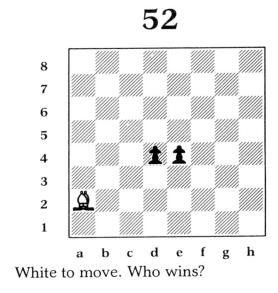

White to move. Who wins?

_____

_____

_____

53

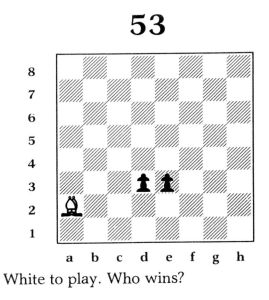

White to play. Who wins?

_____

_____

_____

54

White to move. Who wins?

_____

_____

_____

55

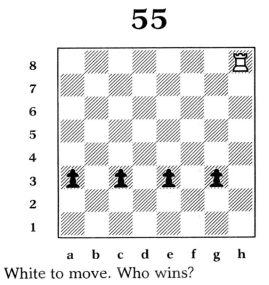

White to move. Who wins?

_____

_____

_____

56

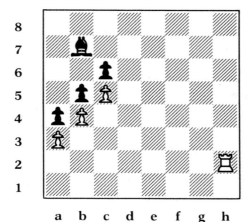

White to play. Who wins?

_____

_____

_____

57

White to play. Can he win?

_____

_____

_____

Remember: a clear and exact mental image of each square of the chessboard is a guarantee of mastering further material. You should prove it to yourself before going further.

Homework Answers

D-48 The White Rook needs ten moves to capture all the Black pawns if they are not allowed to move: 1. **Re2xg2,** 2. **Rg2xh2,** 3. **Rh2xh5,** 4. **Rh5xf5,** 5. **Rf5xf6,** 6. **Rf6xb6,** 7. **Rb6-b7,** 8. **Rb7xa7,** 9. **Ra7-c7,** and 10. **Rc7xc3.**

D-49 The White Bishop needs eleven moves to capture all the Black pawns if they are not allowed to move: 1. **Bc6xb7,** 2. **Bb7xa6,** 3. **Ba6xc4,** 4. **Bc4xe2,** 5. **Be2xg4,** 6. **Bg4-f5,** 7. **Bf5xh7,** 8. **Bh7-g8,** 9. **Bg8xf7,** 10. **Bf7-e8,** and 11. **Be8xa4.**

D-50 White wins with 1. **Rh8-h5 b5-b4** 2. **Rh5xc5 a5-a4** 3. **Rc5-c4 b4-b3** 4. **Rc4xa4 b3-b2** 5. **Ra4-b4 b2-b1Q** 6. **Rb4xb1.** Other solutions are also possible.

D-51 White loses, as one of the Black pawns will reach the first rank safely: 1. **Rh8-h4 b4-b3** 2. **Rh4xc4 b3-b2** 3. **Rc4-b4 a4-a3** 4. **Rb4-b3 a3-a2,** and so on.

D-52 White can win by playing 1. **Ba2-d5.** If Black replies with 1. ... **e4-e3,** then White plays 2. **Bd5-c4** and the Black pawns must perish. If you study the position carefully, you will see that White will win after any starting move except 1. **Ba2-b1.**

D-53 No matter what White plays, Black can win by replying with 1. ... **e3-e2,** and the Black e-pawn will become a Rook or Bishop on the next move.

D-54 White wins with 1. **Rd4-d5 e6-e5** 2. **d3-d4 e5xd4** 3. **Rd5-h5 d4-d3** 4. **Rh5-h3 d3-d2** 5. **Rh3-d3** and so on, or 1. **Rd4-d5 e6xd5** 2. **e4xd5 c7-c6** 3. **d5xc6 d6-d5** 4. **c4xd5 c5-c4** 4. **d3xc4.**

D-55 White wins with 1. **Rh8-h1.** All the Black pawns will be captured as soon as they reach the first rank.

D-56 White wins as the Black Bishop is in a corner and has very few squares (only three) to which it can move. The White Rook controls these squares and then captures the Bishop: 1. **Rh2-h8 Bb7-a6** 2. **Rh8-b8** and captures the Bishop on the next move.

D-57 The position is a draw here since there the Black Bishop has many squares to move to and can protect its pawns from the White Rook.

Lesson Four

How the Queen and Knight Move and Capture

Check Lesson Three Homework if necessary.

Review Questions:

1. Name the square where the third rank crosses the b1-h7 diagonal.
2. Without looking at a chessboard, name the White and Black men and the squares they stand on at the start of the game.
3. Can the White a-pawn (the Queen's Rook Pawn) wind up on the f-file during a game? If so, how?
4. Can a situation with Black pawns on a2, a3, a4, and a5 occur in a game?
5. Without looking at the board, say where the mobility of a Bishop is greater — in the center or in a corner?
6. Without looking at the board, name the maximum number of squares that could be needed by a Rook to get from one square of an empty board to another.
7. Without looking at the board, determine how many moves are needed for a Bishop on a1 to reach h2 on an empty board. How many moves does it need to get from a1 to h6?
8. Which Bishops can never collide?

Answers:

1. d3.
2. White: Ke1, Qd1, Ra1, Rh1, Nb1, Ng1, Bc1, Bf1, P's a2, b2, c2, d2, e2, f2, g2, h2; Black: Ke8, Qd8, Ra8, Rh8, Nb8, Ng8, Bc8, Bf8, P's a7, b7, c7, d7, e7, f7, g7, h7.
3. The White a-pawn can reach the f-file by capturing five times, e.g., **a2 x b3 x c4 x d5 x e6 x f7.**
4. Yes. The pawn on a4 could have got there in one move from b5 by the capture ... **b5 x a4**; the pawn on a3 could have got there in two moves from c5 by the captures ...

c5 x b4 and ... b4 x a3; and the pawn on a2 could have got there in three moves by the captures ... **d5 x c4, ... c4 x b3,** and ... **b3 x a2.** Thus a total of six capturing moves would be needed.

5. A Bishop has 13 moves in the center of the board and only 7 in a corner.
6. Two moves.
7. Two moves to reach h2: **Ba1-e5-h2** and two to reach h6: **Ba1-g7-h6.**
8. Bishops that move on light squares never meet the Bishops that move on dark squares.

How The Queen Moves and Captures

The Queen is the most powerful piece in chess. In appearance, it is taller than any of the other pieces except the King. The Queen combines the moves of the Rook and the Bishop. It can move in any direction (but it cannot change direction in the middle of a move) along the entire length of any rank, file, or diagonal on which it stands, if there are no obstacles in its way. Diagram 58 shows a position in which the Queen controls a total of 27 squares.

58

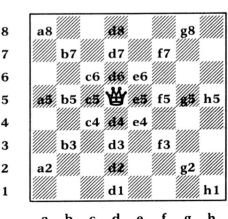

Diagram 59 illustrates one possible move that the Queen in Diagram 58 could make. On the edge of the board the Queen is weaker, as it has only 21 possible moves.

59

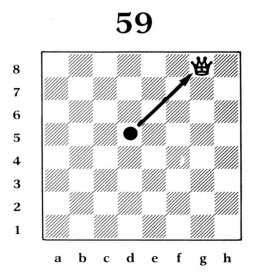

The Queen can have two types of obstacles in its way: friendly men, which cannot be displaced or jumped over, and enemy men, which can be captured and removed from the board. This will become clearer when we examine Diagram 60.

60

The Black Queen there can capture the White Bishop or pawn, but cannot capture the White Knight, which is blocked by the White pawn and thus is safe. The White Rook too is safe, as the Queen's own Knight stands in the way. For all its might, the Queen cannot jump over men. Diagram 61 shows the Black Queen's move ... **Qd7xf7**, capturing the White Bishop.

61

Diagram 62 shows a position where the Black Queen can capture any one of eight White men, while the Queen itself is not under attack by any of them.

62

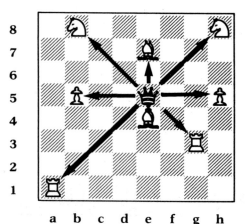

The position in Diagram 63 is another illustration of the Queen's might. By moving **Qb5-g5**, White can attack six Black men simultaneously, although it can only capture one of them on its next move.

63

How the Knight Moves and Captures

Knights have always ridden horses. That is why a Knight in chess has the shape of a horse's head.

The Knight's move is illustrated in Diagram 64, where the Knight on d4 controls the squares c6, e6, f5, f3, e2, c2, b3 and b5.

64

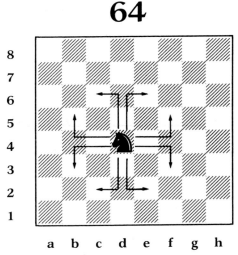

It is clear that a Knight's move in any direction has the shape of a capital L. Good descriptions of the Knight's move are:

a) two squares sideways, then one square up or down;

b) two squares up or down, then one square sideways.

Either of these descriptions can be used to describe any Knight's move.

Diagram 65 shows one of the eight possible moves of a Knight on the central square d4: **Nd4-f3.**

65

Note that a Knight changes the color of its square every time it moves. Thus, starting from the dark square d4 (Diagram 64), it moves to the light square f3 (Diagram 65).

Diagram 66 shows the following Knight's moves: **Na8-b6, ... Nb2-a4, Nf6-h5 and ... Ng1-e2.**

66

A Knight is not allowed to move just one square or two squares and then stop. A Knight in a corner has only two moves.

Like any good horseman, the chess Knight too is able to jump over obstacles. The Knight is the only chess piece with the power to jump over its own and enemy men. Unlike checkers, however, the Knight never captures the men it jumps over. Diagram 67 shows a White Knight on d4 that is surrounded by its own and enemy men.

67

It may jump over any of these men and has a choice of eight different moves, just as it does on the empty board in Diagram 64. If the Knight's destination is occupied by an enemy man, the latter is captured by the Knight. The enemy man is removed from the board and the Knight takes its place instead. Knights operate well in close quarters. A Knight is able to jump into the middle of things and, if it feels uncomfortable there, it can leap right out again.

In Diagram 68, the White Knight can capture the Black Bishop on b3 (**Na1xb3**). This Knight cannot move to c2, since there is already another Knight there.

68

The Knight on c2 is much stronger than the Knight on a1, as it has a choice of four different moves: **Nc2-a3, Nc2-d4**, capturing the Queen by **Nc2xb4** (see Diagram 69), and capturing the Bishop on e3 by **Nc2 x e3.**

69

However, it cannot go to a1 or e1, since these squares are occupied by friendly pieces. The Black Knight on a8 has no moves at all, since the squares b6 and c7 are occupied by Black pieces. The Black Knight on h7 can move to g5 (**Nh7-g5**) or capture the White Queen (**Nh7-f6**). It cannot go to f8, since that square is occupied by a friendly piece, a Black Rook.

A Knight's strength is approximately equal to that of a Bishop. A Knight is stronger than a pawn, but weaker than a Rook or a Queen.

Place a Knight on a board and move it as shown in Diagrams 64–66.

Recommendations

You now know the moves of all the men except the King. Set up these men in the positions they would occupy in an actual full-scale chess game (see Diagram 70).

70

Start playing from this position. The rules are the same as in the Rook, Bishop and Pawn game of Lesson Three, except for Rule 1. The new Rule 1 is:

1. A pawn that reaches the other end of the board can and must be promoted into a Queen, Rook, Bishop, or Knight, after which the game continues.

HOMEWORK
I. Diagrams 71–80
(Answers at the end)

71

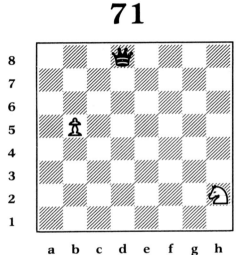

Black to move. Find a square from which the Queen attacks the White Knight and the pawn simultaneously.

_____

_____

_____

72

a) How many possiblities has the White Knight to capture?

b) In how many moves will the White Knight capture all the Black pieces, provided that Black does not move?

_____

_____

_____

73

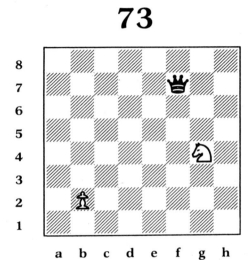

Black to move. Find the square from which the Black Queen attacks the White Knight and the pawn simultaneously.

_____

_____

_____

74

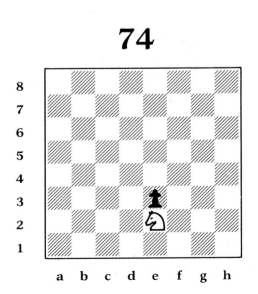

27

In how many moves will the White Knight capture the Black pawn, provided the pawn doesn't move?

_____

_____

_____

75

White to play. Find the square from which the Queen attacks the Black Knight and the Bishop simultaneously.

_____

_____

76

In how many moves will the Black Knight

capture the White pawn if the pawn doesn't move?

_____ _____

_____

_____

77

White to play. Find the square from which the Queen attacks both Black Bishops and the Knight.

_____

_____

_____

78

In how many moves will the White Knight capture all of the Black pawns if they don't move?

_____

_____

_____

79

White to play and win.

_____

_____

_____

80

	a	b	c	d	e	f	g	h
8	31	54	47	8	33	10	27	50
7	46	7	32	53	28	49	34	11
6	5	30	55	48	9	36	51	26
5	56	45	6	29	52	25	12	35
4	43	4	57	20	61	14	37	24
3	58	19	44	1	40	23	62	13
2	3	42	17	60	21	64	15	38
1	18	59	2	41	16	39	22	63

The numbers show the order in which a Knight moves from square to square in making a "Knight's Tour" of the chessboard.

a) In the same order, write down the names of the squares in chess notation.

In a Knight's Tour, a Knight lands on every square of the board without landing on any square twice. Mathematicians have calculated that there are more than 30 million different Knight's Tours possible. Diagram 80 shows just one of them

b) Add up the number of the squares on each rank and on each file and compare them!

Homework Answers

D-71 1. ... **Qd8-b8** attacks the White Knight and pawn at the same time.

D-72 **a)** The White Knight has a choice of eight different captures: **Ne4xd6, Ne4xf6, Ne4xg5, Ne4xg3, Ne4xf2, Ne4xd2, Ne4xc3,** and **Ne4xc5.**

b) If the Black pieces do not move, the White Knight can capture them all in fifteen moves: **1. Ne4xd2, 2. Nd2-e4, 3. Ne4xc3, 4. Nc3-e4, 5. Ne4xc5, 6. Nc5-e4, 7. Ne4xd6, 8. Nd6-e4, 9. Ne4xf6, 10. Nf6-e4, 11. Ne4xg5, 12. Ng5-e4, 13. Ne4xg3, 14. Ng3-e4,** and **15. Ne4xf2.**

D-73 1. ... **Qf7-g7** attacks the White Knight and the pawn at the same time.

D-74 If the Black pawn doesn't move, the White Knight can capture it in three moves: **1. Ne2-c3, 2. Nc3-d5,** and **3. Nd5xe3.**

D-75 1. **Qb6-d8** and 1. **Qb6-e3** both attack the Black Knight and Bishop simultaneously.

D-76 If the White pawn doesn't move, the Black Knight can capture it in four moves: **1. ... Nf1-d2, 2. ... Nd2-e4, 3. ... Ne4-f2,** and **4. ... Nf2xh3.**

D-77 The White Queen attacks the Black Knight and both Black Bishops with the move **1. Qf5-e4.**

D-78 If the Black pawns don't move, the White Knight can capture all of them in 18 moves: **1. Nb1-c3, 2. Nc3-b5, 3. Nb5xa7, 4. Na7-b5, 5. Nb5xc7, 6. Nc7-d5, 7. Nd5xe7, 8. Ne7-f5, 9. Nf5xg7, 10. Ng7-h5, 11. Nh5-f6, 12. Nf6xh7, 13. Nh7-g5, 14. Ng5xf7, 15. Nf7-e5, 16. Ne5xd7, 17. Nd7-c5,** and **18. Nc5xb7.**

D-79 1. **Qa1-h8.** The White Queen will capture the Black pieces, which are boxed in the corner.

D-80 a) 1. d3, 2. c1, 3. a2, 4. b4, 5. a6 6. c5, 7. b7, 8. d8, 9. e6, 10. f8, 11. h7, 12. g5, 13. h3, 14. f4, 15. g2, 16. e1, 17. c2, 18. a1, 19. b3, 20. d4, 21. e2, 22. g1, 23. f3, 24. h4, 25. f5, 26. h6, 27. g8, 28. e7, 29. d5, 30. b6, 31. a8, 32. c7, 33. e8, 34. g7, 35. h5, 36. f6, 37. g4, 38. h2, 39. f1, 40. e3, 41. d1, 42. b2, 43. a4, 44. c3, 45. b5, 46. a7, 47. c8, 48. d6, 49. f7, 50. h8, 51. g6, 52. e5, 53. d7, 54. b8, 55. c6, 56. a5, 57. c4, 58. a3, 59. b1, 60. d2, 61. e4, 62. g3, 63. h1, and 64. f2.

b) The numbers in any file or rank add up to 260.

Lesson Five

How the King Moves and Captures. Check. Checkmate.

Check Lesson 4 homework if necessary.

Review Questions
1. Which men always attack an enemy man in such a way that the enemy man cannot be saved by a man being interposed between it and the attacking man?
2. Which piece can be moved in the starting position before any pawns are moved?
3. How many squares are there on the board from which the Knight can make only two moves?
4. Without looking at a board, count up how many different moves can be made by White and Black in the starting position.
5. Without looking at a board, say where the mobility of the Queen is greater — in the center or in a corner.
6. How many men can a Queen attack simultaneously?
7. Without looking at a board, say whether each of the following squares is dark or light: b2, d3, e7, f4, h3.
8. Without looking at a board, name all the squares on the h2-b8 and the h1-a8 diagonals.

Answers to Review Questions

1. The pawn and the Knight.
2. The Knight, because it can jump over the pawns.
3. The four corners: a1, a8, h1, and h8.
4. White and Black can each begin the game with twenty different moves (16 pawn moves and four Knight moves).
5. The Queen is stronger in the center, where it has 27 moves, compared to only 21 in a corner.
6. The Queen can attack eight men simultaneously.
7. b2-D, d3-L, e7-D, f4-D, h3-L.
8. The h2-b8 diagonal consists of the dark squares h2, g3, f4, e5, d6, c7, and b8, while the h1-a8 diagonal consists of the light squares h1, g2, f3, e4, d5, c6, b7, and a8.

How The King Moves and Captures

The King is the most important piece in chess, the heart and soul of the game. If you lose any other piece except the King, you can still play on. If you lose your King, however, you lose the game.

The King moves like the Queen, but only one square at a time. Thus, it can move forwards, backwards, sideways, or diagonally.

Diagram 81 illustrates the King's moves.

81

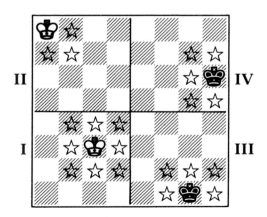

In 81-I, the King controls eight squares, as it always does except when it is on the edge of the board. 81-III and 81-IV show that on the edge the King has only five moves, while 81-II shows that in a corner the King's mobility is restricted even more, to only three squares.

Like all chessmen, the King cannot jump over other men or move onto a square occupied by a man of its own color. Thus, in 82-I, the King can move to b2, b4, d2, and d4, but not to the squares occupied by the White pawns.

82

Similarly, the Black King in 82-II has only one move, to b8, while the White King in 82-III can move only to f1 or h1. In 82-IV, the Black King is completely surrounded by its own pieces and thus has no moves at all.

The King captures the same way as it moves. Diagrams 83 and 84 illustrate how the King captures by showing positions before a capture has been made (see Diagram 83).

83

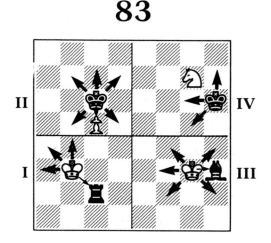

and after a capture has been made (see Diagram 84).

84

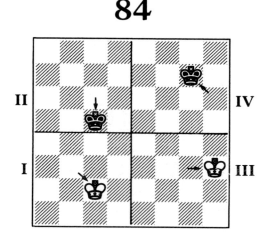

Capturing means taking the opponent's man off the board and moving your man onto the square the opponent's man occupied. Note that capturing is **not** compulsory in chess.

Check

When the King is attacked by an enemy piece, it is said to be "in check." A basic rule of chess is that whenever a player's King is put into check, the player must immediately, on the very next move, get his King out of check. In keeping with this, a King is never allowed to move into check either. That is, a King must never be moved onto a square where it will be within the capturing range of an enemy piece. It follows from this that neither King can put the other into check, and hence the two Kings can never stand on adjacent squares. Nor can a King capture a defended enemy piece, since it would thereby be moving into check. If by mistake a King has been left in check or moved into check, then as soon as the mistake is found out, the position before the King was left in check or moved into check must be set up and another move must be made. Checking is not obligatory, nor is it in itself either good or bad. Many beginners try to check whenever possible simply because they like announcing "check!".

In Diagram 85-I, Black has just moved his Knight (**Nd2-b3**) and put White's King in check. The Knight is directly attacking the White King, who must try to get out of check. 85-II to 85-IV show other examples of check.

85

How To Get Out Of Check

There are three different ways to get out of check:

1. By moving your King to a safe square which is not attacked by any enemy man;
2. by moving one of your own men between your King and the checking piece;
3. by capturing the piece which is checking your King.

The King is in check in each of the four positions shown in Diagram 86, but in each case it has five different ways of getting out of check.

86

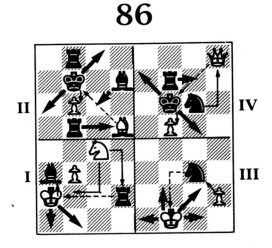

Checkmate

If none of the three ways of getting out of check are possible, then your King is said to be **checkmated** and you lose the game.

A King can be checkmated by any enemy piece except the other King.

Diagrams 87–92 show positions where the King is checkmated. Make sure that in each case you understand why it is checkmated.

87

Queen checkmates

88

Rook checkmates

89

Knight checkmates

90

Bishop checkmates

91

Pawn checkmates

Diagram 92 is a problem where White is to play and checkmate the Black King in one move. There are 47 different ways of doing this.

A move of the Rook on b2 opens up the diagonal of the Bishop on a1, which checkmates the White King. This accounts for fourteen checkmates, since the Rook can move to fourteen squares: (1) **Rb2-a2**, (2) **Rb2-c2**, (3) **Rb2-d2**, (4) **Rb2-e2**, (5) **Rb2-f2**, (6) **Rb2-g2**, (7) **Rb2-h2**, (8) **Rb2-b1**, (9) **Rb2-b3**, (10) **Rb2-b4**, (11) **Rb2-b5**, (12) **Rb2-b6**, (13) **Rb2-b7**, and (14) **Rb2xb8**.

A move of the Bishop on d5 allows the Queen on c5 to checkmate the Black King. This accounts for 11 mates, since the Bishop on d5 can make 11 moves: (15) **Bd5-a8**, (16) **Bd5-b7**, (17) **Bd5-c6**, (18) **Bd5-e4**, (19) **Bd5-f3**, (20) **Bd5-g2**, (21) **Bd5-h1**, (22) **Bd5-a2**, (23) **Bd5-b3**, (24) **Bd5-c4**, and (25) **Bd5-e6**.

A move of the Knight on f5 allows the Rook on g5 to checkmate the Black King. This accounts for seven checkmates: (26) **Nf5-e3**, (27) **Nf5-d4**, (28) **Nf5-d6**, (29) **Nf5-e7**, (30) **Nf5-g7**, (31) **Nf5-h6**, and (32) **Nf5-h4**.

The White Queen can make six moves which checkmate the Black King: (33) **Qc5-c3**, (34) **Qc5-c7**, (35) **Qc5-d4**, (36) **Qc5-d6**, (37) **Qc5-e3**, and (38) **Qc5-e7**.

And, finally, there are nine different pawn moves which checkmate the Black King: (39) **a7xb8 = Q**, (40) **a7xb8 = B**, (41) **d7xe8 = Q**, (42) **d7xe8 = R**, (43) **f7xe8 = Q**, (44) **f7xe8 = R**, (45) **h7-h8 = Q**, (46) **h7-h8 = B**, and (47) **d3-d4**.

Recommendations

Now that you know how all the men move, set them up in the starting position (see Diagram 93) and start playing!

92

93

Don't forget that to win you have to checkmate your opponent's King, not capture all his men. The goal of any real chess game is to checkmate the opponent's King. Don't make your moves in a big hurry. Take your time. It is better to play one good game, taking the time to think, than ten poor ones in a rush.

HOMEWORK
Diagrams 94–103
(Answers at the end)

94

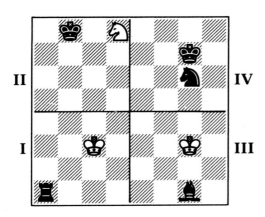

Can the King capture a piece in each quarter?

_____

_____

_____

95

Record all possible moves by the King in each quarter.

_____

_____

_____

96

Record all possible moves which protect the King in each quarter from check.

_____

_____

_____

97

Record all possible moves which protect the King in each quarter from check.

_____

_____

In Diagrams 98–101, White is to move and checkmate in one move.

Write down your answers in the space provided.

98

_____

_____

99

100

This problem has two solutions. Find them and record.

_____

_____

_____

101

_____

_____

_____

102

White to play. Checkmate in one move.

_____

_____

_____

103

This problem has 43 solutions. Find them and record.

_____

_____

_____

_____

_____

HOMEWORK ANSWERS

D-94 In I, II, and III, the King cannot capture the enemy pieces as they are too far away — a King can only move one square at a time. The King in IV cannot capture the Knight next to it since it is of the same color, and capturing your own men is not allowed in chess.

D-95 The King can only move as follows:
In I: **1. Kc2xb1** (only one move)
In II: **1. Kb6-a5; 1. Kb6-a7; 1. Kb6xc7** (three moves)
In III: **1. Kh3-h4; 1. Kh3-g4** (two moves)
In IV: **1. Kh7-g6** (only one move)

D-96 The King can get out of check by:
I: **1. Ba2-b1** (only one move)
II: **1. Ka7-a8; 1. Ka7-b8; 1. Ka7-a6; 1. b6-b7; 1. c6-c7; 1. c6xd7** (six moves)
III: **1. Kg1-f1; 1. Kg1-h1; 1. Nf2xg4; 1. Rh2-g2** (four moves)
IV: **1. ... Nf8-h7; 1. ... Ng8xh6** (two moves)

D-97 The King can get out of check by:
I: **1. Bc2xa4** (only one move)
II. **1. ... Kb6xc5; 1. ... Kb6-a6** (two moves)
III. **1. Ng1-f3; 1. Kh1-h2** (two moves)
IV. **1. ... Kf7-e6; 1. ... Kf7-e7; 1. ... Kf7-f8; 1. ... Kf7-g8; 1. ... Nf6xh5; 1. ... g7-g6** (six moves)

D-98 **1. Qd5xf7 checkmate**

D-99 **1. Ne4-d6 checkmate**

D-100 **1. Ra7-a8 or 1. Rf7-f8 checkmates**

D-101 **1. Bd2-e3 checkmate**

D-102 **1. d5-d6 checkmate**

D-103 **1-6: Kg4-f5/g5/h5/f3/g3/h3.** Each of these six King moves allows the Rook on h4 to checkmate.

7-11: Qd6-c5/b6/e5/f4/f6. Five checkmates with the Queen.

12-25: Re3-a3/b3/c3/d3/f3/g3/h3/e1/e2/e4/e5/e6/e7/e8. Fourteen checkmates by the Bg1 resulting from the moves of the Re3.

26-38: Bd5-a2/b3/c4/e6/f7/g8/a8/b7/c6/e4/f3/g2/h1. Thirteen checkmates by the Qd6 resulting from moves of the Bd5.

39-40: Nd2-b3/f3. Two checkmates by the Nd2.

41-42: Nc7-b5/e6. Two checkmates by the Nc7.

43: c2-c3. One checkmate by the pawn c2.

Total: 6 + 5 + 14 + 13 + 2 + 2 + 1 = 43 possible checkmates!

Lesson Six

En Passant Pawn Captures

Check homework (if necessary).

Review Questions

1. What piece can attack a Queen without itself being attacked by the Queen?
2. Where can a King trap a Knight in such a way that the Knight cannot avoid being captured?
3. How many moves does a Knight need to get from g1 to f1? Name the route.
4. How many moves does a Rook need to get from b1 to h7 on an empty board?
5. Why cannot a King stand next to the opponent's King?
6. Is it possible to checkmate the opponent by a King's move?
7. Is it possible to checkmate the White King and the Black King simultaneously?
8. Record all the moves by which the White Queen can check the Black King in Diagram 104.

104

Answers to Review Questions:

1. The Knight.
2. The King can trap a Knight in a corner. For example, in Diagram 105, wherever the Black Knight moves it will be captured by the King, while if it does not move, White will play **Kc6-b7** and capture the Knight the next move.

105

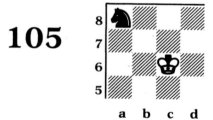

3. A Knight needs three moves to get from g1 to f1: e.g., **1. Ng1-e2, 2. Ne2-g3, 3. Ng3-f1**. The Knight can also get to f1 in three moves via f3 and d2 or via f3 and h2.
4. A Rook needs two moves to get from b1 to f7: **1. Rb1-f1 2. Rf1-f7, or 1. Rb1-b7 2. Rb7-f7.**
5. Because a King is not allowed to move into check, as it would be doing if it moved next to the other King.
6. Yes. For example, in Diagram 106 White can give checkmate with the Rook on h1 by the King move **1. Kh2-g1.**

106

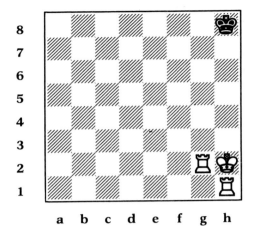

a b c d e f g h

7. No. The players in a game of chess must move by turns, and as soon as one King is checkmated the game is over, and the player whose King has been checkmated is not allowed to make a reply, even if it would checkmate his opponent's King.

8. There are eight different moves by which the White Queen can check the Black King. These are: **1. Qg3-b3, 2. Qg3-d3, 3. Qg3-f3, 4. Qg3-g2, 5. Qg3-g5, 6. Qg3-g8, 7. Qg3-d6, 8. Qg3-e5.** Note that the last two checks are not good since the Black King can capture the White Queen.

En Passant Pawn Captures

You will remember that every pawn, the first time it moves, and only then, has the option of moving two squares forward instead of just one. You will also remember that pawns capture diagonally, and not the way they move. Keeping these facts in mind, look at the following diagrams and learn one final rule — a special pawn move.

107

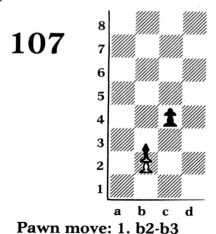

Pawn move: 1. b2-b3

Diagrams 107 and 110 show a White pawn on b2 and a Black pawn on c4. If the White pawn moves one square forward on its first move, the position in Diagram 108 will occur.

108

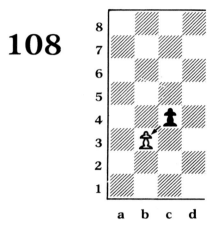

a b c d

Here the Black pawn on c4 can capture the White pawn on b3, and if it does so, the position will be as in Diagram 109.

109

a b c d

110

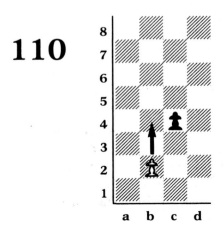

a b c d

If the White pawn shown in Diagram 107 or 110 moves forward **two** squares on its first move, the resulting position will be as shown in Diagram 111, and the White pawn seems to have escaped being captured.

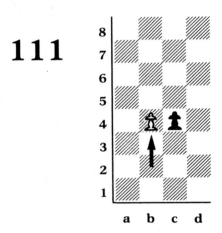

However, a special rule allows the Black pawn to capture the White pawn as if it had only moved one square. The resulting position is shown in Diagram 112.

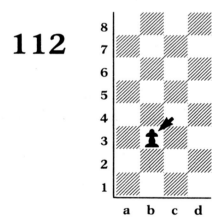

As you can see, it is the same as Diagram 109. Just like in the normal capture shown in Diagrams 108 and 109, the White pawn is removed from the board in the special capture shown in Diagrams 111 and 112. This special way of capturing is called capturing en passant, and is abbreviated e.p. En passant is a French expression meaning "in passing." It is as if the Black pawn in Diagram 111 captured the White pawn while it was passing through the b3 square.

En passant capturing is possible only if all the following conditions are satisfied:

1. The pawn doing the capturing must be on the fifth rank, if it is a White pawn, or on the fourth rank, if it is a Black pawn.
2. The pawn doing the capturing and the pawn being captured must be on adjacent files.
3. The pawn to be captured must be on its original square (second rank for White and seventh for Black.)
4. The pawn to be captured must advance two squares in one move (Diagram 111).
5. In reply, the opposite pawn captures the pawn that has advanced two squares as if it had only advanced one square. (Diagrams 109 and 112).

The option to capture en passant must be exercised by the capturing side on its very first move following the two-square advance of the enemy pawn. If a player chooses not to capture en passant, the position will be as shown in Diagram 111. If, in Diagram 111, Black does not capture en passant and makes some other move instead, the White pawn is safe from being captured en passant for the rest of the game.

An en passant capture is compulsory only when it is the only legal move available — e.g., if it is the only move a player has to get his King out of check (see Diagram 113).

By the move **1. ... g7-g5** the Black pawn checks the King. Only the rule "en passant" can save the White King.

On the other hand, an en passant capture is of course not permitted if it would expose the player's King to check. For example, in Diagram 114 Black to move can checkmate White with the move **1. ... g7-g5.**

114

White cannot get out of check by capturing en passant, since to do so would mean exposing his King to check by the Black Rook along the h-file.

Remember that only pawns can capture en passant and that only pawns can be captured en passant.

HOMEWORK
I. Diagrams 115–120
(answers at the end)

115

What was White's last move?

_____

_____

_____

116

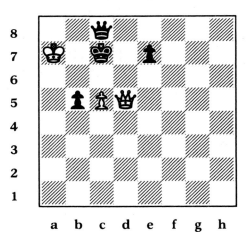

a) White to play and checkmate in one move.
b) What was Black's last move?

_____

_____

_____

In Diagrams 117–120, White is to play and checkmate in one move. Write down your answers in the space provided below.

117

_____

_____

118

_____

_____

119

_____

_____

120

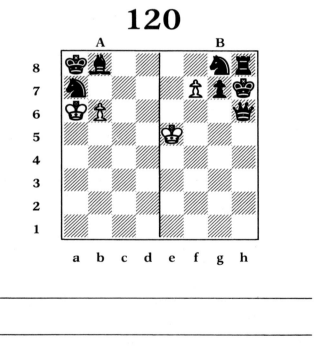

_____

_____

II. Exercises

Write down your answers in the space below.

1. Move the Queen from d1 to g8 via b7 and write down its route.

_____

_____

_____

2. Move the Bishop from c1 to b8 via g7 and write down its route.

_____

_____

_____

3. Without looking at a chessboard name the squares where:

   a) the c1-a3 diagonal crosses the a1-h8 diagonal.

   b) the f1-h3 diagonal crosses the h1-a8 diagonal.

_____

_____

_____

4. Construct:

   a) a position in which a Black pawn could capture en passant **e4xd3** or **e4xf3**, depending on White's previous move.

   b) a position in which either of **two** White pawns could capture a Black pawn en passant.

_____

_____

_____

Homework Answers
I. Diagrams 115–120

D-115 White's last move had to be **1. d5xe6 e.p.** (en passant).

D-116 a) **1. c5xb6 e.p. checkmate**
       b) **b7-b5**

D-117 a) **b6-b7 checkmate**
       b) **g5-g6 checkmate**

D-118 a) **1.c6-c7 checkmate**
       b) **1. g5-g6 checkmate**

D-119 a) **1. b6-b7 checkmate**
       b) **1. h6-h7 checkmate**

D-120 a) **1. b6-b7 checkmate**
       b) **1. f7-f8N checkmate**

II. Exercises

1. **Qd1-d5-b7-b8-g8.** This is just one possibility. There are several other four-move routes possible.

2. **Bc1-b2** (or h6) **-g7-e5-b8.**

3. a) **b2.** b) **g2.**

4. a) White pawn on d4 and f4 and a Black pawn on e4. If White has played 1. **d2-d4** on his last move, Black can capture 1. ... **e4xd3 e.p.**, while if White has just played 1. **f2-f4**, then Black can capture 1. ... **e4xf3 e.p.**

   b) White pawn on d5 and f5 and a Black pawn which has just played 1. ... **e7-e5.** White has a choice between **d5xe6 e.p.** and **f5xe6 e.p.**

Lesson Seven
Castling

Check Lesson Six homework if necessary.

Review Questions:
1. What are the ways of getting out of check?
2. What happens if a King cannot get out of check?
3. How many moves does a Knight need to get from a1 to b2? Give an example.
4. How many moves does a Knight need to get from h1 to a8? Give an example.
5. When will a King that is standing beside a pawn not be within capturing distance of the pawn after the pawn moves?
6. Can a Black pawn on d4 capture en passant if a White pawn moves from e2 to e4?
7. A Black pawn is on e4. White moves d2-d4 and then f2-f4, while the Black pawn is still on e4. After White moves f2-f4, which pawn can be captured en passant?
8. Can en passant captures occur near the end of a game, or only near the beginning?

Answers to Review Questions
1. A player can get out of check in any of three ways:
    a) by moving his King to a safe square;
    b) by interposing any of his men between his King and the checking piece;
    c) by capturing the checking piece.
2. When none of the above methods can be applied, the King is checkmated and the game is over — the player whose King has been checkmated loses.
3. A Knight needs four moves to get from a1 to b2; e.g. **Na1-b3-c1-d3-b2.**
4. A Knight needs six moves to get from h1 to a8: e.g. **Nh1-f2-d3-b4-d5-c7-a8.**

5. When the pawn is in its starting position (on the second rank for a White pawn and on the seventh rank for a Black pawn). For example, in Diagram 121 White to move can play 1. **h2-h4** and the pawn has escaped from the Black King, and Black to move can play 1. ... **b7-b5**, and the Black pawn has escaped from the White King.

121

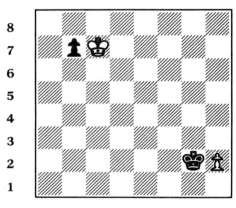

6. Yes.
7. White can capture "en passant" only the f-pawn.
8. The "en passant" rule can be used at any time during a game.

Castling

Castling was introduced into chess in the 14th century. It is an extremely important move. Castling involves moving both the King and the Rook at the same time in a special way, but counts as one move.

Castling helps a player to:
a) provide his King a safe shelter behind his pawns, and

In Diagrams 117-120, White is to play and checkmate in one move. Write down your answers in the space provided below.

119

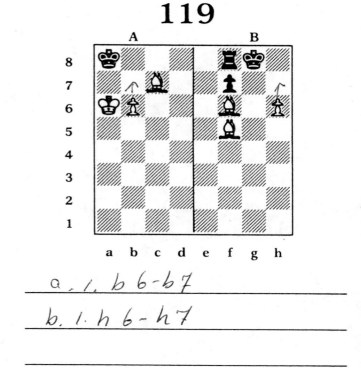

a. 1. b6-b7

b. 1. h6-h7

117

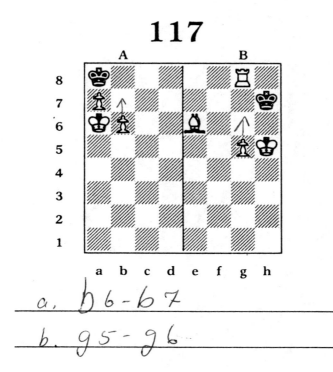

a. b6-b7

b. g5-g6

118

a. 1. c6-c7

b. 1. g5-g6

120

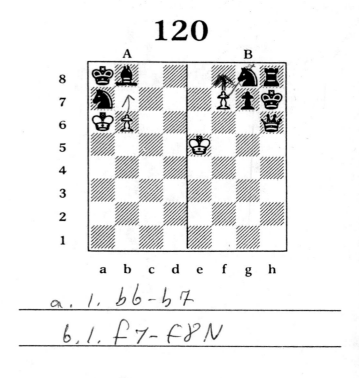

a. 1. b6-b7

b. 1. f7-f8N

b) bring one of his powerful Rooks into a good position either for attack or for defense.

The King's safety is a prime concern in each game, and it is dangerous to leave it in the middle of the board, where it is more exposed to attack. By castling, a player whisks the King away to the security of the Royal Castle, so to speak!

Castling is optional, but it is a useful move that should not be lightly forsaken. In most games, both the players castle.

Diagram 122 shows that both White and Black can castle either on the Kingside or on the Queenside.

122

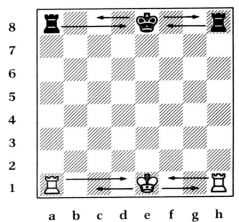

The King moves only two squares in castling, either King's side or Queen's side.

123

White can castle Queen's side or King's side; Black can castle only King's side.

Diagram 124 shows a position where neither players has castled, and Diagram 125 shows the resulting position after White has castled on the Kingside and Black on the Queenside.

124

125

As you can see, in each case, the King moved two squares towards a Rook, and the Rook moved onto the square that the King had crossed. White, when castling on the Kingside, moves his King from e1 to g1 and his Rook from h1 to f1; and when castling on the Queenside moves his King to c1 and his Rook to d1. Black moves his King to g8 and his Rh8 to f8 when castling on the Kingside, and his King to c8 and his Ra8 to d8 when castling on the Queenside.

In chess notation, Kingside castling is written as 0-0, and Queenside castling is written as 0-0-0. Kingside castling is also called castling short, while Queenside castling is also known as castling long.

45

Castling Rules

A player may castle only once in a game, and only according to the following rules:

1. Castling is not permitted if either the King or the Rook used in castling has already moved at any point in the game. See Diagrams 122, 124 and 125.

2. All the squares between the King and the Rook must be empty. Neither can jump over any other pieces. That is why Black in Diagram 123 cannot castle on the Queenside and White in Diagram 126 cannot castle on the Kingside.

3. The King must not be in check (castling is not allowed for the purpose of getting out of check). That is why Black cannot castle in Diagram 127.

4. The King may not move into check. That is why Black cannot castle on the Queenside in Diagram 126.

5. The square which the King jumps over should not be under attack by any enemy man. That is why Black cannot castle on the Kingside in Diagram 126.

Note: Castling is possible when the Rook is under attack and also, in the case of Queenside castling, when the b1 or b8 square is under attack by an enemy man.

Let us examine Diagram 126.

126

Black can't castle.
White can only castle Queenside.

White can only castle on the Queenside. He cannot castle on the Kingside (although he may be able to later) because one of the squares between the King and the King's Rook is occupied by a piece, in this case a Black Knight.

Black cannot castle on either side. He cannot castle on the Queenside (although he may be able to later) because the square on which the King would land, c8, is controlled by an enemy piece, the White Knight on a7. He cannot castle Kingside (although he may be able to later) because in order to do so the King would have to cross a square controlled by an enemy man (the Bishop on a3, or Ba3, attacks the square f8.)

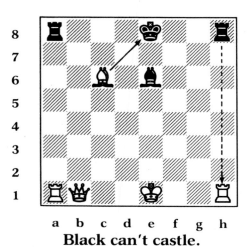

127

Black can't castle.
White can only castle Kingside.

In Diagram 127, Black cannot castle because his King is in check by the White Bishop on c6. If Black gets out of check by capturing the Bishop or interposing a piece on d7, he may be able to castle later on. If he gets out of check by moving his King, he can never castle for the rest of the game (see Rule 1 above). White cannot castle on the Queenside because one of the squares between the King and the Queen's Rook, b1, is occupied by a piece, in this case the White Queen. However, White can castle on the Kingside.

Now you know how to move, capture, and castle. You are ready to play real chess!

HOMEWORK
I. Diagrams 128–133

In Diagrams 128–130, can White castle on either side if it is his turn to move? Can Black to move castle on either side?

128

129

130

In Diagrams 131–133, it is White's turn to move. (Funny Puzzles)

131

Checkmate in one move.

132

Place the Black King so that White checkmates him in one move. Two solutions.

_____

_____

_____

133

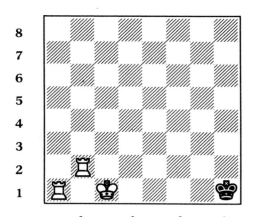

Checkmate in half a move.

_____

_____

_____

II. Exercises

Write down your answers in the spaces provided.

1. How many moves does a Knight on c3 need to get:

    a) to c4? _____

    b) to d4? _____

    c) to c6? _____

    d) to e5? _____

First find all these moves on a board and then try to visualize them on the board without moving the Knight. After that, without looking at the board all, try to imagine a Knight on c3 and name the squares that it will need to cross in order to get to c4, d4, c6 and e5.

2. Construct a position on the diagram below where the White King and two White Bishops have checkmated the Black King.

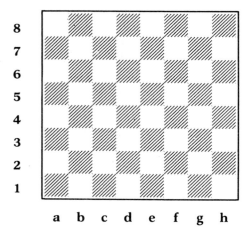

Homework Answers
I. Diagrams 128–133

D-128 White can castle only on the Kingside and Black only on the Queenside.

D-129 Both White and Black can castle on either side.

D-130 Both White and Black can castle only on the Queenside.

D-131 1. 0-0

D-132 The Black King must be place on c1 or

f3, when White can checkmate it by castling on the Kingside (**1. 0-0**).

D-133 White is in the process of castling on the Queenside — he has so far completed half the move by placing his King on c1. By making the other half of the move and shifting the Rook from a1 to d1, White will checkmate Black.

II. Exercises

1. A Knight on c3 needs:

a) 3 moves to reach c4: e.g. **Nc3-e4-d2-c4**;
b) 2 moves to reach d4: e.g. **Nc3-b5-d4**;
c) 3 moves to reach c6: e.g. **Nc3-b5-d4-c6**; and
d) 4 moves to reach e5: e.g. **Nc3-b5-d4-c6-e5**.

2. An example is shown in Diagram 134.

134

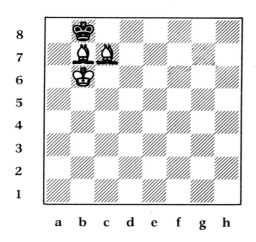

Lesson Eight

Relative Values Of The Chess Forces

Check Lesson Seven homework (if necessary).

Review Questions:
1. What is the name of the move which involves moving a King and a Rook at the same time?
2. Which piece can jump over another one only once in a game?
3. How many moves would a Knight on a1 need to visit all three other corners and then come back to a1?
4. Can a player castle with a Rook if it is under attack?
5. Can a player get his King out of check by castling?
6. Can a player castle if in doing so his King would have to cross a square attacked by an enemy man?
7. Can a player castle if in doing so his Rook has to cross a square attacked by an enemy man, but his King doesn't?
8. Can a player castle if after doing so his King would be in check?

Answers to Review Questions

1. Castling.
2. The King — it jumps over a Rook during castling.
3. A Knight on a1 will need twenty moves to visit the three other corners and then return to a1. For example: 1. Na1-c2 2. Nc2-a3 3. Na3-b5 4. Nb5-c7 5. Nc7-a8 6. Na8-b6 7. Nb6-c8 8. Nc8-e7 9. Ne7-g6 10. Ng6-h8 11. Nh8-f7 12. Nf7-h6 13. Nh6-g4 14. Ng4-f2 15. Nf2-h1 16. Nh1-g3 17. Ng3-f1 18. Nf1-d2 19. Nd2-b3, and 20. Nb3-a1.
4. Yes.
5. No.
6. No.
7. Yes.
8. No.

Relative Values of the Chess Forces

It is very important to know the value of the various men so that in trading men you don't give up a strong one for a weak one. A player who gets an advantage by trading his weaker men for his opponent's stronger ones can use this advantage to force checkmate or to queen a pawn and then force checkmate.

The value of a chessman is determined by its maneuverability and range, by the number of squares it can cross in one move, by the number of squares it can control, by how rapidly and deeply it can infiltrate the enemy positions, and by how dangerous a threat it can pose to the opponent. The experience of many games has shown that the approximate relative values of the chessmen are as follows:

Queen	— 9 points
Rook	— 5 points
Bishop	— 3 points
Knight	— 3 points
Pawn	— 1 point

The King cannot be captured, and so it is not included in the above list. In the center of the board it controls eight squares, while in a corner it is not even half as strong, controlling only three squares (see Diagram 135).

135

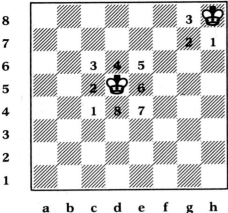

The King differs from the other men, however, in that its value is not determined by its strength. In the opening and the middlegame the King is a weak piece that must be safely guarded. In the endgame, when it is not in danger of being checkmated by the opponent's men, the King gains power considerably, varying in strength between a Bishop (or Knight) and a Rook.

The strongest piece is the Queen. From a central position it controls 27 squares, nearly half the board (Diagram 136).

136

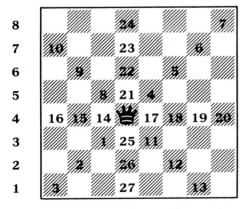

It is weaker in the corner, but still controls 21 squares (Diagram 137).

137

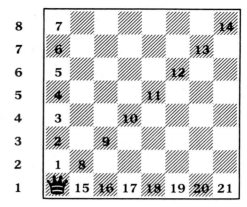

The next strongest is the Rook. No matter where it is on the board, it controls 14 squares (Diagram 138).

138

The Bishop controls 13 squares from a central position (Diagram 139) but only seven squares from a corner (Diagram 140).

139

140

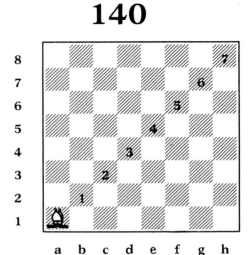

Although i can control almost as many squares as a Rook, the Bishop is much weaker. The reason is that it can move only on squares of one color, and thus cannot threaten enemy pieces on squares of the other color. The Queen, Rook, and Bishop are all long-range pieces, as they can attack hostile pieces at any distance.

The Knight controls eight squares from a central position and only two from a corner (Diagram 141).

141

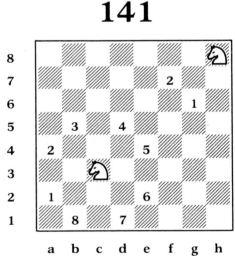

The Knight controls fewer squares than the Bishop, and unlike the Bishop, it is not a long-range piece. It can only attack enemy pieces that are nearby. On the other hand, the Knight has greater maneuverability, being able to jump over other pieces, and it can attack enemy pieces on both light and dark squares. These advantages and disadvantages generally balance out, and so the Knight and Bishop are considered to be of equal value.

Diagram 142 illustrates the attacking capabilities of pawns.

142

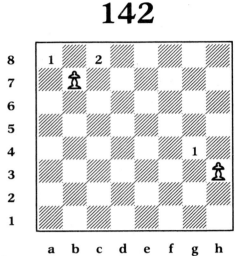

The Rook pawns (a-pawn and h-pawn) control only one square each, while the other pawns all control two squares each. The pawns are the weakest units in the chess army. However, we must not disdain them, since they have the potential of changing into a Queen or any other piece.

Diagrams 143–146 show positions in which the White and Black men are of equal value:

143

Bishop = 3 pawns = 3 points

144

Knight = 3 pawns = 3 points

145

Rook = Bishop + 2 pawns = 5 points

146

Rook = Knight + 2 pawns = 5 points
Similarly, you can figure out that two Bishops are stronger than a Rook, that a Queen

is more valuable than a Rook and a Bishop, and so on.

When playing, you should keep in mind the relative values of the various men, but at the same time never forget that the final goal is to checkmate your opponent's King. It is worth it to sacrifice any number of your pieces if by doing so you can checkmate your opponent's King.

HOMEWORK

In doing the homework, remember that
Queen = 9 points
Rook = 5 points
Bishop = 3 points
Knight = 3 points
Pawn = 1 point

From now on, you should keep track of the point count during your games, but never forget that checkmate is of greater value than any number of points.

I. Diagrams 147–154

147

Who has more points — White or Black?

_____

_____

_____

148

Which position is better and why?

_____

_____

_____

149

Who has more points — Black or White?

_____

_____

_____

150

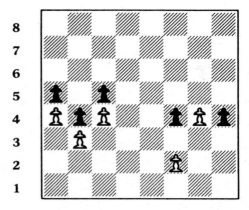

White's last move was **g2-g4**. How many moves has Black in this position?

_____

_____

_____

151

Is castling possible in this position for White and Black?

_____

_____

_____

152

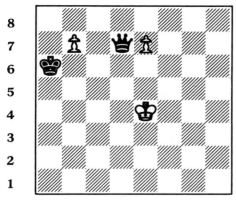

White to play. Can they win?

_____

_____

_____

153

White to play. Can they win?

_____

_____

_____

154

White to move. How will the game end?

_____

_____

_____

II. Exercises

1. Without looking at the board, name the squares that the King crosses in going from e1 to h8 via f5.

_____

_____

_____

2. Move a Rook from a1 in such a way that it lands on every square of the board exactly once and then comes back to a1. (Mark your answer on the diagram below).

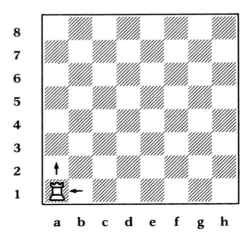

HOMEWORK ANSWERS
I. Diagrams 147–154

D-147   White is one point up and has chances of winning.

D-148   White is two points up and has chances of winning.

D-149   White and Black have each lost six points, and the game is even.

D-150   Black has four moves: **1. ... f4-f3; 1. ... f4xg3 en passant; 1. ... h4xg3 en passant; and 1. ... h4-h3.**

D-151   Neither side can castle: White, because his Rooks have already moved, and Black, because his King has already moved.

D-152   Yes. Although Black is seven points up, White wins here thanks to the wonderful ability of pawns to turn into any other piece when they reach the other end of the board: **1. b7-b8N +** and White captures the Black Queen the next move.

D-153   White can win only if his King and the Rook on h1 have not made any moves at all so far in the game. In that case White can castle and should win, since he is eight points up.

D-154   Black wins although White is a whole 12 points up. Black is threatening checkmate with **1. ... Ra8-a1** and the White Queen and Rook are in such a bad position that they cannot help their King. So the White King can avoid checkmate only by running away with **1. Ke1-d1**, but then Black replies with **Ra8-a1 +**, capturing the White Queen the next move and the White Rook the move after.

II. Exercises

1.   One possibility is: **1. Ke1-e2 2. Ke2-e3 3. Ke3-e4 4. Ke4-f5 5. Kf5-g6 6. Kg6-g7 7. Kg7-h8.**

2.   See Diagram 155.

155

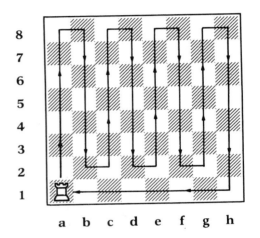

Lesson Nine

How Games Are Drawn

Check Lesson Eight homework if necessary.

Review Questions

What is more valuable:
1. A Knight or a Bishop?
2. A Knight and a pawn, or a Rook?
3. A Queen or two Rooks?
4. A Queen, or two Bishops and a Knight?
5. A Queen, or two Knights and a Bishop?
6. A Knight or four pawns?
7. A Bishop or three pawns?
8. A Rook or two Knights?
9. A Rook, or a Bishop and two pawns?
10. A King or a Queen?

Answers to Review Questions

1. A Bishop and a Knight are each worth three points, so neither is stronger — they are equal in value.
2. A Knight (three points) and a pawn (one point) are worth a total of four points, so they are weaker than a Rook (five points).
3. Since a Rook is worth five points, two Rooks are worth $2 \times 5 = 10$ points, so they are a bit stronger than a Queen (nine points).
4. Two Bishops (three points each for a total of six) and a Knight (three points) are worth a total of nine points and so are equal to a Queen (nine points).
5. Two Knights (three points each for a total of six) and a Bishop (three points) are worth a total of nine points and so are equal to a Queen (nine points).
6. Since a pawn is worth one point, four pawns are worth four points and so are stronger than a Knight, which is worth only three points.
7. Since a pawn is worth one point, three pawns are worth three points and so are equal in strength to a Bishop, which is also worth three points.
8. Since a Knight is worth three points, two Knights are worth six points and so are stronger than a Rook, which is worth only five points.
9. Since a pawn is worth one point, two pawns are worth two points. A Bishop is worth three points. So a Bishop and two pawns together are worth a total of $3 + 2 = 5$ points, and are equal to a Rook, which is also worth five points.
10. The King is of course more valuable than any other chess man.

How Games Are Drawn

Chess games usually end in victory for one player and defeat for the other. In some games, however, neither player is able to checkmate his opponent's King. In such cases, neither player wins, and the game ends in a draw. Here are some ways in which a draw can result: perpetual check, stalemate, or not enough material to force checkmate.

Perpetual Check

Perpetual check is a term which refers to the situation when one player checks the opponent's King endlessly, without, however, being able to checkmate it. Diagrams 156 and 157 show typical cases of perpetual check. It is most often a Queen that give perpetual check, but the Bishop, Rook, and Knight are also capable of doing so.

Diagram 156 shows perpetual check by the Queen.

156

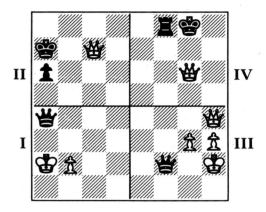

In 156-I, The Black Queen uses d1 and a4 for perpetual check. The only way for White to get out of check in the diagram is to move his King to b1. Then Black moves his Queen to d1 and again checks the White King, which must move back to a2, allowing the Black Queen to check from a4. Black can thus keep checking the White King forever by moving his Queen back and forth between a4 and d1, and so the game is a draw.

In 156-II, the White Queen moves back and forth between c7 and c8. In 156-III, the Black Queen gives perpetual check from f1 and f2, and in 156-IV, the White Queen shuttles back and forth between g6 and h6.

157

In Diagram 157-I, the Black Knight gives perpetual check to the White King by moving from b3 to c1 and back to b3 (... Nb3-c1, ... Nc1-b3), since the White King can only move to and fro between a1 and a2.

In 157-II, the White Rook can give perpetual

check from d8 and d7.

In 157-III, Black has an extra Queen. He should have won earlier, but he made a mistake and allowed the position in the diagram to occur. Here White can get a draw by giving perpetual check. No matter which Black Queen interposes, White can always check either on e4, e1 or h4.

In 157-IV, the White Queen can give perpetual check from g5 and f6, forcing the Black King to move back and forth between g8 and h8.

Perpetual check helps players to escape with a draw in games that they would otherwise lose. All players find it useful at some time or another, even World Champions.

Stalemate

A player can find himself in a situation where, although it is his turn to move, and his King is not in check, he has no legal moves. Any move that he made would put his King in check. Such a situation is called stalemate, and the player is said to be stalemated. The difference between stalemate and checkmate is that in stalemate, the King is not in check, while in checkmate, it is in check and cannot get out of it. A stalemate is a drawn game, while a checkmate is a loss for the player whose King is checkmated.

Stalemate occurs only if the player cannot make any legal moves at all. If his King cannot move, but he can move some other piece, he is not stalemated, and must move the other piece, even it it is dangerous to do so and will cause him to lose the game.

Diagrams 158-161 show typical stalemate positions. In all positions in Diagrams 158 and 159, it is White's turn to move. In each case, the King is not in check, but neither does it have any legal moves, since any move would put it in check.

158

159

In the eight positions in Diagrams 160 and 161, it is Black's turn to play, but any move would put his King in check. Therefore, the game in each case is a draw by stalemate, since Black's King is not in check and at the same time Black cannot make any legal move on his turn.

160

161

At first, the difference between checkmate and stalemate might not seem very big. In both cases, the King has no moves. But in checkmate, the King is in check, and that is very important. Checkmate wins, but stalemate draws.

Stalemate is often the last chance of a player who is losing. If you happen to have more men than your opponent and you think you can win easily, don't start playing carelessly, or else your opponent might escape with a stalemate. On the other hand, if you are losing, you should try to bring about a stalemate position, since a draw is better than a loss. Stalemate often is the result of a mistake by the player who has the advantage, but sometimes it is the logical end to a game in which both players have played equally well.

It is advisable for beginners to announce "stalemate," "check," or "checkmate" although according to the rules of play it is not compulsory to do so.

Not Enough Material

When neither player has enough material to checkmate, the game is a draw. Thus:
a) If each player only has a King left, neither can checkmate the opponent.
b) A King and a Knight alone cannot checkmate a lone King.
c) A King and a Bishop alone cannot checkmate a lone King.
d) If each of the players has only a King and a Bishop, and the Bishops are on the same color, then neither side can checkmate the other.

A King and a Knight (or a Bishop) alone can

only stalemate the enemy King, never checkmate it (see Diagram 161–I, II, III, IV).

HOMEWORK
I. Diagrams 162-169

162

Black to start and make a draw in two ways.

_____

_____

_____

163

How will the game end if White is to move and if Black is to move?

_____

_____

_____

164

Black to move. Can he draw?

_____

_____

_____

165

White to move and draw.

_____

_____

_____

166

White played **Qg4xd7**. Is it a good move?

_____

_____

_____

167

Black to play and draw.

_____

_____

_____

168

Black to move. Can he stop the White pawns?

_____

_____

_____

169

Black to move. Checkmate in one move.

_____

_____

_____

II. Exercises

1. Place five Queens on the diagram below in such a way that together they attack all 64 squares on the board.

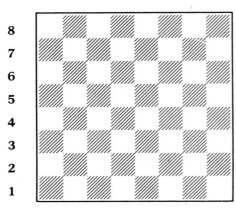

2. Make up a position on the diagram below in which a pawn is not attacked by any enemy men and has a choice of twelve different moves.

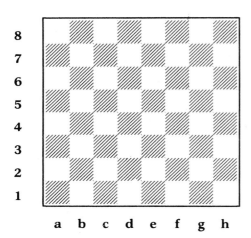

HOMEWORK ANSWERS
I. Diagrams 162-169

D-162 a) **1. ... Qc1-c7 +**. After **2. Qd7xc7** Black is stalemated.

b) **1. ... Qc1-f4 +**. If the White King now retreats to the first rank (**2. Kh1** or **2. Kg1**), then the Black Queen returns to c1 and checks the White King (**2. ... Qc1 +**), giving perpetual check on c1 and f4. If after **1. ... Qc1-f4 +** White does not retreat his King but instead interposes his pawn (**2. g2-g3**), then the Black Queen captures the pawn on f2 (**2. ... Qf4xf2 +**) and gives perpetual check on f2 and f1.

D-163 White to play can draw by giving perpetual check with his Knight by **1. Nf8-g6 + 2. Ng6-f8 +**, etc. Black to play can checkmate White by **1. ... Qf2-h2#**.

D-164 Black to play draws with **1. ... Qf5-g4 +** and after **2. Kh1** the Black Queen gives perpetual check on f3 and g4.

D-165 After **1. Qb3-g8 +**, Black must capture the Queen by **1. ... Kh8xg8**, and White is stalemated.

D-166 **1. Qg4xd7** is a bad move since it stalemates Black. Instead White should have first played **1. Rb5-a5 +** and then captured the Queen on the next move, when Black wouldn't be stalemated any more.

D-167 Black draws by **1. ... Qb4-h4 +**, forcing White to capture the Queen by **52. Kxh4**, after which Black is stalemated.

D-168 No. The Rook cannot hold back both White pawns and one of them will become a Queen.

D-169 **1. ... Qb4-a3#** checkmates White! White cannot capture the Black Queen with his pawn because that would expose his King to check by the Black Bishop on h8.

II. Exercises

1. There are some 4,000 ways of placing five Queens on a chessboard in such a way that together they attack all 64 squares on the board. One way is shown in Diagram 170.

170

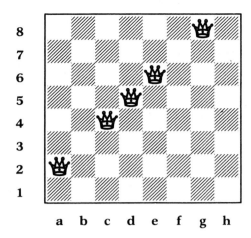

2. In Diagram 171 the White pawn is not attacked and has a choice of twelve different moves: (1) **1. e7xd8Q**; (2) **1. e7xd8R**; (3) **1. e7xd8B**; (4) **1. e7xd8N**; (5) **1. e7-e8Q**; (6) **1. e7-e8R**; (7) **1. e7-e8B**; (8) **1. e7-e8N**; (9) **1. e7xf8Q**; (10) **1. e7xf8R**; (11) **1. e7xf8B**; and (12) **1. e7xf8N**.

171

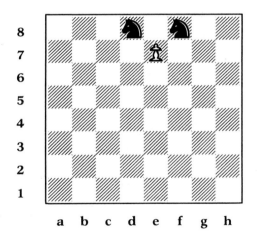

Lesson Ten
How To Record Moves

Check Lesson Nine homework (if necessary)

Review Questions:
1. What is the difference between a check-mate and a stalemate?
2. Make up a stalemate position.
3. Is it possible to win with only a King and a Knight against a lone King?
4. Is it possible to win with only a King and a Bishop against a lone King?
5. White has a King and a Queen, and Black has only his King. Using these pieces only, make up a position in which Black is stale-mated.
6. What is perpetual check?
7. Make up a position in which a pawn on e2 has a choice of four different moves.
8. Is it possible for a position to occur in which there are Black pawns on a2, a3, a4, a5, and a6?

Answers to Review Questions

1. In checkmate one of the Kings is in check and cannot get out of it, while in stalemate neither King is in check.
2. An example is shown in Diagram 172, where Black to move is stalemated.

3. No.
4. No.
5. An example is shown in Diagram 173, where Black to move is stalemated.

6. Perpetual check is a series of endless checks from which the King cannot escape.
7. An example is shown in Diagram 174, where the White pawn on e2 has the choice of moving 1. e2-e3, 1. e2-e4, 1. e2xd3, or 1. e2xf3.

8. Yes. The a6 pawn can get there by advancing from a7 without any captures; the a5 pawn can get there from b6 by capturing (... b6xa5); the a4 pawn can get there from c6 by making two captures (... c6xb5, and ... b5xa4); the a3 pawn can get there from d6 by making three captures (... d6xc5, ... c5xb4, and ... b4xa3);

and the a2 pawn can get there from e6 by making four captures (... e6xd5, ... d5xc4, ... c4xb3, and ... b3xa2). Thus a total of ten enemy men must be captured. This is possible since each side has fifteen men that may be captured during play.

How To Record Moves

In this lesson we will review what we have learned about chess notation. As you know, chess notation is a special kind of language in which each square and man has a name, so that we can record positions and moves. The notation taught in this book is the international algebraic notation.

Once you have mastered the notation system, you will be able to read chess books. Using this system, strong players can even play chess blindfolded.

Algebraic notation is based on a grid system. Each file is designated by a letter, and each rank by a number. Thus, each square is uniquely identified by a symbol consisting of a letter followed by a number.

The files are designated by the letters from a to h, starting from White's left, while the ranks are numbered from 1 to 8, starting from the rank nearest White.

To record a move, you first write down the symbol of the piece that is being moved, then its square of departure, then a hyphen (-), and then the square to which the piece is being moved. If the move is a capture, use an ''x'' instead of a hyphen. If the move is made by a pawn, its symbol is left out, and only the square of departure, an ''x'' or a hyphen, and the square of arrival are indicated. For example, e2-e4 means that the pawn on e2 is moved to e4. Here are some other examples: **Rd1xd6** means that a Rook on d1 captured a man on d6; **a7xb8Q** means that a pawn on a7 captured a piece on b8 and became a Queen; **e7xd8N +** means that a pawn on e7 captured a piece on d8, became a Knight, and gave check to the Black King.

The moves in a game are recorded in two vertical columns, the first for White's moves and the second for Black's moves. Before each of White's moves, there is a number. This number indicates how many moves have been made. Here is an example showing the first five moves in a game:

1.	e2-e4	e7-e5
2.	Ng1-f3	Nb8-c6
3.	Bf1-c4	Ng8-f6
4.	d2-d3	Bf8-e7
5.	0-0	0-0

The position after these moves is shown below in Diagram 175.

175

If you want to refer to Black's move by itself, you put three dots before his move. Thus, if we wanted to refer to Black's second move in the above example, we would write **2. ... Nb8-c6.**

Here is another example:

Qd1-h5# means that the White Queen moves from d1 to h5 and checkmates the Black King.

Chess players often record not only games but also positions. In recording a position, first the positions of White's King, Queen, Rooks, Bishops, Knights, and pawns are given, in that order, and then the positions of the Black men, in the same order.

For example, let us record a position from the homework (Diagram 177):

White: Kg1, Qg2, Re8, P's a5, b4, c3
Black: Kh8, Qg6, Nf8, P's a6, b5, c4.
White to move.

The main symbols used in chess notation are as follows: K for King, Q for Queen, B for

65

Bishop, N for Knight, p for pawn, - for "moves to," x for "captures on," + for "check," # for "checkmate," 0-0 for "castles on the Kingside," 0-0-0 for "castles on the Queenside," ? for bad move, ! for good move, and ... for "Black's move."

The recording of games is obligatory in tournaments and matches. Beginners are advised to start recording their games so that they can later analyze them to try and find out their own and their opponents' mistakes.

HOMEWORK
I. Diagrams 176-181

Write down your answers in the spaces provided.

176

Find and record how on its move:
a) White wins
b) Black draws

_____

_____

_____

177

White played **1. Qg2xg6.** Is it a good move?

_____

_____

_____

178

How can Black, on its move, checkmate in one move, and how can it stalemate the White King?

_____

_____

_____

179

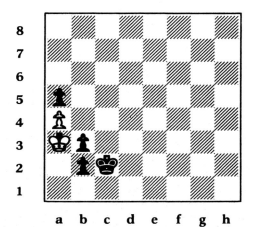

Black to move and checkmate in one move.
Find four ways of stalemating the White King.

_____

_____

_____

180

Record three moves by White and Black
which have been made in this game.

	WHITE	BLACK
1.		
2.		
3.		

181

Record the position of White and Black
pieces after the moves:

1. e2-e4	e7-e5
2. Ng1-f3	Nb8-c6
3. Bf1-c4	Ng8-f6

_____

_____

_____

II. Exercises

Write down your answers in the spaces
below.

1. How many Knights of the same color can
be placed on a board in such a way that none of
them defends another?

_____

_____

_____

2. Is it possible for a position to occur with
White pawns on g2, h2, and h3? If not, why
not? If so, how?

_____

_____

_____

3. Is it possible for a position to occur with Black pawns on a2, a3, and a4? If so, how? If not, why not?

_____

_____

_____

4. Place five Knights on an empty board in such a way that one of them attacks only two squares, another attacks only three squares, a third attacks only four squares, a fourth attacks only six squares, and the fifth attacks eight squares, with none of the Knights attacking any of the same squares as any other Knight.

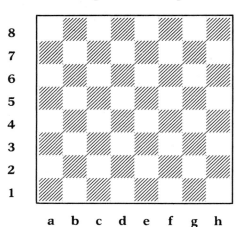

Homework Answers
I. Diagrams 176–181

D-176 a) White to move can checkmate Black with **1. Ra3-a8#.**

b) Black to move plays **1. ... a2-a1Q +**, and after White captures the Queen with **2. Ra3xa1,** Black is stalemated.

D-177 1. Qg2xg6 was a very bad move as it stalemated Black. Instead, White could have won by playing **1. Re8xf8 +.**

D-178 Black can checkmate White by **1. ... Bd7-h3#,** and stalemate him by **1. ... Bd7-b5.**

D-179 Black checkmates White by **1. ... b2-b1N#. 1. ... Kc2-c3, 1. ... b2-b1Q, 1. ... b2-b1R,** and **1. ... b2-b1B** all stalemate White.

D-180 This position can be reached after the following moves:

1. e2-e4		e7-e5
2. Ng1-f3		Nb8-c6
3. Nb1-c3		Bf8-c5

D-181 White: Ke1, Qd1, Ra1, Rh1, Bc1, Bc4, Nb1, Nf3, P's a2, b2, c2, d2, e4, f2, g2, h2.

Black: Ke8, Qd8, Ra8, Rh8, Bc8, Bf8, Nc6, Nf6, P's a7, b7, c7, d7, e5, f7, g7, h7.

II. Exercises

1. Thirty-two, placed on all the light squares or on all the dark squares of the board. This is easy to understand if you remember that a Knight always moves from a light square to a dark square or vice-versa.

2. Such a position (see Diagram 182) is impossible, because a pawn can get to h3 only by moving up from h2 or by capturing from g2.

182

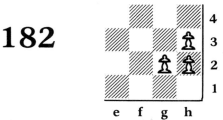

Since both the h2 and the g2 pawns are still in their original positions, there is nowhere for the pawn on h3 to have come from.

3. Yes. The pawn on a4 could move up there from a7, while the other two pawns could get where they are by capturing a total of three times: once (**... b4xa3**) for the pawn on a3 and twice (**... c4xb3** and **b3xa2**) for the pawn on a2.

4. See Diagram 183.

183

Knight 1 (on a1) attacks two squares (b3 and c2);

Knight 2 (on g1) attacks three squares (e2, f3, and h3);

Knight 3 (on d8) attacks four squares (b7, c6, e6, and f7);

Knight 4 (on b6) attacks six squares (a4, a8, c4, c8, d5, and d7);

Knight 5 (on e4) attacks eight squares (c3, c5, d2, d6, f2, f6, g3, and g5);

and none of them attacks any squares attacked by any of the other Knights!

Note that the closer a Knight is to the center, the stronger it becomes.

Lesson Eleven
How To Open a Chess Game

Check Lesson Ten homework if necessary.

Review Questions

1. How many squares are there on a chessboard?
2. What are the different kinds of lines formed by squares on a chessboard?
3. What is meant by the "center" of the chessboard?
4. How many Queens can a player have during a game?

Answer Questions 5–8 without looking at a board.

5. Is e7 a light square or a dark one?
6. Name the squares on which the various Black pieces stand at the start of a game.
7. Name the squares that make up the a1-h8 diagonal. Are they light squares or dark ones?
8. At what square does the b-file cross the fourth rank?

Answers to Review Questions

1. Sixty-four.
2. A chessboard contains eight ranks (1 to 8) and eight files (a to h) and many diagonals.
3. The "center" consists of the four squares d4, d5, e4, and e5.
4. A player can have as many as nine Queens, if in addition to keeping his original one he manages to queen all eight of his pawns.
5. The e7 square is dark square.
6. Ke8, Qd8, Ra8, Rh8, Bc8, Bf8, Nb8 and Ng8.
7. The a1-h8 diagonal is a dark-square diagonal consisting of the squares a1, b2, c3, d4, e5, f6, g7, and h8.
8. Obviously b4!

How to Start a Chess Game

You are now acquainted with the main rules of play. In order to master them better, you need to practise, preferably one hour a day. You can practise against anyone who knows how to play chess, even a computer. Set up the pieces in their starting positions, and away you go!

There are a large number of possibilities for your first move: 16 pawn moves and 4 Knight moves. However, not all of these moves are equally good. Let us look at some examples.

Opening move for White: **1. e2-e4** or **1. d2-d4.**

Opening move for Black: **1. ... e7-e5** or **1. ... d7-d5.** (Diagrams 184 and 185).

184

1. e2-e4 (White) 1. ... e7-e5 (Black)
These are good moves to start a game.

185

1. d2-d4 (White) 1. ... d7-d5 (Black)
These are good moves to start a game.

These are reasonable moves. Lines are opened up for a Bishop and the Queen.

Opening move for White: **1. g2-g4** or **1. h2-h4**

Opening move for Black: **1. ... g7-g5** or **1. ... h7-h5** (Diagrams 186 and 187).

186

1. h2-h4 (White) 1. ... h7-h5 (Black)
Bad moves. Don't start a game this way.

187

1. g2-g4 (White) 1. ... g7-g5 (Black)
Bad moves. Don't start a game this way.

These moves are not only useless, but also harmful, since the King's position after castling on the Kingside will be exposed, and the opponent will find it easier to checkmate the King.

What are the best ways to start a game? Which pawns should be moved? You have already learned, in Lesson Five, that the center includes the squares d4, d5, e4, and e5. Pieces in the center can easily be transferred to any point on the board, either on the Queenside or on the Kingside. In addition, pieces gain in strength and range when they are in or near the center. For example, a Knight has only two moves if it is in a corner, but eight moves if it is in the center.

In general, a player should aim to achieve the following goals in the opening:

1. the quick development (mobilization) of his pieces;
2. the transfer of his pieces towards the center;
and
3. the safety of his King.
Only thus can a player hope to win.

The experience of the best chessplayers in the world over many centuries has shown that it is wise to adhere to the following principles during the opening stages of a chess game:
1. Always keep in mind the relative strength of each piece. Since the Queen is the strongest one, don't bring it out hastily, or else your opponent will attack it with his Knights, Bishops,

or pawns, thereby forcing your Queen to retreat and furthering his development at your expense.

2. Don't make passive waiting moves such as **a2-a3, a7-a6, h2-h3** or **h7-h6.** Each move should either develop a piece or increase the piece's mobility by opening up files, ranks, or diagonals for them.

3. Try to set up a strong pawn center (e.g. pawns on e4 and d4).

4. Don't waste time by moving one and the same piece repeatedly, at the expense of developing the other pieces.

5. Bring out your Kingside Knight and Bishop, thereby getting ready to transfer your King to a safe place by castling on the Kingside, a move which at the same time develops the King's Rook. After castling, develop your Queenside pieces.

6. Don't attack prematurely. First develop your pieces and castle.

The following is an example of correct opening play by both White and Black:

White	Black
1. e2-e4	e7-e5
2. Ng1-f3	Nb8-c6
3. Bf1-c4	Bf8-c5
4. 0-0	Ng8-f6
5. Nb1-c3	0-0
6. d2-d3	d7-d6

The resultant position is shown in Diagram 188.

188

Both sides have achieved a good position in the opening and the outcome of the game will depend on who conducts the rest of the game better.

Now let's look at a game where White blunders in the opening and gets checkmated on the second move. This is the shortest game of chess possible, and it's called the "Fool's Mate."

White: 1. f2-f3?

A bad move that leaves the King open to attack. In addition, the pawn on f3 robs the Knight on g1 of its best square.

Black: 1. ... e7-e5

An excellent move, occupying the central square e5 and opening up a diagonal for the f8 Bishop and the Queen.

White: 2. g2-g4??

A terrible move! White completely opens up the way to his King instead of bringing out his pieces.

Black: 2. ,... Qd8-h4#

Just desserts!

Black had planned to develop his center pawns and then his Knights and Bishops, but after such a terrible move by White, he at once made the most of his opportunity. This example shows you that it is not safe to move your f and g pawns unless you know exactly what you are doing. When your opponent makes such weak moves, try to checkmate him or attack him vigorously.

If your opponent's mistake leads to a situation where you think it is suitable to move your Queen out even in the opening, do so with care, remembering that it is an extremely valuable piece.

The Fool's Mate position is shown in Diagram 189. In this diagram the men have been represented by their letter symbols instead of by their picture symbols. The letters indicating Black men have been circled. Chess players sometimes use this method when solving a problem since it is easy to use; all a person needs is a blank diagram and he can show any position on it. It is advisable to use a pencil, since that way any mistakes can be easily rubbed out and corrected. You will use this method in Chapter Twelve, the test. There are 20 tests altogether and each student will pick one at random and answer all six questions on it. The test will show how well you have learned the material in the course.

189

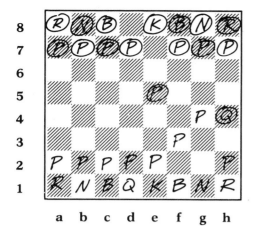

HOMEWORK

1. Review the homework of previous lessons.
2. Teach your parents how to play chess (if they don't know already).
3. Play often, but not more than one hour a day.

You have now finished Level I, **The Rules of Play.**

Test One

1. Where does the a3-f8 diagonal cross the d-file?

190

2. Construct a checkmate position where White has a Queen, Rook, and a King, and Black has only a King.

3. Place a White Queen, two Black Rooks, and the Black King on the board in such a way that Black is checkmated.

4. Place the White King, a White Bishop, the Black King, a Black Bishop, and a Black pawn on the board in such a way that Black is stalemated.

5. Place four White Queens on a quarter-board in such a way that none of them is defended. You can use pawns to represent Queens.

6. Diagram 190. White to move. There is a mistake in the position. Find out what it is and correct it by any means. Once you have done so, White should be able to checkmate Black in one move.

To show different positions on the blank diagrams below use the following symbols:

WHITE: King— K ; Queen— Q ; Rook— R ; Bishop— B ; Knight— N ; Pawn— P
BLACK: King— Ⓚ ; Queen— Ⓠ ; Rook— Ⓡ ; Bishop— Ⓑ ; Knight— Ⓝ ; Pawn— Ⓟ

 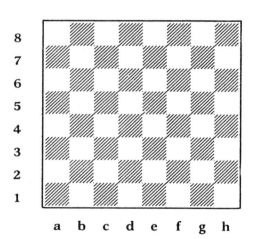

1. Where does the b8-h2 diagonal cross the 4th rank?

191

2. Construct a checkmate position using the White Queen, the White King, and the Black King.

3. Construct a checkmate positon using two White pawns, a White Bishop, and the Black King.

4. Using any men you want, make up a position where White can checkmate Black by playing pawn takes pawn en passant.

5. Place two White Rooks and two White Bishops on a quarter-board in such a way that none of them is defended by another.

6. Where must the Black King be placed in Diagram 191 so that

    a) Black is checkmated?

    b) Black is stalemated?

    c) White to play can checkmate Black in one move?

To show different positions on the blank diagrams below use the following symbols:

WHITE: King— K ; Queen— Q ; Rook— R ; Bishop— B ; Knight— N ; Pawn— P
BLACK: King— Ⓚ ; Queen— Ⓠ ; Rook— Ⓡ ; Bishop— Ⓑ ; Knight— Ⓝ ; Pawn— Ⓟ

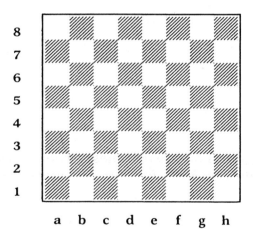

Test Three

1. What is the most number of Queens that a player can have?

---

2. Construct a checkmate position where White has two Rooks and his King and Black has just his King.

3. Construct a position where a White Rook and a White Knight have checkmated Black's King.

4. Find a position in which White can checkmate the Black King in half a move.

5. Place a White King, White Queen, White Rook and White Bishop on a quarter-board in such a way that none of them is defended by another.

6. Diagram 192. In a real chess game, each side can only have one King. But here is a crazy position in which Black has ten Kings! Find a move for White which checkmates all the Black Kings at the same time.

192

To show different positions on the blank diagrams below use the following symbols:

WHITE: King— K ; Queen— Q ; Rook— R ; Bishop— B ; Knight— N ; Pawn— P
BLACK: King— Ⓚ; Queen— Ⓠ ; Rook— Ⓡ ; Bishop— Ⓑ; Knight— Ⓝ ; Pawn— Ⓟ

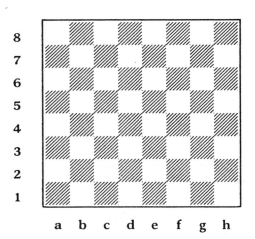

Test Four

1. What is the most number of Rooks that one player can have?

193

2. Construct a position where White, with his King, a Rook, and a Bishop, has checkmated Black's King.
3. Place a Black King, Black pawn, White King, and White Knight on the board in such a way that Black is checkmated.
4. Construct a position in which a pawn has a choice of twelve different moves without itself being under attack any any time, either before or after moving.
5. White has two Rooks, a light-square bishop, and a dark-square Bishop. Place them all on a quarter-board in such a way that each piece defends and is defended by exactly one other piece.
6. Diagram 193. A tricky puzzle! White to checkmate Black in one move.

To show different positions on the blank diagrams below use the following symbols:

WHITE: King— K ; Queen— Q ; Rook— R ; Bishop— B ; Knight— N ; Pawn— P
BLACK: King— Ⓚ; Queen— Ⓠ; Rook— Ⓡ; Bishop— Ⓑ; Knight— Ⓝ; Pawn— Ⓟ

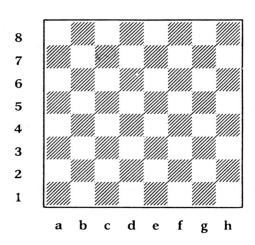

Test Five

1. What is the most number of Bishops that a player can have?

194

---

2. Construct a checkmate position in which White has a King, Rook, and a Knight, and Black has a lone King.

3. Place a Black King and a White Queen on the board in such a way that Black is stalemated.

4. Set up a position where White and Black each have a King and a Knight, and Black has been checkmated.

5. Place a White King, White Queen, White Bishop, and White Knight on a quarter-board in such a way that none of them is defended by another.

6. Diagram 194. Can either player, if it is his turn to move, avoid checkmating the other?

To show different positions on the blank diagrams below use the following symbols:

WHITE: King— K ; Queen— Q ; Rook— R ; Bishop— B ; Knight— N ; Pawn— P
BLACK: King— Ⓚ; Queen— Ⓠ; Rook— Ⓡ; Bishop— Ⓑ; Knight— Ⓝ; Pawn—Ⓟ

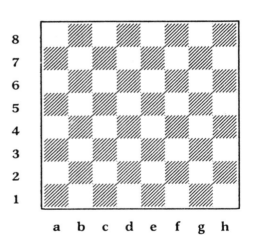

Test Six

1. What is the most number of Knights that one player can have?

---

2. Construct a position in which White, with a King and Rook, has checkmated Black's lone King.

3. Place two White Rooks and a Black King on a board in such a way that Black is stalemated.

4. Construct a position in which White, with two Bishops and a King, has checkmated Black's lone King.

5. Place a White King, Queen, Rook, and Knight on a quarter-board in such a way that none of them is defended by another.

6. Diagram 195. White to play and checkmate Black in one move.

To show different positions on the blank diagrams below use the following symbols:

WHITE: King— K ; Queen— Q ; Rook— R ; Bishop— B ; Knight— N ; Pawn— P

BLACK: King— Ⓚ; Queen— Ⓠ; Rook— Ⓡ; Bishop— Ⓑ; Knight— Ⓝ; Pawn— Ⓟ

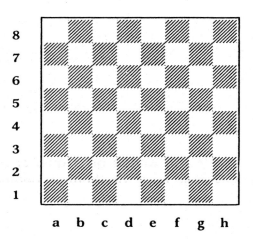

Test Seven

1. Can a pawn remain a pawn when it reaches the last rank, or does it have to turn into a piece?

196

2. Construct a position where White, with a Bishop, Knight, and King, has checkmated a lone Black King.

3. Place a Black King, White Rook, and White Knight on a board in such a way that Black is stalemated.

4. Place a White King, White Bishop, and White Knight on a board in such a way that the Knight has no moves.

5. Place a White Queen, White Rook, White Bishop, and White Knight on a quarter-board in such a way that none of them is defended by another.

6. Diagram 196. White to play and checkmate Black in one move.

To show different positions on the blank diagrams below, use the following symbols:

WHITE: King— K ; Queen— Q ; Rook— R ; Bishop— B ; Knight— N ; Pawn— P

BLACK: King— Ⓚ ; Queen— Ⓠ ; Rook— Ⓡ ; Bishop— Ⓑ ; Knight— Ⓝ ; Pawn— Ⓟ

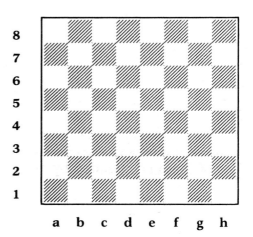

Test Eight

1. When a pawn reaches the last rank, can it turn into a King?

2. Construct a position in which White, with his King and two Knights, has checkmated a lone Black King.

3. Place a Black King, White Rook, and White pawn on a board in such a way that Black is stalemated.

4. White and Black each have a King, Queen, Bishop and Rook. Place all the eight men on a quarter-board in such a way that none of them is attacked by an enemy man.

5. Place a White King, White Rook, White Bishop, and White Knight on a quarter-board in such a way that none of them is defended by another.

6. Diagram 197. White to play and checkmate Black in one move.

197

To show different positions on the blank diagrams below use the following symbols:

WHITE: King— K ; Queen— Q ; Rook— R ; Bishop— B ; Knight— N ; Pawn— P
BLACK: King— Ⓚ ; Queen— Ⓠ ; Rook— Ⓡ ; Bishop— Ⓑ ; Knight— Ⓝ ; Pawn— Ⓟ

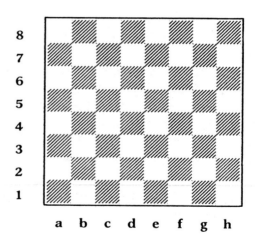

Test Nine

1. Is castling possible when a Rook is under attack?

---

2. Place a Black King, Black Bishop, White King and White Bishop on a board in such a way that Black is checkmated. White's is a dark-square Bishop, and Black's is a light-square one.

3. Place a Black King, White King, and White Rook on a board in such a way that Black has been stalemated.

4. Place eight pawns (four of each color) on the board in such a way that each player has a choice of six different captures.

5. Can White castle if he has his King on d1 and a Rook on a1?

---

6. Diagram 198. White to play and checkmate Black in one move.

198

To show different positions on the blank diagrams below, use the following symbols:

WHITE: King— K ; Queen— Q ; Rook— R ; Bishop— B ; Knight— N ; Pawn— P
BLACK: King— Ⓚ; Queen— Ⓠ; Rook— Ⓡ; Bishop— Ⓑ; Knight— Ⓝ; Pawn— Ⓟ

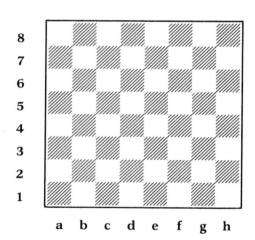

Test Ten

1. Can a player castle if that would involve moving his Rook across a square attacked by an enemy piece, but his King would not have to cross or land on a square attacked by an enemy piece?

199

2. Construct a position where White, with his King and two Pawns, has checkmated a lone Black King.

3. Place a Black King, Black Knight, White King and White pawn on a board in such a way that the White pawn has four ways of checkmating Black in one move by being promoted into a Rook or a Queen.

4. Place the eight Black pieces along with the White King on a quarter-board in such a way that White is not in check and has a choice of three captures.

5. Using a White King, a White Bishop, two White pawns, and a Black King, make up a position in which one of the White pawns can checkmate Black by being promoted into a Bishop.

6. Diagram 199. White to play and checkmate Black in one move.

To show different positions on the blank diagrams below use the following symbols:

WHITE: King— K ; Queen— Q ; Rook— R ; Bishop— B ; Knight— N ; Pawn— P

BLACK: King— Ⓚ ; Queen— Ⓠ ; Rook— Ⓡ ; Bishop— Ⓑ ; Knight— Ⓝ ; Pawn— Ⓟ

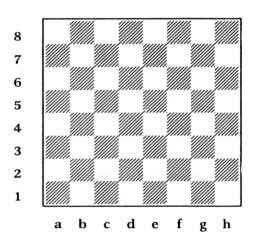

Test Eleven

1. If White has moved his pawn from c2 to c3, and later, on another move, from c3 to c4, can the pawn be captured en passant by a Black pawn on d4?

2. Place a Black King, Black Knight, White King, and White Bishop on a board in such a way that Black has been checkmated.

3. Place a Black King, White King, and White Knight on a board in such a way that Black has been stalemated.

4. Place eight pawns (four of each color) on a board in such a way that none of them can move or capture.

5. Can White castle if he has his King on e1 and a Rook on h1, while Black has a Bishop on g3 and there is no man on f2? _____

6. Diagram 200. White to play and checkmate Black in one move.

200

To show different positions on the blank diagrams below use the following symbols:

WHITE: King— K ; Queen— Q ; Rook— R ; Bishop— B ; Knight— N ; Pawn— P
BLACK: King— (K) ; Queen— (Q) ; Rook— (R) ; Bishop— (B) ; Knight— (N) ; Pawn— (P)

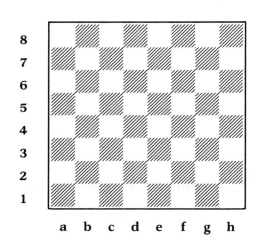

Test Twelve

1. What is the difference between a checkmate and a stalemate?

---

2. Construct a position in which White, with a King, Bishop, and pawn, has checkmated Black's lone King

3. Place a Black King, White King, and White Bishop on a board in such a way that Black is stalemated.

4. Arrange the two Kings along with a White Queen, White Rook, White Bishop, and White Knight on a quarter-board in such a way that each of the four White pieces can checkmate Black in one move.

5. Place a White Rook, White Bishop, Black King, Black Rook, Black Bishop, and two Black pawns on a board in such a way that the White Bishop can give perpetual check.

6. Diagram 201. White to play and checkmate Black in one move.

201

To show different positions on the blank diagrams below use the following symbols:

WHITE: King— K ; Queen— Q ; Rook— R ; Bishop— B ; Knight— N ; Pawn— P

BLACK: King— (K); Queen— (Q); Rook— (R); Bishop— (B); Knight— (N); Pawn— (P)

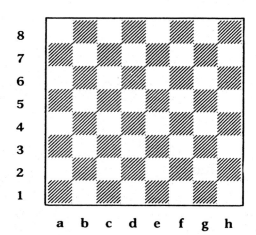

Test Thirteen

1. There is a Black pawn on e4. White first moves d2-d4, and later f2-f4. Which pawn can Black capture en passant after White's move f2-f4?

---

2. Place a Black King, Black Bishop, White King, and White Knight on a board in such a way that Black is checkmated.

3. Place a Black King, Black pawn, and White Queen on a board in such a way that White can give perpetual check to the Black King.

4. Set up a stalemate position using a White King, White pawn, and two Black Rooks without putting any men on any of the board's edges.

5. Diagram 202—I. White to play and checkmate black in one move.

---

6. Diagram 202—II. White to play and checkmate Black in one move. This is a tricky puzzle!

202

I   II

To show different positions on the blank diagrams below use the following symbols:

WHITE: King— K ; Queen— Q ; Rook— R ; Bishop— B ; Knight— N ; Pawn— P
BLACK: King— Ⓚ ; Queen— Ⓠ ; Rook— Ⓡ ; Bishop— Ⓑ ; Knight— Ⓝ ; Pawn— Ⓟ

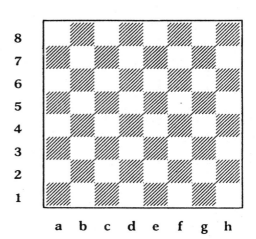

Test Fourteen

1. If you touch one of your pieces which has a legal move, can you move another piece instead?

2. Construct a position in which White, with a King, Knight, and pawn, has checkmated a lone Black King.

3. Arrange a Black King, a Black Rook, a Black Bishop, two Black pawns, and a White pawn on a board in such a way that the White pawn can checkmate Black in one move by being promoted into a Knight.

4. Arrange the two Kings and one White pawn on a board in such a way that the White pawn can checkmate Black in one move by being promoted into a Queen or a Rook.

5. Diagram 203—I. White to play and checkmate Black in one move.

6. Diagram 203—II. White to play and checkmate Black in one move.

203

I   II

To show different positions on the blank diagrams below use the following symbols:

WHITE: King— K ; Queen— Q ; Rook— R ; Bishop— B ; Knight— N ; Pawn— P
BLACK: King—(K); Queen—(Q); Rook—(R); Bishop—(B); Knight—(N); Pawn—(P)

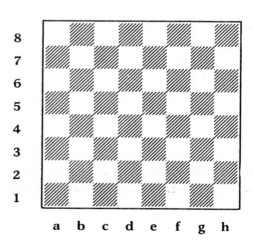

Test Fifteen

1. If you touch an enemy piece which is attacked by one of your own pieces, do you have to capture the enemy piece?

---

2. Place a Black King, Black Rook, White King, and White Knight on a board in such a way that Black has been checkmated.

3. Can White castle if he has his King on f1 and a Rook on h1?

---

4. Construct a position in which a pawn can move to any of four squares without itself being under attack at any time, either before or after moving.

5. Diagram 204—I. White to play and checkmate Black in one move.

---

6. Diagram 204—II. White to play and checkmate Black in one move.

204

I

II

To show different positions on the blank diagrams below use the following symbols:

WHITE: King— K ; Queen— Q ; Rook— R ; Bishop— B ; Knight— N ; Pawn— P
BLACK: King— Ⓚ ; Queen— Ⓠ ; Rook— Ⓡ ; Bishop— Ⓑ ; Knight— Ⓝ ; Pawn— Ⓟ

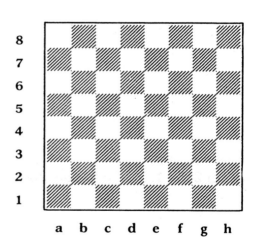

Test Sixteen

1. If a player's King is checked by a Knight or a pawn, can the player get his King out of check by putting one of his men in the way to block the check?

2. Place a Black King, Black Knight, Black pawn, White King, and White pawn on a board in such a way that Black has been checkmated.

3. Can Black castle if he has his King on e8 and a Rook on g8?

4. Set up a position in which each player has only a King and pawn, and Black has been checkmated.

5. Diagram 205—1. White to play and checkmate Black in one move.

6. Diagram 205—II. White to play and checkmate Black in one move.

205

I   II

To show different positions on the blank diagrams below use the following symbols:

WHITE: King— K ; Queen— Q ; Rook— R ; Bishop— B ; Knight— N ; Pawn— P
BLACK: King— Ⓚ ; Queen— Ⓠ ; Rook— Ⓡ ; Bishop— Ⓑ ; Knight— Ⓝ ; Pawn— Ⓟ

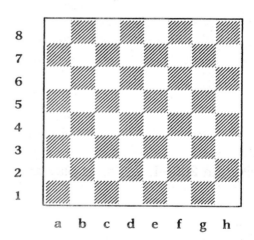

Test Seventeen

1. What is the least number of moves in which a pawn starting from its home square can change into a Queen?

---

2. Construct a position in which White, with a Queen and Bishop, has checkmated a lone Black King.

3. Place a Black King, Black pawn, White King, and White Rook on a board in such a way that White can give perpetual check to the Black King.

4. Place a Black King, a Black Knight, two Black Bishops, and a White Knight on a board in such a way that the White Knight can give perpetual check.

5. Diagram 206—I. White to play and checkmate Black in one move.

---

6. Diagram 206—II. White to play and checkmate Black in one move.

206

I   II

To show different positions on the blank diagrams below use the following symbols:

WHITE: King— K ; Queen— Q ; Rook— R ; Bishop— B ; Knight— N ; Pawn— P
BLACK: King— Ⓚ ; Queen— Ⓠ ; Rook— Ⓡ ; Bishop— Ⓑ ; Knight— Ⓝ ; Pawn— Ⓟ

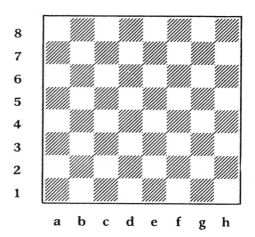

Test Eighteen

1. Is it possible in a game for White to have pawns on g2, h2, and h3 at the same time?

2. Place a Black King, Black Bishop, Black pawn, White King, and White pawn on a board in such a way that Black has been checkmated.

3. Suppose that White has a King and a pawn, and Black has just a King. Make up a position in which White can checkmate Black in one move only by promoting his pawn to a Queen.

4. Suppose that White has a King and a pawn, and Black has just his King. Make up a position in which White would stalemate Black if he promoted his pawn to Queen.

5. Diagram 207—I. White to move and checkmate Black in one move.

6. Diagram 207—II. White to move and checkmate Black in one move.

207

To show different positions on the blank diagrams below use the following symbols:

WHITE: King— K ; Queen— Q ; Rook— R ; Bishop— B ; Knight— N ; Pawn— P

BLACK: King— Ⓚ ; Queen— Ⓠ ; Rook— Ⓡ ; Bishop— Ⓑ ; Knight— Ⓝ ; Pawn— Ⓟ

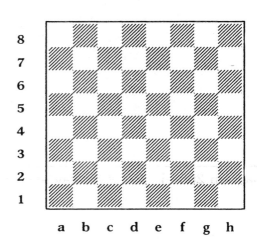

Test Nineteen

1. Can the a-pawn ever get to the e-file? If so, how?

2. Construct a position in which White, with a Queen and a Knight, has checkmated a lone Black King.

3. Suppose that White has his King on e1 and a Rook on h1, while Black has a Bishop on e3 and there is no man on f2. Can White castle?

4. Suppose that White has his King on e1 and a Rook on h1, while Black has a Bishop on h3 and there is no man on g2. Can White castle?

5. Diagram 208—I. White to play and checkmate Black in one move.

6. Diagram 208—II. White to play and checkmate Black in one move.

208

To show different positions on the blank diagrams below use the following symbols:

WHITE: King— K ; Queen— Q ; Rook— R ; Bishop— B ; Knight— N ; Pawn— P
BLACK: King— Ⓚ ; Queen— Ⓠ ; Rook— Ⓡ ; Bishop— Ⓑ ; Knight— Ⓝ ; Pawn— Ⓟ

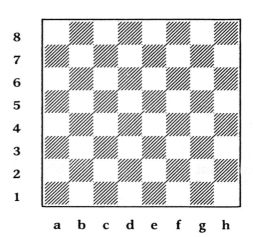

Test Twenty

1. How many moves does a Knight need to get from c3 to e5? Write down its route.

2. Construct a position in which four White pawns, without help from their King or other pieces, have checkmated the Black King.

3. Suppose that White has a King and a pawn, and Black has just his King. Make up a position in which the White pawn can become a Queen, but would stalemate Black if it did so, while by becoming a Rook instead, it could checkmate Black the move after it becomes a Rook.

4. Suppose that White has a King and two pawns, and Black has a King and one pawn. Make up a position in which the White pawn is ready to reach the last rank, but would stalemate Black if it turned either into a Queen or a Rook.

5. Diagram 209—I. White to play and checkmate Black in one move.

6. Diagram 209—II. White to play and checkmate Black in one move.

209

I
II

To show different positions on the blank diagrams below use the following symbols:

WHITE: King— K ; Queen— Q ; Rook— R ; Bishop— B ; Knight— N ; Pawn— P
BLACK: King— Ⓚ ; Queen— Ⓠ ; Rook— Ⓡ ; Bishop— Ⓑ ; Knight— Ⓝ ; Pawn— Ⓟ

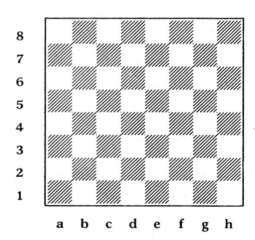

Answers To Test One

1. The a3-f8 diagonal crosses the d-file at d6.
2. Diagram 210.

3. Diagram 211.

4. Diagram 212.

5. Diagram 213.

6. There is one Black pawn too many in Diagram 190. After any one of the nine pawns are removed, White can checkmate Black in one move.

If we remove the pawn on
a) a7, then **1. Qb1-b6#**
b) b7, then **1. Nd8-c6#**
c) c4, then **1. Qb1-b4#**
d) d3, then **1. Qb1-e4#**
e) e3, then **1. Bg1xf2#**
f) f2, then **1. Bg1xe3#**
g) f7, then **1. Nd8-e6#**
h) g6, then **1. Rg8-g4#**
i) h3, then **1. Rh1-h4#**

Answers To Test Two

1. The b8-h2 diagonal crosses the 4th rank at f4.
2. Diagram 214.

3. Diagram 215.

4. Diagram 216. **1. c5xb6#.**

5. Diagram 217.

6. Diagram 191. a) The Black King would be checkmated on e3. b) The Black King would be stalemated on h1. c) If we place the Black King on a8, White could checkmate it with one move by **Qg4-c8#.**

Answers To Test Three

1. The most number of Queens that a player can have is nine (the original Queen plus eight Queens promoted from pawns).

2. Diagram 218.

3. Diagram 219.

4. Diagram 220.

White has made half of his castling move by placing his King on g1. Now he checkmates the Black King by making the other half of the move, i.e. by moving his h1 Rook to f1.

5. Diagram 221.

6. **1. Nd3-e5#** checkmates all ten Black Kings in Diagram 192.

Answers To Test Four

1. The most number of Rooks that a player can have is ten (the two original Rooks plus eight Rooks promoted from pawns).

2. Diagram 222.

3. Diagram 223.

4. Diagram 224.

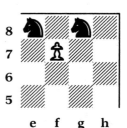

The pawn can turn into any of four different pieces upon reaching the last rank, and since in this case it can reach the last rank in three different ways, it has a total of twelve different possible moves:

   1–4: 1. f7xe8 (Q, R, B, or N)
   2–8: 1. f7-f8 (Q, R, B, or N)
  9–12: 1. f7xg8 (Q, R, B, or N)

5. Diagram 225.

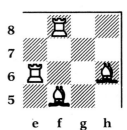

6. The catch in Diagram 193 is that you can't solve the problem without knowing what Black's last move was. It was in fact **... d7-d5.** Now you can see that White can checkmate Black in one move by capturing en passant: **1. e5xd6 e.p.#.**

Answers To Test Five

1. The most number of Bishops that one player can have is ten (the two original ones plus eight Bishops promoted from pawns).

2. Diagram 226.

3. Diagram 227.

4. Diagram 228.

5. Diagram 229.

6. Neither Black nor White can avoid checkmating the opponent in Diagram 194. Any move by White checkmates Black, and any move by Black checkmates White!

Answers To Test Six

1. The most number of Knights that one player can have is ten (the two original ones plus eight Knights promoted from pawns).

2. Diagram 230.

3. Diagram 231.

4. Diagram 232.

5. Diagram 233.

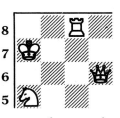

6. White checkmates Black in Diagram 195 by **1. Qc2xh7#.**

Answers To Test Seven

1. A pawn that reaches the last rank cannot remain a pawn, it MUST be promoted to any other piece (except the King) of its own color.

2. Diagram 234.

3. Diagram 235.

4. Diagram 236.

5. Diagram 237.

6. White checkmates Black in one move in Diagram 196 by **1. Qf3xf7#.**

Answers To Test Eight

1. No, a pawn cannot ever turn into a King. When a pawn reaches the last rank, it can and must be promoted into any piece of its own color except a King.

2. Diagram 238.

3. Diagram 239.

4. Diagram 240.

5. Diagram 241.

6. White checkmates Black in one move in Diagram 197 by **1. Qf6-g7#.**

Answers To Test Nine

1. Yes, a player can castle when one of his Rooks is attacked, or even when both of them are.

2. Diagram 242.

3. Diagram 243.

4. Diagram 244.

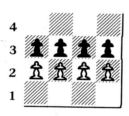

White and Black each have a total of six different pawn moves available.

5. Diagram 245. No.

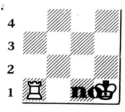

6. White checkmates Black in one move in Diagram 198 by 1. Qc5-f8#.

Answers To Test Ten

1. Yes, castling is permitted if the Rook crosses a square attacked by an enemy man but the King doesn't.

2. Diagram 246.

3. Diagram 247. **a)** 1. c7-c8Q#; **b)** 1. c7-c8R#; **c)** 1. c7xd8Q#; **d)** 1. c7xd8R#.

4. Diagram 248.

5. Diagram 249. **1. b7-b8B#.**

6. White checkmates Black in one move in Diagram 199 by **1. Qg4-d4#.**

119

Answers To Test Eleven

1. No. En passant capturing is only possible when the opponent's pawn has moved two squares in a single move..

2. Diagram 250.

3. Diagram 251.

4. Diagram 252.

5. Diagram 253. No.

6. White checkmates Black in one move in Diagram 200 by **1. Kc6-c7#**.

Answers To Test Twelve

1. Checkmate is when a King is in check and cannot get out of it. Stalemate is when the player whose turn it is to move has no legal moves, but his King is not in check. Checkmate is a win for the player who checkmates his opponent's King, while stalemate is a draw.

2. Diagram 254.

3. Diagram 255.

4. Diagram 256.

a) **1. Qf5-g6#; b)** **1. Rg5-h5#; c)** **1. Bh8-g7#; d)** **1. Ne7-g8#.**

5. Diagram 257.

1. ... Kg8-h7; 2. Be6-f5 + Kh7-g8; 3. Bf5-e6 + Kg8-h7 4. Be6-f5 + etc: perpetual check.

6. White checkmates Black in one move in Diagram 201 by **1. f6-f7#.**

Answers To Test Thirteen

1. Only the pawn on f4 can be captured en passant by the Black pawn on e4. The pawn on d4 could only have been captured en passant as soon as White had played d2-d4..

2. Diagram 258.

3. Diagram 259.

1. ... Ka2-a1 2. Qc2-c1 + Ka1-a2 3. Qc1-c2 + Ka2-a1 4. Qc2-c1 + : perpetual check.

4. Diagram 260.

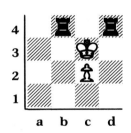

5. In Diagram 202—I, White checkmates by **1. Nd4-c2#.**

6. The catch in Diagram 202—II is that you don't know whether the White King or the Rook on h1 have already moved. Actually, neither one of them has, so that White can castle and checkmate Black: **1. 0-0#.**

Answers To Test Fourteen

1. No. You must move the piece which you touched, if it has a legal move. Don't forget: "Touch — Move"!.

2. Diagram 261.

3. Diagram 262. **1. c7-c8N#.**

4. Diagram 263. **a) 1. d7-d8Q#. b) 1. d7-d8R#.**

5. In Diagram 203—I, White checkmates by **1. Nb5-c7#.**

6. In Diagram 203—II, White checkmates by **1. h7-h8N#.**

Answers To Test Fifteen

1. If you touch one of your opponent's pieces which is attacked by one of your own pieces, you must capture the piece which you touched.

2. Diagram 264.

3. Diagram 265. No.

4. Diagram 266. **a)** 1. f2xe3; **b)** 1. f2-f3; **c)** 1. f2-f4; **d)** f2xg3.

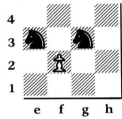

5. In Diagram 204—I, White checkmates by **1. Ra7-a8#.**

6. In Diagram 204—II, White checkmates by **1. Qe4-g2#.**

Answers To Test Sixteen

1. If your King is checked by a pawn or a Knight, the only ways of getting out of check are by moving your King or capturing the checking man..

2. Diagram 267.

3. Diagram 268. No.

4. Diagram 269.

5. In Diagram 205—I, White checkmates by **1. Rd1-d8#.**

6. In Diagram 205—II, White checkmates by **1. Bg4-e6#.**

Answers To Test Seventeen

1. A pawn needs to make at least five moves from its starting position to become a Queen.

2. Diagram 270.

3. Diagram 271.

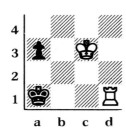

1. ... Ka1-a2 **2.** Rd1-d2+ Ka2-b1 **3.** Rd2-d1+ Kb1-a2 **4.** Rd1-d2+ etc.: perpetual check.

4. Diagram 272.

1. ... Ka2-a1 **2.** Nc1-b3+ Ka1-a2 **3.** Nb3-c1+ Ka2-a1 **4.** Nc1-b3+ etc.: perpetual check.

5. In Diagram 206—I, White checkmates by **1. a4-a5#**.

6. In Diagram 206—II, White checkmates by **1. Re5-e8#**.

Answers To Test Eighteen

1. No. A White pawn can get to h3 only by moving up one square from h2 or by capturing from g2. So when the h2 and g2 pawns are still on their home squares, it is impossible for a White pawn to be on h3.

2. Diagram 273.

3. Diagram 274. **1. d7-d8Q#**.

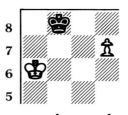

4. Diagram 275. **1. c7-c8Q stalemate.**

5. In Diagram 207—I, White checkmates by **1. Qd6-a3#**.

6. In Diagram 207—II, White checkmates by **1. Qf5xh7#**.

Answers To Test Nineteen

1. The a-pawn can get to the e-file by capturing four enemy men.

2. Diagram 276.

3. Diagram 277. No.

4. Diagram 278. No.

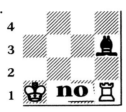

5. In Diagram 208—I, White checkmates by 1. Ra3-a2#.

6. In Diagram 208—II, White checkmates by 1. Qh5xf7#.

Answers To Test Twenty

1. A Knight on c3 needs four moves to get to e5. e.g., **Nc3-e4-c5-d3-e5.**

2. Diagram 279.

3. Diagram 280. a) 1. **f7-f8Q** stalemate; b) 1. **f7-f8R Kh7-h6 2. Rf8-h8#.**

4. Diagram 281. a) 1. **f7-f8Q** stalemate; b) 1. **f7-f8R** stalemate.

5. In Diagram 209—I, White checkmates by 1. Ba3-c1#.

6. In Diagram 209—II, White checkmates by 1. Qg5xg7#.

Level Two
of
A Comprehensive Program of Chess Training
From Beginner to Master

by
Roman Pelts
and
GM Lev Alburt, U.S. Champion

CONTENTS

ACKNOWLEDGEMENTS

I would like to thank my wife for her help in translating the first volume and for the many hours she spent on the endless small tasks necessary to the production of the books. I would also like to thank Jonathan Berry and Mohan for translating the books and Gordon Howe for proofreading.

Roman Pelts
Toronto
May, 1986

I am very grateful to Faneuil Adams, Dewain Barber, Svetozar Jovanovic, Bruce Pandolfini and all others who helped me in my work on the second edition. The time has come to recognize chess as an excellent tool for education.

Lev Alburt
New York
October 1987

Foreword

Welcome to Level II (the first intermediate level) of our comprehensive program of chess instruction. The course can be used to teach chess in schools, colleges, universities and chess clubs, as well as for individual study. The twelve lessons of the book have been specially designed for school children eight years of age (in exceptional cases six years of age) and older, but can also be used by adults of all ages.

The entire program has been conceived to enable an average 8-year-old beginner to reach the strength of a North American national master (2200 rating) by the age of 15 or 16.

Each level of the program entails its own particular methods of teaching and learning, and is directed at students of a specific standard. Level II is aimed at those who have completed Level I. The teaching methods to be followed are explained in the following section.

How To Teach Intermediate Players

The Level II course is aimed at players who are familiar with the main rules of play set forth in the Level I course. Experience has shown, however, that it is useful to review these rules in the first lesson of Level II, since there are always a few players in the class who do not do them thoroughly.

In addition, two new rules are introduced in the first lesson, namely the "triple repetition" rule and the "50-move" rule. Thus, by the end of the first Level II lesson, the player knows all the rules of play.

It is desirable that the teacher should play better than his students and have good coaching abilities. Classes should be small — 10 to 15 students at the most — and meet once a week for one and half to two hours. If the children are eight years old or younger, however, each lesson should only last for one hour. The plan of each lesson is as follows:

Lesson Plan
1. Going over difficulties (if any) in the homework.
2. Revision of previously studied material.
3. Introduction and explanation of new material.
4. Assignment of homework for the next lesson.
5. Practice games (about half the total lesson time).

At the beginning of each lesson, some time should be devoted to the previous lesson's homework, if necessary — that is, if a student has a question concerning one of the problems or if the teacher thinks that some problem is particularly interesting and worth going over in class. The position should be set up on a demonstration board and a student who has answered the problem correctly should explain the solution to the rest of the class.

After going over the homework, the next step is to review previously learned materials, with special attention being given to study of the chessboard. Each chapter contains 10-12 review questions of varying difficulty, but it is enough if the teacher selects five or six of these. In any class, no matter what the level, there will always be above-average, average, and below-average students. The teacher should select easy questions for the poorer students (gradually leading up to more difficult questions) and tough questions for the better students. The point of these questions is not to try and flummox the students but rather to activate their knowledge.

After the review the new material is presented. If at any time during your explanations, you notice that many of the students are getting tired and losing their concentration, it would generally be advisable to break off the theoretical part of the lesson at this point, hand out the homework assignments, and switch over to the practical (game-playing) part of the lesson. The material which still remains to be explained can, if necessary, be made part of the homework, but if possible it should rather be taught at the next class. The teacher must always be certain that the students are assimilating the material. If they are having any difficulty in doing so, it would be best to set aside a few classes for review purposes, even if this means that 16 or so classes are needed to complete 12 lessons of Level II, rather than just 12 classes. Beginners are attracted to chess primarily as a game, and some of them do not have very much patience for studying. The teacher should explain to these students that the more we know about how to play chess well, the greater the enjoyment that we get from the game.

Each student should have a copy of the textbook. This will make the teacher's job easier and save him time. If for some reason, however, this is not possible, the teacher should run off copies of the homework assignments and hand them out at the end of each class. The answers should be included, so that if after working on a problem for 5-10 minutes a student finds that he is getting nowhere, he can look at the solution and try to understand it. It is by no means necessary for a student to do all his homework in a single day; in fact, it is better if he spreads it out over a couple of days.

Each student should preferably be provided with a separate chessboard and chess set so that he can follow the explanations of the teacher, especially if games are being analyzed.

At the end of each lesson in the book you will find some supplementary material for the teacher. If you are studying on your own, without a teacher, we suggest the following method of learning this material: set up the positions on a board, look at the answers, and try to understand them. This will bring you not inconsiderable benefits.

There should be an interval of one or two months between Level II and Level III. This time should be used for practice games and training and also for participating in tournaments, simultaneous exhibitions, and problem-solving contests. These contests can be conducted in the following way. A chess position is displayed on the demonstration board and students are allowed three to five minutes to come up with the correct solution. Three points are awarded for a correct answer and one point is subtracted for a wrong answer. This makes the children think before answering. Such a contest usually consists of three to six problems, and the person who accumulates the greatest number of points is declared the winner.

The Level II course contains a lot of material, but the student can assimilate it successfully if he does his homework assignments and plays several games each week between lessons.

The last lesson of Level II is for testing purposes. There are 20 tests of approximately equal difficulty, consisting of six questions

each. The tests are displayed upside down on a table and each student picks one at random. He is given one hour to answer all six questions on the test. If he fails to answer more than three questions, he can be allowed to try another test. The first five questions in each test are worth 15 percent each, while the last, (on pawn endings) is worth 25 percent (if a problem has two solutions, the student is given half the total marks for each solution). The coach will decide who is to be promoted to the next level.

The Mistake of Memorization

In some books, the explanation of the rules is immediately followed by a section on opening theory. To be sure, the prospect of being able to correctly play the first 10 to 15 moves of a game is a very tempting one indeed! Unfortunately, however, opening theory is based on subtleties which can be grasped only by strong players. A weak player can learn to parrot opening variations without understanding them. Such a procedure, however, is clearly harmful, as the goal of a chessplayer must be to play each game in a thoughtful manner. He should know the purpose of every move that he makes. What happens otherwise is illustrated by the case of those amateurs who stuff their heads with opening variations. If the opponent of such a player makes a bad move that is not in the book, the player is entirely at a loss, and all his memorization has been wasted. Such amateurs are quite helpless even in simple positions.

Mindless memorization is harmful not only in the case of opening variations but also in the case of all the principles of play and other material that the student is taught. What is needed is to understand the principles and the reasons underlying them. Once a student has done this, he will remember the material almost effortlessly.

Chess books usually tell you *what* to learn but almost nothing about *how* to learn it. In many books the material is laid out by chapters, with one chapter devoted to endgames, another to the middlegame, another to the various openings, and so on. Experience, however, has shown that beginners are not particularly keen on studying the endgame. Consequently, the best way to teach the endgame is gradually, devoting a small part of each lesson to it.

The lessons place considerable emphasis on tactics (combinations). This is not accidental. It is very important to master the various tactical weapons in order to be able to make combinations, find hidden possibilities in positions, understand the opponent's plans, and play creatively. Many outstanding chess masters began their careers as tacticians, and only later on successfully mastered the subtleties of positional play (i.e., play without combinations).

Taking into account the inadvisability of teaching opening variations to beginners, the early lessons of the present course instead acquaint the student with the general principles of piece development in the opening and give guidelines on how to avoid mistakes. For a beginner, this is quite enough in order to be able to put up a good fight in his games.

Visualization

The ability to mentally picture the position as it will be after a few moves have been made is absolutely indispensible to a chessplayer. Visualising the chessboard with the position of the men changed from the way it is on the real board in front of them is the main difficulty experienced by beginners. This specifically chess-related ability must be gradually developed. The first step for a beginner is to learn to clearly visualize in his mind all the squares of an empty board. A series of exercises have been devised to aid in the achievement of this goal.

Depending on his own abilities, a beginner will need two to eight hours in order to acquire the ability to mentally visualize the chessboard. However, the player would be unwise to skimp on this aspect of his chess studies, as it is an indispensible pre-requisite for future success in chess. The player must have a perfect knowledge of the board, and visualising the board must become an automatic habit. Knowing the chessboard is to a chessplayer what knowing the multiplication tables is to a student of arithmetic.

Gradually, step by step, the board in the visualization exercises will become "peopled" by more and more men, and the student will de-

velop the important ability to mentally form a clear picture of the position as it will be a few moves later.

Practice and the Analysis of Games

A chessplayer can make progress only if he coordinates study and practice. Practice means playing games, and in a game a player has to go through the opening, the middlegame, and sometimes the endgame as well. That is why in our program each lesson has something about the endgame and something about the middlegame, and sometimes also entire games that allow the student to get acquainted with an opening in a context.

A total of some 100 games are presented in this course, with almost all of them specially annotated for students of Level II. The games in each lesson have been chosen so as to illustrate the themes discussed in that lesson. For example, Lesson 8 contains games employing the idea of pinning, while Lesson 10 contains games with back-rank mates. You should try to analyze and understand these games. Don't be surprised to find, for instance, only one game by our great World Champion Robert James Fischer. The reason is that many strong players have very complicated playing styles. Level II players would not understand or derive any benefit from the games of such champions.

Beginners react poorly to their opponent's threats. They often commit gross blunders. Often a player who is up several pieces loses because he falls into an elementary checkmate. In order to reduce the number of such mistakes to a minimum, beginners must play often.

Players should always abide by the rules and never take back moves. They should not play numerous quick games during the practice session but rather just one or two games conducted in a serious manner, with each move being carefully thought out.

Most chessplayers know something about the history of chess. Beginners should also be introduced to chess history, but in a gradual fashion. For example, if one of Fischer's games is being studied, the teacher should spend two or three minutes to explain who Fischer is and when he played chess. Or, to take another example, if a game starting with Philidor's Defense is being studied, the teacher could say a few words about Philidor.

A few words now about tournaments. Beginners are advised to take part in tournaments only after they have acquired a certain amount of elementary knowledge and have had some experience in playing games.

It happens not infrequently that several early defeats demoralize a student so much that he gives up chess. A modern aid to help us deal with this problem is the chess computer, to which a student can lose without his ego suffering too much! All the same, the teacher should constantly remind the students at every lesson that they should not be afraid of losing, since a player learns from his losses. In fact, former World Champion Jose Capablanca said that he learned more from a single game that he lost than from many victories.

The students will benefit greatly from an analysis of their games. However, since it is not possible to analyse fully all games played during a session, the teacher, while observing the play of his students, should take note of particularly instructive points that occur in the games and then demonstrate them to the class. For example, a player might have overlooked a possibility of checkmating his opponent, another player might have made particularly effective use of the material that he had learned in class, etc.

Level II players should acquire the habit of recording their games. This will stand them in good stead later, when they start playing in tournaments. In addition, by recording his games a student will have the possibility of analysing it later with the help of his teacher.

Lesson One

Many of you already know the rules of play, but we shall review them briefly here for the benefit of those whose mastery of them is perhaps a bit shaky.

1. What is the ''touch-move'' rule?
2. Can you change a move after playing it?
3. What do the words ''Kingside'' and ''Queenside'' mean?
4. What are the relative values of the various chess pieces and pawns?
5. What is chess notation and what is its purpose?
6. How do you record a game?
7. What reward does a pawn get for reaching the last rank?
8. What other special pawn rule do you know?
9. What is the strongest move possible in a game?
10. When is a player considered to have won the game?
11. What is the name of a move which involves both the King and a Rook at the same time, and when can such a move be made?
12. What is stalemate?
13. Do we have to say ''check,'' ''checkmate,'' or ''stalemate'' during a game?
14. What happens when one of the players keeps checking his opponent endlessly?
15. Do you know the ''three-time repetition of position'' rule? What is it?
16. What is the 50-move rule?
17. When is a game considered to be a draw?

Answers

1. A player who touches one of his men *must* move that man. If he touches one of his opponent's men, he *must* capture it. However, if a player touches one of his own men but the man has no legal move, or if he touches one of his opponent's men but there is nothing to capture it with, then there is no penalty. If certain men are untidily placed on the board and you want to center them in their squares, you must first say ''I adjust'' or ''j'adoube'' to your opponent.

2. If a player moves a man and lets go of it with his hand, the move is considered to be completed and cannot be taken back. However, if the player is still holding on to the man after moving it, the move is not considered to be finished and the players has the right to place that man on any legally allowed square.

3. The ''Kingside'' is that half of the board on which the two Kings stand at the beginning of a game, while the ''Queenside'' is the other half of the board. See Diagram 1.

1

4. The praxis of many generations of chessplayers has shown that the men have the following relative values:

Man	Points
Queen	9
Rook	5
Bishop	3
Knight	3
Pawn	1

From these values we can see that a Knight = a Bishop = 3 pawns or that a Rook = a Knight + 2 pawns, and so on. The King is invaluable, as a game cannot continue without it.

It must always be kept in mind, however, that the exact value of a given man varies according to position on the board. Sometimes a pawn can be stronger than the entire adverse army, as a look at the crazy position in Diagram 2 will convince you.

2

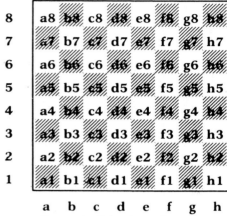

a b c d e f g h

5. Chess notation is a system of symbols for designating the squares of the chessboard. It is used in order to help us to record games or positions. Let us look at the algebraic system of notation, which is what we shall be using.

The chessboard consists of 64 squares forming eight vertical lines known as files and eight horizontal lines known as ranks. The files are designated by the letters **a**, **b**, **c**, and so on to **h** (starting from White's left), and are correspondingly called the a-file, b-file, c-file, etc. The ranks are designated by the numbers from **1** to **8** (starting from White's side of the board) and are correspondingly called the 1st rank, 2nd rank, etc. For example, in the starting position (see Diagram 1) all the White pawns are on

the 2nd rank while all the Black pawns are on the 7th rank. Since each square is at the intersection of a file and a rank, it can be designated by a letter and a number.

The board with the designations of all the squares is shows from White's side in Diagram 3 and from Black's side in Diagram 4.

3

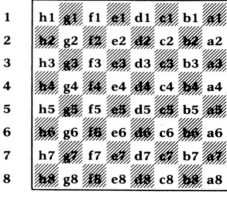

a b c d e f g h
from White's side

4

h g f e d c b a
from Black's side

The board can also be divided into diagonals, which are named by indicating their end squares. For example, the a1-h8 diagonal refers to the diagonal beginning with **a1** and ending with **h8**. All the squares in a given diagonal are of the same color, i.e., a diagonal can be either light-squared or dark-squared.

6. In order to record chess moves or positions, we have to know certain symbols. The major ones are given in the following table.

Main Symbols Used in Chess Notation

Symbol	Meaning
K	King
Q	Queen
R	Rook
B	Bishop
N	Knight
P	Pawn
–	moves to
x	captures
+	check
#	checkmate
0-0	castles King's side
0-0-0	castles Queen's side
?	bad move
!	good move

The symbols for designating the men and the squares allow us to record the moves of pieces and pawns. First, the symbol for the piece moved is indicated, then the symbol for the square on which the piece stood before the move, then a hyphen, and then the symbol for the square on which the piece stands after the move. If we are recording a pawn move, the symbol for the pawn (P) is left out.

Let us now go over a sample game.

Game 1

1. e2-e4
The numeral "1" indicates the number of the move, while the "e2-e4" means that the White pawn from e2 moves to e4.

1. ...   **e7-e5**
The three dots before the move indicate that it is Black's move. Black's King pawn moves from e7 to e5.

2. Qd1-h5?   **Nb8-c6**
The White Queen moves from d1 to h5. The symbol "?" indicates that the move is a poor one. The Black Knight moves from b8 to c6.

3. Bf1-c4   **Ng8-f6?**
The White Bishop moves from f1 to c4, while Black brings out his Knight from g8 to f6, a mistake.

4. Qh5xf7#
The Queen on h5 captured the pawn on f7. The symbol "#" means checkmate. Remember the final position, shown in Diagram 5.

5

It occurs many times in beginners' games and is called the Scholar's Mate.

7. A pawn that reaches the last rank (8th rank for White and 1st rank for Black) must turn into a piece of its own color. Usually the strongest piece, the Queen, is chosen, but in some cases a Knight, Bishop, or Rook is chosen instead. Thus it is possible to have 9 Queens of the same color on the board at one time, or 10 Knights, and so on, if all the pawns are promoted to pieces and added to the already existing ones.

Some beginners mistakenly think that it is always good to promote a pawn to a Queen. That this is not so can be seen from Diagram 6.

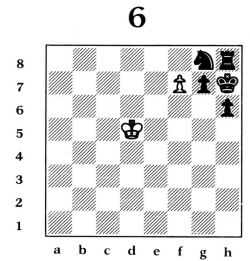

6

If White promotes his pawn to a Queen he will lose it after 1. ... Ng8-f6 +, while by promoting it to a Knight (1. f7-f8N#) he can checkmate Black (see Diagram 7).

3

7

8. Another special pawn rule is the "en passant capture." This is illustrated in the position in Diagram 8, which occurred in a school tournament.

8

The boy playing Black moved 1. ... b7-b5 and joyfully announced "Mate!" (see Diagram 9). "No, it's your King which is mated!", replied his opponent, playing 2. a5xb6# (see Diagram 10).

9

10

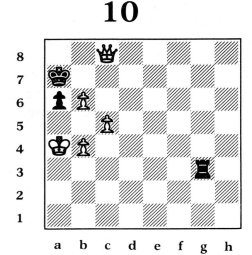

Only the tournament director's intervention settled the dispute, which had arisen because the boy with the Black pieces did not know the "en passant capture" rule. An "en passant capture" is possible when a pawn moves two squares from its starting position and ends up side by side with an enemy pawn, which can then capture it as if it had moved up not two squares, but only one. A player who wishes to capture en passant must do so on his first turn after the opposing pawn has moved up two squares.

9. The strongest move in a game is obviously a move which checkmates the opponent's King, since after that the game is finished.

11

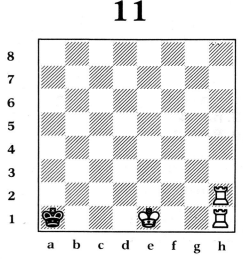

In Diagram 11, White to play mates in 1 move. This problem can be solved provided neither the White King nor the Rook on h1 has moved during the game. The solution is 1. 0-0#.

10. A game is won
  a) when one of the players checkmates the opponent's King, or
  b) when one of the players resigns, considering further resistance to be useless, or
  c) when one of the players loses on time.

11. Each players can make a simultaneous move with his King and a Rook once in a game. The move is called **castling**. A player may castle either with the King's Rook (castling short or castling K-side) or with the Queen's Rook (castling long or castling Q-side). Castling is only possible under the following conditions:

  i. Castling is not permitted if either the King or the Rook used in castling has already moved at any point in the game.

  ii. All the squares between the King and the Rook must be empty. Neither can jump over any other pieces.

  iii. The King must not be in check (castling is not allowed for the purpose of getting out of check).

  iv. The King may not move into check.

  v. The square which the King jumps over should not be under attack by any enemy man.

Now let us analyze the following game.

Game 2
Feuer–O'Kelly
Liege, 1934

1. e2-e4	e7-e5
2. Ng1-f3	Nb8-c6
3. Bf1-b5	a7-a6
4. Bb5-a4	d7-d6
5. Ba4xc6 +	b7xc6
6. d2-d4	f7-f6
7. Nb1-c3	Ra8-b8
8. Qd1-d3	Ng8-e7
9. h2-h4	h7-h5
10. Bc1-e3	

"What! It looks like he's blundered his pawn on b2!", thought Black with surprise. Finding no reason why he shouldn't, he decided to take the pawn.

10. ...	Rb8xb2?
11. d4xe5	d6xe5?

Of course he had to take on e5 with the other pawn. (11. ... fxe5). The Black player later became a grandmaster, but at the time of this

game he wasn't very strong.

12. Qd3xd8 +	Ke8xd8

See Diagram 12.

12

Black has lost his right to castle in this game, as his King has already moved. White, however, can castle on either side. Naturally, he chose to castle long, 11. 0-0-0, since that allowed him to win a Rook (see Diagram 13).

13

The White Rook checked Black's King and at the same time the White King attacked the Black Rook on b2. So Black resigned.

12. "Stalemate" is a position where the player whose turn it is to move is not in check but has no legal moves either with his King or with any of his other men. When a stalemate occurs, the game is considered drawn. Stalemate can arise if a player makes a thoughtless move when attempting to mate his opponent's lone King. Carelessness in winning positions is the main cause of stalemate.

14

15

For example, in Diagram 16 Black to move could mate in two moves: 1. ... Re8-e1 + 2. Kg1-f2 g2-g1Q#. However, it was White's turn to move and he found an interesting stalemate idea. The White King has only one possible move, to f2. So White played:

1. Rg7-h7 +   Kh3-g3

Now the White King cannot go even to f2, since the Black King controls that square.

2. Rh7-e7!

White gives up his Rook for nothing, since once it is gone the position will be a stalemate.

2. ...   Re8-a8

The Black Rook tries to get away, but in vain!

3. Re7-a7!

The draw is inevitable! The White Rook keeps sacrificing itself along the 7th rank (see Diagram 17).

17

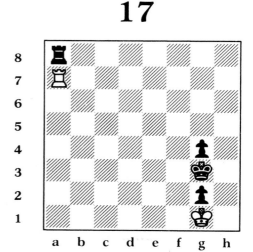

A Rook like this is called a desperado Rook.

In Diagram 14, White unthinkingly played 1. Qe1xe6? and the game was drawn, since the resulting position was a stalemate (see Diagram 15). Any other move (except of course 1. Qe1-e4??) would have led to a win.

However, stalemate is not always the result of a gross blunder. Sometimes it is planned as a method of saving an otherwise lost position.

13. It is not compulsory to announce "check," "mate," or "stalemate."

14. A series of checks from which the King cannot escape is known as "perpetual check," and the game is considered to be drawn.

16

18

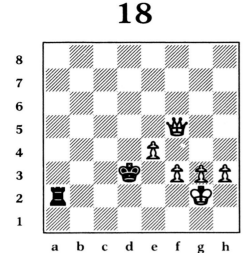

For example, in Diagram 18 Black gives perpetual check by checking the White King continuously from a2 to a1. The White King has nowhere to hide and the draw is forced. Just like stalemate, perpetual check too can be planned in advance by a player. Sometimes players even sacrifice pieces in order to obtain a draw by perpetual check.

Now let us look at a game played between two World Champions in the year 1914. White was 22-year-old Alexandre Alekhine, who became World Champion in 1927 by defeating the Cuban Jose Raoul Capablanca. Black was the reigning World Champion Emanuel Lasker, who won the title in 1894 and kept it for 27 years, until he lost it to Capablanca in 1921.

Game 3
Alekhine–Lasker

1. e2-e4	e7-e5
2. Ng1-f3	Nb8-c6
3. d2-d4	

This opening is called the "Scotch Game," because it was a favorite opening of Scottish players many years ago. The early opening up of the center does not cause Black any difficulties. By the way, do you remember what is meant by the "center" of a chess board? Right!

The center consists of the four squares d4, d5, e4, and e5.

3. ...	e5xd4
4. Nf3xd4	Ng8-f6
5. Nb1-c3	Bf8-b4
6. Nd4xc6	b7xc6
7. Bf1-d3	d7-d5
8. e4xd5	c6xd5

9. 0-0	0-0
10. Bc1-g5	Bc8-e6
11. Qd1-f3	Bb4-e7
12. Rf1-e1	h7-h6

See Diagram 19.

19

Both sides have played very well and if White had now retreated his Bishop from g5, the game would have been even. However, Alekhine was impatient to get a draw against the World Champion and so he sacrificed the Bishop for a pawn, and then his Rook on e1 for the Bishop on e6.

13. Bg5xh6	g7xh6
14. Re1xe6	f7xe6

Now the Black King is exposed and White can give perpetual check.

15. Qf3-g3 +	Kg8-h8

Not 15. ... Kg8-f7, because of 16. Qg3-g6#.

16. Qg3-g6!	

The players agreed to a draw here! See Diagram 20.

20

Black is up a Rook for a pawn, but he cannot avoid perpetual check. For example, 16. ... Qd8-e8 17. Qg6xh6 + Kh8-g8 18. Qh6-g5 + Kg8-h8 19. Qg5-h6 + etc.

15. If the same position with the same player to move occurs three (or more) times in a game, the game is drawn by three-time repetition of position. Incidentally, perpetual check is a case of three-time repetition of position.

21

In Diagram 21, White has lost a pawn and decides that it is better to draw by three-time repetition of position than to lose the game. There followed:

1. Ra1-b1	Qb2xa3
2. Rb1-a1	Qa3-b2
3. Ra1-b1	

The first time.

3. ...	Qb2-a2
4. Rb1-a1	Qa2-b2
5. Ra1-b1	

The second time.

5. ...	Qb2-a3
6. Rb1-a1	Qa3-b2
7. Ra1-b1	

The third time. The Black Queen cannot get away from the attacks of the White Rook. White claimed a draw.

16. If 50 moves (a "move" here actually means a pair of moves, one by each side) go by with no capture or pawn move being made, either player can claim a draw. For example, a player with a King and Queen against a lone King must know how to mate within 50 moves.

17. A game is considered drawn
  a) when the two players agree to a draw;
  b) if stalemate occurs;
  c) if a player gives perpetual check;
  d) if a player claims a draw by three-time repetition of position;
  e) if a player claims a draw by the 50-move rule;

and finally,

  f) if neither side has enough material to mate the opponent's King:
    i) A King alone can never checkmate another King.
    ii) A King and Knight alone cannot checkmate a lone King.
    iii) A King and Bishop alone cannot checkmate a lone King.
    iv) A King and Bishop alone cannot checkmate a lone King and Bishop if the Bishops move on diagonals of the same color (see Diagram 22).

22

HOMEWORK
(Answers at the end)

I. Diagrams 23–30

23

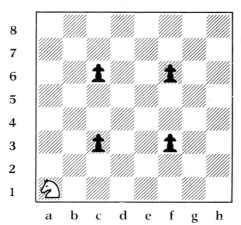

Only White moves. Write down the route that the Knight must take to visit the other three corners and then come back. In doing so, the Knight must not put itself under attack by any of the Black pawns, nor must it capture any of the pawns, nor must it land on any square more than once.

Write your answer

_____

_____

24

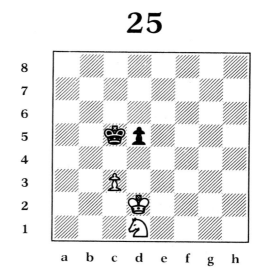

How should the game end
a) with White to move?
b) with Black to move?

Write your answer

_____

_____

_____

25

How should the game end
a) with Black to move?
b) with White to move?

Write your answer

_____

_____

_____

26

White to play and mate in two moves (the Rooks and Kings have not yet moved in the game).

Write your answer

	WHITE	BLACK
1.		
2.		

	WHITE	BLACK
1.		
2.		

28

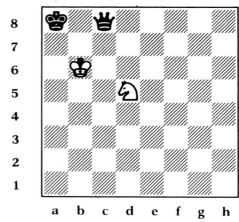

White to play. How should the game end?

Write your answer.

_____

_____

_____

27

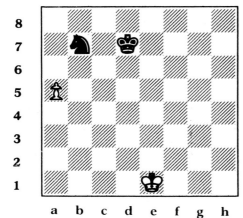

White to play and win.

Write your answer

_____

_____

_____

29

White to play and draw.

Write your answer

_____

_____

_____

30

a b c d e f g h

Black to play. How should the game end?

Write your answer

_____

_____

_____

II. Board Study Exercises

Write down your answers in the space below.
1. Place the board so that you are playing White. Find the squares d4, f7, and c3.
2. Looking at the board from Black's side, find the squares c6, h2, d3, and a5.

Answer questions 3–5 without looking at a board.
3. What color are the following squares: c3, h5, d6, b4?

_____

_____

4. Name all the squares making up the h2-b8 and d1-h5 diagonals.

_____

_____

5. Name the diagonals running through d5. Name the squares making up these diagonals.

_____

_____

III. Games for Analysis

Game 4
1. e2-e4	e7-e5
2. Bf1-c4	Bf8-c5
3. Qd1-f3?	Ng8-h6?

3. ... Ng8-f6 was the correct move.
4. d2-d4!	e5xd4
5. Bc1xh6	g7xh6?
6. Qf3xf7#	

See Diagram 31 for the final position.

31

a b c d e f g h

Game 5

1. e2-e4	e7-e5
2. Ng1-f3	d7-d6
3. Bf1-c4	Bc8-g4
4. c2-c3	Nb8-c6
5. Qd1-b3	Bg4xf3?

5. ... Nc6-a5! was the correct move.
6. Bc4xf7 +	Ke8-e7
7. Qb3-e6#	

See Diagram 32 for the final position.

32

HOMEWORK ANSWERS
I. Diagrams 23–30

D-23
Na1-b3-c5-a6-c7-a8-b6-d7-f8-g6-h8-f7-h6-f5-g3-h1-f2-d1-e3-c2-a1. Twenty moves in all. Other routes are also possible.

D-24
a) White to play wins with 1. b7-b8Q+! Kh2-h3 2. Qb8xc8+ etc.
b) Black to play wins with 1. ...g2xf1Q+ 2. Kb5-c6 Nc8-e7+ and Black will win the pawn in a few moves.

D-25
a) Black to move plays 1. ... d5-d4, exchanging off the last White pawn, after which the game is a draw!
b) White to play should win after 1. Kd2-d3.

D-26

| 1. 0-0-0! | 0-0 |

On any other move White would play 2. Rd1-d8#.

| 2. Rd1-g1# |

D-27
1. a5-a6 Kd7-c7 2. a6-a7! and the White pawn Queens.

D-28

1. Nd5-c7 +	Ka8-b8
2. Nc7-a6 +	Kb8-a8
3. Na6-c7 +	

Drawn by perpetual check. If Black gives up his Queen for the Knight, it's still a draw.

D-29

| 1. Rb1-b8 + ! | Ka8-a7 |

If the King takes the Rook, it's stalemate.

| 2. Rb8-b7! + | Ka7-a6 |
| 3. Rb7-b6 + | |

The desperado Rook keeps offering itself as a sacrifice. The game is a draw.

D-30

| 1. ... | Bb3-c4 + |

Or else the White pawn will Queen.

| 2. Kf1-f2 | Bc4xa6 |

Stalemate

II. Exercises
You can easily check your answers to the board study questions by looking at a chessboard.

SUPPLEMENTARY MATERIAL

for use at the teacher's discretion

In Diagrams 33–38 the stalemate idea is used; Diagrams 39–42 contain the perpetual check theme; Diagram 43 illustrates a three-time repetition of position; and Diagram 44 uses an en passant capture.

33
L. Ponziani, 1769

White to play and draw

1. Kg4-g5	Ra1-g1 +
2. Kg5-h6	a2-a1Q
3. Ra7-a8 + !	Qa1xa8

Stalemate

34

L. Ponziani, 1769

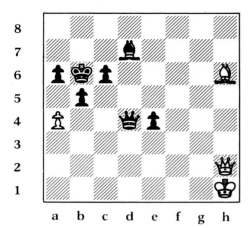

White to play and draw

1. Bh6-e3!	**Qd4xe3**
2. Qh2-f2!	**Qe3xf2**

Not 2. ... Qc5, because of 3. a4-a5 + winning the Queen.

3. a4-a5 +	**Kb6xa5**
Stalemate	

35

E. Cook

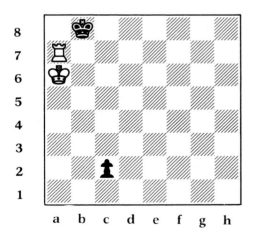

White to play and draw

1. Ra7-b7 +	**Kb8-c8**
2. Rb7-b5	**c2-c1Q**
3. Rb5-c5 +!	**Qc1xc5**
Stalemate	

36

Marshall–McClure, New York 1923

White to play and draw.

1. Rf6-h6!	**Rh5xh6**
2. h7-h8Q +	**Rh6xh8**
3. b4-b5	

and all moves by Black produce a stalemate!

37

White to play and draw.

1. Qg1-c5 +!	**b6xc5**

If Black moves his King, he loses his Queen on f8.

2. Kb4-a3!	

and all moves by Black produce a stalemate.

38

H. Rinck, 1912

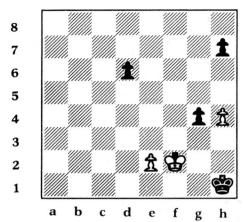

White to play and draw

1. Kf3-g3	h7-h5
2. e2-e4	Kh1-g1
3. e4-e5	d6xe5
Stalemate	

Black could not play 3. ... d6-d5, as White would have won by Queening his pawn.

40

Black to play and draw

1. ...	Nh6-g8 +
2. Ke7-e8	Ng8-f6 +
3. Ke8-e7	Nf6-g8 +

Or 3. ... Nf6-d5 +, and the White King cannot escape from perpetual check without losing a Rook.

39

White to play and draw

1. Nc7-e8 +	Kf6-e6
2. Ne8-c7 +	Ke6-f6
3. Nc7-e8 +	

Perpetual check.

41

From a game played by A. Neuman

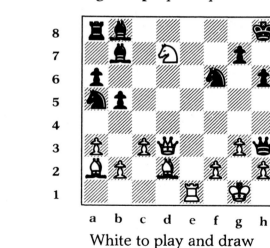

White to play and draw

1. Re1-e8 +!	Nf6xe8
2. Qd3-h7 +!	Kh8xh7
3. Nd7-f8 +	Kh7-h8
4. Nf8-g6 +	Kh8-h7
5. Ng6-f8 +	

Perpetual check.

42

White to play and draw

1. Qh1-d5 +	Kg8-h8
2. Nh4-g6 + !	h7xg6
3. Qd6-h1 +	Kh8-g8
4. Qh1-d5 +	

Perpetual check.

44

D. Ulyanov

White to play and mate in 3 moves

1. Bb1-a2	d6-d5
2. d2-d4!	c4xd3
	(en passant)
3. Ba2xd5#.	

Checkmate.

43

Lipnizky (Master)–Boleslavsky (Grandmaster)
Moscow 1950

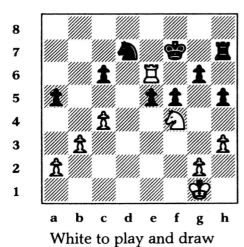

White to play and draw

1. *Re6-d6*	Kf7-e7
2. Rd6-e6 +	Ke7-f7
3. *Re6-d6*	Kf7-e7
4. Rd6-e6 +	Ke7-f7
5. *Re6-d6*	

Drawn by three-time repetition of position.

Lesson Two

A. Check Lesson 1 homework (if necessary).

B. *Review Questions:*
1. What is the most powerful move in a chess game?
2. Can a player pass his turn?
3. Which pieces can be moved before any pawn moves have been made?

Try to answer Questions 4–8 without looking at a chessboard.

4. Name the squares on which each of the White men stands at the start of a game.
5. What color (light or dark) is each of the following squares: a1, a8, h1, h8?
6. Name the squares making up the a1–h8 diagonal. What color are they?
7. Name the square where the e1-h4 and g1-a7 diagonals cross.
8. Name the square where the 4th rank crosses the h1-a8 diagonal.

45

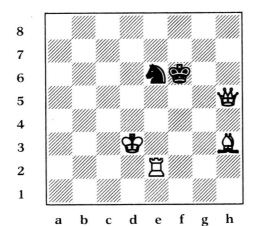

What move by the Black Knight will attack all the White pieces at the same time?

46

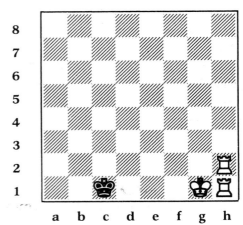

A trick puzzle! How can White checkmate Black in half a move?

Answers to Review Questions:
1. Checkmate.
2. No.
3. Knights.
4. Ra1, Nb1, Bc1, Qd1, Ke1, Bf1, Ng1, Rh1, pawns a2, b2, c2, d2, e2, f2, g2, and h2.
5. a1 and h8 are dark squares, and h1 and a8 are light squares.
6. a1, b2, c3, d4, e5 f6, g7, and h8. They are all dark squares.
7. f2.
8. e4.

D-45. 1. ... Ne6-f4 + .

D-46. White is in the middle of castling short. He has made half the move (King to g1) and by completing the move (by jumping the Rook from h1 over to f1) he will checkmate Black. The whole move is 1. 0-0#.

C. *Abbreviated Notation*

Beginners usually record their games using

the "full" algebraic notation, where the square on which a man stands before making a move is first indicated and then the square on which it stands after completing its move. As players become more experienced, however, they often switch over to the "abbreviated" notation, where the square from which a man starts out is omitted and only the square on which it lands is indicated. For example, 1. Nb1-c3 is written in abbreviated form as 1. Nc3. In the case of a pawn capture, the file (but not the square) from which the pawn starts out is also indicated.

47

For example, the move 28. b6xa7 in Diagram 47 would be written as 28. bxa7.

Suppose now that White plays 28. Ra1-c1 in Diagram 47. This would be written in abbreviated notation as 28. Rac1. By giving the file of departure ("a") we make it clear that it is the Rook on a1 and not the Rook on f1 which moves to c1.

Sometimes in order to remove an ambiguity, we have to indicate the rank from which a piece starts out. If, for example, in Diagram 47 White plays 28. Nd4-f3, it would not be enough to write 28. Nf3, since both White Knights can go to f3. However, if we write 28. N4f3, it becomes clear that it is the Knight on the 4th rank which moves to f3.

From now on we shall be using both the full and abbreviated types of notation. The main moves in games and puzzles will be given in full notation, while in the commentaries ab-

breviated notation will be used.

Now let us analyze a game recorded in full notation. This encounter from the 1924 Paris Championship is the shortest game ever played in a major tournament.

Game 6
Gibeau–Lazard

1. d2-d4	**Ng8-f6**
2. Nb1-d2?	

An unfortunate move that blocks the dark-square Bishop. 2. c4 or 2. Nf3 would be better.

2. ...	**e7-e5**

Black hopes to set up an attack by means of this pawn sacrifice.

3. d4xe5	**Nf6-g4**
4. h2-h3?	

White is playing hastily, without thinking out his moves carefully. He wants to chase back the advanced enemy Knight right away even though it is not threatening anything dangerous. A possible alternative is:

4. Ngf3 Bc5 5. e3 Nc6 6. Nc4 b5 7. Ncd2 a6 8. a4, with a slightly better position for White.

4. ...	**Ng4-e3!**

(see Diagram 48)

48

White resigns. He must lose his Queen, since if 5. fxe3, then 5. ... Qh4+ 6. g3 Qxg3 #.

Here is how this game would be recorded in abbreviated notation:

Gibeau–Lazard
(Paris, 1924)

1. d4	Nf6
2. Nd2?	e5
3. dxe5	Ng4
4. h3?	Ne3!

White resigns

0–1

Some Chess Terms and Concepts

Let us look at some frequently used chess terms.

Any arrangement of pieces and pawns on the chessboard is called a **POSITION**.

Pieces and pawns are known as **MATERIAL**.

At the start of a game, therefore, the two opponents are in a state of **MATERIAL EQUALITY**.

If one player has extra material (even if it is only a pawn) or material of greater value (*e.g.* a Queen for his opponent's Rook), he is said to have a **MATERIAL ADVANTAGE**.

49

Diagram 49 shows another kind of advantage. Black is up a Rook for only a pawn, but the Rook is trapped — it cannot make any moves without being captured. As a result, it is White who has chances of winning. In positions like this we say that White has a **POSI-**

TIONAL ADVANTAGE. That is, his pieces and pawns are better placed, and in Diagram 49 that more than makes up for Black's **MATERIAL SUPERIORITY** (another term for "material advantage").

Queens and Rooks are called **MAJOR PIECES**, while Bishops and Knights are known as **MINOR PIECES**.

A player who captures a Rook in exchange for a minor piece is said to **WIN THE EXCHANGE**, and his opponent is said to **LOSE THE EXCHANGE**.

Voluntarily giving up material in order to achieve some goal is called a **SACRIFICE**.

Thus, if a player voluntarity gives up a Rook for a minor piece (Knight or Bishop), he is said to **SACRIFICE THE EXCHANGE**.

It is worthwhile to sacrifice almost all your material if you can checkmate your opponent's King with what you have left.

Virtually every game contains **THREATS**. A **THREAT** is an intention to make a move that is unpleasant for the opponent. For example, if you make a move which opens up the possibility of checkmating the enemy King the next move, you are threatening checkmate. Similarly, if you check the enemy King, that is a threat, since you intend to capture the King next move. A player can also threaten to win material or occupy some important square with one of his men.

Many chess terms originated in military usage. Examples are **ATTACK**, which is a combination of aggressive actions, and **COUNTERATTACK**, which is an attack unleashed by a player in reply to his opponent's attack.

50

18

In Diagram 50, White played 1. Rf1xf6 — an **EXCHANGE SACRIFICE** with the **THREAT** of 2. Qxh7 #. White is thus **ATTACKING** the Black King. Black replied with a **COUNTERATTACK**: 1. ... Ba7xe3 +; 2. Kg1-h1 Be3xg5. Black has repulsed White's attack and won a pawn. In this case, Black's **COUNTERATTACK** proved stronger than White's **ATTACK.**

Attack and Defense. Trades.

Sometimes, as for example in the "Scholar's Mate", a direct attack on the King brings a game to a rapid finish even before any men have been captured by either side. However, this does not happen very often. Usually each player tries to eliminate the opponent's men and starts a mating attack only when the enemy King has lost most of its army.

To eliminate an enemy man, you must first **ATTACK** it. This is a different meaning of the word "attack." Here it means to "threaten to capture."

An attack can be one-way or mutual. A pawn that attacks an enemy pawn, Bishop, Queen, or King is itself under attack by the enemy man. These are cases of mutual attack. On the other hand, a pawn that attacks a Knight or Rook is not itself under attack from the enemy man. These are examples of one-way attack.

When attacking, defending, or exchanging men, you must take into account the relative worth of the men involved. For example, let us analyze the position in Diagram 51.

White decided to attack the pawn on a7 by playing 1. Ra1, and Black replied with 1. ... Ra8, defending the pawn. White could now capture the a7 pawn with 2. Rxa7, but after the reply 2. ... Rxa7 White would have lost a Rook for only a pawn. So White played 2. Rea2. Now the pawn is attacked twice but defended only once (see Diagram 52).

52

If Black does not defend it again, White could continue with 3. Rxa7 Rxa7 4. Rxa7, and Black has lost a pawn. Black could strengthen the pawn's defense by playing 2. ... Nc8, but then after 3. Bxc8 Rgxc8 (an equal trade) 4. Rxa7 Rxa7 5. Rxa7 Black still winds up losing the pawn.

Coming back to Diagram 51, let us see what might happen if Black replies to 1. Ra1 with 1. ... Nc6. White could then continue with 2. Rea1 (see Diagram 53).

51

53

Now the a7 pawn is attacked twice but defended only by the Knight on c6. Does this mean that White is threatening to capture the pawn? Let's figure it out:

3. Rxa7 Nxa7 4. Rxa7.

White has lost a Rook in return for a Knight and a pawn (or, in other words, he has lost the Exchange for a pawn). Since we know that a Rook is worth a Knight and two pawns, it is clear that the captures have resulted in White losing about a pawn's worth of material.

So the answer to the above question is that White was not really threatening to capture the a7 pawn in Diagram 53. When you attack an enemy man, it is important to take into account not only the *number* of your own men that are attacking it, but also the value of these men. It is not worthwhile to begin attacking an enemy man with a piece of your own that is more valuable than the defender.

All the same, 1. ... Nc6 in Diagram 51 is not a good defense against 1. Ra1. White will play 2. Bf3, threatening to trade on c6 and then capture the a7 pawn. The simplest defense for Black is 1. ... a6. Now White could pile up on the a-pawn with his Bishop and other Rook, but even then capturing the pawn would not be worth it, since White would get only two pawns for his Bishop. Thus it is pointless to use pieces to attack a pawn that is defended by another pawn.

Here is another example.

Game 7

1. e2-e4	**e7-e5**
2. Ng1-f3	

The Knight attacks the pawn on e5.

2. ...	**d7-d6**

Black defends the pawn on e5 with a pawn on d6, so that now it will be useless for White to attack the e-pawn with pieces alone. So White played:

3. d2-d4

White threatens to win the pawn on e5, which is now attacked twice and defended only once. So Black defends the pawn a second time with:

3. ...	**Nb8-c6**

(see Diagram 54)

54

Now 4. d4xe5 Nc6xe5 5. Nf3xe5 d6xe5 6. Qdxd8 + Ke8xd8 would only be an equal trade of a White pawn, Knight, and Queen for the same Black men, although the resulting position, show in Diagram 55, is slightly better for White as Black has lost the right to castle.

55

Now let us look at the next example.

Game 8

1. e2-e4	**e7-e5**
2. Ng1-f3	**Nb8-c6**

Black defends the pawn on e5, which the Knight on f3 was threatening to capture.

3. Bf1-c4

The Bishop attacks the pawn on f7, which, however, is defended by the Black King.

3. ...	**Bf8-c5**

This attack on the f2 pawn is also not dangerous for the time being.

4. d2-d3	**Ng8-f6**
5. Nf3-g5?	

(see Diagram 56)

White increases the pressure on the f7 pawn and threatens to take it with his Bishop or Knight. So Black must defend the pawn again. 5. ... Qe7, although it defends the pawn a second time, will not do, as you will see from the following variation:

6. Bxf7 + Qxf7 7. Nxf7 Kxf7
(see Diagram 57)

57

White has lost two minor pieces worth a total of six points but in return has gained Black's Queen and a pawn, worth a total of ten points, so that Black has ended up losing four points worth of material

Let us go back to Diagram 56. Another way for Black to defend the f7 pawn is with 5. ... Rf8. Now after 6. Nxf7 Rxf7 7. Bxf7 + Kxf7 White has given up a Bishop and a Knight (6 points) for a Rook and a pawn (6 points). That is, an equal trade has taken place.

In the resulting position, shown in Diagram 58, White and Black are materially equal, but Black has a positional advantage because he has developed (i.e., brought out) three minor pieces while all of White's pieces are still sitting at home.

In spite of this, 5. ... Rf8 is a bad move, because White does not have to capture the pawn on f7 but can instead play 6. 0-0, while Black has lost the right to castle Kingside and will have difficulty in transferring his King to a safe spot.

The correct move in Diagram 56 is 5. ... 0-0!, castling and at the same time re-defending the f7 pawn.

In playing 5. Nf3-g5? White counted on Black making a mistake. The correct defence by Black, 5. ... 0-0!, however, shows up White's move to have just been a time-wasting error.

Now let us look at Diagram 59.

59

The Black pawn on d5 is attacked four times (by the Bishop, Queen, and two Rooks) and defended only three times (by the Bishop and two Rooks). In spite of that, it would be bad for White to capture it:

1. Bxd5? Bxd5 2. Rxd5 Rxd5 3. Qxd5? Rxd5 4. Rxd5

60

The result is shown in Diagram 60. White has lost his Queen (9 points) for a Rook (5 points) and a pawn (1 point). That is, White has lost 9 − (5 + 1), or 3, points worth of material. This happened because the White Queen was the third attacker and the Black pawn was defended three times.

Let us change Diagram 59 just a bit by shifting the White Queen from d3 to b5. The result is shown in Diagram 61.

61

White is still attacking the d5 pawn four times and Black is still defending it three times.

However, now White can win the pawn:

1. Bxd5 Bxd5 2. Rxd5 Rxd5 3. Rxd5

This is the difference! In the previous example White was unable to capture with his Rook on the third move and instead captured with his Queen. Now, however, after

3. ... Rxd5 4. Qxd5

White is a pawn up (see Diagram 62).

62

Let us follow the thought processes of a chessplayer faced with the problem of whether or not to capture the Black pawn on d5 in Diagram 61:

"I'm attacking it four times and he's defending it only three times. Now let's check the value of the attackers and defenders. I have two Rooks and a Bishop attacking the pawn and he also has two Rooks and a Bishop defending it. But in addition I have my Queen hitting the pawn, and, what's more important, I can use the Queen to make the final capture and thus hold on to it."

Only after thinking things out like this will the player make the move 1. Bxd5.

A player must learn not only to see his opponent's threats but also to take proper defensive measures against them and in addition create threats of his own. In his desire to create threats, however, a player should avoid attacking this opponent's men aimlessly and at random. Rather, he should attack a man only when he sees that he can gain some advantage by doing so. Otherwise he will just be wasting time to the detriment of his position.

In conclusion, let us see how we can defend against the "Scholar's Mate."

Game 9

1. e2-e4   **e7-e5**

2. Qd1-h5?   **Nb8-c6**

Defending the pawn on e5.

3. Bf1-c4

What is White's threat? *(4. Qxf7#)*

3. ...   **g7-g6**

Defending f7 and simultaneously attacking the Queen.

4. Qh5-f3?

Does White threaten anything now? *(5. Qxf7#)*

44. ...   **Ng8-f6**

The best defense. Black develops a piece and defends against mate at the same time.

5. Qf3-b3?

White is stubborn. He attacks the f7 pawn, which is defended only once, a second time. However, he is no longer threatening mate (see Diagram 63).

63

5. ...   **Nc6-d4!**

Black does not defend the f7 pawn but rather *counterattacks* by threatening the White Queen.

6. Qb3-c3

Only now does White realise that 6. Bxf7+ would lose a piece after 6. ... Ke7 7. Qc4 b5!.

6. ...   **d7-d5!**

Black could have captured the pawn on e4 but he decides that it is more expedient to open up a path for his light-square Bishop and quickly bring it into play.

7. e4xd5   **Bc8-f5**

What does Black threaten? *(8. ... Nxc2+; the pawn on c2 is now attacked by two Black pieces and defended only once).*

8. d2-d3

See Diagram 64.

64

How can Black win the White Queen now?

8. ...   **Bf8-b4!**

Black sacrifices a Bishop!

9. Qc3xb4

There is nothing better, since if 9. Bb5+, then 9. ... Bd7 10. Bxd7+ Qxd7 leaves White with the same problem. Who can find Black's winning move now?

9. ...   **Nd4xc2+!**

See Diagram 65.

65

White resigns. The Black Knight is simultaneously attacking the White King (check), the White Queen, and a White Rook. The King must move out of check, after which the Knight will capture the Queen, leaving White with only a Bishop for a Queen, that is a material disadvantage of six points.

White lost quickly because he made more

than half his moves with his Queen (the most valuable piece). This enabled Black to bring his minor pieces into play with gain of time by attacking White's Queen or creating various threats.

Conclusion: Do not rush to bring your Queen into play before you have prepared your attack properly.

HOMEWORK
(Answers at the end)
I. Diagrams 66–73

66

Black to play will pile up on the e5 pawn. Can White defend it?

_____

_____

_____

67

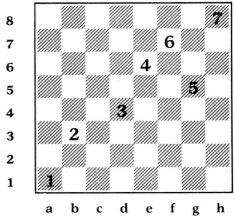

Name in order the squares marked 1 to 7. First do this with the help of the letters and numbers printed on the edges of the diagram, then cover up the file numbers on the left edge with a piece of paper and repeat the exercise, and finally cover up both the file numbers and the letters indicating the ranks and do the exercise once more.

68

Can White to play win the pawn on d5?

_____

_____

_____

69

Will Black lose his e-pawn if he plays 1. ... e6-e5?

_____

_____

_____

70

What is the difference between this position and Diagram 69? Is 1. ... e6-e5 a good move for Black in this changed position?

_____

_____

_____

71

Same question as for Diagram 70.

_____

_____

_____

72

Can White to play hinder Black from castling?

_____

_____

_____

73

```
8  . . . ♛ . ♜ ♚ .
7  . . ♟ ♞ ♟ ♜ ♟ .
6  . . ♟ . ♞ . ♟ .
5  . . ♘ ♟ . . . ♝... 
4  . ♙ . ♘ . . . ♗
3  ♙ . ♙ . . ♕ ♙
2  . . . . . ♖ ♙ .
1  . . . . . ♖ ♔ .
   a b c d e f g h
```

Can White to play win material?

_____

_____

_____

II. Exercises

Write your answers in the space below.

1. Change 1. bxc8N+ to full notation.

_____

_____

_____

2. The White King is on g1 and there are White pawns on g2 and f2. Describe two different ways for the King to get to f3 in three moves.

_____

_____

_____

Try to answer the following questions without looking at a chessboard.

3. Name all the squares in a) the h1-a8 diagonal, and b) the a1-h8 diagonal.

_____

_____

_____

4. Name the diagonals running through the square b2. Which squares make up these diagonals?

_____

_____

_____

5. At which square does the 2nd rank cross the c1-a3 diagonal?

_____

_____

_____

III. Games For Analysis
Game 10

1. e2-e4	e7-e5
2. Bf1-c4	Ng8-f6
3. d2-d4	Nf6xe4
4. d4xe5	c7-c6
5. Ng1-e2	Ne4xf2
6. 0-0!	

Black had counted on 6. Kxf2, after which 6. ... Qh4+ would win back the piece.

| 6. ... | Nf2xd1? |

6. ... Bc5! was necessary.

| 7. Bc4xf7+ | Ke8-e7 |
| 8. Bc1-g5# | |

See Diagram 74 for final position.

74

Game 11

1. e2-e4	**e7-e5**
2. Ng1-f3	**Nb8-c6**
3. Bf1-c4	**Bf8-c5**
4. c2-c3	**Ng8-f6**
5. d2-d4	**Bc5-b6?**

5. ... exd4 was correct.

6. d4xe5	**Nf6xe4**

6. ... Ng4 was better.

7. Qd1-d5	**Ne4xf2?**
8. Qd5xf7#	

Of course, Black would have done better to give up the Knight than to get mated. See Diagram 75 for the final position.

75

Homework Answers
I. Diagrams 66–73

D-66 Yes, because White can match a defender for each of Black's three attackers.

D-67 a1, b3, d4, e6, g5, f7, h8.

D-68 Yes. The pawn on d5 is attacked seven times and also defended seven times. However, the preliminary exchanges will open up the c-file, after which the Black Knight on c7 will not be able to move as it must shield its King against the White Queen. So the number of Black defenders will be reduced by one and White will win the pawn.

D-69 No. The pawn on e5 will be attacked six times and defended six times as well. In addition, the defenders and attackers are of equal value. Thus, Black can safely play 1. ... e6-e5.

D-70 No. This position differs from Diagram 69 in that the White Queen is on c2 instead of d2. This change is enough to make 1. ... e6-e5 a bad move, since after the preliminary exchanges on e5, White can exchange Queens by Qxc7. As a result, one of the defending pieces will be eliminated and the attackers will outnumber the defenders.

D-71 No. This position differs from Diagram 69 in that Black's h-pawn is on its home square instead of on h6. As a result of this seemingly insignificant change, Black cannot play 1. ... e6-e5. The sequence of exchanges on e5 would result in the disappearance of all the minor pieces and Rooks and conclude with the Black Queen capturing on e5 (7. ... Qxe5). At that point, however, the Black King's fate would be sealed as White would play 8. Qd2-d8+ and mate next move. If the pawn were on h6, the King would have an escape hole and be safe.

D-72 In this position from the game Morphy–Stanley, New York 1857, White played 1. Bc1-a3!, fixing the Black King in the center, and later worked up a strong attack.

D-73 No. The Knight on f6 is attacked 5 times and defended 5 times as well (the pawn on g7 cannot be counted a defender since it shields the King against the White Queen). So the defense is adequate.

II. Answers to the Exercises

1. 1. bxc8N +, indicating a pawn promoting to a Knight, would be described in full algebraic notation by 1. b7xc8N +.

2. a) Kf1-e2-f3; b) Kh2-g3-g3.

You can check the answers to the remaining questions easily by looking at a chessboard.

SUPPLEMENTARY MATERIAL

for use at the teacher's discretion

Positions 76–81 illustrate the theme of "Attack and Defense."

76

White to play and win a pawn.

    1. Rd1-d4!   **Rd8-d6**
    2. Rb1-d1   **Rf8-d8**

The two attackers are matched by the two defenders, but White has a third attacker in reserve.

    3. c2-c4!   **b5xc4**
    4. b3xc4

And White wins the pawn on d5.

77

Can White play and win the pawn on f7?
No. Although White has three attackers against only two defenders, the Queen is the first attacker and will be captured by the Black Rook:

    1. Qf3xf7 +   **Re7xf7**
    2. Rf2xf7 +   **Kf8-g8**

And White has lost his Queen for a Rook and a pawn, a material disadvantage of $9-(5+1)=3$ points.

78

White to play and win a pawn.

    1. Ra1-a7!   **Rf8-c8**
    2. Re1-c1

And Black cannot defend the c7 pawn a second time. Note that 1. Rec1 would not win since after 1. ... Rb7 2. Rc3 Black can defend the pawn a second time by 2. ... Rc8.

79

Can White play and win the pawn on d4?

No. White can attack the pawn four times, but Black has four defenders of the same value as White's attackers:

1. Bg3-f2	Ng7-e6
2. Rc2-d2	Bf8-g7
3. Rf1-d1	Re8-d8

80

Can Black play and win the pawn on e4?

No. The attacking pieces are worth more than the defenders, and Black would lose the Exchange for a pawn (i.e., a loss of one point.):

1. ...	Nd6xe4
2. Bd3xe4	Re7xe4
3. Nf2xe4	Re8xe4

81

Can Black move and win a pawn?

Yes. The White Knight is attacked three times by Black and defended only twice:

1. ...	Bg4xf3
2. g2xf3	Qf7xf3
3. Qd3xf3	Rf8xf3

And Black has won a pawn.

Examples of Games with Opening Mistakes

Game 12

1. e2-e4	b7-b6
2. Bf1-c4	Bc8-b7
3. Qd1-f3?	

3. d3 is better.

3. ...	Ng8-f6
4. Ng1-h3	Bb7xe4?

4. ... e6 is better.

5. Nf3-g5?

White should win back the pawn by 5. Bxf7+ Kxf7 6. Ng5+ Ke8 7. Nxe4.

5. ...	Be4xf3?

5. ... d5 is necessary.

6. Bc4xf7#

See Diagram 82 for the final position.

82

Game 13

   1. d2-d4   **f7-f5**
   2. Bc1-g5   **h7-h6**
   3. Bg5-h4

White tempts his opponent to open up the Black King's position.

   3. ...   **g7-g5**
   4. Bh4-g3   **f5-f4?**

4. ... Nf6 is correct.

   5. e2-e3   **h6-h5**

Black defends against the threat of 6. Qh5#.

   6. Bg1-d3   **Rh8-h6?**

Black has to play instead 6. ... Bg7 7. exf4 h4.

   7. Qd1xh5 + !   **Rh6xh5**
   8. Bd3-g6#

See Diagram 83 for the final position.

83

Game 14

   1. e2-e4   **e7-e5**
   2. Bf1-c4   **Qd8-f6?**
   3. Ng1-f3   **Qf6-g6?**

It is bad play to move only your Queen in the opening.

   4. 0-0!   **Qg6xe4?**
   5. Bc4xf7 + !   **Ke8-d8**

5. ... Kxf7 would be bad as Black would lose his Queen after 6. Ng5 + .

   6. Nf3xe5!

White sacrifices a Knight.

   6. ...   **Qe4xe5?**

It was high time Black started bring out his other pieces.

   7. Rf1-e1   **Qe5-f6?**
   8. Re1-e8#

See Diagram 84 for the final position.

84

Game 15

   1. e2-e3

1. e4 is better.

   1. ...   **e7-e5**
   2. Qd1-f3?   **d7-d5**
   3. Nb1-c3   **e5-e4**
   4. Qf3-f4?

A gross blunder, instead of which White should have retreated his Queen (4. Qd1).

   4. ...   **Bf8-d6!**

85

White resigns, as he cannot save his Queen.

Lesson Three

A. Check Lesson 2 homework (if necessary).

B. *Review Questions*
1. What difference, if any, is there between an attack and a counterattack?
2. Can a player have a positional advantage even if the two sides have equal material?
3. Which pieces are called minor pieces and which are called major pieces?
4. What is meant by a sacrifice?
5. What does the phrase "sacrifice the Exchange" mean?
6. Without looking at a chessboard, name all the squares in the g1-a7 diagonal. Are they light or dark squares?

87

Is the Black pawn on d5 sufficiently defended?

86

Is the Black pawn on d5 sufficiently defended?

88

How can White checkmate Black in one move?

89

How can White checkmate Black in one move?

Answers to Review Questions:

1. A counterattack is an attack undertaken by a player in reply to his opponent's attack.
2. Yes. A **positional advantage is a better** *arrangement* of pawns and pieces (material) and can occur even when the two sides have equal material.
3. The Bishops and Knights are the **minor pieces** and the Queen and Rooks are the **major pieces.**
4. A **sacrifice** is when a player voluntarily gives up material in order to achieve some goal.
5. The difference in value between a Rook and a minor piece is known as the **Exchange.** So to **sacrifice the Exchange** means to voluntarily give up a Rook for a Bishop or a Knight.
6. g1, f2, e3, d4, c5, b6, a7 (all are dark squares.)

D-86 The pawn is attacked by two pieces and defended by only one. So it is not adequately defended and needs additional protection.

D-87 The two defenders are matched by two attackers of corresponding value, but White has a third attacker as well. So the pawn is not adequately defended and needs additional protection.

D-88 1. Qa5-d8#.

D-89 1. Qf4-f5#.

More Symbols and Terms

We are already acquainted with a number of symbols that help us to record and analyse chess games. Now here are some more useful symbols.

Symbols	Meaning
!!	excellent (beautiful) move
??	gross blunder
?!	risky (dubious) move
u	any move
=	White and Black have equal positions
+ / −	White's position is better
− / +	Black's position is better

And now let us get acquainted with a few more chess terms and concepts. You will sometimes come across expressions such as "White has a **forced** win", "an exchange of pieces is **forced**", "the pawn Queens **by force**", "Black **forced** a draw", etc. In chess, to say that something is **forced** means that it cannot be avoided by one of the players if his opponent wants it.

90

For example, in Diagram 90, we say that White has a forced mate in five moves. That means that Black cannot avoid getting checkmated in five moves or less no matter what he does:

| 1. Rh5-e5 + | Ke4-d4 |
| 2. Qg3-e3 + | Kd4-c4 |

(see Diagram 91)

91

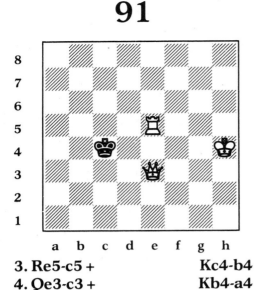

3. Re5-c5 +	Kc4-b4
4. Qe3-c3 +	Kb4-a4

(see Diagram 92)

92

5. Rc5-a5#

You can see that Black cannot avoid the above series of five moves. Such a series of moves in which one player cannot avoid is known as a **forced variation**, in this case a five-move forced variation.

A **variation** is a series of moves united by a common idea. In Diagram 90, White's idea was to drive the Black King to the edge of the board and checkmate it.

A **combination** is a forced variation containing a sacrifice and permitting the achievement of some **aim** desired by the player who makes the combination. The **aim** of a combination can be to mate the opponent's King, obtain a draw, win material, improve your position, etc.

93

Diagram 93, from the game Steinberg–Makarov, Kiev 1956, shows an example of a combination. White had sacrificed a pawn and then an Exchange for the attack, but after a while it became clear that Black had defended successfully while at the same time retaining his material advantage. Realizing that he was more likely to lose than to win, White decided to force a draw in the position of Diagram 93 by means of a **combination:**

    1. Nd5xe7!

White sacrifices the Knight with the **idea** of eliminating the pawn that defends Black's Knight on f6.

    1. ...   **Nc6xe7**

    2. Qb2xf6 + !

Now White sacrifices his Queen with the idea of drawing the Black King out of his shelter.

    2. ...   **Kxf6**

(see Diagram 94)

94

3. Be3-d4 +

And now White forces a draw by a perpetual check that Black cannot avoid!

3. ...	Kf6-g5
4. Bd4-e3 +	Kg5-h4
5. Be3-f2 +	Kh4-g5
6. Bf2-e3 +	

Draw

Another commonly used chess term is **Zugzwang.** A player is said to be in **Zugzwang** if it is his turn to move and, although he is not threatened with anything, any move that he makes will lead to a loss or to a worsening of his position.

95

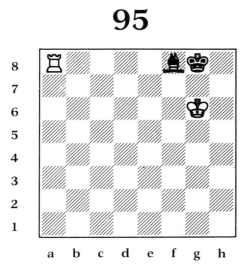

Diagram 95 is an example. Black to play loses because he is in **Zugzwang.** If he could stay put without making any moves he would not lose, but since the rules of chess do not allow a player to pass his turn Black must make the only move available to him, 1. ... Kg8-h8, although it leaves his Bishop undefended and allows White to checkmate him with 2. Ra8xf8#.

Let us examine the position again, but this time with White to move. We observe that Black, if it were his turn to play, would be in Zugzwang. Therefore White must somehow transfer his turn to Black, while conserving the elements of the position that make a Zugzwang possible. White can achieve this by making a **waiting move** with his Rook along the 8th rank, for example 1. Ra8-c8. Now Black is in Zugzwang and after the forced move 1. ... Kg8-h8 he is mated by 2. Rxc8xf8#.

How to Start a Game

A chess game can be divided into three stages: the opening (the starting moves of a game), the middlegame, and the endgame. In this section we shall discuss the opening.

All that a beginner needs to know about the opening is the basic principles of piece development that will help him to choose the right moves in the starting stages of a game. Here is a list of these principles:

1. It is best for White to start a game with 1. e2-e4 or 1. d2-d4, opening up a pathway for a Bishop and the Queen and attacking important **central squares.** Black should reply correspondingly with 1. ... e7-e5 or 1. ... d7-d5.

2. From the very first moves you should fight for control of the center (the d4, d5, e4, and e5 squares). Pieces are much stronger in the center of the board than on an edge. For example, a Knight controls (i.e., attacks) eight squares from the center, four squares from an edge, and only two squares when it has been driven into a corner.

3. The main opening principle is **rapid development** of your pieces. What this means is that you should bring your pieces into play as quickly as possible. Begin by developing your Kingside minor pieces (Knight and Bishop). This clears the way for Kingside castling, which enables you to put your King in safety and develop your Rook at the same time. After castling, bring out your Queenside pieces.

The reason for developing rapidly is that the player who succeeds in bringing his pieces into play before his opponent can obviously start attacking first and will have better chances of making effective combinations and winning the game.

A great master at exploiting advantages in development was the brilliant American chessplayer Paul Morphy. Before examining examples of his play, let us first take a brief look at some highlights of Morphy's chess career, one of the most remarkable in the annals of chess.

Morphy learned to play chess at the age of ten and within just two years became the strongest player in his hometown of New Orleans. in 1857, at the age of twenty, he easily brushed aside all opposition in winning the First American Chess Congress and was on the path to becoming a chess celebrity. Not finding worthy opponents in America, Morphy went to Europe in 1858 and played a number of matches in London and then Paris. The fantastic ease with which he defeated the strongest players of the day earned him an unequalled reputation. In 1859 Morphy returned to America and, to everyone's surprise, never took part in any more tournaments.

Now let us examine one of Morphy's brilliant games. This game was played under extremely odd circumstances. The date was October 1859, and the place was the Grand Opera in Paris. the boxes and stalls were occupied by the cream of Parisian society, the "beau monde", who had come to watch a performance of the opera *The Barber of Seville*. Among these spectators were two aristocrats, the well-known Duke of Brunswick and the little-known Count Isouard. They were both chess amateurs, and by the standards of those days they did not play too badly. By a coincidence, another person who had come to the opera that night was none other than Paul Morphy, who played excellent chess — by the standards of *any* period. During the interval the Count and the Duke invited Morphy to their box and suggested a game of chess. Morphy agreed. Here is the immortal game that was played.

Game 16

White: Paul Morphy

Black: Count Isouard and the Duke of
       Brunswick (in consultation)

1. e2-e4	e7-e5
2. Ng1-f3	d7-d6
3. d2-d4	Bc8-g4?

3. ... Nf6 or 3. ... Nd7 are the correct moves.

| 4. d4xe5 | Bg4xf3 |

After 4. ... dxe5 White would win a pawn by 5. Qxd8+ Kxd8 6. Nxe5.

| 4. Qd1xf3 | d6xe5 |

(see Diagram 96)

96

The Black Bishop made two moves and was exchanged for the White Knight, which had only made one. As a result, White has gained a development advantage over his opponent.

6. Bf1-c4

What is White threatening? *(Qxf7#.)*

| 6. ... | Ng8-f6 |

Black defends against the mate but has not noticed the other threat created by Morphy's last move. 6. ... Qd7 would be a better move, although Black would still be faced with a difficult defense after the possible White moves 7. Qb3, 8. Nc3, 9. 0-0, and 10. Rfd1.

7. Qf3-b3

(see Diagram 97)

97

White attacks two Black pawns at the same time. The Queen attacks the pawn on b7, while the Bishop, supported by the Queen, threatens the pawn on f7. Black cannot defend both of them.

| 7. ... | Qd8-e7 |

Relatively the best. Although he must lose a

pawn, Black wants to at least force an exchange of Queens after 8. Qxb7 Qb4+ and thereby hinder White's attack.

Why would 7. ... Qd7 8. Qb7 Qc6 be bad? *(Because of 9. Bb5 winning Black's Queen).*

What would happen if Black played 7. ... Nxe4? *(8. Bxf7+ Kd7 9. Qe6#).*

8. Nb1-c3!

With this move Morphy emphasizes that it is more important in the opening to develop your pieces than to capture enemy pawns.

8. ...   **c7-c6**

In order to defend his pawn, Black is forced to make yet another pawn move instead of developing his pieces.

8. Bc1-g5

White has now completed the development of his minor pieces.

9. ...   **b7-b5?**

Black expects the White Bishop to retreat, after which he could play ... Nbd7 and gradually develop his pieces. But 9. ... Qc7 would be better. See Diagram 98.

98

10. Nc3xb5!!

An important moment in the game. Morphy sacrifices the Knight in order to open up lines along which his other pieces can attack the Black King. This sacrifice is not an accident, but rather a manifestation of one of the principles which govern chess struggles. According to this principle, the player who has developed faster than his opponent must strive to open up lines since his pieces are ready to seize control of them. Conversely, a player who is behind in development should avoid moves that lead to the opening of lines since his pieces are not ready to use them and they will be taken over by the opponent's pieces.

10. ...   **c6xb5**
11. Bc4x b5 +   **Nb8-d7**
12. 0-0-0

By castling long White enables the Queen's Rook to immediately enter the struggle along the d-file. What is White's threat now? *(13. Bxd7+, and Black cannot recapture with 13. ... Nxd7 since he would lose his Queen.)*

12. ...   **Ra8-d8**

Why doesn't Black play 12. ... Qb4? *(Because of 13. Bxf6 Qxb3 14. Bxd7#, or 13. Bxf6 gxf6 14. Bxd7+, winning back the piece and maintaining a devastating attack.)* See Diagram 99.

99

13. Rd1xd7!   **Rd8xd7**
14. Rh1-d1

White sacrificed the Exchange in order to eliminate the important defensive Knight and now brings up fresh reserves in the form of the h1 Rook. Black on the other hand has conducted the opening so poorly that neither his Rook on h8 nor his Bishop on f8 can help him in his defense.

14. ...   **Qe7-e6**

Why is 14. ... Qb4 no good? *(Because of 15. Bxf6 followed by 16. Bxd7+.)*

15. Bb5xd7 +   **Nf6xd7**

See Diagram 100

100

a b c d e f g h

Find the combination which Morphy made to checkmate Black in two moves.

  16. Qb3-b8 + !!   **Nd7xb8**
  17. Rd1-d8#

A brilliant finish!

If it weren't for this game, nobody in the world would have heard of Count Isouard. As it is, however, his name is known to millions of chess lovers. Thus did a genius make the Count immortal!

We learned earlier on that it is bad to bring out your Queen at the beginning of a game. How is it then that Morphy "violated" this principle and still won a beautiful game? The reason is that Morphy rapidly developed *all* his pieces. As for his Queen, it was safe because the Black pieces were not in a position to attack it. There was good co-operation among all of White's pieces (i.e., they helped one another) and White was even able to sacrifice the Queen in order to checkmate Black.

So Morphy did not really break any opening rules. We must keep in mind furthermore that exceptions to the rules are possible and that everything depends on the actual situation on the board.

The Endgame
Checkmate with Queen and Rook

Checkmate in the opening is possible only as the result of a gross blunder by one of the players and occurs rarely among strong chess-players. Nor is it possible in every game to checkmate your opponent in the middlegame, when there are still a lot of pieces on the board. Thus games are often in fact decided only in the endgame, when the number of pieces on

the board has been considerably reduced as a result of exchanges.

The main goal of a player in the endgame is generally not an immediate checkmate, as there are usually too few pieces left to organize a mating attack. Rather, the player strives first of all to queen a pawn, after which checkmating the opponent will not be difficult.

To begin with, however, here is a very simple endgame where White already has a Queen, along with a Rook and his King, while Black has only his King (see Diagram 101).

101

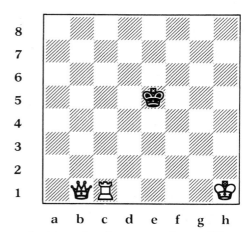

a b c d e f g h

In order to checkmate a lone King that is away from the edge of the board, you have to control the eight squares around it as well as a ninth square: the one on which the King is standing. If the King is on an edge, however, it has only 5 escape squares, while in a corner it has only 3 escape squares. So it is obviously easier to checkmate a King on an edge than one in the center, and even easier to checkmate a King in a corner.

A Queen and a Rook can checkmate a lone enemy King without the help of their own King by driving it over to an edge. In Diagrams 90–92 we saw a commonly occurring type of mate with Queen and Rook against King, but now let us look at the main mating method, known as "row-by-row mating."

Diagram 102 shows the typical pattern resulting from "row-by-row mating." (We call the situation in Diagram 102 a pattern rather than a position because a real position always has two Kings, while in Diagram 102 the White King has been left out as not being relevant to what we want to illustrate). The idea of this mating pattern is simple: one piece controls the back row, where the enemy King stands, and the other piece controls the second-last row, cutting off the King's escape.

Now let us return to Diagram 101 and try to drive the Black King over to an edge.

1. Rc1-c4

The Rook takes control of the 4th rank and cuts the King off from half the board.

1. ...   Ke5-d5

The King attacks the White Rook. See Diagram 103.

103

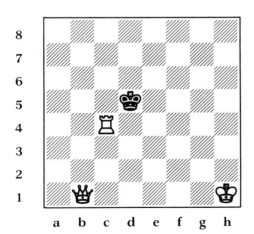

2. Qb1-b5 +

The Queen takes control of the 5th rank and at the same time protects the Rook.

2. ...   Kd5-d6

Since White controls the 4th and 5th ranks, the Black King is forced to retreat to the 6th rank. See Diagram 104.

104

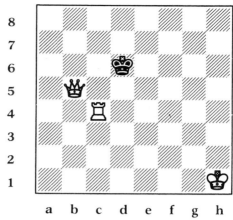

3. Rc4-c6 +

The White Queen having cut the Black King off from the 5th rank, the White Rook now takes control of the 6th rank.

3. ...   Kd6-d7

Since the Rook now guards the 6th rank, the Queen is able to move over to the 7th rank.

4. ...   Kd7-d8

The end of the road.

5. Rc6-c8#

See Diagram 105.

105

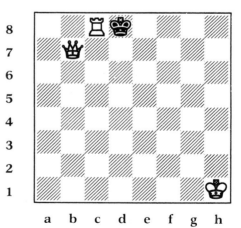

This way of mating is called the row-by-row method because the Queen and Rook in turn cut the King off from one row after another until they have driven it to the edge row (file or rank), where they can checkmate it. The Queen and the Rook are arranged in such a way that the Rook is always defended by the Queen. Thus the two pieces help each other and their joint efforts are enough to checkmate the opposing King. This is an example of good **piece co-operation.**

106

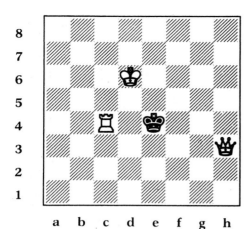

Diagram 106 shows another example. The Black King has been checkmated in the center of the board thanks to the fine co-operation of all the White pieces (including the King). The White King controls d5 and e5, the Rook guards the 4th rank and attacks the Black King, and the Queen controls the 3rd rank and f5.

HOMEWORK
(Answers at the end)

I. Diagrams 107–112

107

White to play and mate in six moves.

	WHITE	BLACK
1.		
2.		
3.		
4.		
5.		
6.		

108

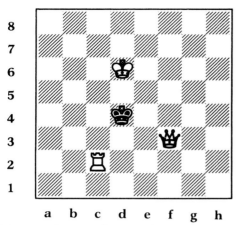

White to play and mate in two moves.

	WHITE	BLACK
1.		
2.		

110

White to play and mate in two moves.

	WHITE	BLACK
1.		
2.		

109

White to play and mate in two moves.

	WHITE	BLACK
1.		
2.		

111

Black to play and mate in two moves.

	WHITE	BLACK
1.		
2.		

112

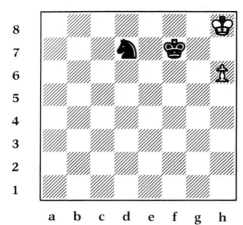

Black to play and mate in two moves.

	WHITE	BLACK
1.		
2.		

II. Board Study Exercises

Write down your answers in the spaces below.

1. Place eight Queens of the same color on an empty board in such a way that none of them defends any of the others.

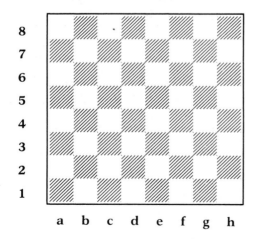

_____

_____

_____

2. Find any one of the paths in which a Black King on f8 can reach a4 in the shortest number of rows. Write it down in chess notation.

_____

_____

_____

3. Suppose you are playing Black. Name the square where the fourth row (counting from your side) crosses the fourth file (counting from your left).

_____

_____

_____

4. Write down any one of the paths in which a Knight on a8 can reach b7 in the shortest number of moves.

_____

_____

_____

5. Record one of your games in full algebraic notation and then play it over to check if you recorded it correctly.

SCORESHEET

Date: _____ 19 _____

WHITE: _____

BLACK: _____

WHITE	BLACK		WHITE	BLACK
1.			21.	
2.			22.	
3.			23.	
4.			24.	
5.			25.	
6.			26.	
7.			27.	
8.			28.	
9.			29.	
10.			30.	
11.			31.	
12.			32.	
13.			33.	
14.			34.	
15.			35.	
16.			36.	
17.			37.	
18.			38.	
19.			39.	
20.			40.	

RESULT:

WHITE WON   DRAW   BLACK WON

43

III. Games for Analysis

Game 17
Spielman–Flamberg, Mannheim, 1917

1. e2-e4	e7-e5
2. Nb1-c3	Ng8-f6
3. f2-f4	

White plays a **Gambit.** A gambit is an opening in which a player sacrifices a pawn or a piece in order to develop very quickly.

3. ...	d7-d5!

The right move, counterattacking in the center.

4. f4xe5	Nf6xe4

Threatening 5. ... Qh4 +, and if 6. g3, then 6. ... Nxg3.

5. Ng1-f3	Bc8-g4
6. Qd1-e2	

White sets up two threats. One is to win a pawn by 7. Nxe4, and the other is play 7. Qb5 + and then take the pawn on b7.

6. ...	Ne4-c5?

Black should exchange Knights, complete his development and castle on the Kingside.

7. d2-d4!	

Sacrificing a pawn.

7. ...	Bg4xf3
8. Qe2xf3	Qd8-h4 +
9. g2-g3	Qh4xd4

Black has won a pawn, but at great cost. White's Queen has occupied an attacking position and the other White pieces are ready to enter the fray without loss of time.

10. Bc1-e3!	Qd4xe5

Black wins a second pawn, but gets even farther behind in development.

11. 0-0-0!	c7-c6

White has developed his Queen, a Knight, a Bishop, and a Rook, while Black has managed to bring out only his Queen and a Knight, and even they occupy poor positions. Such disregard for development cannot remain unpunished.

12. Nc3xd5!	

When you have more pieces active, you must act energetically so as not to give your opponent a breather.

12. ...	c6xd5
13. Rd1xd5	Qe5-e6
14. Bf1-c4	Qe6-e4

White was threatening 15. Rxc5 or 15. Rd8 +.

15. Be3xc5!
See Diagram 113.

113

White sacrifices his Queen. Black resigns, because if 15. ... Qxf3, then 16. Re1 + Be7 17. Rxe7 + Kf8 18. Rd8#.

Rudolf Spielmann, who commanded the White army in this brilliant game, was a famous Austrian grandmaster.

HOMEWORK ANSWERS
I. Diagrams 107–112

D-107

1. Rc1-c3 +	Kb3-b4
2. Qa1-a3 +	Kb4-b5
3. Rc3-c5 +	Kb5-b6
4. Qa3-a5 +	Kb6-b7
5. Rc5-c7 +	Kb7-b8
6. Qa5-a7#	

D-108 (by G. Carpenter)

1. Qf3-h3	

Black is in Zugzwang. He is forced to play

1. ...	Kd4-e4

And give up control over c4, allowing

2. Rc2-c4#	

D-109

Solution 1:

1. Ke3-d3	Kd5-e5
2. Qg1-g5#	

Solution 2:

1. Qg1-c1	

Black is in Zugzwang and must give up control over c5.

        1. ...   Kd5-e5
        2. Qc1-c5#
D-110 (by P. Morphy)
        1. Rh1-h6
    Black is in Zugzwang. If he did not have to
move, White could not checkmate him, but
since he must move, he loses:
a)   1. ... g7xh6 2. g6-g7#
b)   1. ... Bg8-anywhere 2. Rh6xh7#
D-111
        1. ...   Nd4-c2
    Zugzwang.
        2. b2-b4   c4xb3#
C-112
        1. ...   Nd7-f8
    Zugzwang.
        2. h6-h7   Nf8-g6#

II. Exercises

1.   See Diagram 114. Ninety-two solutions to
     this problem were already known more
     than a hundred years ago.

114

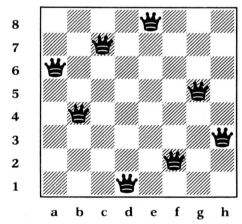

2.   Kf8-e7-d6-c5-b4-a4 (five moves).
3.   e5.
4.   Na8-c7-b5-d6-b7 (4 moves).

SUPPLEMENTARY MATERIAL

for use at the teacher's discretion

In Diagrams 115–120 White wins by putting
Black in Zugzwang.

115

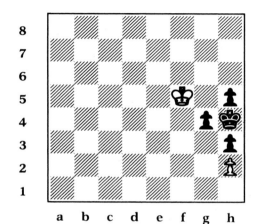

White to play and mate in two moves.
        1. Kf5-f4   g4-g3
        2. h2xg3#

116

G. Greco, 1624

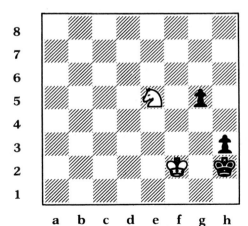

White to play and mate in three moves.
        1. Ne5-g4 +   Kh2-h1
        2. Kf2-f1   h3-h2
        3. Ng4-f2#

117

White to play and mate in two moves.
1. Ba8-h1   Kh2xh1
2. Rh7xh3#

118

White to play and mate in two moves.
1. Ke6-f7   Bh6-u
2. Be5xg7#

119

M. Yudovich

White to play and mate in two moves.
1. f2-f4   ...
  a)/... e4xf3   2. Qg3xe5#
  b)/... e5xf4   2. Be1-c3#
  c)/... g4xf3   2. Qg3xg5#
  d)/... g5xf4   2. Qg3-h4#

120

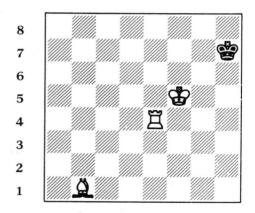

White to play and mate in two moves.
1. Kf5-f6   ...
  a)/... Kh7-h8   2. Re4-e8#
  b)/... Kh7-h6   2. Re4-h4#

121

White resigns. He has to give up his Queen by 13. Qxg4 in order to avert immediate mate.

Game 18
Four Knights Game
H. Dickson–H. N. Pillsbury, New Orleans
1900

1. e2-e4	e7-e5
2. Ng1-f3	Nb8-c6
3. Nb1-c3	Ng8-f6
4. Bf1-b5	Bf8-c5
5. 0-0	0-0

H. N. Pillsbury, who played Black in this game, was an outstanding American grandmaster and one of the strongest players in the world in the late 1800s and early 1900s. This game was played in what is known as a simultaneous blindfold exhibition. That is, Pillsbury was blindfolded and was playing many games against different opponents (who were not blindfolded!) at the same time.

6. Nf3xe5	Qd8-e7

After 6. ... Nxe5 7. d4 White would win back his piece with a good game.

7. Ne5xc6?

Trying to hang on to his extra pawn, White makes poor moves. He should instead play 7. Nf3 Nxe4 8. d4, when the Black Queen will come under fire along the open e-file.

7. ...	d7xc6
8. Bb5-d3??	

He had to play instead 8. Bc4 Nxe4 9. d3, giving up the pawn but completing his development.

8. ...	Qe7-e5
9. h2-h3	

The final mistake! Even now White could have averted disaster by playing 9. Be2.

9. ...	Bc8xh3!

By sacrificing the Bishop, Black exposes the White King's position.

10. g2xh3	Qe5-g3 +
11. Kg1-h1	Qg3xh3 +
12. Kh1-g1	Nf6-g4

Game 19
Giuoco Piano
Greco–Amateur, Rome 1619

1. e2-e4	e7-e5
2. Ng1-f3	Nb8-c6

The Italian master Greco, White in this game, was the strongest player of his time.

3. Bf1-c4	Bf8-c5
4. c2-c3	Qd8-e7

4. ... Nf6 is played more often in this position.

5. 0-0	d7-d6
6. d2-d4	Bc5-b6
7. Bc1-g5	f7-f6?
8. Bg5-h4	g7-g5?

Black's last two moves are poor. It is more important to develop your pieces in the opening that to move pawns. 7. ... Nf6 followed by 8. ... 0-0 would be better.

9. Nf3xg5!

White sacrifices the Knight! Only by such energetic measures can Black's incorrect play be refuted.

9. ...	f6xg5
10. Qd1-h5 +	Ke8-d7
11. Bh4xg5	Qe7-g7
12. Bc4-e6 + !	

A pretty sacrifice leading to mate.

12. ...	Kd7xe6
13. Qh5-e8 +	Qg7-e7
14. d4-d5#	

See Diagram 122 for the final position.

122

Lesson Four

A. Check Lesson 3 Homework (if necessary).

B. *Review Questions*

1. Is e2-e4 is good first move? If yes, why exactly?
2. What is the "opening"?
3. Do you know the meaning of the word "gambit"?
4. When does the endgame start?
5. What is meant by the word "forced"?
6. What is a "variation"?
7. What is a "combination"?

Try to answer questions 8–10 without looking at a chessboard.

8. What color (light or dark) is the g2 square?
9. How many moves does a Knight need to get from g4 to f5? Name these moves. Give two solutions.
10. Suppose you are playing Black. Name the square where the third row (counting from your side) crosses the a1-h8 diagonal.

Answers to Review Questions

1. 1. e2-e4 is a very good first move because it opens a path for the Queen and a Bishop. In addition, the pawn occupies a central square and controls the important squares d5 and f5.
2. The *opening* is made up of the first 10–15 moves of a game.
3. A *gambit* is an opening in which one of the players sacrifices a pawn or sometimes even a piece in order to gain an advantage in development over his opponent and whip up a quick attack.
4. The *endgame* begins when, apart from the Kings and pawns, only a few pieces remain on the board, the rest having been exchanged off.
5. To say that something is *forced* means that it cannot be avoided.
6. A *variation* is a series of moves united by some idea. If these moves compel the opponent to make certain replies, the variation is called a *forced variation*. For example, in Diagram 123 White (to play) wins by means of a forced variation:

123

1. b7-b8N +	Ka6-b6
2. Nb8xc6	Kb6xc6
3. h6-h7	u
4. h7-h8Q	etc.

Theoretically speaking, other moves too were possible, but the moves we have given are the best for both White and Black.

7. A *combination* is a forced variation in which one or more sacrifices (of a pawn, an Exchange, or a piece) are made in order to achieve a particular aim. An example is shown in Diagram 124:

124

1. Qh1xh7+!   **Kh8xh7**

Black's reply is forced.

2. Rg1-h1#

8. Light.

9. Two moves: Ng4-e3-f5 or Ng4-h6-f5.

10. f6.

Mistakes in the Opening

Every time somebody loses a game, it is because he has made some mistake. Sometimes even a mistake in the opening can be so serious as to decide the outcome of the whole game. In chess as in life we must pay for our mistakes, and the more serious the mistake the more severe the penalty.

Let us go over some opening principles whose violation results in mistakes:

1. It is bad to bring out your Queen early in the game. If you do, your opponent will be able to develop his minor pieces with gain of tempo by attacking your Queen, which, being the more valuable piece, will have to retreat.

2. Do not make passive waiting moves in the opening such a2-a3, a7-a6, h2-h3, or h7-h6. Every move should be used either to bring out a piece or to open a line (rank, file, or diagonal) for a piece.

3. Do not waste time (tempos) in the opening by unnecessarily moving the same piece several times.

4. An attack conducted with meager forces before you have completed your development and castled is premature unless your opponent has committed some gross blunder that allows you to make a combination that wins by force.

5. Do not go chasing after some small material advantage (such as a pawn) in the opening at

the cost of lagging behind in development or getting a bad position.

Now let us look at some games featuring typical opening mistakes.

Game 20

1. e2-e4	e7-e5
2. d2-d4	e5xd4
3. c2-c3	d4xc3
4. Bf1-c4	c3xb2
5. Bc1xb2	

This opening is known as the Danish Gambit. White sacrifices two pawns in order to develop his Bishops on active diagonals without loss of time.

5. ...   **Bf8-b4+**

A solid defense is 5. ... d5!, with the idea of giving back one (or perhaps even both) of the pawns in order to achieve full piece development. A possible variation is 6. Bxd5 Bb4+ 7. Nc3 Bxc3+ 8. Bxc3 Nf6 9. Nf3 Nxd5 10. exd5 Qe7+ 11. Kf1 0-0 12. Qd4 Qf6 13. Qxf6 gxf6 14. Bxf6 Nd7=

6. Nb1-d2   **Qd8-g5?**

As you no doubt remember, it is not good to bring your Queen out early in the game. However, Black has decided that in the given position he can gain an advantage by doing so since the Queen on g5 not only defends g7 but also attacks the White pawn on g2. In addition, Black is threatening to exchange Queens by 7. ... Qxd2+, which would be good for him since he is two pawns up. See Diagram 125.

125

7. Ng1-f3!

White sacrifices a third pawn and continues

to rapidly bring his pieces into play.

7. ...	Qg5xg2
8. Rh1-g1	Bb4xd2 +

See Diagram 126

126

This is the position that Black had in mind when he played 6. ... Qg5. What is White to do now? If he recaptures the Bishop with his Queen he will lose his Knight, if he recaptures it with his Knight he will lose his Rook, and if he recaptures it with his King (9. Kxd2) he will lose his pawn on f2 with check.

9. Ke1-e2!!

This move, overlooked by Black, allows White to continue with a devastating attack.

9. ...	Qg2-h3
10. Qd1xd2	

See Diagram 127.

127

Someone who came upon this position without seeing what led up to it might be forgiven if

he thought for an instant that only White had been moving for most of the game! Black has three (!) extra pawns but has paid dearly for them. All his pieces (except the Queen) are in a deep slumber, so to speak, while all the White pieces control important files and diagonals and are ready to launch an attack. It is therefore no surprise that the struggle is over in just a few more moves.

10. ...	Ng8-f6
11. Bc4xf7 + !	Ke8-d8

If 11. ... Kxf7, then 12. Ng5+ wins the Queen, while if 11. ... Kf8, then 12. Ba3 + d6 13. Bxd6 + cxd6 14. Qxd6 + Kxf7 15. Ng5 again wins the Queen.

12. Rg1xg7	Nf6xe4
13. Qd2-g5 + !	Ne4xg5

How does White mate next move?

14. Bb2-f6#

The final position is shown in Diagram 128.

128

This didactic game shows how dangerous it is go to "pawn-grabbing" in the opening. As a result of his gambit, White obtained an overwhelming superiority of forces on the Kingside and in the center, and this advantage in development created excellent conditions for attaining victory.

Game 21

1. e2-e4	e7-e5
2. Ng1-f3	f7-f6?

A poor way of defending the pawn on e5. The pawn on f6 deprives the Knight on g8 of its natural developing square, the Black King's position becomes exposed, and White is able to work up an irresistible attack by sacrificing his

Knight. Black should instead play 2. ... Nc6, 2. ... d6, or 2. ... Nf6. (See Diagram 129 for the position after 2. ... f7-f6?).

129

3. Nf4xe5!   **f6xe5?**

3. ... Qe7 would be better, although even then White would develop with tempo (gain of time) by 4. Nf3 Qxe4+ 5. Be2 Nc6 6. Nc3.

     4. Qd1-h5 +!

This early Queen sortie is justified here since White has a forced win.

     4. ...   **Ke8-e7**

If 4. ... g6, then 5. Qxe5+ Qe7 6. Qxh8.

     5. Qh5x5 +   **Ke7-f7**
     6. Bf1-c4 +

White develops his pieces with tempo (since the moves by the Black King are useless) and works up an irresistible attack.

     6. ...   **Kf7-g6**

Black could prolong his resistance by 6. ... d5, although after 7. Bxd5 + Kg6 (f5 is now controlled by the Bishop on c8) 8. h4 h6 9. Bxb7! Bd6 (if 9. ... Bxb7, then 10. Qf5#) 10. Qa5 Nc6 11. Bxc6 White has four (!) extra pawns.

     7. Qe5-f5 +   **Kg6-h6**

How should White continue his attack?

     8. d2-d4 +

The Bishop on c1 enters the fray with tempo.

     8. ...   **g7-g5**

How can White bring up fresh reserves now?

     9. h2-h4!

The h-pawn and the Rook on h1 join the attack.

     9. ...   **d7-d5**
     10. Qf5-f7   **d5xc4**

How can White mate next move?

     11. h4xg5#

130

All the Black pieces looked on idly from their home squares while their King perished.

The Endgame Mate
With Two Rooks Against a King

You already know how to mate a lone King with a Queen and a Rook using the *row-by-row* method. Two Rooks too can, without the help of their own King, mate the opposing King by using the same method. The mating pattern (see Diagram 131) is also almost the same.

131

Now let us look at Diagram 132.

132

The Black King must be driven to an edge, preferably the nearest one. So let us try to drive it to the h-file. To do that, we must first prevent the King from escaping to the Queenside.

1. Rg7-d7

The Rook controls the d-file and cuts the King off from the Queenside.

1. ...   **Ke5-e6**

See Diagram 133.

133

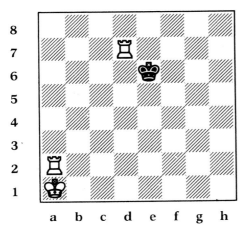

The King attacks the Rook. White moves the Rook far away, to the first rank (not to the second, where it would interfere with the other Rook). Now one Rook will be acting along the first rank and the other along the second.

2. Rd7-d1   **Ke6-e5**

Next White forces the Black King to abandon the e-file.

3. Ra2-e2 +   **Ke5-f4**

4. Rd1-f1 +

The persecution continues.

4. ...   **Kf4-g3**

See Diagram 134

134

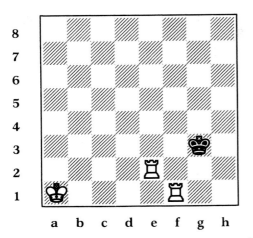

The Rook on f1 controls the f-file and White would now like to take over the g-file with the Rook from e2. However, the Rook cannot give a check immediately on g2, as it would be captured by the Black King. So White moves the Rook as far away as possible, to the other end of the board. We can now see the difference between mating a lone King with two Rooks and mating it with a Queen and a Rook. If the Rook on f1 were a Queen, the Rook on e2 would not have to run away to the other end of the board but could instead go to g2 (5. Rg2 +), since it would be supported by the Queen.

5. Re2-e8   **Kg3-g2**

Attacking the Rook on f1, which must also be moved as far away as possible, but not to the 8th rank, where it would interfere with the other Rook. So now the Rooks will be acting along the 7th and 8th ranks.

6. Rf1-f7   **Kg2-g3**

7. Re8-g8 +   **Kg3-h4**

8. Rf7-h7#

135

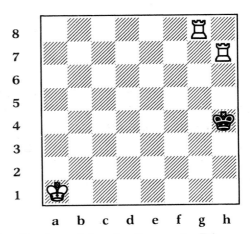

The final position is shown in Diagram 135. The Black King has nowhere further to retreat, so it's checkmate!

Two Rooks can mate the opposing King in the middle of the board as well, but only if they are aided by their own King. Diagram 136 shows an example.

136

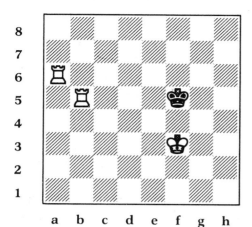

As you know, nine squares must be controlled in order to mate a King that is not on an edge. In our example, the White pieces each control a separate group of three of these nine squares, so that together they control all the nine squares, thus checkmating the Black King.

HOMEWORK
(Answers at the end)
I. Diagrams 137–142

137

White to play. Find the best move.

_____

_____

_____

138

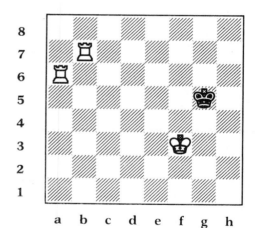

White to play. Find the best move.

_____

_____

_____

139

White to play. Mate in two moves. Find two solutions.

	WHITE	BLACK
1.		
2.		

	WHITE	BLACK
1.		
2.		

140

White to play. Mate in four moves. Find two methods.

WHITE	BLACK
1.	
2.	
3.	
4.	

WHITE	BLACK
1.	
2.	
3.	
4.	

141

White to play. Mate in two moves.

WHITE	BLACK
1.	
2.	

142

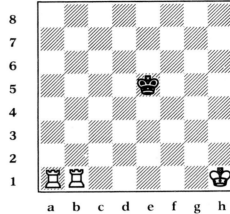

White to play. How many moves are needed to checkmate Black? What are these moves?

WHITE	BLACK

II. Exercises

Write down your answers in the space below.

Try to answer questions 1–3 without looking at a board.

1. Can a position with White pawns on a2, a3, and b2 occur in a game?

_____

_____

_____

2. How many moves will it take a Black Knight on c7 to capture a White pawn on e7?

_____

_____

_____

3. Name the diagonals running through e4. Which squares make up these diagonals?

_____

_____

_____

4. Set up several random positions with a King and two Rooks or a King, Queen and Rook against a lone King and practice checkmating the King until you can do it quickly and confidently.

5. Record one of your games in abbreviated notation and then play it over to check if you did it correctly.

III. Games With Opening Mistakes For Analysis

Game 22

1. f2-f4

This is not considered to be one of the strongest first moves since it does not open lines for the White pieces or help White's development. Furthermore, it exposes the White King's position.

1. ... e7-e5

A strong move. Black sacrifices a pawn (i.e., he is playing a gambit) but gets more than enough in return: paths are opened up for his Queen and dark-square Bishop and he can develop rapidly. 1. ... d5, freeing the way for the Queen and the light-square Bishop, would also be good.

2. f4xe5

White loses time by capturing the pawn instead of developing. The best move would be 2. e4, with White in his turn offering Black a gambit.

56

2. ... d7-d6
3. e5xd6

Bringing out a piece by 3. Nf3 would be better.

3. ... Bf8xd6
4. Nb1-c3??

White blithely ignores the exposed position of his King. He had to play 4. Nf3.

4. ... Qd8-h4 + !

This check is good here because it has a definite follow-up that leads to victory.

5. g2-g3 Qh4xg3 + !

Black sacrifices his Queen for a pawn. 5. ... Bxg3 + ! would have led to the same result also.

6. h2xg3 Bd6xg3#

The final position is shown in Diagram 143.

143

White lost quickly because he neglected the development of his pieces.

The next game also finishes very quickly.

Game 23

1. f2-f4 e7-e5
2. e2-e4

This time White plays a better move than 2. fxe5. The pawn sacrifice offered by White is called the "King's Gambit."

2. ... Bf8-c5

Black follows the very sensible policy of developing his pieces instead of grabbing a pawn. Also, he correctly avoids 2. ... Qh4 + . Beginners love to check whenever they can, but checks are often useless or even harmful. For example, White would reply to 2. ... Qh4 + with 3. g3. The attacked Queen would have to retreat and Black would just have lost time.

3. f4xe5?

White should have followed Black's example and developed a piece with 3. Nf3.

    3. ...   **Qd8-h4 + !**

Now this check is good!

    4. Ke1-e2   **Qh4xe4#**

See Diagram 144 for the final position.

144

White could have avoided checkmate by playing 4. g3, but after 4. ... Qxe4 + he would have lost a Rook. In this game too White got carried away by the idea of winning a pawn and neglected his development.

Answers to the Homework
I. Diagrams 137–142

D-137

    1. Qd1-d5   **Ng8-h6**

    2. Bc1xh6   **0-0**

3. Qxf7 was threatened.

    3. Bh6-e3

And so on. The diagram position arose after the opening moves 1. e4 e5 2. Nf3 d6 3. Bc4 Nd7 4. d4 Be7? 5. dxe5 dxe5??.

D-138   The solution is exactly the same as for D-137, although this position arose from a different opening (1. e4 e5 2. d4 exd4 3. Bc4 Bb4 + 4. c3 dxc3 5. bxc3 Be7??).

D-139

Solution a):

    1. Rb7-b5 +   **Kg5-h4**

    2. Ra6-h6#

Solution b):

    Rb7-h7

Zugzwang.

    1. ...   **Kg5-f5**

    2. Rh7-h5#

D-140

Solution a):

    1. Rb1-e1 +   **Ke7-f6**

    2. Rd2-f2 +   **Kf6-g5**

    3. Re1-g1 +   **Kg5-h4**

    4. Rf2-h2#

Solution b):

    1. Rb1-b6   **Ke7-f7**

    2. Rd2-d7 +   **Kf7-e8**

    3. Rd7-a7   **Ke8-d8**

    4. Rb6-b8#

D-141

    1. Qc2-xh7 + !   **Kh8xh7**

    2. Ra2-h2#

D-142   Black can be mated in seven moves. There are many ways of doing this. Here is one:

    1. Ra1-a4   **Ke5-d5**

    2. Rb1-b5 +   **Kd5-c6**

    3. Rb5-h5

As far away from the King as possible.

    3. ...   **Kc6-b6**

    4. Ra4-g4

So that the Rooks don't get in each other's way.

    4. ...   **Kb6-c6**

    5. Rg4-g6 +   **Kc6-d7**

    6. Rh5-h7 +   **Kd7-e8**

    7. Rg6-g8#

II. Exercises

1.   No. Such a position is impossible because the only ways a pawn can get to a3 are either by advancing from a2 or by capturing from b2, but both these pawns are still on their home squares.

2.   Two moves: 1. ... Nc7-d5 2, ... Nd5xe7.

3.   You can easily check the answers your selves by looking at a chessboard.

SUPPLEMENTARY MATERIAL

for use at the teacher's discretion

Positions 145 and 146 illustrate opening mistakes and Diagrams 147–150 demonstrate the linear mate idea.

145

Black to play. What is White's threat and how can Black defend against it? This position arose after the following opening moves:

1. e2-e4	e7-e5
2. Ng1-f3	Nb8-c6
3. Bf1-c4	Ng8-f6
4. Nb1-c3	d7-d6?
5. Nf3-g5	

White threatens 6. Ng5xf7. Black is forced to give up a pawn, whether by 6. ... Bc8-e6 (defended once, attacked twice), 6. ... d6-d5 (defended twice, attacked three times), or 6. ... Bc8-g4 7. Bc4x7+ Ke8-d7 8. f2-f3

146

From the game Petrosian–Ree, Beverwijk 1971. White to play and win a piece. This position arose after the following opening moves:

1. c2-c4	e7-e5
2. Nb1-c3	Nb8-c6
3. Ng1-f3	Ng8-f6
4. e2-e3	Bf8-b4
5. Nc3-d5	Nf6xd5?
6. c4xd5	e5-e4??

White now wins by:

7. d5xc6	e4xf3
8. Qd1-b3!	a7-a5
9. a2-a3!	Bb4-d6
10. c6xb7	Bc8-b7
11. Qb3xb7	

with an extra piece.

147

From the game Goglidze–Botvinnik, Moscow 1935. Black to play mates in three moves.

1. ...	Qe2xf1 +!
2. Kg1xf1	Rb8-b1 +
3. Kf1-e2	Rc8-c2#

148

From the game Schlechter–Tarrasch, Cologne 1911. Black resigned after 1. Rd1-d3. Why?

Because he had no good defense against the threat of 2. Qxh6+ Kxh6 3. Rh3#.

149

From the game Pillsbury–Maroczy, Paris 1900. White to play wins

1. Qf4-h6

Threatening 2. Qg7# or 2. Qf6#.

1. ...	**Qb2xe5**
2. Qh6xh7+!!	**Kh8xh7**
3. Kh3-g2#	

150

From the game Budrich–Gumprich, Berlin 1950. White to play wins.

1. Bg2xd5+!

To clear the c-file.

1. ...	**c6xd5**
2. Qe7xf8+!	**Kg8xf8**
3. Rc2-c8+	**Bg5-d8**
4. Rc8xd8#	

Sample Games Containing Opening Mistakes

Game 24
Three Knights Opening
Reti–Dunkelblum, Vienna, 1914

1. e2-e4	**e7-e5**
2. Ng1-f3	**Nb8-c6**
3. Nb1-c3	**Bf8-c5?!**

This "active" move is not very good as it allows White to gain an advantage in the center by means of a temporary sacrifice.

4. Nf3xe5!	**Nc6xe5**
5. d2-d4	**Bc5xd4?**

Better would be 5. ... Bd6 6. dxe6 Bxe5.

6. Qd1xd4	**Qd8-f6?**

It would be better to defend the Knight by 6. ... d6, when 7. f4 would be dangerous for White because of 7. ... Qh4+ 8. g3 Nf3+. In bringing his Queen out to f6, Black has been tempted by the chance to threaten to win White's Queen by 7. ... Nf3+.

7. Nc3-b5!

The more stereotyped reply 7. Be3, developing a piece, would also have given White an advantage, but in this particular position the talented grandmaster Richard Reti realizes that he can better exploit Black's opening mistakes by moving his Knight a second time before completing his development, although such a move goes against a general opening principle.

7. ...   **Ke8-d8?!**

7. ... c6 would undoubtedly be better, but Black's position would remain difficult in any case after 8. Nd6+.

8. Qd4-c5!

Black resigns, as he cannot defend against both 9. Qf8# and 9. Qxc7+ at the same time. See Diagram 151 for the final position.

151

This game shows us that while as a rule we must play in accordance with the major opening principles, exceptions to these rules are sometimes possible.

Game 25

1. e2-e4	e7-e5
2. Ng1-f3	Nb8-c6
3. Bf1-c4	Bf8-c5

Both sides have played well in bringing out their Bishops to strong positions. This opening is called the Giuoco Piano.

4. d2-d3

Opening a path for the other Bishop.

4. ...   **Ng8-e7?**

A poor move. The Knight would be better placed on f6.

5. Nf3-g5!

Attacking the pawn on f7 a second time.

5. ...   **0-0?**

After this mistake, Black can no longer save himself. He should instead defend with 5. ... d5.

6. Qd1-h5!

If White plays 6. Nxf7 instead, then after 6. ... Rxf7 7. Bxf7+ Kxf7 he will have given up a Bishop and a Knight in return for a Rook and a pawn, a disadvantageous trade in the opening stages of a game. After 6. Qd1-h5!, on the other hand, White threatens mate on h7 and simultaneously attacks the pawn on f7 a third time. Black cannot defend against both threats at once.

6. ...   **h7-h6**

The only defense against mate, since 6. ... Re8 would be followed by 7. Bxf7+ Kf8 8. Nxh7#.

7. Ng5xf7   **Rf8xf7**

Black has to give up the Exchange. After 7. ... Qe8 he would be mated in three moves: 8. Nxh6++ (double check) Kh8 9. Nf7++ (another double check!) Kg8 10. Qh8#.

8. Bc4xf7+   **Kg8-f8**

If 8. ... Kh8, then 9. Bxh6 gxh6 10. Qxh6#.

9. Bf7-b3   **Qd8-e8**

White was threatening to mate with the Queen on f7.

10. Qh5xh6

Instead of this Queen sacrifice, White could also play 10. Qf3+ Nf5 11. Qxf5, with an extra Rook and an easy win.

10. ...   **g7xh6?**

11. Bc1xh6#

See Diagram 152 for the final position.

152

Instead of capturing the Queen, Black could have played 10. ... Ng8, which would have been followed by 11. Qh8 Ne7 12. Bg5 d5 13. Bxe7 Qxe7 14. Bxd5 Be6 15. Bxe6 Qxe6. In order to exploit his material advantage of an Exchange and three pawns, White should now strive to simplify the game by exchanging the Queens and other pieces and going into an endgame.

Lesson Five

A. Check Lesson 4 Homework (as necessary).

B. *Review Questions*

1. What is the difference between an opening and a gambit?
2. What does "Zugzwang" mean?
3. If a pawn moves from e2 to e3, and then the next move from e3 to e4, can a Black pawn on d4 capture it en passant?

Try to answer questions 4-6 without looking at a board.

4. Name the squares on which Black's Bishops stand at the start of a game. What color (light or dark) are they?
5. On which square does White's Queen stand at the start of the game? Is it a light or dark square?
6. At what square do the a3-f8 and e1-a5 diagonals cross? What color (light or dark) is it?

Answer the next questions directly from diagrams, without setting up the men on a board.

153

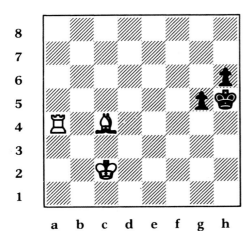

White to play and mate in one move.

154

White to play and mate in one move.

155

White to play and mate in two moves.

156

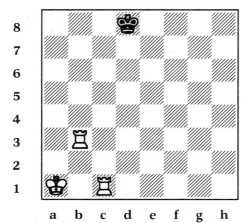

White to play and mate in two moves.

Answers to Review Questions

1. The "opening" refers to the first few moves of a game. A "gambit" is a special kind of opening in which a player sacrifices material in order to develop his pieces more rapidly.

2. A player is said to be in "Zugzwang" when all the moves available to him will worsen his position but he is forced to make one of them anyway because you are not allowed to pass your turn in chess. An example is shown in Diagram 156 (for solution see No. 10 below).

3. No. A Black pawn on d4 can capture a White e-pawn en passant only when the latter goes to e4 in a single move, i.e., e2-e4. Furthermore, if Black wants to take en passant (...d4xe3), he can only do so on the move with which he replies to White's e2-e4 — on succeeding turns the pawn on e4 will be safe from en passant captures.

4. c8 (light) and f8 (dark).
5. d1 (light.
6. b4 (dark).
D-153: 1. Bc4-f7#.
D-154: 1. Qa1-e5#.
D-155: 1. Qb8xf8+ Kg8xf8 2. Rb7-b8#.
D-156:

    1. Rb3-b7

Black is now in Zugzwang.

    1. ...   **Kd8-e8**

A forced King move that loses control of c8, allowing the White Rook to occupy it.

    2. Rc1-c8#

Opening Traps

Many battles in the history of warfare have been won as a result of some cunning stratagem. Similarly, chess battles too are often decided when we catch our opponent in a trap or when we ourselves fall into a trap.

What exactly is a trap? Simply put, a trap is an *enticement to make a mistake*. It is a cunning move containing some hidden, disguised threat which the trap-setter hopes his opponent will overlook. A regular characteristic of a trap is that it entices the opponent to make some tempting, natural, and apparently advantageous move or variation which, however, will meet with an unexpected refutation. Every chessplayer has at one time or another fallen into traps, even the World Champions.

Traps can be good or bad. **A trap is bad (or unsound) if it is a risky gamble** that will give you an advantage if your opponent falls into it but that will rebound to your disadvantage if your opponent sees and avoids it. That is, an unsound trap is based **only on the hope that the opponent will make a mistake.**

A trap is good (or sound) if there is no risk associated with it. If your opponent makes a mistake and falls into the trap, so much the better, but even if he sees and avoids your clever ruse, your position must not suffer. A sound trap will take into account the opponent's best replies and make sure they are not harmful.

Let us now look at some games whose outcomes were decided by a trap.

We will begin with an old trap which occurred in a game played in Paris in 1787. The 85-year-old chess master de Kermur sire de Legal was playing White, while the commander of the Black army was a weak chessplayer called Saint-Brie. Legal had been the strongest chessplayer in Paris for many years, until he acquired a talented pupil by the name of Francois Andre Danican Philidor who one fine day started winning from his teacher. Philidor later became not only the strongest chessplayer in the world but also a famous musician and composer. Legal, although overtaken by Philidor, nevertheless remained the second-best player in Paris right to the end of his life. In our days, too, pupils often start defeating their teachers. Right?

Game 26
Legal–Saint-Brie

1. e2-e4	e7-e5
2. Ng1-f3	d7-d6

This opening is called Philidor's Defense. That's right! The same Philidor who was Legal's pupil!

3. Bf1-c4	Nb8-c6
4. Nb1-c3	Bc8-g4

See Diagram 157.

157

Until now both sides have played well. At this point, however, Legal touched the Knight on f3 and then quickly took his hand away, whereupon his opponent reminded him about the "touch-move" rule. The many onlookers confirmed that Legal had in fact touched the Knight and they too insisted that he move it. Legal agreed, but he said he wanted to think a bit more about where to move it, and finally he played:

5. Nf3xe5?!

The Chevalier Saint-Brie immediately snapped up the Queen, thinking that White was giving it up just like that.

5. ...   **Bg4xd1??**

This is the move that White's highly risky trap was based on. But if Black had thought the position over carefully, he would have realized that the Queen could not be taken but that the simple 5. ... Nxe5, on the other hand, would leave Black a piece up.

6. Bc4xf7 +	Ke8-e7
7. Nc3xd5#	

158

Nobody knows today whether Legal's touching the Knight really was accidental or whether it was just a ploy calculated to catch an inexperienced opponent in a pretty trap that Legal, although he knew it was unsound, was unable to resist playing.

Although the trap worked in this case, you would do well not to set such traps. Don't forget, if Black had seen through the trap, he could have won a piece.

This mate became known as "Legal's Mate", and it has been repeated many times since then in a variety of forms.

The idea of Legal's mate continues up to the present day to form the basis of threats or traps even in the games of strong players. Here is an example.

Game 27
Cheron–Jeanlose, Leysin 1929

This game was played in a "simultaneous exhibition" — Andre Cheron, many times champion of France, was playing many games at the same time against different opponents.

1. e2-e4	e7-e5
2. Ng1-f3	Nb8-c6
3. Bf1-c4	d7-d6
4. Nb1-c3	Bc8-g4

The position in which Legal set an unsound trap with 5. Nxe5.

5. h2-h3!!

The temptation to follow Legal might be great, but logic is more important! However, the move 5. h2-h3 too sets a cunning trap.

5. ...   **Bg4-h5?**

After 5. ... Bxf3 6. Qxf3 Nf6 (defending

against 7. Qxf7#) 7. d3 White's position would be better but it would still be a hard fight. See Diagram 159 for the position after 5. ... Bg4-h5?.

159

6. Nf3xe5!

Now this Legal-style Queen sacrifice is absolutely sound.

    6. ...   **Bh5xd1??**

Black should resign himself to the loss of a pawn by 6. ... Nxe5 7. Qxh5 Nxc4 8. Qb5+ c6 9. Qxc4 (or 6. ... dxe5 7. Qxh5).

    7. Bc4xf7 +   **Ke8-e7**

    8. Nc3-d5#

See Diagram 160 for the final position.

160

The trap in this game not only worked but, unlike Legal's trap, it was also sound. Even world champions are not averse to setting such traps!

You should make a study of both "good" and "bad" traps — the good ones so that you can use them, and the bad ones so that you can avoid them.

Let us now look at another very popular trap.

Game 28
Mullok–Kostic, Cologne 1912
    1. e2-e4   e7-e5
    2. Ng1-f3   Nb8-c6
    3. Bf1-c4   Nc6-d4?!
See Diagram 161.

161

Black sets an unsound trap! White could now gain a development advantage over Black by playing 4. c3 Nxf3+ 5. Qxf3, while even the simple 4. d3 or 4. Nxd4 would give White the better game. Of course, Grandmaster Kostic realized that 3. ... Nc6-d4?! was far from the best move, but he counted on his weak opponent being tempted by the pawn that Black leaves undefended.

    4. Nf3xe5?

The first step toward disaster. The Black pawn on e5 was a "poisoned pawn."

    4. ...   **Qd8-g5!**

See Diagram 162.

The Queen simultaneously attacks the Knight and the pawn on g2. White, however, can hardly believe his eyes and thinks, *"How can a grandmaster make such blunders? I can take his pawn on f7 with my Knight and fork his Queen and Rook!"* (*"Fork"* means to *"simultaneously attack"*).

5. Ne5xf7??

And this is the second and final step towards disaster. The trap has clapped shut! Why would 5. Ng4 be a bad move?

(Because of 5. ... d5, winning the Knight or the Bishop).

White could still have saved the game by playing 5. Bxf7+ Kd8 6. 0-0 Qxe5 7. c3 followed by 8. d4. In return for his piece he would then have two pawns and chances of working up an attack against the Black King stranded in the center. In such cases White is said to have compensation for his lost piece.

5. ...   **Qg5xg2**

6. Rh1-f1

If White played 6. Nxh8, how would Black reply?

(6. ... Qxh1+ 7. Bf1 Qxe4+ 8. Be2 Nxc2+ 9. Qxc2 and Black wins the Queen. If 9. Kf1, then 9. ... Qh1#).

6. ...   **Qg2xe4+**

7. Bc4-e2?

It's better to lose the Queen by 7. Qe2 than to get mated.

7. ...   **Nd4-f3#**

See Diagram 163.

White's King is completely surrounded by its own men but none of them can help. Such a mate is called a "smothered mate."

The trap in this game was pretty but unsound — it was based entirely on the presumption that the opponent would blunder.

How can you safeguard yourself from falling into a trap? Chess abounds in innumerable traps, so it is obviously impossible to memorize them all, but in spite of that strong players very rarely get taken in by them. The reason is that they follow the "major principles of piece development," the very ones that you have studied in previous lessons.

The most important thing is to always play carefully and never capture enemy pawns and pieces (even the Queen) without first thinking it over and making sure there's no trap.

Mating with a Queen in the Endgame

You already have some experience in mating a lone King and know that you must first drive it to one of the edges of the board. The Queen, the strongest chess piece, can do this all by itself, without the help of its King. Let us look at the position in Diagram 164.

164

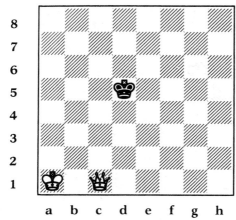

The best method is to chase the King to the nearest corner, which in our example is a8. However, if the King voluntarily heads for another corner (h8), we can mate it there as well.

1. Qc1-f4

The Queen controls the fourth rank and the f-file, cutting off several of the Black King's escape routes.

    1. ...   **Kd5-e6**

    2. Qf4-g5

The Black King having given up the fifth rank, the White Queen immediately occupies it.

    2. ...   **Ke6-d6**

    3. Qg5-f5

Now the Black King is cut off from the f-file.

    3. ...   **Kd6-c6**

    4. Qf5-e5   **Kc6-b6**

    5. Qe5-d5

See Diagram 165.

165

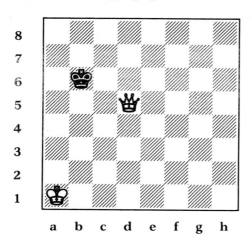

Note the technique: the Queen does its job without giving a single check, always staying a Knight's move away from the Black King, which, unable to attack the Queen, is constantly forced to give way and lose control over more squares.

    5. ...   **Kb6-c7**

Abandoning the 6th rank.

    6. Qd5-e6   **Kc7-b7**

    7. Qe6-d6   **Kb7-c8**

Leaving the second last rank.

    8. Qd6-e7   **Kc8-b8**

    9. Qe7-d7   **Kb8-a8**

    10. Qd7-c7???

See Diagram 166.

166

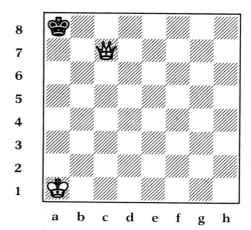

Oh, no! What have we done? The Black King is laughing and the White King is crying. And no wonder: it's stalemate, the game's a draw!

White's last move was a **gross blunder**, but beginners often fall into this trap.

In a real game, you cannot take back moves, but here let's take back our terrible last move so that you can learn how to checkmate (rather than stalemate)! See Diagram 167.

167

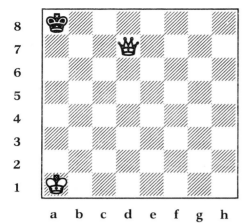

In driving the King into the corner, you have to be very careful and not make hasty moves. Leave the enemy King **two** squares on which it can move (in this case a8 and b8) and begin moving up your own King.

10. Ka1-a2	**Ka8-b8**
11. Ka2-a3	**Kb8-a8**
12. Ka3-a4	**Ka8-b8**
13. Ka4-a5	**Kb8-a8**
14. Ka5-b6	**Ka8-b8**

See Diagram 168.

168

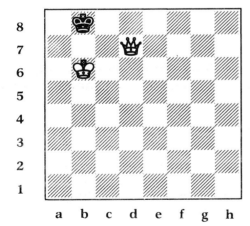

Now the White King controls a7, b7, and c7 and allows the Queen to deliver a fatal check (mate!) to the Black King.

15. Qd7-b7#

See Diagram 169 for the final position.

169

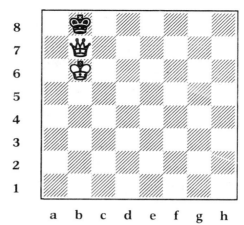

Did White have other ways of mating in one move in Diagram 168?
(Yes. 15. Qd8# and 15. Qe8#.)

We pushed back the enemy King using only our Queen. This is the easiest method for beginners. If we bring our King into play right from the start the joint action of the King and Queen will allow mate to be given more quickly. In that case, however, we must play even more carefully because stalemate can occur more often.

With correct play, a Queen and King can mate a lone enemy King within 10-15 moves. However, if you make a lot of mistakes you will run the risk of not winning the game because of the 50-move rule. Do you remember this rule?
(If 50 consecutive moves go by with no man captured and no pawns moved, then the game is a draw!)

So when mating a lone King, you have to make sure you do it within 50 moves.

Now here are a number of frequently encountered standard positions in which a Queen and King mate a lone enemy King. Remember these positions!

See Diagrams 170 and 171.

170

171

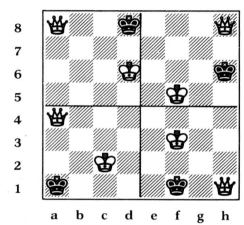

A different position is shown in each quarter-diagram. In the positions in Diagram 170, the Queen, defended by its own King, mates the enemy King from an adjoining square, while in the positions in Diagram 171, the Queen mates the enemy King from afar, while its own King takes away flight squares.

I. Diagrams 172-177

172

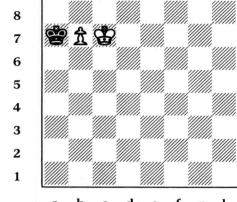

White to play. Mate in two moves.

	WHITE	BLACK
1.		
2.		

173

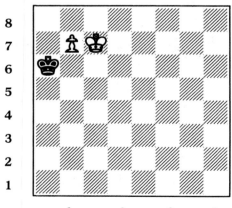

White to play. Mate in three moves.

	WHITE	BLACK
1.		
2.		
3.		

174

White to play. Mate in two moves.

	WHITE	BLACK
1.		
2.		

175

White to play. Mate in two moves.

	WHITE	BLACK
1.		
2.		

176

White to play. Mate in two moves.

	WHITE	BLACK
1.		
2.		

177

White to play. Mate in four moves.

	WHITE	BLACK
1.		
2.		
3.		
4.		

II. Exercises

1. Write down the position after the moves 1. e4 e5 2. Nf3 Nc6 3. Bc4 Nf6. First write down White's position, and then Black's. In giving the locations of more than one man of the same kind, (i.e., pawns, Bishops, etc.), list them in order from the a-file to the h-file. If several men of the same kind are located on the same file, then begin with the one on the lowest rank (i.e., the one nearest White's side.)

_____

_____

_____

2. Set up several random arbitrary positions with King and Queen against King and practice mating until you can do it rapidly and confidently.

Try to answer Questions 3-5 without looking at a board.

3. What color (light or dark) is f3?

4. At which square does the a3-f8 diagonal cross the d-file?

5. At which square does the h2-b8 diagonal cross the 4th rank?

III. Games Containing Opening Traps for Analysis

Game 29

1. e2-e4	e7-e5
2. Ng1-f3	Nb8-c6
3. Bf1-b5	

This opening is called the "Ruy Lopez."

3. ...	Ng8-f6
4. d2-d3	Nc6-e7?

It is against the principles of development to move the same piece twice in the opening before developing your other pieces. On top of that, the Knight is poorly placed on e7, blocking the Queen and the Bishop. In making the move, Black relies entirely on his opponent making a mistake.

5. Nf3xe5?

White falls for the bait and captures the poisoned pawn.

5. ...   c7-c6!

Here is the point of the trap. If the Bishop now retreats, Black will win a Knight for pawn by 6. ... Qa5+ followed by 7. ... Qxe5. Although it worked in this case, the trap was an unsound one. For starters, if White hadn't taken the pawn on e5 and instead had just continued his development, Black would have simply lost time. On top of that, the trap is too obvious. The ostentatious removal of the e-pawn's defender should put even a very inexperienced player on his guard.

6. Ne5-c4

Rather than lose the Knight, White decides to "give away" the Bishop.

6. ...   c6xb5??

Black is so happy at catching White in his trap that he doesn't pay any attention to White's last move and quickly snaps up the Bishop, thereby falling into a counter-trap.

7. Nc4-d6#

See Diagram 178.

178

A smothered mate! Instead of greedily grabbing the Bishop, Black could have won a piece for two pawns by playing 6. ... d6 7. Ba4 b5 8. Bxb5 cxb5. While Black's trap was no good, White's trap, on the other hand, was both sound and beautiful. White had to lose a piece anyway, so he decided to "give away" the Bishop, setting a pitfall into which Black duly fell. As the old proverb says, "Don't dig a grave for somebody else, you might fall in yourself."

Game 30
Pirc Defense
Hamlisch–N.N., Vienna 1899

1. e2-e4   **d7-d6**

This defense was developed into a system and introduced into master play by the Yugoslav grandmaster Vasja Pirc.

2. d2-d4   **Nb8-d7?!**

An inaccuracy. Today Black usually plays 2. ... g6, putting off the development of the Queen's Knight.

3. Bf1-c4   **g7-g6**
4. Ng1-f3   **Bf8-g7?**

Black does not sense the danger looming over him.

5. Bc4xf7 + !!   **Ke8xf7**

5. ... Kf8 would be better, but after 6. Ng5 Black would still be in bad shape.

6. Nf3-g5 +   **Kf7-f6**

Black does not want to retreat his King to f8 or e8 because in both cases 7. Ne6 would win his Queen.

7. Qd1-f3#

See Diagram 179.

179

White played well and did not violate the principles of development. Black has only himself to blame for blundering into an opening trap.

HOMEWORK ANSWERS
I. Diagrams 172-177

D-172

    1. b7-b8Q +   **Ka7-a6**
    2. Qb8-b6#

D-173

    1. b7-b8Q   **Ka6-a5**
    2. Qb8-b3!

Cutting off the Black King's escape and forcing it to return to its original square because of Zugzwang.

    2. ...   **Ka5-a6**
    3. Qb3-b6#

D-174

    1. Kh5-g6!

Controlling the important squares f7, g7, and h7.

    1. ...   **Kh8-g8**
    2. Qg2-a8#

D-175

    1. Qc1-f4!

Controlling the important squares b8 and f8.

    1. ...   **Kc8-d8**
    2. Qf4-f8#

D-176

    1. Ke3-f4!

Controlling the important squares g3, g4, and g5.

a)   **1. ...**   **Kh4-h5**
    2. Qb1-h7#
b)   **1. ...**   **Kh4-h3**
    2. Qb1-h1#

D-177

    1. Kh8-h7!

Controlling the important squares g6 and g7.

    1. ...   **Kf6-e7**

Forced, because of Zugzwang.

    2. Kh7-g6

Now the King controls the important squares f6 and f7.

    2. ...   **Ke7-e8**

If 2. ... Kf8, then 3. Qf7#.

    3. Kg6-f6

Now the Black King is again in Zugzwang. If it could stay put, it could not be mated next move, but it is forced to move onto a fatal square.

    3. ...   **Ke8-f8**
    4. Qd5-f7#

II. Exercises

1. White: Ke1, Qd1, Ra1, Rh1, Bc1, Bc4, Nb1, Nf3, P's a2, b2, c2, d2, e4, f2, g2, h2.
Black: Ke8, Qd8, Ra8, Rh8, Bc8, Bf8, Nc6, Nf6, P's a7, b7, c7, d7, e5, f7, g7, h7.

You can easily check your answers to the other questions by looking at a chessboard.

SUPPLEMENTARY MATERIAL

for use at the teacher's discretion

Sample Games with Opening Traps

Game 31

1. e2-e4	e7-e5
2. Ng1-f3	Ng8-f6

This is Petroff's Defense, named after the first Russian chess master (1794–1867).

3. Nf3xe5	Nf6xe4?

Black must first drive the Knight away with 3. ... d6 and only then take the e-pawn.

4. Qd1-e2!

A strong move that at the same time sets a trap!

4. ...	Ne4-f6??

It is better to lose a pawn than the Queen: 4. ... d5 5. d3 Qe7 6. dxe4 Qxe5 7. exd5, or 4. ... Qe7 5. Qxe4 d6 6. d4.

5. Ne5-c6+!

See Diagram 180.

180

This is the point of the trap! The Knight attacks the enemy Queen and at the same time clears the way for its own Queen to check the enemy King. Such a check is known as a "discovered check." Black resigns, since he cannot avoid losing his Queen.

Game 32
Petroff's Defense

1. e2-e4	e7-e5
2. Ng1-f3	Ng8-f6
3. Nf3xe5	Nf6xe4?
4. Ne5xf7?	

White should play 4. Qe2 Qe7 5. Qxe4 d6 6. d4 f6 7. Nc3! dxe5 Nd5 Qd6 9. dxe5 fxe5 10. Bf4 Nc6 11. 0-0-0 with irresistible threats. Instead he plays for a trap, hoping for 4. ... Kxf7 5. Qh5+ Kf6 (or 5. ... Kg8 6. Qd5#, or 5. ... Ke7 6. Qe5+, or 5. ... g6 6. Qd5+) 6. Qf3+ Ke5 7. d4+ Kxd4, after which it is only a matter of time before Black is mated.

4. ...	Qd8-e7!

An excellent move that incidentally sets a counter-trap.

5. Nf7xh8??

It is of course better to lose a Knight by 5. Be2 than the Queen.

5. ...	Ne4-c3+!

A discovered check. See Diagram 181.

181

White resigns, since he has to lose his Queen and the Knight in the corner won't get out alive either.

Game 33
Petroff's Defense

1. e2-e4	e7-e5
2. Ng1-f3	Ng8-f6
3. Nf3xe5	Nb8-c6?

A mistake. Better would be 3. ... d6 followed by 4. ... Nxe4.

4. Ne5xc6	d7xc6
5. e4-e5?!	

5. Nc3, developing a piece, would be better.

5. ...	Nf6-e4
6. d2-d3?	

Even now it would be better to bring out the Knight, by 6. Nc3.

6. ...	Bf8-c5!

By wasting time (tempos) with unnecessary pawn moves, White has fallen into a trap.

7. d3xe4?

7. Be3 Bxe3 8. fxe3 Qh4 + 9. g3 Nxg3 would be slightly better, although White would still be in a bad state.

    7. ...   **Bc5xf2 + !**

    8. Ke1xf2

If 8. Ke2, then 8. ... Bg4 wins the Queen.

    8. ...   **Qd8xd1**

See Diagram 182.

182

White resigns.

Game 34
Four Knights Game

    1. e2-e4   **e7-e5**

    2. Ng1-f3   **Nb8-c6**

    3. Nb1-c3   **Ng8-f6**

This opening is known as the Four Knights Game.

    4. Bf1-b5   **Bf8-b4**

    5. 0-0   **0-0**

    6. d2-d3   **d7-d6**

Black copies White for too long and soon falls into a trap. Here the right way to play is 6. ... Bxc3 7. bxc3 d6.

    7. Bc1-g5   **Bc8-g4**

    8. Nc3-d5   **Nc6-d4**

    9. Nd5xb4   **Nd4xb5**

It's very dangerous to copy your opponent's moves for so long.

    10. Nb4-d5   **Nb5-d4**

    11. Qd1-d2   **Qd8-d7**

    12. Bg5xf6   **Bg4xf3**

    13. Nd5-e7 +

Black can no longer copy and gets mated in a few moves.

    13. ...   **Kg8-h8**

    14. Bf6xg7 +   **Kh8xg7**

    15. Qd2-g5 +   **Kg7-h8**

    16. Qg5-f6#

See Diagram 183 for the final position.

183

Game 35
Mieses–Equist, Nuremberg, 1895

    1. e2-e4   **d7-d5**

This move is the Center Counter Defense.

    2. e4xd5   **Qd8xd5**

As you can see, the disadvantage of this defense is that Black has to bring his Queen into play very early.

    3. Nb1-c3   **Qd5-d8**

Instead of this move, which leaves White with a clear advantage in development, 3. ... Qa5 would be more active.

    4. d2-d4   **Nb8-c6?**

A mistake, as White can easily attack the Knight with a pawn. 4. ... c6 or 4. ... Nf6 would be safer.

    5. Ng1-f3   **Bc8-g4?**

When you are behind in development you should avoid making ambitious moves. Here, for example, 5. ... e6 could be played. White would of course have an advantage, but Black would not lose right away.

    6. d4-d5   **Nc6-e5?**

The final mistake. Black falls into a pretty trap. Black should play 6. ... Nb8 and try to defend his very difficult position.

    7. Nf3xe5!

See Diagram 184.

184

Black resigns, since 7. ... Bxd1 would be followed by 8. Bb5+ c6 9. dxc6 a6 (if 9. ... Qb6, then 10. cxb7+ followed by 11. bxa8Q+) 10. c7+ etc.

Game 36

1. d2-d4	d7-d5
2. c2-c4	d5xc4

This opening is called the Queen's Gambit Accepted.

3. e2-e3	b7-b5?

It is better not to try to hang on to the pawn and instead continue with 3. ... e6 4. Bxc4 c5!. 3. ... e5! would also be a good reply.

4. a2-a4	c7-c6?

Of course not 4. ... a6 5. axb5, and Black cannot recapture the pawn on b5 because he would lose the Rook on a8. The relatively best reply was 4. ... bxa4 5. Bxc4 e6, giving back the pawns.

5. a4xb5	c6xb5?
6. Qd1-f3!	

See Diagram 185.

185

Even a computer couldn't count all the beginners who have fallen into this trap! Black now has the choice of parting with his Rook, Knight, or Bishop. The least of the evils is to give up his Knight by 6. ... Nc6 7. Qxc6 Bd7. Thus Black's pawn hunting has cost him a piece.

Game 37
The Queen's Gambit Declined

1. d2-d4	d7-d5
2. c2-c4	e7-e6
3. Nb1-c3	Ng8-f6

Black ignores White's pawn sacrifice and instead develops his pieces.

4. Bc1-g5	Nb8-d7

A good move that incidentally sets a trap which often catches beginners.

5. c4xd5	e6xd5
6. Nc3xd5?	

White takes the bait. He feels sure that the Knight on d5 cannot be captured.

6. ...	Nf6xd5!

A temporary Queen sacrifice that results in Black winning a piece for a pawn.

7. Bg5xd8	Bf8-b4+

An insidious check.

8. Qd1-d2	Bb4xd2+
9. Ke1xd2	Ke8xd8

See Diagram 186.

186

White's position is lost.

Game 38

1. d2-d4   d7-d5
2. c2-c4   e7-e5

This is the Albin Counter Gambit.

3. d4xe5   d5-d4

In return for his sacrificed pawn, Black gets a strong pawn on d4 that hinders the development of White's pieces.

4. e2-e3?

White attempts to exchange off Black's central pawn while preserving his extra material. However, it was better not to try to hold on to the extra pawn but rather develop his pieces by 4. Nf3, 5. g3, 6. Bg2, 7. 0-0, etc.

4. ...   Bf8-b4 +
5. Bc1-d2   d4xe3!

A devious trap. Black sacrifices the Bishop.

6. Bd2xb4?

White decides that he can safely accept the "gift." However, 6. fxe3 must be played, although it results in doubled pawns.

6. ...   e3xf2 +
7. Ke1-e2

White cannot recapture the pawn on f2 because his Queen would be left undefended and Black would win it by 7. ... Qxd1. But now White is in for a surprise.

7. ...   f2xg1N + !

See Diagram 187.

187

This is the point of the trap! A rare situation! A Black pawn reaches the first rank, captures a White Knight, itself becomes a Knight, and delivers a fatal check to the White King, causing White to resign immediately. It would be much less effective to promote the pawn to a Queen, since after 7. ... fxg1Q White would have time to exchange Queens by 8. Qxd8 + and after 8. ... Kxd8 capture the newborn Queen with his Rook. In Diagram 187, if the White Rook takes the Knight, 8. ... Bg4 + is decisive, while 8. Ke1 is met by 8. ... Qh4 + with a devastating attack.

Game 39
Caro-Kann Defense
Keres–Arlamovskii
Szczawno-Zdroj 1950

1. e2-e4   c7-c6

Black prepares ... d7-d5. This defense was invented in the 19th century by the German chessplayers Caro and Kann.

2. Nb1-c3   d7-d5
3. Ng1-f3   d5xe4
4. Nc3xe4   Ng8-f6
5. Qd1-e2

A good move. Grandmaster Keres defends the Knight and prepares to castle on the Queenside. The light-square Bishop will be developed on g2.

5. ...   Nb8-d7??

The master playing Black was afraid of the move 6. Nxf6 and decided to defend the Knight on f6 with his other Knight. He made his move instaneously and was duly punished with the utmost severity.

6. Ne4-d6#

A smothered mate. See Diagram 188.

188

Black fell into a "children's" trap that has caught many chessplayers of varying strengths.

Game 40
Sicilian Defense
Fischer–Reshevsky, USA 1959

At the time of this game Fischer was 15 years old.

1. e2-e4   **c7-c5**

The Sicilian Defense. One of the most popular openings today, it got its name more than 500 years ago.

2. Ng1-f3   **Nb8-c6**
3. d2-d4

White is played by the brilliant American chessplayer Robert Fischer, who won the World Championship in 1972:

3. ...   **c5xd4**
4. Nf3xd4   **g7-g6**
5. Nb1-c3   **Bf8-g7**

The player of the Black pieces is no beginner either but rather the well-known grandmaster Samuel Reshevsky, a former child prodigy who at the age of eight was already touring many European cities, giving simultaneous exhibitions on 20-25 boards against adult opponents.

6. Bc1-e3   **Ng8-f6**
7. Bf1-c4   **0-0**
8. Bc4-b3   **Nc6-a5?**

Until now both grandmasters have played very well, but here Reshevsky blunders and falls into a subtle opening trap. The right moves are 8. ... Qa5 or 8. ... d6.

9. e4-e5!   **Nf6-e8**

After 9. ... Nxb3 10. exf6 Nxa1 11. fxg7 White

has a clear advantage.

10. Bb3xf7 + !   **Rf8xf7**
11. Nd4-e6!

See Diagram 189.

189

Black could resign here as his position is hopeless. Nor would 10. ... Kxf7 have saved him since White wins after 11. Ne6 Kxe6 12. Qd5 + Kf5 13. g4 + Kxg4 14. Rg1 + Kh5 15. Qd1 + . No one is immune to mistakes!

Lesson Six

A. Check Lesson 5 homework (as necessary).

B. *Review Questions*

1. How many squares are there on a chessboard?
2. Can you castle if your Rook is under attack?
3. Is it a good idea to set a trap whose worth depends entirely on your opponent blundering?

Try to answer Questions 4-6 without looking at a chessboard.

4. On what squares do the Black Rooks stand at the start of a game? What color (light or dark) are these squares?
5. How many different moves can White make in the starting position?
6. At which square does the h1-a8 diagonal cross the third rank and what color (light or dark) is it?

Answer the next questions directly from the Diagrams, without setting up the men on a board.

Black to play and mate in two moves.

191

White to play and mate in two moves.

190

192

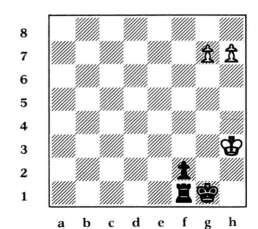

White to play and mate in two moves.

193

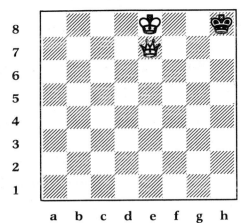

a b c d e f g h

White to play and mate in two moves.

Answers to the Review Questions

1. 64.
2. Yes.
3. No. Such a trap is unsound (bad) and if your opponent sees through it you can expect nothing but trouble.
4. a8, a light square, and h8, a dark square.
5. 20.
6. f3, a light square.

D-190

1. ...	Rc8-c2 +
2. Kb2-b1	Re8-e1#

A straight-line mate.

D-191

1. Qf5xh7 +	Kh8xh7
2. Rf2-h2#	

A straight-line mate.

D-192

1. g7-g8Q +	Kg1-h1
2. Qg8-g2#	

D-193

1. Ke8-f7!

Controls the important squares g6, g7 and g8.

1. ...	Kh8-h7
2. Qe7-h4#	

The Concept of Planning

There are often moments in a person's life when he has to choose a course of action that will enable him to make best use of his abilities. At the same time, he must also find ways of overcoming any obstacles that may hinder his progress along his chosen path. He achieves all this by working out a definite plan. You can-

not always hit upon the correct plan at first shot — mistakes sometimes occur. One of the very useful things that a chessplayer learns is the art of making appropriate plans.

During a game, a player sets certain goals for himself: to win the game, to checkmate the opponent, to avoid losing, etc. He must then form a plan of play which charts out what he has to do in order to achieve these goals.

A plan indicates the main channels along which a player chooses to direct the course of the game. For example, he can make a plan to attack the enemy King or a plan to carry out a Queenside attack.

Now let us analyze the position in Diagram 194.

194

a b c d e f g h

It is White's turn to play. His goal is to first eliminate the dangerous Black pawn on d2 and then checkmate the Black King. Let us form a plan of play to achieve this goal. First, we must control the d1 square, or else the pawn will promote to a Queen. Can we control d1 and at the same time attack the pawn on d2? Yes, from either of two squares — d4 and d7. So we can play, for example, 1. Qg7-d4 and the next move capture the pawn. With that, the first part of our goal has been achieved. Now let us form a further plan consisting of two stages: 1) driving the Black King to one of the board's edges, and 2) moving in with the White King, and with its help, mating the Black one. You already know how to do this.

Plans are important! Former world champion Emanuel Lasker used to say that is better to follow even a bad plan than to play without any plan at all.

Exploiting a Large Material Advantage

Who among us has not had the experience of being one or two pieces up but then drawing or even losing as a result of not finding the correct plan! Two methods of play can be recommended for exploiting a large material advantage:
1. Exchange off pieces and transpose into a winning endgame, or
2. Use your superior force to land an attack on the enemy King.

The main method is exchanging off pieces, because simplifying the position makes it easier to exploit a material advantage. Let us look at some examples.

195

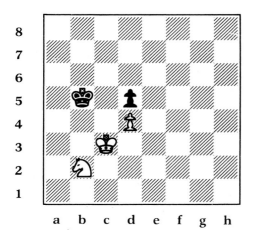

In Diagram 195, it is White's turn to move. He is up a Knight and should, of course, win. But the question is, how?

Let us form a plan:
1. Win the Black pawn.
2. Promote the White pawn to a Queen.
3. Drive the Black King to an edge.
4. Mate the Black King by the combined action of the White King and Queen (and possibly also the Knight).

Let us put this plan into action:

| 1. Nb2-d1 | Kb5-c6 |
| 2. Nd1-e3 | |

The Knight attacks the Black pawn. It would not have been as good to play 1. Nd3 followed by 2. Nb4 since the Knight would then block the path of its own King.

| 2. ... | Kc6-d6 |

Continuing to defend the pawn.

| 3. Kc3-b4 | |

The King sets off towards the Black pawn in order to attack it a second time.

| 3. ... | Kd6-c6 |
| 4. Kb4-a5 | |

The White King pushes back the Black King by making use of Zugzwang.

| 4. ... | Kc6-d6 |

Because of Zugzwang, the King is forced to give up control of b5 and b6.

| 5. Ka5-b6 | Kd6-e6 |

Now Zugzwang forces the Black King to give up c5 and c6.

| 6. Kb6-c6 | Ke6-e7 |
| 7. Ne3xd5 + | |

Now the Knight and King will help the pawn to queen. See Diagram 196.

196

| 7. ... | Ke7-d8 |
| 8. Nd5-b6 | |

The Knight controls c8 and frees the way for the pawn.

| 8. ... | Kd8-e7 |
| 9. Kc6-c7! | |

Now the King controls the important squares d6, d7, and d8, thereby clearing the way for the pawn to queen.

9. ...	Ke7-e6
10. d4-d5 +	Ke6-e7
11. d5-d6 +	u
	(any move)
12. d6-d7	u
13. d7-d8Q	

Only the last stage of our plan remains, i.e., to mate the lone Black King, but you already know how to do this by yourself.

197

Diagram 197, with White to play, is our next example. Here too White should try to win quickly, but he must watch out for the danger of Black trying to draw by giving up his two pawns in return for the lone White pawn. For example, if White attacks the Black e-pawn by 1. Nf7, then Black will reply 1. ... f4+ and obtain a draw by exchanging off White's last pawn. So let us form a plan:

1. The White pawn must be preserved from being exchanged, and so the White King must be moved to another square.
2. The Knight must attack and capture the Black pawns.
3. The White pawn must be queened, and so on.

Here is the execution of the plan:

    1. Ke3-f3!   **Ka8-b7**

Now if 1. ... f4, then the White pawn queens by force after 2. g4.

    2. Nh8-f7   **e5-d4+**

2. ... f4 doesn't save Black since after 3. g4 he loses both his pawns.

    3. Kf3-f4   **Kb7-c6**

    4. Nf7-h6

See Diagram 198.

198

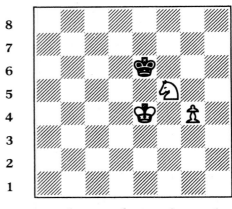

4. Kxf5 is not as good since after 4. ... e3 there is a danger of the Black pawn queening.

    4. ...   **Kc6-c5**

    5. Nh6xf5   **Kc5-d5**

    6. g3-g4

Now Black must give up his last pawn.

    6. ..   **Kd5-e6**

    7. Kf4xe4

See Diagram 199.

199

The next part of our plan is to queen the pawn with the help of the King and the Knight and then mate the lone enemy King. You can do that by yourself.

The first rule that a beginner should learn about exploiting a material advantage is to avoid all hastiness. Who among us does not remember instances where we had a large material advantage but were robbed of our victory because of just one hasty move! So remember: **Don't be hasty.**

Mating with a Rook and King against a Lone King

A Rook and King can mate a lone King only on an edge or in a corner. Diagram 200 shows four standard "Rook and King against lone King" mating positions (each quarter of the diagram shows a different position).

200

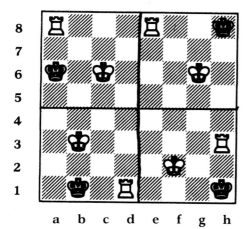

To mate a King on the edge of the board we must control all five of the squares to which it could move, and in addition a sixth square, the one on which the King stands, must be attacked by our Rook.

The Rook can control two flight squares and attack the King, while the other three squares must be controlled by our own King. When the Kings are placed such that each of them controls three of the other's flight squares, they are said to be **in opposition**. This happens when the Kings face each other with a single square between them. In Diagram 200 , for example, the Kings on b1 and b3 are in opposition, as are the Kings on a6 and c6. If the lone King is in a corner (for example, h8 or h1, as in Diagram 200), then mate is possible even without opposition.

201

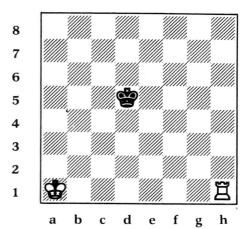

In Diagram 201, White must first of all decide which edge he wants to drive the Black King to. Let's suppose he decides to mate the Black King on the eighth rank. Then we have to form a plan:

1. Cut the Black King off from the lower half of the board.
2. Move the White King towards the center, because the Rook is much weaker than the Queen and cannot chase the enemy King to a corner or an edge by itself.
3. Drive the King into a corner by the combined action of the Rook and the King.
4. Checkmate the Black King!

Here is the execution of the plan:
1. Rh1-h4
The Black King is cut off from the lower half of the board.

1. ...	**Kd5-e5**
2. Ka1-b2	

Only with the help of its King can the Rook push back the enemy King.

2. ...	**Ke5-d5**
3. Kb2-c3	**Kd5-e5**
4. Rh4-d4!	

202

Protected by its own King, the Rook cuts the Black King off from the Queenside.

4. ...	**Ke5-f5**
5. Kc3-d3	

The King now controls e4.

5. ...	**Kf5-e5**
6. Kd3-e3!	

6. Re4+ would be a mistake because of 6. ... Kd5, and the Black King would escape to the Queenside.

6. ...	**Ke5-f5**

The Black King does not in the least want to leave the center of the board, where it is in safety, but it is forced to do so because of Zugzwang. 6. ... Ke6 would be no better because of 7. Kf4 Kf6 8. Rd6+ Ke7 9. Ke5 etc.

7. Rd4-e4	

Taking possession of the e-file.

7. ...	**Kf5-f6**

Black was again in Zugzwang. If 7. ... Kg5, then 8. Rf4 cuts the King off from the f-file.

8. Ke3-f4	

Controlling the important squares f5 and g5. Note how the White King and Rook help each other.

8. ...	**Kf6-g6**

If Black could pass his turn, he wouldn't lose. But . . . This "but" is called Zugzwang.

9. Re4-e6+!	

See Diagram 203.

203

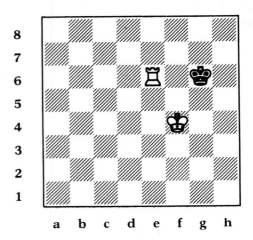

The Black King must retreat to the seventh rank, since after 9. ... Kh5 a waiting move by the Rook along the sixth rank, e.g., 10. Rf6, would again put Black in Zugzwang, forcing him to move his King into opposition by 10. ... Kh4, allowing 11. Rh6#.

9. ...	**Kg6-f7**
10. Kf4-f5	**Kf7-g7**
11. Re6-e7+	

Forcing Black to the last rank, since 11. ... Kh6 would allow mate in two moves by 12. Rf7 (Zugzwang) Kh5 (opposition) 13. Rh7#.

11. ...	**Kg7-f8**
12. Kf5-f6	**Kf8-g8**
13. Kf6-g6!	**Kg8-f8**

See Diagram 204.

204

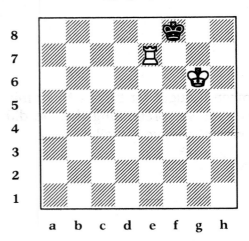

White to play and mate in two moves. Remember this method! There are six solutions. Any waiting move of the Rook along the e-file (except 14. Re8+) will put Black in Zugzwang, forcing him to play 14. ... Kf8-g8 and allow 15. Re6-e8#.

We have executed all the stages of our plan and mated Black in fifteen moves. In general, with correct play you should be able to mate with King and Rook against King in 15-20 moves starting from any position. If you do make mistakes, however, you must be very careful not to make so many as to let Black draw by the 50-move rule.

In conclusion, let us look at a short but interesting game.

Game 41
Queen's Gambit Declined
Fine–Yudovich, Moscow 1937

1. d2-d4	d7-d5
2. c2-c4	e7-e6
3. Nb1-c3	

The American grandmaster Reuben Fine, White in this game, was one of the strongest players in the world at the time.

3. ...	Ng8-f6

His opponent was the little-known Soviet master Mikhail Yudovich.

4. Ng1-f3	c7-c5

Yudovich was of course quite excited at the prospect of playing such a fearsome opponent. He prepared for the encounter by playing over a large number of Fine's games. In one of them he noticed the Fine had won by catching his opponent in an opening trap. Yudovich found, however, that Fine's trap could be refuted by a remarkable countertrap, and so decided that in his own game with Fine he would "fall into" White's trap.

5. Bc1-g5	c5xd4
6. Nf3xd4	e6-e5

Yudovich thought for two or three minutes over each move, pretending that he did not know this opening very well.

7. Nd4-b5

See Diagram 205.

205

Everything is going according to Yudovich's plan. One more move , and he can "fall into" Fine's trap. Although Yudovich already had his next move figured out before the game, he pretended to think here for twenty minutes. He did not want to reply quickly, for fear that Fine would get suspicious and discover Black's idea.

7. ...	a7-a6
8. Nc3xd5?	

See Diagram 206.

206

White has to play instead 8. Qa4, with a complicated game. Fine, however, glanced slyly at his opponent, thinking he had caught yet another inexperienced master in his trap, and played 8. Nc3xd5? instantaneously.

8. ...	a6xb5!

207

Yudovich was very excited! After all, he had managed to catch one of the world's strongest players in a trap! And, looking not at the board but at his opponent, he instantly captured the Knight. The grandmaster first recoiled from the board, and then sank into deep thought. He remembered how he had won a pretty game with this same variation after 9. Nxf6+ gxf6 10. Qxd8+ Kxd8 11. Bxf6+ Ke8 12. Bxh8 etc. This was the trap in which he had wanted to catch Yudovich. But now he saw his opponent's plan and realized that he himself had fallen into a beautifully prepared ambush. He regretted that he had made his eighth move without thinking, but it was too late now.

    9. Nd5xf6+   **Qd8xf6!!**
See Diagram 208.

208

This is the "present" that Yudovich had prepared at home for the grandmaster and which he had artfully led up to. Fine had not considered this temporary Queen sacrifice in his calculations.

    10. Bg5xf6   **Bf8-b4+**
Before capturing on f6, Black makes an in-between move, checking with his Bishop.

    11. Qd1-d2
White is forced to return the Queen.

    11. ...   **Bb4xd2+**
    12. Ke1xd2   **g7xf6**
and Black, with a material advantage and an excellent position, quickly won.

The famous grandmaster played very well in the tournament and deservedly took first place, but in this game he was taught a good lesson! And indeed, the game was a good lesson for many amateurs as well.

HOMEWORK
(Answers at the end)

I. Diagrams 209–214.
Form a plan and find the solution.

209

White to play and win.

_____

_____

_____

84

210

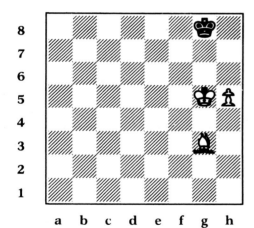

White to play. Mate in two moves.

	WHITE	BLACK
1.		
2.		

212

White to play. Mate in two moves.

	WHITE	BLACK
1.		
2.		

211

White to play and wins.

213

White to play and wins.

214

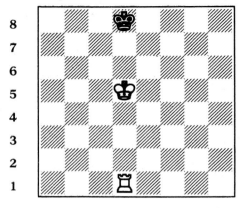

a b c d e f g h

White to play. Mate in three moves.

	WHITE	BLACK
1.		
2.		
3.		

II. Exercises

Try to answer Questions 1–3 without looking at a chessboard.

1. Write down the locations of all the pieces in the starting position.

   _____

   _____

   _____

2. Which lines (rank, file, and diagonal) run through e5?

   _____

   _____

   _____

3. What color (light or dark) is e6?

   _____

4. Set up some random positions with King and Rook against King and practice mating until you can do it quickly and confidently.

5. Think up a position in which Black to play can mate in two moves.

III. Game For Analysis
Game 42
Nimzovich–Alapin, Riga 1913

1.	e2-e4	e7-e6
2.	d2-d4	d7-d5

This opening is called the French Defense.

3.	Nb1-c3	Ng8-f6

Aron Nimzovich, White in this game, was one of the strongest players in the world.

4.	e4xd5	Nf6xd5

It would be better to play 4. ... exd5 so as not to give White a superiority in the center.

5.	Ng1-f3	c7-c5

A loss of time. 5. ... Be7 followed by 6. ... 0-0, 7. ... b6, and 8. ... Bb7 would be better.

6.	Nc3xd5	Qd8xd5

Better would be 6. ... exd5, opening up the light-square Bishop's diagonal.

7.	Bc1-e3	c5xd4
8.	Nf3xd4	a7-a6
9.	Bf1-e2!	

White's position is considerably better. He has brought out all his minor pieces while the master playing Black has developed only his Queen.

9. ...		Qd5xg2?

Instead of this further loss of time, Black should be thinking about developing his minor pieces.

10.	Be2-f3	Qg2-g6
11.	Qd1-d2	e6-e5

Black's position is difficult, but in any case he had to start developing his pieces instead of pushing pawns.

12.	0-0-0!!	

Magnificent! Nimzovich gives up his Knight for a pawn but in return all his remaining pieces rapidly enter the fray.

12. ...		e5xd4
13.	Be3xd4	Nb8-c6

Although a piece up, Black is lost. White's manifest advantage in development allows him to finish off the game with a scintillating combination.

14. Bd4-f6!

Clearing the way for the Queen. White now threatens 15. Qd8+ Nxd8 16. Rxd8#, or if 14. ... Be7, then 15. Bxc6 bxc6 16. Qd8+ Bxd8 17. Rxd8#.

14. ...   Qg6xf6

15. Rh1-e1+

Black is already two pieces up but he gets mated by force.

15. ...   Bf8-e7

If 15. ... Be6, then 16. Qd7#; if 15. ... Ne5, then 16. Rxe5+ Qxe5 17. Qd8#; if 15. ... Qe7, then 16. Bxc6 bxc6 17. Qd8#.

16. Bf3xc6+   Ke8-f8

If 16. ... bxc6, then 17. Qd8#.

17. Qd2-d8+!   Be7xd8

18. Re1-e8#

See Diagram 215.

215

Answers to the Homework
I. Diagrams 209–214

D-209 The plan:
1. Queen the pawn.
2. Drive the Black King to an edge or corner.
3. Checkmate the Black King.

The execution of the plan:

1. Ne3-f5+	Kd6-d7
2. Kd4-e5	Kd7-c7
3. d5-d6+	Kc7-d7
4. Nf5-g7	Kd7-d8
5. Ke5-e6	Kd8-c8
6. Ke6-e7	u
	(any move)
7. d6-d7	u

8. d7-d8Q

and so on. The above variation is only one possibility; other moves also lead to the goal.

D-210 The plan:
1. Put the Black King in Zugzwang.
2. Checkmate Black.

The execution of the plan:

1. Ke5-d6!   Ke8-d8

Because of Zugzwang the King is forced to take the opposition.

2. Rf1-f8#

D-211 The plan is similar to that for D-209. The execution:

1. Kg5-g6	Kg8-h8
2. h5-h6	Kh8-g8
3. h6-h7+	Kg8-f8
4. h7-h8Q+	

and so on. If 3. ... Kh8, then 4. Be5#. Other solutions (with different moves) are also possible.

D-212 The plan is similar to that for D-210. The execution:

1. Ra5-f5!   Ke8-d8

Because of Zugzwang the King is forced to take the opposition.

2. Rf5-f8#

D-213 The plan:
1. Penetrate with the King to d5.
2. Transfer the Knight to c4.
3. Eliminate all the enemy pawns.
4. Queen the pawn, and so on.

The execution of the plan:

1. Kd3-c4   Kc6-c7

If 1. ... d5+, then 2. exd5+ Kd6 3. Nd2 wins.

2. Kc4-d5	Kc7-d7
3. Nf3-d2	Kd7-c7
4. Nd2-c4	Kc7-d7
5. Nc4xd6	Kd7-e7
6. Kd5xe5	Ke7-d7
7. Ke5-d5	Kd7-e7
8. Kd5xc5	Ke7-e6
9. Nd6-c4	Ke6-d7
10. Kc5-d5	Kd7-e7
11. e4-e5	Ke7-d7
12. e5-e6+	Kd7-e7
13. Nc4-e5	Ke7-d8
14. Kd5-d6	Kd8-e8
15. Ne5-c6	

Careful! 15. e7?? is stalemate.

15. ...	Ke8-f8
16. Kd6-d7	u

216

17. e6-e7   u
18. e7-e8Q

and so on. Other solutions (with different moves) are also possible.

D-214 The plan:

1. Take the opposition and confine the King to the eighth rank.
2. Put Black in Zugzwang.
3. Checkmate Black.

The execution of the plan:

1. Kd5-d6

and now a)

1. ...	**Kd8-e8**
2. Rd1-f1	

Putting Black in Zugzwang.

2. ...	**Ke8-d3**
3. f1-f8#	

or b)

1. ...	**Kd8-c8**
2. Rd1-b1	

Putting Black in Zugzwang.

2. ...	**Kc8-d8**
3. Rb1-b8#	

II. Exercises

1. White: Ke1, Qd1, Ra1, Rh1, Bc1, Bf1, Nb1, Ng1, P's a2, b2, c2, d2, e2, f2, g2, h2. Black: Ke8, Qd8, Ra8, Rh8, Bc8 Bf8, Nb8, Ng8, P's a7, b7, c7, d7, e7, f7, g7, h7.

2. Four lines pass through e5: a) the fifth rank; b) the e-file; c) the h2-b8 diagonal; and d) the a1-h8 diagonal.

3. Light.

SUPPLEMENTARY MATERIAL

for use at the teacher's discretion

Positions 216–221 deal with the theme "Plan for exploiting a large material advantage." Positions 222–227 illustrate the combined action of a King and a Rook against a lone King.

White to play and win. The plan:

1. Put Black in Zugzwang.
2. Win the pawn on c5 or the one on g5.
3. Queen the c-pawn or the g-pawn, and so on.

The execution:

1. Bd1-f3

With the Kings facing one another in opposition, any Bishop move puts the Black King in Zugzwang.

1. ...	**Ke5-d6**

Taking the opposition and barring the White King's access to the Black pawns.

2. Ke3-e4	**Kd6-e6**
3. Bf3-h1	

This waiting move with the Bishop makes it Black's turn to move, but Black does not have any good moves.

3. ...	**Ke6-e7**

Losing control over the important squares d5, e5, and f5.

4. Ke4-f5

4. Kd5 would also win.

4. ...	**Ke7-f7**
5. Kf5xg5	**Kf7-g7**
6. Kg5-f5	**Kg7-f7**
7. g4-g5	**Kf7-g7**
8. g5-g6	**Kg7-g8**
9. Kf5-f6	**Kg8-f8**
10. g6-g7 +	**Kf8-g8**
11. Bh1-d5 +	

White must be careful: 11. Kg6 or 11. Be4 is stalemate.

11. ...	**Kg8-h7**
12. g7-g8Q +	**Kh7-h6**
13. Qg8-h8#	

Other solutions (with different moves) are also possible.

217

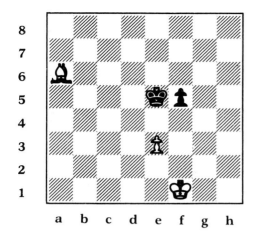

White to play and win. The plan:
1. Guard your pawn from being exchanged.
2. Win the Black pawn.
3. Queen your pawn, and so on.

The execution:

    1. Ba6-b7

Controlling e4. 1. Bd3 is also possible.

    1. ...   **f5-f4**

Trying to exchange off the White pawn.

    2. e3-e4!

Saving the pawn from being exchanged.

    2. ...   **Ke5-e6**

    3. Kf1-f2   **Ke6-f6**

    4. Kf2-f3   **Kf6-e5**

    5. Bb7-d5

A waiting move with the Bishop, making it Black's turn to move and thus putting Black in Zugzwang.

    5. ...   **Ke5-f6**

    6. Kf3xf4   **Kf6-e7**

    7. Kf4-e5

Taking the opposition and pushing back the Black King.

    7. ...   **Ke7-d7**

    8. Ke5-f6

Freeing the way for the pawn and controlling e6 and e7.

    8. ...   **Kd7-e8**

    9. e4-e5

and so on.

218

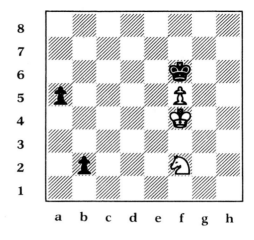

White to play and win. The plan:
1. Hold back the Black pawns.
2. Queen the f-pawn.
3. Checkmate the Black King.

The execution:

    1. Nf2-e4 + !

Only with this check can White stop the Black pawns.

    1. ...   **Kf6-e7**

    2. Ne4-c3

Controlling b1.

    2. ...   **a5-a4**

Threatening 3. ... a3 followed by the queening of one of the pawns.

    3. Nc3-b1!

Now both the critical squares, b1 and a3, are controlled by the Knight, which thus prevents the advance of both Black pawns.

    3. ...   **Ke7-f6**

If 3. ... Kd6, then 4. f6 wins.

    4. Nb1-a3

A waiting move that puts Black in Zugzwang by making it his turn to move.

    4. ...   **Kf6-f7**

    5. Kf4-e5   **Kf7-e7**

Taking the opposition.

    6. f5-f6 +   **Ke7-f7**

    7. Ke5-f5   **Kf7-f8**

Because of Zugzwang.

    8. Kf5-e6   **Kf8-e8**

Taking the opposition.

    9. f6-f7 +   **Ke8-f8**

    10. Na3-b1!

Only with this waiting move can White win. 10. Kf6? is bad because of 10. ... b1Q 11. Nxb1 a3, when 12. Nxa3 stalemates Black!

10. ...   **Kf8-g7**

Because of Zugzwang.

    11. Ke6-e7   **Kg7-g6**

    12. f7-f8Q

and so on.

219

Black to play and win. The plan:

1. Attack White's Queenside pawns with the Rook.
2. Stop the advance of White's Kingside pawns.
3. If necessary, give up the a-pawn in order to eliminate all of White's pawns.
4. Checkmate with King and Rook against King.

The execution:

    1. ...   **Rf8-c8**

    2. f4-f5

If 2. Ke4, then 2. ... Rc2 3. Kd4 Rxa2 4. b4 Rf2 5. Kc5 Rxf4 6. b5 Rxg4 7. Kc6 Rg5 8. Kb7 Rxb5 + etc.

    2. ...   **Rc8-c2**

    3. g4-g5   **Rc2xa2**

    4. Kf3-f4   **Ra2-b2**

    5. f5-f6   **Rb1xb2**

    6. g5-g6   **a7-a5**

    7. Kf4-e5   **a5-a4**

    8. Ke5-e6   **a4-a3**

    9. Ke6-e7

Threatening 10. f7+ followed by 11. f8Q.

    9. ...   **Rb3-e3 +**

and the Black pawn will go on to become a Queen!

220

Grandmaster Schlechter–Grandmaster Marshall
Vienna 1908

White to play should win. He has a Bishop for two pawns and in addition will win Black's pawn on d5 next move. They continued as follows:

    27. Qd3xd5

Being ahead in material, White tries to exchange Queens.

    27. ...   **Qd7-e7**

    28. Qd5-d6   **Qe7xd6**

If 28. ... Qg5, then 29. Qb8 + Kh7 30. Be4 + etc.

    29. e5xd6   **Rb2-d2**

    30. Bg2xb7   **Rd2xd6**

    31. Kh1-g2

Bringing the King towards the center.

    31. ...   **g7-g6**

    32. Rf1-f2

Controlling the second rank.

    32. ...   **Kg8-g7**

    33. Rf2-c2

and Black resigned. If Black had played on, White should have tried to exchange Rooks and bring his King up to the center. Another good goal would be to occupy the seventh rank with the Rook so as to attack the a7 and f7 pawns.

In Diagram 220, White had an alternative way of exploiting his advantage: 27. Bxd5, threatening the pawn on f7. Then 27. ... Qh3 would not work because of 28. Bxf7 + Kh8 29. Qd8 + and 30. Qg8#. Finally, a third method of winning was shown by Tarrasch: 27. Rxf7 Qxf7 28. Bxd5 or 27. ... Kxf7 28. e6 + Qxe6 (28. ... Kxe6 29. Bh3 +) 29. Bxd5 Rb1 + 30. Kg2 Rb2 + 31. Kf3. However, such a method is not to be recommended. Try to choose the simplest means of exploiting your advantage, because it is easy to make mistakes in complicated variations.

221

White to play. He is up an Exchange. How can he exploit his material advantage?

Black is threatening 1. ... Qh1#. The Black Queen and Bishop can cause a great deal of unpleasantness for White, since his King is exposed. Consequently, the best method for White to exploit his advantage is to exchange Queens:

1. Qf2-d4 +	Kh8-g8
2. Qd4-d5 + !	Qc6xd5
3. c4xd5	Bb7xd5

White has sacrificed a pawn but in return has managed to exchange Queens. Now the b-pawn assures him of an easy win.

4. b2-b4	Kg8-f8
5. b4-b5	Kf8-e7
6. b5-b6	Ke7-d6

If 6. ...Ke6, then 7. Rc7 h5 8. b7 Bxb7 9. Rxb7 and White must win.

7. Rc1-d1!	Kd6-c6
8. Rd1xd5!	Kc6xd5
9. b6-b7	

and the pawn will queen.

Diagrams 222–227. The theme in all these positions is the same: the confinement of the Black King by the combined action of the White pieces.

222

White to play. Mate in six moves.

The plan: Drive the Black King to the a1 corner and checkmate it. It is not hard to win, but there is only one way of mating in six moves:

1. Rb2-b5

Placing the Rook under the protection of its King and at the same time putting Black in Zugzwang.

1. ...   **Ka4-a3**

Black is compelled by Zugzwang to give up control over the a5 square.

2. Kb6-a5!

Attacking the a4 square.

2. ...   **Ka3-a2**

Because of Zugzwang.

3. Ka5-a4

Driving the Black King into the corner.

3. ...   **Ka2-a1**

Black was again in Zugzwang.

4. Ka4-b3!

White must be careful: 4. Ka3 would be stalemate.

4. ...   **Ka1-b1**

5. Rb5-c5

The Rook controls the c-file and keeps the King in the corner. Black is now in Zugzwang for the last time!

5. ...   **Kb1-a1**

6. Rc5-c1#

223

8 7 6 5 4 3 2 1
a b c d e f g h

White to play. Mate in seven moves.

The plan: Keep the Black King confined to the a8 corner and checkmate it. The idea is the same as in D-222.

1. Kh4-g5	**Ka8-b8**
2. Kg5-f6	**Kb8-c8**
3. Kf6-e7	

Defending the Rook and simultaneously attacking the d8 square.

3. ...	**Kc8-b8**

The Black King is forced to give way because of Zugzwang.

4. ...	**Ke7-d8!**

Continuing to keep the Black King in the corner.

4. ...	**Kb8-a8**

Forced because of Zugzwang.

5. Kd8-c7

White must be careful — 5. Kc8 would be stalemate.

5. ...	**Ka8-a7**
6. Rd7-d6	

The Rook controls the sixth rank and thus keeps the Black King in the corner.

6. ...	**Ka7-a8**

Again forced due to Zugzwang.

7. Rd6-a6#

224

8 7 6 5 4 3 2 1
a b c d e f g h

White to play. Mate in seven moves.

The plan: Confine the Black King to the h8 corner and checkmate it.

1. Rf8-f4

Placing the Rook under the King's protection and cutting Black off from the fourth rank.

1. ...	**Kg5-g6**

If 1. ... Kh5, then 2. Rg4 Kh6 3. Kh4 Kh7 4. Kh5 Kh8 5. Kg6 Kg8 6. Rf4 Kh8 7. Rf8#. If 1. ... Kh6, then 2. Rh4 Kh5 3. Kf4 Kh6 4. Kf5 Kh5 (or 4. ... Kh7 5. Kf6 Kh8 6. Kh7 7. Rh4#) 5. Re4 Kh6 6. Re7 Kh5 7. Rh7#.

2. Kg3-h4

Avoiding the square g4, which might be needed for the Rook.

2. ...	**Kg6-h7**

If 2. ... Kh6, then 3. Rg4 Kh7 4. Kh5 gives us a familiar position. If 2. ... Kg7, then 3. Kg5 Kh7 4. Kf6 Kh8 (or 4. ... Kg8 5. Rh4 Kf8 6. Rh8#) 5. Kf7 Kh7 6. Rh4#.

3. Kh4-g5	**Kh7-g7**

5. Rf4-f1

A waiting move that puts Black in Zugzwang.

5. ...	**Kg7-h7**

If 4. ... Kg8, then 5. Kg6 Kh8 6. Rf8#. If 4. ... Kh8, then 5. Kg6 Kg8 6. Rf2 Kh8 7. Rf8#.

6. Kg5-f6	**Kh7-g8**

If 5. ... Kh8, then 6. Kf7 Kh7 7. Rh1#.

6. Rf1-h1	**Kg8-f8**

Forced due to Zugzwang.

7. Rh1-h8#

92

225

White to play. Mate in eight moves.

The plan: Confine the Black King to the a1 corner and checkmate it. We solve this problem easily by applying the method that is now familiar to us:

1. Rb2-b7	**Ka6-a5**
2. Kb8-a7!	**Ka5-a4**

The Black is continually in Zugzwang.

3. Ka7-a6	**Ka4-a3**
4. Ka6-a5	**Ka3-a2**
5. Ka5-a4	**Ka2-a1**
6. Ka4-b3	

White must be careful: 6. Ka3 would be stalemate.

6. ...	**Ka1 – b1**
7. Rb7-c7	

Putting Black into Zugzwang for the final time.

7. ...	**Kb1-a1**
8. Rc7-c1#	

226

White to play. Mate in seven moves.
The plan: Confine the Black King to the a8

corner and checkmate it.

1. Kb1-c2!	**Ka3-a4**
2. Kc2-c3	**Ka4-a5**

If 2. ... Ka3, then 3. Rb4 Ka2 4. Kc2 Ka3 5. Rc4 Ka2 6. Ra4#

3. Kc3-c4	**Ka5-a6**

If the King returns to a4 (3. ... Ka4), it will be in opposition to the White King and get checkmated by 4. Ra2#.

4. Kc4-c5	**Ka6-a7**
5. Kc5-c6	**Ka7-a8**
6. Kc6-c7	**Ka8-a7**

Unable to retreat any more, the Black King is forced to return and stand opposite its White counterpart.

7. Rb2-a2#

227

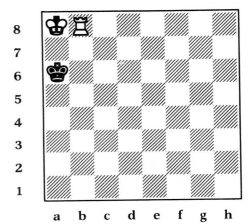

White to play. Mate in eight moves.
The plan: Drive the Black King to the a1 corner and checkmate it. By now, this problem will seem a cinch.

1. Rb8-b7

A waiting move.

1. ...	**Ka6-a5**
2. Ka8-a7	**Ka5-a4**
3. Ka7-a6	**Ka4-a3**
4. Ka6-a5	**Ka3-a2**
5. Ka5-a4	**Ka2-a1**
6. Ka4-b3	

You of course remember that 6. Ka3 can't be played, because of stalemate.

6. ...	**Ka1-b1**
7. Rb7-c7	

The final Zugzwang for Black.

7. ...	**Kb1-a1**
8. Rc7-c1#	

In all the examples the King and Rook helped each other, i.e, they co-operated well.

Lesson Seven

A. Check Lesson 6 Homework (as necessary).

B. *Review Questions*

1. How many moves are you allowed for mating if you have a Rook and King against a lone King?

2. What is meant by a "plan" in a chess game and why is it needed?

3. What is the purpose of waiting moves?

4. What is the best method of play if you have a large material advantage?

Try to answer Questions 5 & 6 without looking at a chessboard.

5. There is a White pawn on a6 and a Black one on b7. Black plays ... b7-b5. Can White capture en passant?

6. How many moves does a Knight need to get from h1 to f3? What are these moves?

Answer the next questions directly from the diagrams, without setting up the men on a board.

229

White to play and mate in two moves.

230

Black to play and mate in two moves.

228

White to play and mate in two moves.

231

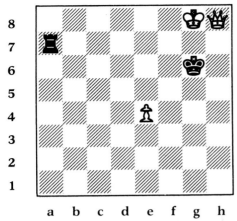

White to play. Who should win?

Answers to Review Questions

1. 50 moves. If you take more, the game's a draw!

2. A plan is a program of action that tells us what we have to do in order to attain the goal that we have set for ourselves.

3. Sometimes your opponent will be in Zugzwang, i.e., he will not have any good moves. In such cases you can profitably play a waiting move, which will make it your opponent's turn to play without changing the position significantly.

4. Exchanging pieces and transposing into an endgame.

5. No. White could capture en passant only if his pawn were on a5, and not on a6.

6. Four: Nh1-f2-e4-g5. Other routes are also possible.

D-228
　　1. Qd1-d7 +
Or 1. Qb1, or 1. Qb3.
　　1. ...　　　　　　**Ka7-a8**
　　2. Qd7-b7#
D-229
　　1. Qb1xh7 +　　　**Kh8xh7**
　　2. Ra5-h5#
A line mate.
D-230
　　1. ...　　　　　　**Rh8-a8**
Putting White into Zugzwang.
　　2. Kb1-c1　　　　**Ra8-a1#**

D-231 Black should win. He is threatening 1. ... Ra8# and the White Queen is so badly

placed that it cannot help its King. The White pawn only helps Black, since without it White could win by 1. Qh1, controlling the critical square a8. But in the position as it is, the best White has is:

　　1. Kg8-f8　　　　**Ra7-a8 +**
　　2. Kf8-e7　　　　**Ra8xh8**

Black has won the Queen and in a few moves he will win the White pawn and go on to win the game.

Tactics

You already know that the **plans** that a player forms during a game answer the question of **what** must be done in order to attain a certain goal. The question of **how** to execute a plan belongs to the realm of **tactics**, which consists of combinations, exchanges, tactical themes, etc.

Tactical themes which are often encountered in positions that share certain features are known as **typical** tactical themes.

Let us now look at Diagram 232.

232

a b c d e f g h

White to play and win. After

　　1. Rh6-h7 +　　　　**Kd7-d8**
　　2. Kd5-e6

Black cannot prevent White from executing his plan of playing Rh7-d7 followed by Rd7xd6, giving up his Rook for the Bishop but winning all of Black's pawns in return. Here White's plan consists of exchanging his Rook for Black's Bishop and pawns, while the **tactical device** employed is the **deflection** of the Black King from the defense of the pawn on d6.

Double Attack

Games often contain opportunities for a player to win by a beautiful combination but unfortunately these opportunities frequently go by unnoticed. A knowledge of **typical tactical devices** will help in spotting combinations. Today we shall look at one of the most important of these tactical devices, known as **double attack.**

Diagrams 233 and 234 show various double attack patterns. In each of the quarter-diagrams, the double attack is carried out by a different man.

233

234

A **double attack** occurs when a piece or pawn simultaneously attacks two enemy men. Double attack sare also known as **forks.**

The most dangerous forking pieces are the Queen and the Knight, both of which attack in eight directions simultaneously.

A double attack is particularly effective when one of the pieces attacked is the King. Checking the King and simultaneously attacking another man often leads to the win of material.

Let us now look at some simple examples of double attack.

In Diagrams 235–240, White is to play and win material using the tactical device of double attack. Solve these exercises without moving the men.

235

236

237

238

239

240

Now here are some material-winning combinations based on the tactical device of "double attack." White moves first in Diagrams 241–246.

241

How can you win Black's Bishop?

242

How can you win Black's Bishop?

243

How can you win Black's Knight?

244

How can you win Black's Queen?

245

How can you win Black's Queen and draw the game?

246

How can you win Black's pawn and draw the game?

Answers

D-241

   1. Re3xh3!

By sacrificing the Exchange White decoys the Black Rook onto the h3 square.

   1. ...   **Rh6xh3**

Otherwise White would be a piece up.

   2. Bc4xe6 +

A double attack which will leave White up a Bishop.

D-242

   1. Rg4xg7 +!

By giving up his Rook for the Bishop, White decoys the Black King onto g7.

   1. ...   **Kh7xg7**

Or else 2. Qxh6# would follow.

   2. Qd2-d4 +

This check wins the Rook, leaving White a Bishop up.

D-243

   1. Qe2xe6!

The Queen sacrifices itself for the Knight, which controls f8.

   1. ...   **Qd5xe6**

If 1. ... Qd8, then 2. Qf5 + and 3. f8Q etc.

   2. f7-f8N +!

If the pawn promoted to a Queen the game would be a draw, but by promoting to a Knight it immediately creates a fork that will leave White a Knight up.

D-244 Black, with a material advantage, was dreaming of winning, but White made a magnificent combination and gained the victory.

1. Be6-d7+!

To decoy the Black King or Queen onto the treacherous square d7, the White Bishop sacrifices itself for the sake of a double attack. But its loss will be avenged by the Knight!
Variation a):

1. ...   **Ke8xd7**

2. Ng4-e5+

A Knight fork.

2. ...   **Kd7-d6**

3. Ne5xc6   **Kd6xc6**

Variation b):

1. ...   **Qc6xd7**

2. Ng4-f6+

Again a fork.

2. ...   **Ke8-d7**

3. Nf6xd7   **Ke7xd7**

White has gained three points.

In both variations White finishes two pawn up and should win.

D-245

1. Rc1-c5!

Black has a big material advantage and felt sure of winning, but . . . . White finds a saving combination. By sacrificing the Rook, he forces the Black Queen to occupy c5.

1. ...   **Qd5xc5**

All other moves would lose.

2. d2-d4+

Forking the Queen and the King.

2. ...   **Qc5xd4**

It's better to give up the Queen for two pawns like this than for just one.

3. e3xd4+   **Ke5xd4**

4. Kf2-g3

A draw is inevitable, as Black's last pawn will be eliminated. As a result of the combination White gained three points.

D-246 The Black pawn is threatening to queen. 1. Bc3 a2 2. Ka4 a1Q+ 3. Bxa1 Nxa1 does not save White since Black should win with his Knight and Bishop against White's lone King, although only strong and experienced players know the winning technique. However, White can save himself by a forking combination in which the King itself plays the main role.

1. Bb4xa3

The Bishop sacrifices itself for the dangerous pawn on a3 and at the same time decoys the Black Knight onto that square.

1. ...   **Nc2xa3**

If Black doesn't capture the Bishop the game should be a draw anyway.

2. Ka5-b4

Now either the Knight or the Bishop will be lost and the game will be drawn.

Note that in each of the above examples something was sacrificed in order to achieve a goal — a combination is just that.

Pawn Endgames. The Rule of the Square

We now begin the study of pawn endgames. You will often have to deal with such endgames in your games. They arise when all the pieces have been exchanged off and each side is left only with his King and some pawns.

Pawn endings demand accurate play, since a single incorrect move can change the outcome of the struggle.

Sometimes one of the players obtains an advantage of a single pawn. Is this advantage enough for victory? Should he strive to exchange off all the pieces and go into a pawn ending or should he avoid such exchanges? A player can correctly answer these questions only if he has a mastery of pawn endings.

Today we shall look at some very simple examples, in which a pawn tries to advance to the queening square without the help of its King.

247

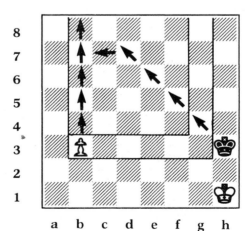

White to play wins. Black to play draws.

In Diagram 247, White to play wins and Black to play draws. With White to play we get:

1. b3-b4   **Kh3-g4**

2. b4-b5   **Kg4-f5**

The Black King approaches the White pawn along the diagonal, which is the shortest route.

3. b5-b6	Kf5-e6
4. b6-b7	Ke6-d7
5. b7-b8Q	

The Black King was unable to catch the White pawn, which has successfully queened.

Now let us look at the same position (Diagram 247) with Black to play:

1. ...	Kh3-g4
2. b3-b4	Kg4-f5
3. b4-b5	Kf5-e6
4. b5-b6	Ke6-d7
5. b6-b7	Kd7-c7

The King slightly deviates from its diagonal path because c8 is controlled by the White pawn.

6. b7-b8Q +	Kc7xb8

The Black King caught the White pawn in time and captures it.

Good chessplayers can tell in advance whether or not the King can catch the pawn in such situations. They do this by making use of the **Rule of the Square**, which states:

Draw a square one side of which is the line extending from the pawn to its queening square. If the defending King on its move can enter this square, it can catch the pawn.

When such positions occur in a game, players draw a mental picture of such squares.

Returning now to Diagram 247, we see that with **White to play** the Black King is unable to enter the smaller square b4-b8-f4-f8 and so the pawn queens, whereas with **Black to play** his King can enter the larger square b3-g8-g3-g8 and catch up with the pawn.

When applying the rule of the square to a pawn on its home square (2nd rank for a White pawn and 7th rank for a Black pawn) we must remember that the pawn can advance two squares at once on its first move. As a result we must draw the square from the third rank (for a White pawn) or the sixth rank (for a Black pawn).

248

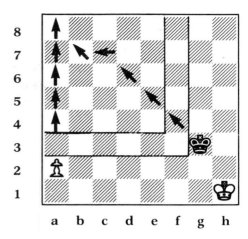

In Diagram 248, for example, White to play wins by 1. a2-a4, the Black King being unable to enter the small square a4-a8-e4-e8. Black to play, on the other hand, draws:

1. ...	Kg3-f4

The King enters the large square a3-a8-f3-f8 and catches the White pawn.

1. a2-a4	Kf4-e5
3. a4-a5	Ke5-d6
4. a5-a6	Kd6-c7
5. a6-a7	Kc7-b7
6. a7-a8Q +	Kb7xa8

The King usually chases the pawn along the diagonal because that is the shortest route. If there is some obstacle on the diagonal, the rule of the square becomes inapplicable.

For example, let us look at Diagram 249:

249

Black to play and White wins.

1. ...	Ka3-b4

The King enters the square but because there

is an obstacle (the Black pawn on d6) in its path (the a3-f8 diagonal), Black loses anyway. Nor would 1. ... d5 save Black: 2. f5 d4 3. f6 d3 4. f7 d2 5. f8Q + Kb3 6. Qf1 Kc2 7. Qb1 + Kc3 8. Ka2 and White will attack the pawn with his King, winning it and with it the game as well.

    2. f4-f5   **Kb4-c5**

    3. f5-f6   **Kc5-c6**

The King is forced to lose time (a tempo) in going around his own pawn.

    4. f6-f7   **Kc6-d7**

    5. f7-f8Q

Black fell one move (tempo) short of drawing the game.

Now let us use our newly-acquired knowledge to make some combinations.

250

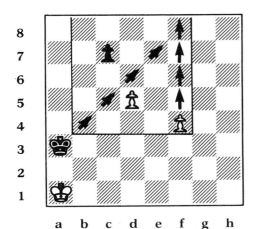

Black to play and White wins.

    1. ...   **Ka3-b4**

With this move the Black King enters the square of the pawn and Black thought that the game would be drawn, but . . . .

    2. d5-d6!

A combination! The White pawn sacrifices itself in order to decoy the Black pawn onto d6.

    2. ...   **c7xd6**

Or else the White d-pawn would queen.

    3. f4-f5

And White wins in exactly the same manner as in the previous example. The Black pawn on d6 blocks its King's path.

251

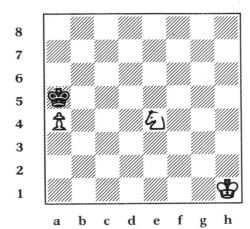

White to play wins.

    1. Ne4-c3!

Otherwise the game would be drawn: 1. Nc5 Kb4 2. Kg2 Kxc5 3. a5 Kb5, and the King is the a5-a8-d5-d8 square and easily wins the pawn.

    1. ...   **Ka5-b4**

    2. Kh1-g2!

A combination! The Knight is sacrificed in order to deflect the Black King from the a5-a8-d5-d8 square.

    2. ...   **Kb4xc3**

Otherwise the White King will approach and, together with the Knight, will escort the pawn to its queening square.

    3. a4-a5

Now the pawn cannot be stopped.

    3. ...   **Kc3-b4**

    4. a5-a6   **Kb4-b5**

    5. a6-a7   **Kb5-b6**

    6. a7-a8Q

and so on.

252

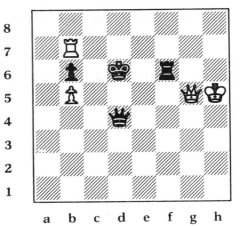

White to play wins.

1. Qg5xf6 + !

A temporary Queen sacrifice with the ultimate goal of assuring the queening of the pawn on b5. Sacrificing the Rook instead does not work: 1. Rxb6 + Qxb6 2. Qxf6 + Kc5 3. Qxb6 + Kxb6 and the White pawn is lost, as the Black King is in the b5-b8-e5-e8 square.

1. ...	Qd4xf6
2. Rb7xb6 +	Kd6-e5
3. Rb6xf6	Ke5xf6
4. b5-b6	

And the pawn queens as the Black King cannot enter the b6-b8-d6-d8 square.

4. ...	Kf6-e6
5. b6-b7	Ke6-d6
6. b7-b8Q	

and so on.

To conclude this lesson, let us look at some very short games in which a double attack decided the outcome of the struggle right in the opening.

Game 43
Combe–Hasenfuss, Folkestone 1933

| 1. d2-d4 | c7-c5 |

If White replies 2. dxc5 can Black win back the pawn? Yes, with the move 2. ... Qa5+, a double attack on the King (check) and the pawn.

| 2. c2-c4 | |

2. d5 would be a good move.

| 2. ... | c5xd4 |
| 3. Ng1-f3 | |

White doesn't want to bring out his Queen with 3. Qxd4.

| 3. ... | e7-e5 |

Black defends the pawn on d4 and at the same time sets a trap that should be "child's play" to avoid. See Diagram 253.

253

What is the trap?

4. Nf3xe5??

White falls for the bait and takes the poisoned pawn. Instead of attempting to regain the sacrificed pawn, he should play a gambit with 4. e3. But he is greedy and loses immediately.

| 4. ... | Qd8-a5 + |

A double attack. The Queen forks the King and the Knight. White resigns. See Diagram 254.

254

This game is the shortest ever played in the World Chess Olympics.

Game 44
French Defense

1. e2-e4	e7-e6
2. d2-d4	d7-d5
3. Nb1-c3	d5xe4
4. Nc3xe4	Ng8-f6
5. Bf1-d3	

A good move that incidentally contains a trap.

5. ...   **Bf8-e7**

Black sees through the trap: 5. ... Qxd4 would cost him his Queen after 6. Bb5 + .

6. Ng1-f3   **0-0**
7. Qd1-e2   **b7-b6?**

Until now both sides have played well but here Black overlooks a double attack of White's. He should play instead 7. ... Nbd7 followed by 8. ... b6.

8. Ne4xf6 +   **Be7xf6**
9. Qe2-e4!

See Diagram 255.

256

Find all the possible double attacks with White to play and with Black to play (do not move a piece to a square where it can be captured for nothing or by a less valuable man).

_____

_____

_____

255

Black resigns, as he must lose his Rook. The White Queen is simultaneously threatening to mate on h7 (10. Qxh7#) and capture the Rook on a8 (10. Qxa8).

HOMEWORK
(Answers at the end)

I. The solutions to Diagrams 256–261 involve the tactical device of "double attack."

257

White to play. Find all the possible double attacks. Which is the best? (Do not put your Queen under attack.)

_____

_____

_____

258

Black to play. Find the best move.

	WHITE	BLACK
1.		
2.		
3.		
4.		

260

White to play and win Black's Queen.

	WHITE	BLACK
1.		
2.		
3.		
4.		

259

Black to play and win a piece.

	WHITE	BLACK
1.		
2.		
3.		
4.		

261

White to play and win a piece.

	WHITE	BLACK
1.		
2.		
3.		
4.		

II. In Diagrams 262-267 find combinations that use the tactical device of "double attack."

262

White to play and win a piece.

	WHITE	BLACK
1.		
2.		
3.		
4.		

263

White to play and win Black's Queen.

	WHITE	BLACK
1.		
2.		
3.		
4.		

264

White to play and win.

	WHITE	BLACK
1.		
2.		
3.		
4.		

265

White to play and win.

	WHITE	BLACK
1.		
2.		
3.		
4.		

266

White to play and win a piece.

	WHITE	BLACK
1.		
2.		
3.		
4.		

267

What will happen if Black captures the pawn on d6?

	WHITE	BLACK
1.		
2.		
3.		
4.		

III. The solutions to Diagrams 268–273 make use of the "rule of the square."

268

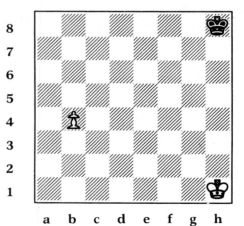

What happens if it is White to play? If it is Black to play?

269

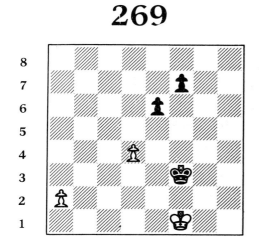

White to play. How should the game end?

	WHITE	BLACK
1.		
2.		
3.		
4.		

271

White to play and win.

	WHITE	BLACK
1.		
2.		
3.		
4.		

270

Can Black to play win?

	WHITE	BLACK
1.		
2.		
3.		
4.		

272

White to play. Queen your own pawn while stopping Black's.

	WHITE	BLACK
1.		
2.		
3.		
4.		

273

White to play and win.

	WHITE	BLACK
1.		
2.		
3.		
4.		

Answers to the Homework

D-256 With White to play: Kg1-g2; Qe1-b4; Qe1-e2; Ng6-e7+; Ng6-h4; b2-b3.

With Black to play: Qc8-e6; Qc8-e8;Rf3-e3; Ba4xc2; Nc4-e3.

D-257 Qf3-b3+ is the best move as it wins the Rook, the most valuable Black piece on the board. Other moves are: Qf3-b7; Qf3-c6+; Qf3-e4+; Qf3-h3+.

D-258 Variation a):

	1. ...	Nd4-c2+
	2. Ke1-d2	Nc2xa1
	3. Rg1xa1	

Black has won a Queen (9 points) and lost a Knight (3 points) for a net gain of 6 points.

Variation b):

	1. ...	Nd4xf3+
	2. Ke1-f2	Nf3xg1
	3. Kf2xg1	

In this case Black has won a Bishop (3 points) and a Rook (5 points) and lost a Knight (3 points). That is, he has won 5 points.

So we conclude that 1. ... Nc2+ is the best move, since it gains one point more than 1. Nxf3+.

D-259 (Based on the game Reti–Alekhine, Baden-Baden 1925). 1. ... Be6-d5 wins either the Rook or the Knight.

D-260 1. Rh5-d5+. This check wins a Queen for a Rook, a gain of four points for White.

D-261

	1. Kc5-b6	Na7-c8+

If 1. ... Kg4, then 2. Kb7 wins a piece.

	2. Kb6-b7	

The King attacks two pieces simultaneously and one of them must perish.

D-262

	1. Qd2xd7+!	

This Queen sacrifice eliminates the Bishop defending the pawn on e6.

	1. ...	Rd8xd7
	2. Nf4xe6+	

Now the Knight is able to capture the pawn on e6 and fork the Queen and King.

	2. ...	u
	3. Ne6xf8	

and White is a Knight up. Black has lost four points.

D-263

	1. Rd2xd4+!	

This exchange sacrifice decoys the Black King onto d4.

	1. ...	Kd5xd4

Otherwise the Rook would take the Queen.

	2. Ng5-e6+	

Our old friend the fork.

	2. ...	u
	3. Ne6xd8	

And White is up a Knight. Black has lost a Queen and Bishop for a Rook, i.e., a total of seven points.

D-264 Black is threatening 1. ... Qg2# and apparently there is no defense. However, White is saved by an "exchanging" combination:

	1. Qa8-h8+!	

The Queen is sacrificed to decoy the Black King onto h8.

	1. ...	Kh7xh8
	2. Nd6-f7+	

Again a fork.

	2. ...	u
	3. Nf7xg5	

Now we see the idea behind the combination. White has exchanged off the dangerous Black Queen and now can win easily, since his King is within the square of the Black pawn (f1-f3-h1-h3) while the Black King hasn't the faintest hope of making it to the square of the White a-pawn (a6-a8-c6-c8).

D-265

1. Bf4-d2 + !

A fine Bishop sacrifice that decoys the Black King onto d2.

1. ...   Kc3xd2

If 1. ... Kxb2, then White plays 2. Bxa5 followed by queening the pawn.

2. Nb2-c4 +

A fork. It is not for nothing that chessplayers consider horses to be dangerous beasts.

2. ...   u

3. Nc4xa5

and the a-pawn will queen as the Black King cannot enter the a6-a8-c6-c8 square.

D-266

1. Rc1xc2!

An exchange sacrifice to decoy the Black Rook onto c2.

1. ...   Rd2xc2

Or else White will remain a Bishop up.

2. Bh3-f5 +

A check winning the Rook. White will be up a Bishop.

D-267 (From Ljublinskii–Kamyshov, Moscow 1949).

1. ...   Kd7xd6?

was followed by

2. Rb1-d1 +   Kd6-e7

3. Rd1xd8!   Ke7xd8

4. Be3xb6 +

A check winning the Rook. Black resigns, as he has lost a piece.

D-268 White wins in both cases as the Black King cannot make it in time to the b4-b8-f4-f8 square and the White pawn will queen.

D-269 White should win:

1. d4-d5!

The pawn is sacrificed in order to establish a Black pawn in the Black King's path. 1. a4 would not work because of 1. ... Ke4 2. a5 Kd5, when the Black King, having entered the a5-a8-d5-d8 square, can stop the a-pawn.

1. ...   e6xd5

Otherwise the d-pawn would queen.

2. a2-a4   Kf3-e4

It doesn't help to move 2. ... d4 3. a5 d3, because of 4. Ke1! and the White King can easily stop Black's pawn. At the same time, the

Black King cannot stop the White pawn on the a-file.

3. a4-a5   Ke4-e5

The King is forced to lose a decisive move (tempo) in going around its own pawn.

4. a5-a6   Ke5-d6

5. a6-a7   Kd6-c7

6. a7-a8Q

Black was just one move short of catching the pawn.

D-270 Yes.

1. ...   Ba1-e5!

The Bishop is sacrificed in order to deflect the White King from the c1-c4-f1-f4 square.

2. Ke4xe5

Otherwise Black will bring his King up to accompany the pawn and win easily

2. ...   f4-f3

and the pawn will queen.

D-271

1. Nc4-b2!

Only this Knight sacrifice wins. 1. Ne5 would be met by the double attack 1. ... Kd4, winning the pawn.

1. ...   Kc3xb2

Or else the White King will come up to help the pawn queen.

2. d3-d4

and White wins, since the Black King cannot stop the pawn.

D-272

1. Kf1-g2!

1. a4 would be a mistake because of 1. ... g2 +, winning for Black (the Bishop can easily stop the a-pawn). So White first keeps the Bishop out of play. Even though it now becomes Black's turn to play, his King still cannot make it in time to the square of the pawn.

1. ...   h6-h5

The only chance.

2. a2-a4   h5-h4

3. a4-a5   h4-h3 + !

Black offers a pawn in an attempt to free his trapped Bishop.

4. Kg2-h1!!

White ignores the pawn on h3. 4. Kxh3 would allow Black to win by 4. ... Bg1, but as it is the Bishop still cannot break loose.

4. ...   g7-g5

Yet another pawn hurries to the aid of the Bishop.

| 5. a5-a6 | g5-g4 |
| 6. a6-a7 | g3-g2 + ! |

Black gives up his Bishop in a final attempt to save the game.

| 7. Kh1xh2 | g4-g3 + ! |

The pawns on g3 and h3 are under attack now, but they are both "poisoned pawns." If the King captures either of them, the pawn on g2 will queen.

8. Kh2-g1!!

The Black pawns have been stopped!

8. ...	h3-h2 +
9. Kg1xg2	Kh8-g7
10. a7-a8Q	

and so on.

The White King successfully coped with a Black Bishop and three (!) Black pawns while nothing could hold back the White a-pawn. This happened because the Bishop was caught in a disastrous situation and the Black King was too far away from both the Bishop and the White pawn.

D-273 (From Petrosian–Taimanov, Moscow 1957). The future world champion played **1. Rd8-d1** and Black resigned. 1. ... Ra2 is no good because 2. Kb3 snares the Rook. If 1. ... Rxd1, then 2. Kxd1 and the Black King cannot reach the square of the a-pawn (a3-a8-f3-f8), while the White King can easily stop any of the Black pawns.

SUPPLEMENTARY MATERIAL

for use at the teacher's discretion

Defending Against a Double Attack

274

Black to play. White's Bishop is forking the King and the Knight. Can Black save his piece?

Yes, he can, by using a tactical device known as **defending against a check by interposition**:

| 1. ... | Bf7-g6 |

Now both the King and the Knight are protected.

| 2. Be4xc2 | Bg6xc2 |

Pieces of equal value have been traded.

275

White to play. The Black pawn on e4 is forking the King and the Rook. Does White have to lose a Rook?

No. White can save himself by using a tactical device known as **counterattacking**:

1. Kf3-g2!

The King gets out of check and at the same time attacks Black's Rook.

    1. ...   **e4xd3**

    2. Kg2xh1

White has lost nothing. All that has occurred is a trade of Rooks.

277

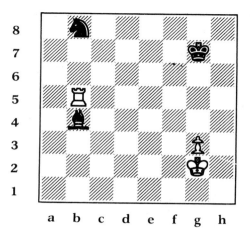

Black to play. The White Rook is forking two Black pieces. Can Black save them?

Yes, by using the tactical device known as **defending one attacked piece with the other attacked piece**:

    1. ...   **Bb4-d6**

The defenses 1. ... Nc6 and 1. ... Na6 would be insufficient since after the new fork 2. Rb6! Black would lose a piece after all.

    2. Rb4-b6   **Bd6-e5**

    3. Rb6-b5   **Kg7-f6**

with an equal position.

276

White to play.

    1. e5-e6

The pawn forks the Rook and the Bishop. Can Black avoid losing a piece?

Yes, by using the tactical device known as **in-between check**:

    1. ...   **Rd7-b7 +**

Black moves away one of his attacked pieces with check. White has no time to capture the other piece because he must firt save his King. Note that the in-between check 1. ... Rd1 + would not work because of the counterattack 2. Kc2, when White would win a piece after all.

    2. u   **Bf7-e8**

Black has saved his piece.

278

Can either White or Black to play win material? White to play wins a piece:

    1. Qd1-h5 +

A check winning the Knight on a5. 1. Qa4 + also simultaneously attacks the King and the Knight, but would not win a piece. Black could defend in two ways: a) 1. ... Nc6 (one attacked piece protects the other) or b) 1. ... c6 (the pawn covers the check and at the same time opens a diagonal along which the Queen defends the Knight).

Black to play cannot win material in spite of the fact that he can make a triple attack!

    1. ...   **Qd8-h4 +**

The Queen simultaneously attacks the King, the Knight, and the e-pawn.

    2. Nh3-f2!

One attacked piece protects the two other attacked men: the Knight moves away from the attack and at the same time covers the check and defends the e-pawn.

279

White to play. Is 1. Be4-d5 a good move?

No. Although the Bishop forks two Black pieces, the move is still a blunder. Black can win a piece by using the tactical device known as **eliminating the defender**:

    1. ...   **Rc4xf4!!**

With this exchange sacrifice Black simultaneously eliminates the Bishop's defender and attacks the White Queen.

    2. Qf1xf4

2. Bxf7 would be even worse since after 2. ... Rxf1 + Black would be a piece up.

    2. ...   **Qf7xd5 +**

As a result of his combination Black has won a Knight and a Bishop (6 points) for a Rook (5 points), i.e., he has gained one point.

You are now acquainted with the major ways of defending against double attacks. There are, however, other methods as well, and you will be introduced to them later on.

Sample Games Containing The Theme of Double Attack

Game 45
Sicilian Defense

    1. e2-e4   **c7-c5**
    2. d2-d4   **c5xd4**
    3. Ng1-f3

White could win back his pawn by 3. Qxd4, but he does not want to bring his Queen out so early. He expects that the Black pawn cannot be defended in any case.

    3. ...   **e7-e5**

Black defends the d-pawn and sets a trap at the same time.

    4. Nf3xe5??

How often we fall into traps! White thinks that the e-pawn is a gift. It would be better to play a gambit: 4. c3 dxc3 5. Nxc3 d6 6. Bc4, and the aggressive development of the White pieces makes up for the lost pawn.

    4. ...   **Qd8-a5 +!**

See Diagram 280.

280

This simple Queen check was overlooked by White in his calculations when he made his last move. Black will capture the Knight on e5 and have excellent chances of winning the game.

Game 46
Vitalii Kozlov (age 12)–Kolya Petuhov (age 14)
Schoolchildren's Tournament, USSR 1974

    1. d2-d4   **Ng8-f6**
    2. Bc1-g5   **c7-c6**

A fairly good move that at the same time sets a trap.

3. e2-e3??

Who sees the strongest reply for Black? White has not noticed a double attack and pays with a piece. Instead 3. Nf3 would lead to an even game.

3. ...   Qd8-a5 + !

Of course, this is the strongest move. A check winning the Bishop. See Diagram 281.

281

White resigned, but it would make sense for a beginner to fight on in such a situation since his opponent might in turn make a blunder.

Can Black be said to have made a **combination** in this game? *No. A combination has to contain a sacrifice. Black's move 3. ... Qa5 + is a tactical device known as double attack.*

Game 47
Ruy Lopez

1. e2-e4	e7-e5
2. Ng1-f3	Nb8-c6
3. Bf1-b5	

This move initiates the most popular opening of our times, the Ruy Lopez, named after a Spaniard in whose hands it was a fearful weapon some 400 years ago.

3. ...   a7-a6

Black often makes this move, which involves a temporary pawn sacrifice.

4. Bb5xc6   d7xc6

Black could also reply 4. ... bxc6, e.g. 5. Nxe5 Qg5 (attacking both the Knight and the pawn on g2) 6. Ng4 d5! (a fresh double attack, this time on the Knight on g4 and the pawn on e4) 7. Ne3 dxe4.

5. Nf3xe5?!

White is in a hurry to win a pawn. He would do better to continue his development by 5. 0-0 or 5. Nc3.

5. ...   Qd8-d4!

A double attack allowing Black to win back his pawn. Also possible is 5. ... Qg5 (again a double attack) 6. d4 Qxg2. Not as good, however, would be 5. ... Qe7 6. d4 f6 7. Nf3 Qxe4 + 8. Be3, when Black is behind in development.

6. Ne5-f3	Qd4xe4 +
7. Qd1-e2	Qe4xe2 +
8. Ke1xe2	

See Diagram 282.

282

Black's position is preferable. White has lost the right to castle while Black can rapidly bring out his pieces and castle on the Queenside.

Game 48
Fima Rokhman (age 11)–Dima Shapiro (age 12)
Schoolchildren's Tournament, USSR 1972

1. c2-c4	d7-d5
2. c4xd5	Ng8-f6

Black could play 2. ... Qxd5 but he doesn't want to bring his Queen out so early and plans to capture the pawn with his Knight.

3. e2-e4

White decides to defend the pawn, at the same time setting a "childishly simple" trap.

3. ...   Nf6xe4??

Black can blame only himself for playing so carelessly. He grabs the pawn without noticing White's simple reply. Instead, Black should play a gambit, i.e., sacrifice a pawn in return for good play. For example: 3. ... c6 4. dxc6 Nxc6.

4. Qd1-a4 +!

A check winning the Knight. See Diagram 283.

283

Black resigns. Of course *you* won't make such "typical mistakes," right?

Game 49

1. e2-e4	**e7-e5**
2. Ng1-f3	**Nb8-c6**
3. Bf1-e2	

A passive move. 3. Bc4 or 3. Bb5 would be better.

3. ...	**Bf8-c5**
4. 0-0	**d7-d6**
5. c2-c3	

Preparing 6. d4.

5. ...   **Bc8-e6?**

A blunder that costs a piece. 5. ... Bg4 or 5. ... Nf6 would be better.

6. d2-d4

Before making this move, White had to count how many times the pawn would be attacked by the Black men and how many times it would be defend.

6. ...   **Bc5-b6**

Black cannot win the pawn on d4 because the three attackers do not outnumber the three defenders.

7. d4-d5!

See Diagram 284.

284

A fork which wins a piece. This is what Black overlooked when playing 5. ... Be6?. Now Black's affairs are in a bad way.

Game 50

1. e2-e4	**e7-e5**
2. Ng1-f3	**Ng8-f6**
3. d2-d3	

White defends his pawn on e4 and plans to capture the Black pawn on e5, but the move is passive and blocks the light-square Bishop. More active possibilities are 3. d4 or 3. Nxe5 d6 4. Nf3 Nxe4 5. d4.

3. ...   **c7-c6**

An interesting move that prepares 4. ... d5 and at the same time indirectly defends the pawn on e5.

4. Nb1-c3

White sees through Black's *first* trap: 4. Nxe5 would be bad because of 4. ... Qa5+ winning the Knight on e5.

4. ...   **d7-d5!**

Black again offers the pawn on e5, but seizes the center.

5. Nf3xe5?

Black's *second* trap catches White! If White wants to win the e-pawn, he should play the following line, although Black gets enough compensation for the pawn: 5. exd5 cxd5 6. Nxe5 d4 7. Qe2! (an in-between move with the Queen that prevents 7. ... dxc3 since the discovered check 8. Nc6+ would win Black's Queen) 7. ... Be7 8. Nd1 (now the Knight on e5 is defended by the Queen and White does not have to fear the double attack 8. ... Qa5+).

5. ...   **d5-d4!**

This is the move the White underestimated in his calculations.

6. Nc3-e2	**Qd8-a5 +**

The same old check winning a Knight that occurs in so many games! See Diagram 285.

285

Game 51
Queen's Gambit Declined

1. d2-d4	**d7-d5**
2. c2-c4	

White sacrifices a pawn for quick development.

2. ...	**Ng8-f6**

Black declines the gift, but a better way of doing so would be by 2. ... e6, defending the d-pawn with another pawn.

3. c4xd5	**Nf6xd5**
4. Ng1-f3	**Nb8-c6**

A mistake. The Black Knights are now convenient targets for the White pawns. It would be better to play 4. ... e6 or 4. ... c6, controlling the central square d5.

5. e2-e4	**Nd5-f6**
6. d4-d5!	

The White·pawns occupy the center and chase the Black Knights away from there.

6. ...	**Nf6xe4?**

Black plays for a trap. He expects 7. dxc6 Qxd1 + 8. Kxd1 Nxf2+ 9. Ke1 Nxh1, when he would be up an Exchange and two pawns. However, it would be better to move the Knight back to its home square with 6. ... Nb8.

7. Bc1-e3!	

Now the pawn on f2 is defended by the Bishop and White really threatens to capture the Knight on c6. Black has fallen into a **countertrap.**

7. ...	**Nc6-a5**

8. Qd1-a4 +!	

See Diagram 286.

286

A triple attack on the King and two Knights! Black can defend the Knight on a5 with 8. ... c6 (opening a line of defence for the Queen) but he cannot save the Knight on e4. The double attack that Black planned to execute with his Knight on e4 has been forestalled by the White Queen's triple attack. White winds up with both a material advantage and a better position.

Game 52
Borbesch–Kovacs, Zurich 1948
Sicilian Defense

1. e2 e4	**c7-c5**
2. Ng1-f3	**d7-d6**
3. d2-d4	**c5xd4**
4. Qd1xd4	

Much rarer than 4. Nxd4 but not at all bad.

4. ...	**Nb8-c6**
5. Bf1-b5	**Bc8-d7**
6. Bb5xc6	**b7xc6**
7. Nb1-c3	**Ng8-f6**
8. Bc1-g5	**Ra8-b8?**

Apparently a good move, for Black attacks the pawn on b2 and probably plans to meet 9. 0-0-0 with 9. ... Qb6. The thing is, however, that White does not have to defend the b-pawn at all. The correct move was 8. ... e5 with an equal game.

9. e4-e5!	**d6xe5**
10. Nf3xe5	**Rb8xb2?**

A blunder. Black overlooks a double attack. The right move is 10. ... Rb7, defending the pawn on a7 and the light-square Bishop. As it is, White gets an idea based on attacking the Black Rook by castling on the Queenside.

11. Bg5xf6

Eliminating the Knight that defends the Bishop on d7.

11. ...   g7xf6?

Black does not sense the danger, or else he would play 11. ... exf6, opening the a3-f8 diagonal for his Bishop and intending to try and complicate the game by replying to 12. Nxd7 with the in-between move 12. ... Rb4.

12. Ne5xd7!

The only way! 12. Qxd7+ Qxd7 13. Nxd7 would be wrong because of the in-between move 13. ... Rxc2, when both White Knights would be under attack.

12.   ...   Qd8xd7

13. Qd4xd7+

Forcing the Black King onto the d-file.

13.   ...   Ke8xd7

14. 0-0-0+!

See Diagram 287.

287

A check winning the Rook on b2. After this pretty move Black resigned right away. We have already come across a similar idea in Foyer–O'Kelly (game 2).

Game 53
Karaklajic–Fuderer, Yugoslavia 1955
Philidor's Defense

1. e2-e4	e7-e5
2. Ng1-f3	d7-d6
3. d2-d4	Nb8-d7

A good move. 3. ... Nc6 could be met with 4.

Bb5, continuing to put pressure on the pawn on e5.

4. Bf1-c4

White develops his Bishop and at the same time sets a trap. 4. Bb5 would yield nothing after the simple reply 4. ... c6.

4. ...   Bf8-e7?

The natural-looking move turns out to be a mistake. Black must first play 4. ... c6, and only then 5. ... Be7.

5. d4xe5   Nd7xe5

5. ... dxe5 would be even worse because of 6. Qd5!, winning (see lesson 4, D-137).

6. Nf3xe5   d6xe5

7. Qd1-h5!

288

The Queen forks the pawns on e5 and f7. Black cannot defend them both and must lose one of them.

The player of the Black pieces in this game, Fuderer, was a Yugoslav master. Interestingly enough, the winner of the game, Yugoslav master Karaklajic, caught another master player, Nedeljkovic, in exacly the same opening trap in another game played five years later, also in Yugoslavia. Nor was Liberzon, who later became a grandmaster, able to avoid falling into this trap in the game he played against the master Estrin in 1958, in Moscow. As you can see, even strong chessplayers sometimes blunder!

Game 54
Imbisch–Goering, 1899
Vienna Game

1. e4-e4	e7-e5
2. Nb1-c3	Ng8-f6
3. Bf1-c4	

White would do better to play a gambit by sacrificing a pawn with 3. f4 and then quickly develop his pieces.

3. ...	Nf6xe4

A temporary piece sacrifice. 4. Nxe4 would be met by 4. ... d5, forking the Knight and Bishop and winning back the sacrificed piece with a good position.

4. Bc4xf7 +

White decides to expose the Black King's position by means of this counter-sacrifice.

4. ...	Ke8xf7
5. Nc3xe4	Nb8-c6?

Material is even, but Black could obtain a positional advantage by 6. ... d5! 6. Qf3 + Kg8 7. Ng5 Qd7! (not 7. ... Qxg5 8. Qxd5 + Be6 9. Qxe6#). Black has the better position after 7. ... Qd7! because of his strong pawn center, and he can easily drive away the White Knight from g5 by 8. ... h6.

6. Qd1-f3 +	Kf7-g8??

Here this move is a grave error indeed! The only way for Black to avoid immediate disaster is 6. ... Ke8, although even then his position is worse due to his King being stuck in the center.

7. Ne4-g5!

See Diagram 289.

289

White plays the strongest move, forcing Black to capitulate immediately. There is no satisfactory defense against the double threat of 8. Qf7# and 8. Qd5#.

Lesson Eight

A. Check Lesson 7 Homework (as necessary).

B. *Review Questions*

1. How many moves does a Knight need to get from f6 to h8 and what are these moves? Try to answer this question without looking at a chessboard.
2. What is meant by a "forced variation"?
3. What is the difference between tactics and a plan?
4. What is the difference between combinations and tactical devices?

Find the solutions to questions 5–8 directly from the diagrams, without setting up the men on a board.

291

White to play. Can he win a piece?

290

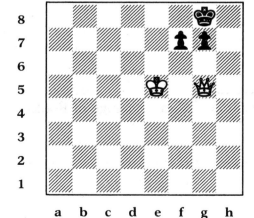

Black to play. How should the game end?

292

Black to play. Find his best move.

293

Black to play. Can he escape from the fork?

294

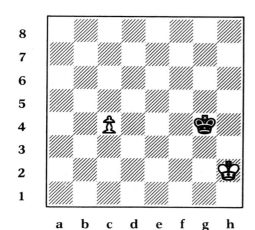

White to play. How should the game end?

295

White to play. How should the game end?

Answers To the Review Questions

1. Four moves. Nf6-g8-h6-f7-h8 (other routes are also possible).

2. A **forced variation** is a series of moves united by a common purpose and which **cannot be avoided** by at least one of the players. For example, we can say that in Diagram 290 the game should finish with a forced variation.

3. A **plan** shows **what** must be done to achieve a certain goal, while **tactics** answer the question of **how** it can be done.

4. **Tactical devices** are a number of methods used in chess combat that **do not entail sacrifices of material** (pawns, pieces, Exchanges, etc.) An example is the double attack (see Diagram 290). A **combination** is a tactical device that is accompanied by the **sacrifice of material**. An example is shown in Diagram 291.

D-290 The game should be drawn:

1. ...		f7-f6 +

(A fork.)

2. Qg5xf6		g7xf6 +
3. Ke5xf6		

D-291 Yes:

1. Qf3-d5 + !

A combination with a Queen sacrifice! The Black Queen is decoyed onto d5.

1. ...		Qd7xd5
2. Nf5xe7 +		

A fork that will leave White a piece up.

2. ...		u
3. Ne7xd5		

D-292 The White Knight is forking two Black pieces but Black can use the tactical device of "counterattack," moving his Bishop to safety and at the same time attacking the White Rook:

1. ...		Bc5-d4
2. Ne4xf6		Bd4xa1

The result is just an exchange of Rooks.

D-293 In this position Black escapes from the Knight fork by employing the tactical device known as the "in-between check":

1. ...		Bc5-b4 +

The Bishop flees the Knight's attack and checks the White King. After White's reply, Black will move his Rook away from the Knight's attack.

D-294 The game should be drawn as the Black King is inside the square of the pawn (c4-c8-g4-g8):

1. c4-c5	Kg4-f5
2. c5-c6	Kf5-e6
3. c6-c7	Ke6-d7
4. c7-c8Q +	Kd7xc8

D-295 White should win. Although the Black King is inside the square of the pawn, its path is blocked by an obstacle — the Black pawn on e6:

1. c4-c5	Kg4-f5
2. c5-c6	Kf5-f6

The Black King is forced to go around the pawn.

3. c6-c7	Kf6-e7
4. c7-c8Q	

Black was one move (tempo) short of eliminating the White pawn.

Pinning

The tactical device known as **pinning** occurs in almost every game. Pinning involves three men standing in a line (diagonal, rank, or file): the **pinning** piece (Queen, Rook, or Bishop), the **pinned man** (any piece or pawn except the King) in the middle, and the man beyond the pinned man (the **shielded man**). The pinning piece is of a different color from the other two men.

296

Diagram 296 shows various pinning patterns. In each quarter-diagram a different man is pinned and unable to defend its King from checkmate.

It is costly for a pinned piece to leave its post since that will expose to attack another — more

valuable or undefended — piece. If this other piece is the King, as in Diagram 296, then we have what is called an **absolute pin.** That is, the pinned piece is totally paralyzed and immobilized. If, however, the other piece is **not** the King, then the pin is known as a **relative pin.** Here the pinned piece can at times, in order to achieve some specific goal, move from its post, sacrificing the more valuable piece (even the Queen) that it was pinned against. Remember Legal's Mate? (See game 26.)

Now let us look at some more examples. In Diagrams 297–302 it is White's turn to play. Find the best continuation in each case. Make use of the tactical device of pinning. Work out the solutions in your head, without moving the men about.

297

298

299

300

301

302

Answers

D-297   1. Qd2-h6#

White makes use of a pin. The Black pawn cannot capture the Queen because it is pinned against its King by the White Bishop.

D-298   1. Rh2-h8#

The Rook can be captured neither by the Knight, pinned against the King by the Bishop on b3, nor by the Bishop, pinned against the King by the Rook on g1.

D-299

    1. Rf1-e1

The Rook pins the Knight against the King along the e-file.

    1. ...   **f7-f5**

The pawn defends the Knight

    2. f2-f3

And the Knight must perish.

D-300

    1. Ba4-c2

A diagonal pin.

    1. ...   **Kh7-g6**

The King defends the Rook.

    2. g2-g4

Winning the rook.

D-301   1. Bd3-e4

White wins a piece. In this case the pin is **relative**, but if Black moves his Knight he will lose his Rook.

D-302   1. Be3-f4

Black loses a piece due to the relative pin of the Knight on b8. The pin is relative because the Knight has the right to move, but if it does the Rook on a8 will be lost.

Now let us try our hand at combinations

based on the tactical device of "pinning." Find the strongest continuation in Diagrams 303–308.

303

Black to play.

304

White to play.

305

White to play.

306

White to play, from the game Ragozin (grandmaster) – Boleslavskii (grandmaster), Moscow 1945.

307

White to play, from the game Averbakh (grandmaster) – Penrose (master), London 1954.

308

White to play, from the game Szabo (grandmaster) – Donner (grandmaster), Goteborg 1945.

Answers

D-303

    1. ...   **Bc7xe5!**

With this Bishop sacrifice Black decoys the White Queen onto the e-file.

    2. Qc3xe5

Any retreat of the Queen would lose the Rook on a1.

    2. ...   **Rc8-e8**

Using a vertical pin, Black wins the White Queen for a net gain of two points (Queen and pawn for Rook and Bishop).

D-304

    1. Rc1xc6!

The Black Rook is decoyed onto the c6 square.

    1. ...   **Rc7xc6**

Now the Black Rook is pinned by the White Bishop.

    2. b4-b5   **a6xb5**

    3. a4xb5

White will win the Rook and will have made a net gain of a Bishop.

D-305

    1. Qc3xg7 + !   **Qf8xg7**

    2. Re1-e8#

The Black Queen is diagonally pinned by the White Bishop and so cannot defend the King.

A second solution is also possible:

    1. Re1-e8   **Kh8-g8**

If 1. ... Qe8, then 2. Qxg7#.

    2. Qc3xg7#

The Black Queen is pinned along the rank and so cannot capture the White one.

D-306

    1. e7-e8Q +

A sacrifice to decoy the Black King onto e8.

    1. ...   **Kf7xe8**

    2. Bc2-a4

Black resigned. Thanks to the pin, White will have won a Rook for a pawn (a net gain of four points.)

D-307

    1. Bb2xd4!

A Bishop sacrifice that Black is forced to accept, since otherwise his Queen, pinned along the diagonal, will be lost.

    1. ...   **Qf6xd4**

The Queen has been decoyed onto d4.

    2. Nh4xf5 +

Black resigns. He will end up having lost a Queen and two pawns for a Bishop (i.e., eight points). This combination made use of two tactical devices: a Knight fork on f5 and a pin on the g6 pawn.

D-308

    1. Ne5xg6 + !

This Knight sacrifice pins the Black Bishop on g7 and exposes the Black King's position.

    1. ...   **h7xg6**

Forced.

    2. Qc1-h6 +   **Bg8-h7**

    3. Qh6xg7#

Endgame with King and Two Pawns versus King

A King and two pawns almost always wins against a lone King. Let us look at some examples in Diagrams 309–314.

309

Black wins no matter who plays first.

310

White wins no matter who moves first.

311

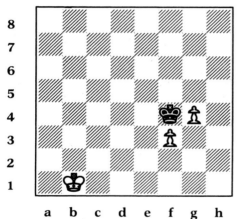

White wins no matter who moves first.

312

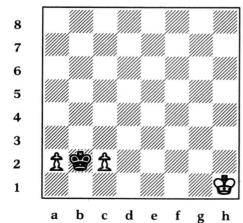

White wins no matter who moves first.

313

White to play wins. Black to play draws.

314

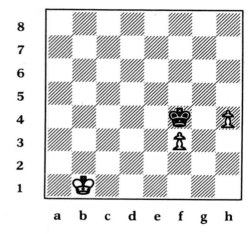

White wins no matter who moves first.

D-309 Black wins no matter who plays first:

    1. Kd4-c4

If the pawns are far removed from each other (at least three files between them) they win easily even without the help of their King.

    1. ...   **f4-f3**

    2. Kc4-d3

Capturing the b-pawn would put the White King outside the square of the f-pawn.

    2. ...   **b4-b3**

While chasing one of the pawns advancing towards its queening square, the White King is forced to leave the square of the other pawn.

    3. Kd3-c3   **f3-f2**

and so on.

D-310 White wins no matter who moves first:

    1. ...   **Kf7-e6**

    2. h5-h6

If the pawns are separated by two files and

are both on the opponent's half of the board, they can always win without the help of their King.

2. ...	Ke6-f7

2. ... Kxe5 would lose because of 3. h7, and the Black King cannot reach the square of the h-pawn.

3. h6-h7	Kf7-g7
4. e5-e6	

And one of the two pawns will queen by force.

D-311 White wins no matter who moves first:

1. ...	Kf4-g5

The point is that the pawn on f3 is invulnerable, since capturing it would take the Black King outside the square of the g-pawn, which would then become a Queen. E.g., 1. ... Kxf3 2. g5 Kg4 3. g6 Kg5 4. g7 Kg6 5. g8Q+ etc.

2. Kb1-c2	

The White King approaches the pawns to help them queen.

Thus we see from this example that two pawns on neighboring squares protect each other against capture by the enemy King.

D-312 White wins no matter who moves first.

1. ...	Kb2-c3

Capturing either of the pawns would take the King out of the other pawn's square. E.g., 1. ... Kxa2 2. c4, and the c-pawn will queen.

2. Kh1-g2	

Taking advantage of the fact that the pawns are safe from capture, the White King comes up to help them queen.

D-313 White to play wins. Black to play draws. White to play:

1. b3-b4	

Controlling the c5 square and forcing the Black King to leave the square of the pawn on b5.

1. ...	Kd5-c4
2. b5-b6	

and the pawn will queen.

Black to play:

1. ...	Kd5-c5
2. b5-b6	Kc5xb6
3. Ke7-d6	Kb6-b5

and Black will capture the pawn on b3 as well and draw.

D-314 White wins no matter who moves first.

1. ...	Kf4-f5

1. ... Kxf3 would lose because of 2. h5, and the Black King cannot reach the square of the h-pawn. At the same time, the Black King has difficulty in attacking the h-pawn, needing three moves to approach it.

2. Kb1-c2	

With the pawns safe from capture, the White King has time to come to their aid.

2. ...	Kf5-g6

Black now threatens to win the h-pawn by 3. ... Kh5.

3. f3-f4!	Kg6-h5

3. ... Kf5 would be followed by 4. h5!.

4. f4-f5!	

The point. Now the h-pawn is immune from capture.

4. ...	Kh5-h6

The only move to stop the f-pawn from queening.

5. Kc2-d3	

With the pawns safe once more, the White King can continue its journey towards them to help them queen.

5. ...	Kh6-g7
6. h4-h5!	

Take note of this tactical device: the pawns stay abreast (i.e., on the same rank) as long as they are not under attack, but when one of them is attacked, the other advances to the same rank as the King.

6. ...	Kg7-f6
7. h5-h6	Kf6-f7
8. Kd3-e4	Kf7-f6
9. Ke4-f4	

A waiting move.

9. ...	Kf6-f7
10. Kf4-g5	Kf7-g8
11. f5-f6	Kg8-h8
12. f6-f7	Kh8-h7

Watch out, a trap!

13. Kg5-h5!	

A waiting move. 13. f8Q or 13. f8R would be stalemate. Now, however, Black is in Zugzwang and must move his King to the eighth rank.

13. ...	Kh7-h8
14. f7-f8Q+	

And mate next move.

We thus see that pawns separated by only a single file can defend each other **indirectly**, no matter where their King might be.

Two pawns of the same color on the same file are called **doubled pawns.** While, as you saw earlier, two pawns on neighboring files can easily defend each other, doubled pawns are unable to do so and are usually easy to attack.

HOMEWORK
(Answers at the end)

I. Use the tactical device of "pinning" in the solutions to Diagrams 315–320.

315

Find all the possible pins both with White to play and with Black to play.

_____

_____

_____

316

White to play. How can he win the Black Knight?

_____

_____

_____

317

White to play. How can he win the Black Knight?

_____

_____

_____

318

White to play. Find the best move.

_____

_____

_____

319

White to play and win a piece.

_____

_____

320

White to play and mate in two moves.

	WHITE	BLACK
1.		
2.		

II. Diagrams 321–326. In each position find a combination based on the tactical device of "pinning."

321

White to play and mate in two moves.

	WHITE	BLACK
1.		
2.		

322

White to play and mate in two moves.

	WHITE	BLACK
1.		
2.		

323

White to play. How can he win the Exchange?

_____

_____

_____

324

White to play. How can he win the Exchange?

_____

_____

_____

325

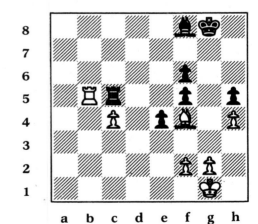

White to play and win a piece.

_____

_____

_____

326

White to play and win.

_____

_____

_____

III. In Diagrams 327-332 use the "rule of the square of the pawn" to find the solutions.

327

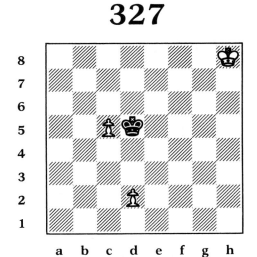

How should the game end with White to play? With Black to play?

_____

_____

_____

328

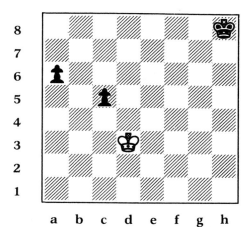

Can Black win if it is his turn to play? And if it is White's turn?

_____

_____

_____

329

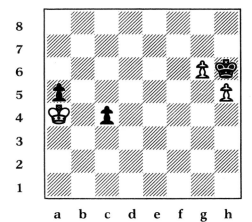

Find the draw both with White to play and with Black to play.

_____

_____

_____

330

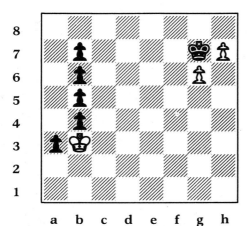

a b c d e f g h

Is it possible for this position to occur? How should the game end (whether it is White or Black to play)?

_____

_____

_____

331

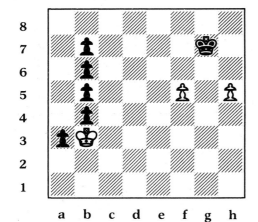

a b c d e f g h

Find the draw both with White to play and with Black to play.

_____

_____

_____

332

a b c d e f g h

Is it possible for this position to occur? Find the draw both with White to play and with Black to play.

_____

_____

_____

Answers to the Homework

D-315 _With White to play_ we can pin the Rook on d5 with **1. Be2-c4** or the Bishop on c7 with **1. Ra1-a7.**

With Black to play there are again two pins possible: **1. ... Bc7-b6,** pinning the Knight on c5, and **1. ... Rd5-d2,** pinning the Bishop on e2.

D-316

    1. Ra1-a4

A horizontal pin of the Knight.

    1. ...   **e7-e5**

    2. e2-e3

and the Knight is lost.

D-317

    1. Nc3-b5 + !   **u**

Neither the pawn on c6, pinned by the Rook, nor the Knight on d6, pinned by the Bishop, can capture the White Knight.

    2. Nb5xd6

winning the Knight.

D-318

    1. Bb5-c4!

and the Black Queen perishes because of the pin (Black ends up losing six points).

D-319

1. Rc1-c6!

The Black Bishop is pinned. White's task is to double Rooks along the c-file and at the same time keep the Black King from coming to the defense of the Bishop. Thus 1. Rc4 would not do because of 1. ... Kd6, defending the Bishop a second time.

1. ...   Ke5-d5

2. Rd1-c1

Defending the Rook on c6 and attacking the Bishop a second time. Black must lose a piece, as he cannot defend the Bishop with a second piece.

D-320

1. Qe4-g6!

This move is possible only because the pawn on f7 is pinned by the White Bishop.

1. ...   u

2. Qg6xg7#

D-321

1. Qf3xf7 + !

By sacrificing his Queen White deflects the Black Rook from the last rank and pins it.

1. ...   Rf8xf7

Or else 2. Qxf8# would follow.

2. Re1-e8#

The Black Rook is pinned and cannot cover its King.

D-322

1. Qf4-f6!

Threatening 2. Qg7#.

1. ...   e7xf6

Black is forced to accept the "gift," though the pawn on e7 is pinned by the White Rook.

2. Re1xe8#

Checkmate is worth more than the Queen!

D-323

1. Nc4-b6!

This Knight sacrifice clears the way for the White Bishop and at the same time forks the Black Queen and Rook.

1. ...   Qd7-d8

It goes without saying that accepting the sacrifice by 1. ... cxb6 would be worse because of 2. Bb5, pinning and winning the Black Queen.

2. Nb6xa8   Qd8xa8

and Black has lost the Exchange.

This example made use of two tactical devices: "double attack" and "pinning."

D-324

1. Qd3xd4!

Decoying the Black Queen onto d4.

1. ...   Qg7xd4

Forced.

2. Bd2-c3

A diagonal pin that dooms the Black Queen.

2. ...   Qd4xc3 +

3. b2xc3

As a result of his combination, White has exchanged the Queen and won the Exchange (a Rook for a Bishop).

D-325

1. Rb5-b8!

Pinning the Black Bishop and threatening to win it by 2. Bd6 or 2. Bh6.

1. ...   Kf8-f7

Now the Black Bishop is no longer pinned by the Rook on b8 and can move. White, however, can play a combination based on a "double attack."

2. Rb8xf8 + !   Kf7xf8

3. Bf4-d6 +   u

4. Bd6xc5

and White is up a Bishop.

D-326

1. Rf3xf6!

White's plan is to exchange off all the pieces and queen a pawn. To achieve his aim he makes use of the tactical device of "pinning" and the "rule of the square." It would be no good to play 1. Bxf6 Rxf6 2. Rxf6 Kxf6 3. b4 Ke6 4. b5 Kd6 5. b6 axb6 6. axb6 Kc6, and the Black King catches the pawn two moves before it can reach the queening square. White could instead try 6. a6 Kc7 7. a7 Kb7, and although again the Black King reaches the square of the a-pawn in time, the pawn is only *one* move short of queening.

1. ...   Rf7xf6

2. b3-b4!

The point! Since the Black Rook is pinned and cannot move, White does not hurry to capture it but first gains a tempo (a move, time).

2. ...   Kg7-f7

Black is forced to lose a move (tempo). 2. ... a6 would not save him, because of 3. b5! axb5 4. a6 and the pawn queens by force.

3. Bb2xf6

The Rook must be captured now or else it will run away.

3. ...	Kf7xf6
4. b4-b5	Kf6-e6
5. b5-b6	a7xb6
6. a5-a6!	

The only way! If 6. a5xb6, then 6. ... Ke6-d6 allows the Black King to reach the square of the pawn (b6-b8-d6-d8).

6. ...	Ke6-d6

Now the Black King cannot enter the square (a6-a8-c6-c8) and the pawn can queen.

7. a6-a7	Kd6-c6
8. a7-a8Q +	

and White should win. Black was just one move short of catching the pawn, the move that he had to lose because of the **pin** on his Rook.

D-327 *White to move wins.*

1. d2-d4!	Kd5-c6

1. ... Kxd4 would lose because the c-pawn would queen after 2. c6.

2. Kh8-g7	

The White King will join the pawns and help them queen.

Black to play draws:

1. ...	Kd5xc5

and the second pawn must perish too.

D-328 *Black to play wins:*

1. ...	a6-a5
2. Kd3-c4	a5-a4!
3. Kc4-c3	

If 3. Kxc5, the Black pawn cannot be stopped after 3. ... a3.

3. ...	Kh8-g7

When the pawns are safe, the King approaches.

4. Kc3-b2	

Now the pawn on a4 is in danger.

4. ...	c5-c4!
5. Kb2-a3	

If 5. Kc3, then 5. ... a3!.

5. ...	c4-c3!

The pawn on c3 indirectly defends the other pawn, as 6. Kxa4 would be followed by 6. ... c2 and the queening of the pawn.

6. Ka3-a2	Kg7-f6
7. Ka2-a3	

7. Kb1 loses immediately, as after 7. ... a3 one of the pawns must queen.

7. ...	Kf6-e5

The Black pawns are absolutely safe, but they cannot queen without the help of their King. So the King goes to them.

If White starts in Diagram 328, he can draw easily:

1. Kd3-c4	a6-a5
2. Kc4xc5	

and since the King is in the square of the pawn (a1-a5-e1-e5) it will eliminate the second pawn too.

D-329 The game should be drawn no matter who moves first. For example:

1. Ka4-a3	

Of course, taking the pawn is a no-no since it would put the King outside the square of the other pawn.

1. ...	Kh6-g7

For the same reason the Black King too cannot capture the pawn.

2. Ka3-a4	

If 2. Kb2, then 2. ... a4 again makes the Black pawns invulnerable.

2. ...	Kg7-h6

Draw! The Kings can keep a watch on the enemy pawns but not capture them. Nor can either players push his pawns without losing. For example, if Black played 2. ... c3, he would lose after 3. Kb3.

D-330 Such a position will hardly ever occur in a game, but it is *theoretically* possible. For example, the pawn from e7 could have got to b4 by making three captures: 1. ... e7xd6, 2. ... d6xc5, 3. ... c5xb4. By continuing in this vein, we can see that Black must have made a total of six pawn captures to reach this position, and that is possible since White has lost men.

The position is a draw because the Kings can ward off the enemy pawns but cannot capture any one of them without leaving the square of another. The White King will shuttle back and forth between a2 and b3 and the Black King between g7 and h8.

D-331 This too is a draw, the only difference being that the Black King must now shuttle back and forth between f6 and f7 or h6 and h7. For example:

1. ...	Kg7-f6
2. h5-h6	Kf6-f7
3. Kb3-a2	Kf7-f6
4. Ka2-b3	

Draw.

D-332 This position is possible only theoretically and would not occur in a game. Thirteen men have disappeared from the board, and that is exactly the number of pawn captures that White had to make to get to this position.

Once again, the result should be a draw, as the Kings can stop the enemy pawns from queening but cannot capture them. For example:

>   **1. h4-h5**   **Kh7-h6!**

The only move. All other moves lose: e.g., after 1. ... Kg8 2. h6, Black is in Zugzwang and must let one of the White pawns queen.

>   **2. h3-h4**   **Kh6-h7**

Naturally the King cannot leave the f6-f8-h6-h8 square.

>   **3. f6-f7**   **Kh7-g7**
>   **4. h5-h6 +**   **Kg7xf7**

The pawn sacrifice has not achieved anything.

>   **5. Ka1-b2**   **Kf7-f6!**

Again the only move. If 5. ...Kf8, then 6. f6 Kg8 7. f5 and Black loses due to Zugzwang.

>   **6. Kb2-a1**   **Kf6-f7!**

Draw.

SUPPLEMENTARY MATERIAL

for use at the teacher's discretion

Fighting Against a Pin

The fewest opportunities for unpinning (escaping from a pin) occur when a piece is pinned against its King, i.e., if the pin is "absolute." The following **tactical devices** for unpinning are possible in such cases:

1. **Chasing away** the pinning piece.
2. **Interposing** a man between the pinning piece and the King.

For example, let us look at Diagram 333.

333

Black to play is faced with the threat of d4-d5, attacking the pinned Knight with a pawn. Black can defend by 1. ... Bc8-d7, **interposing** on the a4-e8 diagonal and thus **unpinning** the Knight.

But he can also play 1. ... Bc8-g4, since 2. d4-d5 can be parried by 2. ... a7-a6 3. Bb5-a4 b7-b5, **chasing away** the Bishop from the a4-e8 diagonal and thereby **unpinning** the Knight.

3. **Pinning** the pinning piece.

For example, let us look at Diagram 334.

334

Can Black to play save his Queen?

Yes, he can, by 1. ... Bd7-c6!, pinning the White Bishop along the h1-a8 diagonal and thus saving the Black Queen.

4. Playing an **in-between check.**

For example, look at Diagram 335.

335

Can White to play win the Black Queen?

Yes. This position differs from the last one in that the White Queen is on g1, a circumstance which allows the White King to be moved away with **discovered check:**

1. Kg2-f2 + !

The White Bishop could not capture the Black Queen because it was pinned along the h1-a8 diagonal. The King move **unpins** the Bishop and at the same time unblocks the g-file, allowing the White Queen to give an **in-between check.** The Black King must move out of check and then White can capture the Queen.

5. Eliminating the pinning piece.

For example, look at Diagram 336.

336

The Knight on f3 is pinned and attacked twice. How can White to play escape from the pin?

By the following combination:
1. Rh4xg4!
Unpinning the White Knight by eliminating the pinning piece.
1. ...   h5xg4
1. ... Nxf3 would be even worse because of the fork 2. Rf4 +.
2. Nf3xd4
As a result, White has won a Knight and Bishop for a Rook (i.e., he had made a net gain of one point.)

6. Moving the King out of the pin with the concurrent creation of strong threats.

See Diagram 337.

337

Can White to play save his piece?

Yes, he can. He must temporarily sacrifice his Knight on c3 but he can then win back a piece by making use of the idea of "double attack."
1. Ke1-e2!
The King gets out of the pin, thereby unpinning the Knight.
1. ...   Ba5xc3
Or else the Knight on c3 can run away.
2. Ke2-d3!
Both Black pieces are under attack and one of them must perish. The net result will be that White and Black have exchanged pieces of equal value.

7. Creating counter-threats.

See Diagram 338.

338

Can White to play win the Black Queen?

No, because 1. Bc4-b5? can be met by the powerful counterstroke 1. ... Na5-b3 + . Taking advantage of the fact that the pawn on c2 is pinned along the file, Black forks the White King and Queen. After 2. ... Nb3xd4 3. Bb5xc6 + Nd4xc6 Black will have won a piece.

If a piece is pinned not against the King but against some other piece, the pin is a **relative** one and additional methods of unpinning become possible:

1. Moving the pinned piece with check.

See Diagram 339.

339

Is 1. Rg1-e1 a good move?

No, because Black can sacrifice his Rook

with check and at the same time attack the White Queen with his own:

    1. ...   Re3xa3 + !
    2. b2xa3   Qg5xd2

and Black has won a Queen and pawn for a Rook.

2. Moving the pinned piece with strong threats.

See Diagram 340.

340

Can White to play save his pinned Knight?

Yes.

    1. Ne5-g4!

Sacrificing the Rook against which the Knight was pinned. However, the Knight has unpinned itself with a strong threat.

    1. ...   **Re8xe2?**

Black's best reply is 1. ... Ne6.

    2. Ng4-h6#

Checkmate is worth more than a Rook!

3. Moving the piece shielded by the pinned piece, either with check or with strong threats.

See Diagram 341.

135

341

Can Black to play unpin his Rook?

Yes, in two ways.

a)   1. ...   Qf7-g6 +

The Queen gets out of the pin and at the same time gives an **in-between check**, thereby **unpinning** the Black Rook.

b)   1. ...   Qf7-f6

The Queen gets out of the pin and attacks the White Rook.

    2. Bb3xd5   **Qf6xa1**

The net result is an exchange of Rooks.

4.   Moving the pinned piece to a square where it defends the piece it was pinned against.

    See Diagram 342.

342

White to play. How does he win a pawn?

    1. Nc3xe4!

The Knight gets out of the pin and at the same time defends the Bishop that it was pinned against.

    1. ...   **Bb4xd2**

    If 1. ... Nxe4, then 2. Bxb4.

    2. Ne4xd2

and White has won a pawn as a result of his combination.

Game 55

Center Counter Defense

    1. e2-e4   **d7-d5**

    2. e4xd5   **Qd8xd5**

    3. Nb1-c3

This shows up the drawback of the Center Counter Defense. White brings out his Knight and attacks the Black Queen at the same time, forcing Black to lose a move (tempo) by retreating the Queen. The usual move here for Black is 3. ... Qa5, although even then it is somewhat more pleasant to be playing White.

    3. ...   **Qd5-c6??**

A gross blunder.

    4. Bf1-b5

Black resigns, as the pin will cost him his Queen. See Diagram 343 for the final position.

343

Game 56
Petroff's Defense

    1. e2-e4   **e7-e5**

    2. Ng1-f3   **Ng8-f6**

    3. Bf1-c4

White sacrifices a pawn to develop his pieces as rapidly as possible.

3. ...	Nf6xe4
4. Nb1-c3	Ne4xc3
5. d2xc3	d7-d6
6. 0-0	Bc8-g4?

He had to play 6. ... Be7 and then castle.

7. Nf3xe5!

The Knight breaks out of the pin and puts its Queen under attack. This combination is possible because the Knight creates mating threats.

7. ...	Bg4xd1

Other replies, too, lose for Black. E.g., 7 ... dxe5 8. Bxf7 + Kxf7 (if 8. ... Ke7, then 9. Bg5 +) 9. Qxd8, or 7. ... Be6 8. Bxe6 fxe6 9. Qh5 + g6 (or 9. ... Ke7 10. Qf7#) 10. Nxg6 hxg6 11. Qxh8.

8. Bc4xf7 +	Ke8-e7
9. Bc1-g5#	

See Diagram 344 for the final position.

344

In this game too the "pin" brought nothing but disenchantment.

Game 57
Center Counter Defense

1. e2-e4	d7-d5
2. e4xd5	Ng8-f6

Black plays a gambit. He disregards the pawn and instead quickly brings out his pieces.

3. c2-c4

A dubious move. Instead of being greedy, White would do better to bring out his pieces.

3. ...	c7-c6
4. d5xc6	

Another mistake. It was not too late to get an even game with 4. d4 cxd5 4. Nc3. White, however, is very keen on having an extra pawn.

4. ...	Nb8xc6

5. d2-d3	e7-e5

Black's position is better in spite of White's extra pawn.

6. Nb1-c3	Bf8-c5
7. Bc1-g5?	

He had to develop his Kingside with 7. Be2 and castle at the first opportunity.

7. ...	0-0
8. Nc3-e4??	

A suicidal move. Legal died a very long time ago, but his idea is immortal.

8. ...	Nf6xe4!
9. Bg5xd8	

If 8. dxe4, then 8. ... Qxg5 leaves Black a piece up.

9. ...	Bc5xf2 +
10. Ke1-e2	Nc6-d4#

See Diagram 345 for the final position.

345

Game 58
Falkbeer–Amateur, Vienna 1847
Scotch Gambit

1. e2-e4	e7-e5
2. Ng1-f3	Nb8-c6
3. d2-d4	

This is the Scotch Game.

3. ...	e5xd4
4. Bf1-c4	

When White doesn't retake the pawn on d4, the opening becomes the Scotch Gambit.

4. ..	d7-d6
5. c2-c3	

White sacrifices a pawn but brings out his pieces quickly.

| 5. ... | d4xc3 |
| 6. Nb1xc3 | Bc8-g4 |

An unfortunate move to which the best reply is 7. Qb3. Black should have played 6. ...Nf6 or 6. ... Be6.

| 7. 0-0 | Nc6-e5?? |

He had to play 7. ... Bxf3 8. Qxf3 Ne5 9. Qe2 Nxc4 10. Qxc4 Qd7, although even in this variation White has good play for his pawn.

| 8. Nf3xe5! |

Once again the great Legal's mate!

| 8. ... | Bg4xd1 |
| 9. Bc4xf7 + | Ke8-e7 |
| 10. Nc3-d5# |

See Diagram 346 for the final position.

346

Game 59
Nimzo-Indian Defense

| 1. d2-d4 | Ng8-f6 |

The Knight controls e4 and prevents White from playing 2. e4.

| 2. c2-c4 | e7-e6 |
| 3. Nb1-c3 |

The Knight attacks e4 and White now threatens 4. e4.

| 3. ... | Bf8-b4 |

This is the key move of the Nimzo-Indian Defense, named after the outstanding grandmaster Aron Nimzovich. The Bishop pins the Knight and thus prevents 4. e4. The Knight on c3 is paralyzed by an **absolute** pin.

| 4. Qd1-c2 | c7-c5 |
| 5. d4xc5 | Bb4xc5 |
| 6. Bc1-g5? |

Now the White Bishop pins the Black Knight, but the pin is a **relative** one since

under certain circumstances the Knight can break out of the pin even if it means exposing the Queen.

| 6. ... | Bc5xf2 +! |

This is the combination that White did not notice. The Bishop sacrifices itself in order to decoy the White King onto f2.

| 7. Ke1xf2 | Nf6-g4 + |

The Knight breaks out of the pin with check, and at the same time the Black Queen attacks the White Bishop.

| 8. Kf2-e1 | Qd8xg5 |

See Diagram 347.

347

The Bishop which was pinning the Knight has perished. Black has won a pawn and has chances of winning. As you can see, pinning does not always lead to success.

Game 60

| 1. e2-e4 | c7-c6 |

This is the Caro-Kann Defense, named in honor of two 19th century German chessplayers.

| 2. d2-d4 | d7-d5 |

The White pawns have occupied the center, but Black immediately attacks them.

3. Nb1-c3	d5xe4
4. Nc3xe4	Nb8-d7
5. Bf1-c4	Ng8-f6
6. Ne4xf6 +	Nd7xf6

Now you can understand why Black played 4. ...Nbd7: in order to have the opportunity of replying here with 6. ... Nxf6.

| 7. Ng1-f3 | Bc8-g4? |

In his eagerness to pin the Knight, Black

overlooks that White can play the following combination: 8. Bxf7 + ! Kxf7 9. Ne5 + Ke8 10. Nxg4, and White is a pawn up with an excellent position. White saw this combination, but he wanted more.

8. Nf3-e5?

A poor trap, based solely on the possibility 8. ... Bxd1 9. Bxf7#.

9. ...   **Qd8-a5 + !**

This in-between check was a surprise for White.

10. Bc1-d2   **Qa5xe5 + !**

A fresh surprise and again an in-between check.

11. d4xe5   **Bg4xd1**
12. Ra1xd1   **Nf6-d5**

See Diagram 348.

348

a b c d e f g h

White does not have even a single extra pawn. Needless to say, he should not have let himself be tempted by an unsound trap, pretty though it might have been.

Game 61
Brikhta–Botur, Budapest 1951
Giuoco Piano

1. e2-e4   **e7-e5**
2. Ng1-f3   **Nb8-c6**
3. Bf1-c4   **Bf8-c5**

These moves constitute the Giuoco Piano, an opening which was very popular in Italy as far back as 500 years ago!

4. c2-c3

Controlling a central square and preparing to play d4.

4. ...   **Bc5-b6**

More often Black plays 4. ... Nf6, developing another piece.

5. d2-d4   **Qd8-e7**

In this particular position it is not dangerous for Black to bring out his Queen since the White pieces will find it difficult to attack it.

6. 0-0

6. d5 would be bad, since the pawn would block its own Bishop while the Black Knight would simply retreat to d8.

6. ...   **d7-d6**

Some of you might be thinking that Black could have won a pawn, but in reality he couldn't have! The reason is that 6. ... exd4 7. cxd4 Qxe4 would be followed by 8. Re1, pinning and winning the Black Queen.

7. Nf3-g5

The usual continuation is 7. h3, forestalling the pin 7. ... Bg4 and thus making the pawn on d4 more secure.

7. ...   **Ng8-h6**
8. Bc1-e3   **0-0**

After 8. ... exd4 9. cxd4 Nxd4 10. Nxf7 (if 10. Bxd4, then 10. ... Qxg5) Nxf7 11. Bxd4 White's game is more comfortable.

9. f2-f4?

A premature move. White had to play 9. h3, keeping the Black Knight out of g4.

9. ...   **e5xd4**
10. c3xd4   **Nh6-g4**
11. f4-f5

White is forced to take this desperate step since no way to defend the pawn on d4 can be seen.

11. ...   **Ng4xe3**
12. Qd1-h5

Threatening 13. Qxh7#.

12. ...   **h7-h6??**

He had to sacrifice his Queen by 12. ... Qxg5. After 13. Qxg5 Bxd4! (but not 13. ... Nxc4, because of 14. f6 g6 15. Qh6) 14. f6 Nxf1 + 15. Kxf1 Bxf6, White would have had to pay for his overly venturesome play. As it is, however, White beautifully refutes Black's gross blunder.

13. f5-f6!

Destroying Black's castled position.

13. ...   **Bc8-g4**

After 13. ... gxf6 Black would be mated in two moves: 14. Qg6 + Kh8 15. Qh7#.

14. Qh5-g6!

See Diagram 349.

349

White threatens both 15. Qh7# and 15. Qxg7#. Since the pinned pawn on f7 cannot help, Black resigns.

Game 62
Steinitz–Amateur, Berlin 1863

Wilhelm Steinitz was the first official World Chess Champion, reigning from 1886 to 1894. In this game he played without his Rook on a1.

Vienna Game

1. e2-e4	e7-e5
2. Nb1-c3	Nb8-c6
3. f2-f4	

White sacrifices a pawn in order to seize the center and quickly develop his pieces.

3. ...	e5xf4
4. Ng1-f3	Bf8-b4

An unfortunate move that allows White to set up a powerful center.

5. Nc3-d5	Bb4-a5
6. Nd5xf4	d7-d6
7. c2-c3	Ba5-b6
8. d2-d4	

White has a strong pawn center while Black's Bishop has moved three times and still ended up poorly placed.

8. ...	Bc8-g4
9. Bf1-b5	

Steinitz pins the Knight and threatens to win it by 10. d5.

9. ...	Ke8-f8?

A poor method of breaking the pin. It would have been better to move the Bishop back to d7.

10. 0-0	Nc6-e5?

Black makes a "pretty" but losing move. He wants to exchange on f3 and thereby close the dangerous f-file. However, he has miscalculated. While the pawn on d4 is pinned absolutely, for it shields the King, the Knight on f3, although it too is pinned by a Bishop;, nevertheless has the right to move:

11. Nf3xe5!	Bg4xd1??

How the hand itches to grab the Queen! However, Black should resist the temptation and instead play 11. ... dxe5 12. Qxg4 exf4.

12. Nf4-g6 +	h7xg6
13. Ne5xg6#	

See Diagram 350.

350

Black forgot that his pawn on f7 would be pinned by the Rook. White has few pieces left but they are working. Black, on the other hand, has many pieces, but they are sleeping.

Game 63
Alekhine–Mikulka, Paris 1928
King's Gambit

1. e2-e4	e7-e5
2. f2-f4	

This is the King's Gambit, a popular opening in the 19th century. White sacrifices a pawn in order to seize the center and rapidly mobilize his pieces.

2. ...	e5xf4

The challenge is accepted!

3. Ng1-f3	

This game was played by World Champion Alekhine in a simultaneous blindfold exhibition.

| 3. ... | g7-g5 |
| 4. d2-d4 | h7-h6 |

Black could also play more aggressively with 4. ... g4, which could be met by the Knight sacrifice 5. Bc4 gxf3 6. Qxf3, with chances for both sides.

5. Nb1-c3	Bf8-g7
6. Bf1-c4	Nb8-c6
7. Nc3-d5	d7-d6

On 7. ... g4 Alekhine would have probably continued with 8. c3 (it was for this reason that he played 7. Nd5) gxf3 9. Qxf3, with an attack for the sacrificed piece.

8. c2-c3	Ng8-e7
9. 0-0	Ne7xd5
10. Bc4xd5	Nc6-e7

Being a pawn up, Black tries to exchange off the active White pieces.

| 11. Bd5-b3 | Ne7-g6 |
| 12. g2-g3 | |

White tries to open the f-file and organize an attack against the pawn on f7.

| 12. ... | f4xg3? |

12. ... g4 13. Ne1 f3, keeping the f-file closed, was worthy of consideration. The world champion would probably have sacrificed his Knight by 14. Nxf3 gxf3 15. Qxf3, with a very sharp and unclear position.

13. Nf3xg5!

With the threat of 14. Bxf7 + .

| 13. ... | 0-0 |
| 14. Qd1-h5 | |

14. Nxf7 could have been met by 14. ... Qh4, with the threat of 15. ... Qxh2#.

| 14. ... | g3xh2 + |
| 15. Kg1-h1! | |

After 15. Kxh2 the White King would have been totally exposed, while now it is shielded and protected by the Black pawn.

| 15. ... | h6xg5 |
| 16. Qh5xg6 | |

This move is possible only because the pawn on f7 is pinned by the Bishop on b3.

| 16. ... | Qd8-e8? |

Black defends the pawn on f7 a third time. However, a better chance would have been 16. ... d5, unpinning the pawn on f7. White cannot play 17. Bxd5 because Black would eliminate the pinning Bishop by 17. ... Qxd5 and then capture the White Queen. Instead White must reply with 17. Qh5, maintaining the attack.

17. Bc1xg5

Yet another piece joins the attack against the Black King.

| 17. ... | Bc8-e6 |

Alekhine's opponent thinks that by blocking the diagonal of the Bishop on b3 he has warded off all the threats: a retreat of the White Queen would be followed by 18. ... Bxb3 and 19. ... Qxe4 + , while after 18. Bxe6 Qxe6 the attack has been beaten off. However, he has not noticed the world champion's brilliant combination:

| 18. Rf1xf7! | Be6xf7? |

After 18. ... Rxf7 19. Bxe6 Black would end up "only" a pawn down in an endgame: 19. ... Kf8 20. Bxf7 Qxf7 21. Qxf7 + Kxf7 22. Kxh2. As it is, however, pins by the White Bishops do him in.

19. Bg5-f6!
See Diagram 351.

351

In order to counter the threat of 20. Qxg7#, Black is forced to give up his Queen by 19. ... Qxe4 + , but after 20. Qxe4 Bxf6 21. Bc2 White would have a material advantage while retaining his attack. So Black resigned.

Game 64
Sangla–Karpov, U.S.S.R. 1968

| 1. d2-d4 | Ng8-f6 |

Black was played by 17-year-old Anatoly Karpov.

2. Ng1-f3	e7-e6
3. Bc1-g5	c7-c5
4. c2-c3	

An unfortunate move. White's usual con-

tinuation in this variation is 4. e3, and if 4. ...
Qb6, then 5. Nbd2, sacrificing the pawn on b2.

| 4. ... | c5xd4 |
| 5. c3xd4 | Qd8-b6 |

The Queen attacks the pawn on b2 and at the
same time unpins the Knight on f6.

| 6. Qd1-b3 | Nf6-e4 |
| 7. Bg5-f4 | |

After 7. Qxb6 axb6 8. Bf4 Nc6 Black's position is a trifle better because his Rook controls
the a-file.

7. ...	Nb8-c6
8. e2-e3	Bf8-b4 +
9. Nb1-d2?	

Of course pieces must be developed, but in
the present situation White had to interpose
the other Knight (9. Nfd2). The Knight on d2 is
pinned and attacked twice. Although it is also
defended twice, Black now removes one of the
defenders by force.

| 9. ... | g7-g5! |

A combination based on the tactical devices
of "pinning" and "double attack."

| 10. Bf4xg5 | |

After 10. Be5 f6 11. Bg3 g4 White would lose
a piece.

| 10. ... | Bb4xd2 + |

See Diagram 352.

352

After 11. Nxd2 the Bishop on g5 would be
undefended, allowing the double attack 11. ...
Qa5, forking the Bishop on g5 and the Knight
on d2 (but not 11. ... Nxg5, because of 12. h4,
winning the Knight on g5). So White resigned.

Lesson Nine

A. Check Lesson 8 Homework (as necessary).

B. *Review Questions*

In the positions shown on Diagrams 353-358, it is White's turn to play. Find his best continuation in each case. Solve the exercises directly from the diagrams, without setting up the men on a board.

353

354

355

356

357

358

Find the solutions to Diagrams 359-364 directly from the diagrams, without setting up the men on a board.

359

White to play and win a piece.

360

White to play. Find a combination.

361

Black to play. How can he get rid of the pin?

362

White to play. Can he save his Knight?

144

363

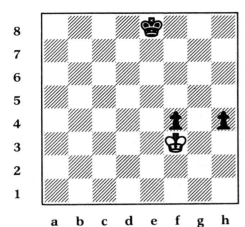

Black to play. How should the game end?

364

Black to play. Can he win?

Answers to Review Questions

D-353 1. Ng5-e6#

D-354 1. Qc3xg7#

D-355 1. Qb3-f7#

D-356 1. Rd1-d4#

D-357

1. Qc1-h6 + Kh8-g8 2. Qh6xg7#

D-358

1. Qe5xg7 + Qg8xg7 2. Re1-e8#

D-359

1. Nf3xd4 Bg4xe2 2. Nd4xe2!,remaining a piece up. If 1. ... exd4, then by 2. Bxg4 White still wins a piece.

D-360

1. Nf3xe5!

The Legal's mate idea.

| 1. ... | Bg4xd1 |

If 1. ... dxe5, then Black loses a piece after 2. Qxg4.

| 2. Bc4xf7 + | Ke8-e7 |
| 3. Nc3-d5# | |

D-361

| 1. ... | Rb6-b1 + |

With this move Black not only gets rid of the pin but also wins a piece.

| 2. Kg1-f2 | Bb7xe4 |
| 3. Rb8xb1 | |

If 3. fxe4, then the Rook is lost by 3. ... Rxb8.

| 3. ... | Be4xb1 |

D-362

1. Bg5-d2!

Only with this move can White save the Knight. 1. Rc1 and 1. Kd2 do not work, because of 2. ... d4, winning the Knight. After 1. Bg5-d2!, however, the Bishop has not only defended the Knight but also shielded the King.

| 1. ... | d5-d4 |
| 2. Nc3-e2 | |

and so on.

D-363 Black wins after

| 1. ... | h4-h3 |
| 2. Kf3-f2 | |

Capturing the pawn on f4 would put the King outside the square of the pawn on h3, which would then go on to queen.

| 2. ... | Ke8-e7 |
| 3. Kf2-g1 | |

If the King returned to f3, the Black King would join its pawns and help them to queen.

| 3. ... | f4-f3 |
| 4. Kg1-h2 | |

4. Kf2 would meet with the decisive reply 4. ... h2, followed by queening.

| 4. ... | f3-f2 |

and so on.

D-364 Black wins after

| 1. ... | g7-g5 |

Now White cannot touch the Black pawns.

| 2. Kg4-f3 | |

Taking the pawn on g5 would put the King outside the square of the pawn on f4, which would then queen.

| 2. ... | Ka4-b4 |

The King approaches its pawns to help them queen.

The Skewer

The tactical device known as the skewer occurs very often in games. As in a pin, three pieces take part in a skewer.

365

In a pin (Diagram 365), the pinned piece must shield a more valuable piece that is behind it.

366

In a skewer (Diagram 366), however, a piece, usually an important one such as the King, the Queen, or a Rook, has to move off a line when attacked by a Queen, Rook, or Bishop, leaving the piece behind it exposed to capture.

Let us look at some examples. In Diagrams 367–372 find the best continuation. Use the "skewer" tactical device. Solve the problems directly from the diagrams, without setting up the men on a board.

367

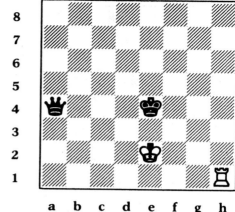

White to play.

368

White to play.

369

White to play.

370

Black to play.

371

White to play.

372

White to play.

How Combinations are Created

As you already know, a combination is a forced variation containing a sacrifice and designed to achieve a definite aim (checkmate, win of material, draw in an inferior position, etc.) Combinations can occur both in attack and in defense, and in the opening as well as in the middlegame or endgame. A successfully conducted combination is a source of great pleasure to a chessplayer and remains in his memory for a long time.

However, combinations are not possible in

all positions, and no one can say *a priori* whether a given position contains a combination or not. We must learn to **find** and **create** combinations that we can use and also to **find** and **disrupt** our opponents' combinations.

Every combination consists of three elements — the situation, the idea, and the goal.

The situation is the position of certain White and Black men that warns us, "Be careful, a combination might be possible!" The possibility of a combination usually arises when a position contains some weakness such as an undefended piece, a pinned piece, an exposed King or, conversely, a smothered King, etc. A material advantage too can sometimes serve as the basis of a combination.

The idea is the method used in carrying out a combination. For example, the tactical devices of "double attack," "pinning," and "skewer" are combinational ideas.

The goal is the desired result of the combination, e.g., the win of a piece, checkmate, or stalemate.

During a game, many interesting conceptions, ideas, and combinations will occur to a player. They must be verified and the impractical ones discarded. Sometimes a player thinks along the following lines: "If it weren't for . . . , I could set up a beautiful fork", etc. Often we come to the conclusion that a combination is not possible in a given position. Sometimes, however, one of the ideas turns out to be practical and we have our combination!

Before beginning a combination, a player must have a clear picture of the **final position** in his mind.

Chessplayers usually do not memorize individual positions, but they firmly commit to memory the **ideas** behind various combinations. The reason is that a given arrangement of men on the board might not be repeated (although even that does happen sometimes!) but the ideas of the combinations are repeated time and time again. Strong players know hundreds or sometimes even thousands of **ideas.** During a game they mentally construct numerous positions that could occur in the game and in which combinations might be possible, and at the same time they try to **discover** the **ideas** of the opponent in order to **counteract** them. Sometimes just a "little"

pawn (your own or your opponent's) stands in the way of some fine combination. While analyzing some game played by world champions, you might sometimes think, "How boringly they play! Not a single combination in the whole game." Such a conclusion would be erroneous. Many ideas and combinations run through the minds of strong players during a game, but each of the two players guesses the thoughts of the other and prevents him from putting them into practice.

There are also numerous **unsound** (incorrect) combinations. These occur when a player sacrifices material without noticing some strong reply by the opponent.

It is of course always painful to lose, especially if you had a winning position. However, a player **always has only himself to blame** for his losses.

It is not the end of the world if you make mistakes, but it **is** bad if you **repeat** them. That is why every time you lose you must find out the **reason** for the loss and try not to repeat the mistake.

A player can develop his combinative abilities by **studying the various tactical devices**, by getting to know the games of masters and grandmasters, and by analysing his own games.

Now try your hand at making combinations based on the "skewer" tactical device. Set up positions 373–378 on a board and in each case find the strongest combination.

373

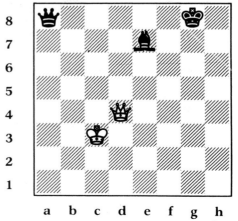

Black to play.

374

8
7
6
5
4
3
2
1

a b c d e f g h

White to play.

375

8
7
6
5
4
3
2
1

a b c d e f g h

White to play.

376

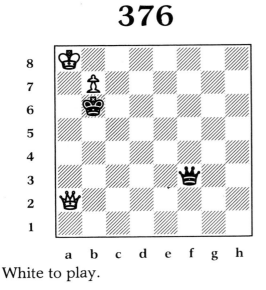

8
7
6
5
4
3
2
1

a b c d e f g h

White to play.

377

8
7
6
5
4
3
2
1

a b c d e f g h

White to play.

378

8
7
6
5
4
3
2
1

a b c d e f g h

White to play.

Answers

D-373 What is there in this position that suggests that a combination might be present? Well, the White King and Queen are on the same diagonal, a1-h8, and we could employ the "skewer" tactical device by playing 1. Qa1 + . However, the White King would move to c4 or d3, defending the Queen. Obviously, such an approach will not bring us victory. Thinking some more, however, we are struck by the idea that it would be nice if the White King and Queen were on the same diagonal, but at some distance from each other. And then we find the combination that helps us do this:

    1. ...   **Be7-f6!**

The Bishop is sacrificed with the idea of drawing the White Queen away from the King while keeping them on the same a1-h8 diagonal.

2. Qd4xf6

Forced, because of the pin.

  2. ...   **Qa8-a1 +**

Now this move wins the game.

  3. u   **Qa1xf6**

Black has won a Queen for a Bishop (six points).

D-374 A look at the position shows us that the Black King and Queen are on the same file, namely the b-file. This suggests the idea of a combination. However, the skewering move 1. Qb3 + does not lead to the desired result since the Queen on b6 is defended by the King, a Rook, and a pawn. How can we **deflect** the Black Queen from b6 while keeping it on the b-file?

  1. Rg8-b8!

A familiar idea! The Rook is sacrificed.

  1. ...   **Qb6xb8**

Forced, because of the pin.

  2. Qh3-b3 +

Now the skewer winds up the combination.

  2. ...   **u**

  3. Qb3xb8

White has won the Queen for a Rook (four points).

D-375 We notice here that the Black King and Queen are both on the 7th rank, a fact which tells us that under certain circumstances a combination might be possible. That is, if White could employ the skewer on the seventh rank, Black would lose his undefended Queen. We find the move 1. Qh7 +, but h7 is controlled by the Black Bishop. However, we should not let that scare us. Rather, we should count up how many points we will be sacrificing and how many we will be winning. Only after this simple calculation should we decide on our move.

  1. Qh2-h7 + !

Such a sacrifice is called a **temporary** Queen sacrifice.

  1. ...   **Bg6xh7**

  2. Rh1xh7 +   **u**

  3. Rh7xa7

As a result of the combination, White has exchanged Queens and won a Bishop (three points).

D-376 The pawn wants to queen, but it is pinned by the Black Queen and there does not

seem any way to unpin it. There is, in fact, a combination that will decide the outcome of the struggle, but to be able to play it we must be acquainted with the following tactical devices: double attack, decoying, anti-pinning methods, pawn promotion, and, finally, the skewer.

  1. Qa2-b3 +

This move makes use of three ideas:

  1. The White Queen **forks** the Black King and Queen.

  2. The Black Queen is **decoyed** onto the b-file.

  3. The pawn is **unpinned.**

  1. ...   **Qf3xb3**

Forced.

  2. b7-b8Q +

A move containing two ideas: queening the pawn and skewering the Black King and Queen.

  2. ...   **u**

  3. Qb8xb3

Naturally White decided upon the **temporary** Queen sacrifice only after visualizing the **final position**, in which he is a Queen up.

D-377 Looking at the position, we notice that the Black King and Queen are on the same file, a fact that would make the skewer possible under certain conditions. In particular, if we removed the Bishop from the board then Qd8 + would win the Black Queen. So what we have to do is to somehow **deflect** the Black Bishop from d5.

  1. Nf2xe4 + !

The Knight sacrifices itself so that the combination can be carried out. The move contains two ideas: forking and deflection.

  1. ...   **Bd5xe4**

Forced.

  2. Qh4-d8 + !

Now the skewer decides the outcome.

  2. ...   **u**

  3. Qd8xd2

As a result of the combination, White has won a Queen and a pawn for a Knight (10 − 3 = 7 points).

D-378 What strikes our attention here is the line-up of the three Black pieces and the White Rook on the e-file. As a result, we are led to look for a combination based on the skewering idea.

1. Re1xe4!

An Exchange sacrifice with the idea of **decoying** the Black Queen onto e4.

1. ...   Qe7xe4

Or else Black would be a Knight down.

2. Rf1-e1

A skewer that wins material. Note that if there had not been a Black pawn on c6 or on f7 the Black Queen could now have defended the Rook by 2. ... Qc6 or 2. ... Qg6. Or if the Rook on e8 had been defended by another piece in addition to the Queen, White's combination would again have been impossible.

2. ...   Qe4xe1 +

With this move Black ends up losing a Queen and a Knight for two Rooks (12 – 10 = 2 points), while if the Queen had moved away, then after 3. Rxe8 + the net result would have been that a pair of Rooks had been exchanged and Black had lost a Knight (three points).

3. Nf3xe1

Endgames with King and Rook Pawn Against Lone King

An extra pawn in the endgame often makes it possible to win the game. However, there are also positions in which an extra pawn is not enough for victory. Chessplayers at all levels should have a firm knowledge of what fate awaits a given extra pawn: will it become a Queen or won't it? For this purpose, a player must know which positions are **won positions** and which ones are **drawn positions.**

The most difficult pawns to queen are the Rook pawns. Let us look at some examples. Set up each of the positions in Diagrams 379–384 on a board.

379

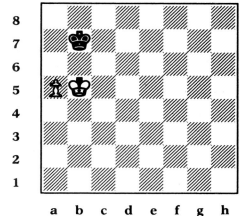

Drawn with either player to move.

380

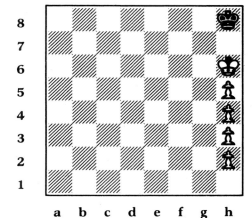

Drawn with either player to move.

381

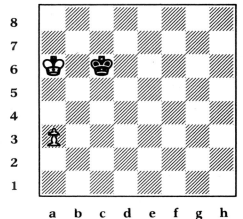

Drawn with either player to move.

382

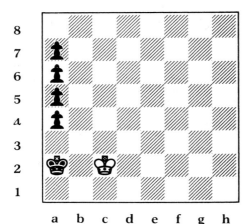

Drawn with either player to move.

383

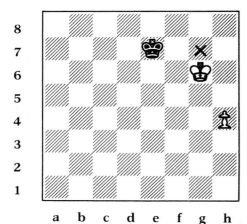

White to play wins; Black to play draws.

384

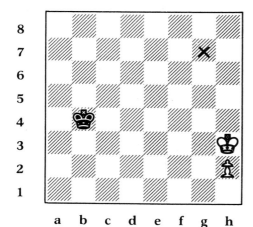

White to play wins; Black to play draws.

D-379 If the King of the weaker side is (or can get) in the way of the Rook pawn (*i.e.,* onto one of the squares in front of it), the game is always drawn.

1. a5-a6 +	Kb7-a7
2. Kb5-a5	Ka7-a8
3. Ka5-b6	Ka8-b8
4. a6-a7 +	Kb8-a8
5. Kb6-a6	Stalemate!

This is the whole point. If the weaker side's King does not lose touch with the corner square, stalemate always occurs.

D-380 You already know that by reaching the corner square in front of an enemy Rook pawn, a King can stop it from queening. In this example, Black draws in the same manner as the last one, even though here the White King is in front of its pawns.

1. Kh6-g6	Kh8-g8
2. h5-h6	Kg8-h8

Nobody can make the Black King abandon h8.

3. h4-h5	Kh8-g8
4. h3-h4	

White has four pawns on the h-file but they cannot win. It would have been better to have just a single extra pawn, but on a different file.

4. ...	Kg8-h8
5. h6-h7	Stalemate

The draw was unavoidable.

D-381 A draw also occurs when the King of the stronger side is in front of its Rook pawn but the defending (lone) King manages to lock it into the corner:

1. a3-a4	Kc6-c7

The Black King heads for a8.

2. Ka6-a7

The White King does not allow the enemy into the corner.

2. ...	Kc7-c8
3. a4-a5	Kc8-c7

The Black King stays close to the a8 corner.

4. a5-a6	Kc7-c8
5. Ka7-a8	

Or 5. Kb6 Kb8 followed by 6. ... Ka8.

5. ...	Kc8-c7
6. a6-a7	Kc7-c8

Stalemate.

D-382 No matter how many pawns there might be on the a-file, White draws in the same way as in the preceding example:

1. Kc2-c1	**a4-a3**

If 1. ... Kb3, then 2. Kb1 followed by 3. Ka1.

2. Kc1-c2	**Ka2-a1**
3. Kc2-c1	**a3-a2**
4. Kc1-c2	

The White King goes back and forth between c1 and c2 and doesn't let the Black King out of the corner. As soon as Black uses up all his pawn moves, he will be stalemated!

D-383 This example shows what the stronger side must aim for in order to win.

1. Kg6-g7!

The g7 square is a **critical** square. By occupying it, the White King assures the queening of the pawn. 1. h5 would be a mistake because of 1. ... Kf8 2. h6 Kg8, when the Black King gets into the coveted corner. If 2. Kh7, then 2. ... Kf7, again with an unavoidable draw.

1. ...   **Ke7-e6**

The King cannot hinder the pawn from queening.

2. h4-h5

And so on. If in Diagram 383 Black moves first, he draws easily by 1. ... Ke7-f8!, controlling the critical g7 square.

D-384 We know by now that if White succeeds in occupying the critical square g7 with his King, he will win, while if the Black King manages to gain control of g7 and keep the enemy King out, the game will be a draw. The result of the game depends on whose turn it is to move. White to move succeeds in his efforts:

1. Kh3-g4	**Kb4-c5**
2. Kg4-g5	**Kc5-d6**
3. Kg5-g6	**Kd6-e7**
4. Kg6-g7!	

And Black cannot stop the advance of the pawn.

With Black to move, the picture is different:

1. ...	**Kb4-c5**
2. Kh3-g4	**Kc5-d6**
3. Kg4-f5	**Kd6-e7**
4. Kf5-g6	**Ke7-f8!**

Controlling the critical square g7.

5. Kg6-h7

If White does not play this move, the Black King will get into the corner and it will be impossible to drive it out.

5. ...	**Kf8-f7**
6. h2-h4	**Kf7-f8**
7. h4-h5	**Kf8-f7**
8. h5-h6	**Kf7-f8**

And White can only choose how to draw: stalemate the Black King or let his own King be stalemated.

HOMEWORK
(Answers at the end)

I. Diagrams 385–390. Use the skewer tactical device in the solutions.

385

White to play and wins the Rook.

	WHITE	BLACK
1.		
2.		
3.		
4.		

153

386

White to play and win a piece.

	WHITE	BLACK
1.		
2.		
3.		
4.		

388

White to play and wins the Exchange.

	WHITE	BLACK
1.		
2.		
3.		
4.		

387

White to play and wins the Rook.

	WHITE	BLACK
1.		
2.		
3.		
4.		

389

White to play. How does he win?

	WHITE	BLACK
1.		
2.		
3.		
4.		

390

White to play and draw.

	WHITE	BLACK
1.		
2.		
3.		
4.		

II. In Diagrams 391–396 find a combination that uses the skewer tactical device.

391

How does White win? (2 solutions)

	WHITE	BLACK
1.		
2.		
3.		
4.		

	WHITE	BLACK
1.		
2.		
3.		

392

White to play and win material.

	WHITE	BLACK
1.		
2.		
3.		
4.		

393

Find a forced win for White.

WHITE	BLACK
1.	
2.	
3.	
4.	

WHITE	BLACK
1.	
2.	
3.	
4.	

394

How can White win material?

396

Black to play and win material.

WHITE	BLACK
1.	
2.	
3.	
4.	

WHITE	BLACK
1.	
2.	
3.	
4.	

395

White to play. Can he win the Knight?

III. Diagrams 397–402 deal with Rook-pawn endgames.

397

White to play and draw.

	WHITE	BLACK
1.		
2.		
3.		
4.		

398

How should the game end with White to play? With Black to play?

	WHITE	BLACK
1.		
2.		
3.		
4.		

	WHITE	BLACK
1.		
2.		
3.		
4.		

399

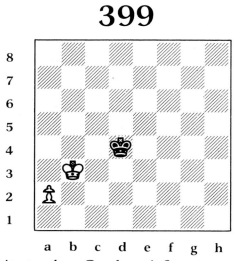

White to play. Can he win?

WHITE	BLACK
1.	
2.	
3.	
4.	

400

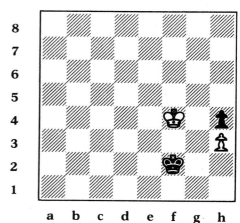

Black to play. Can he save himself?

WHITE	BLACK
1.	
2.	
3.	
4.	

401

Can this position occur in a game? If yes, can White avoid losing if it is his turn to play?

402

Black to play and draw.

WHITE	BLACK
1.	
2.	
3.	
4.	

Answers to the Homework

D-385 **1. Bd2-g5 +** and the Rook perishes.

D-386 **1. Ra1-d1 +**, winning the Bishop. 1. Ra4 + would be no good since the Knight is defended by the Bishop.

D-387

1. Rh8-h3 + !

(forcing the King onto the 4th rank)

    1. ...   **any move**

    2. Rh3-h4 +

(winning the Rook.)

D-388 **1. Bd2-g5** forces the Black Queen to move, whereupon **2. Bg5-f6 +** wins the exchange.

D-389

    1. b5-b6   **h4-h3**

The Black King cannot hold back the White pawn since it is not in the pawn's square.

| 2. b6-b7 | h3-h2 |
| 3. b7-b8Q | h2-h1Q |

The Black pawn too has become a Queen, but not for long!

4. Qb8-b7 +

This check wins the Black Queen.

D-390

1. Bc1-g5!

1. Bh6 was also possible. If Black now queens his a-pawn, he will lose it immediately after 2. Bf6 + . 1. Bd2 + would lose to 1. ... Kc2.

| 1. ... | h4-h3 |
| 2. Ke2-f2 | |

The King is within the square of the h-pawn.

| 2. ... | h3-h2 |

Black sets a pretty trap.

3. Bg5-f6 + !

Only this **in-between check** allows White to draw. 3. Kg2 would lose to 3. ... h1Q+! (decoying the King onto the first rank) 4. Kxh1 a1Q + , and White doesn't have time to play 5. Bf6 + since his King is in check.

| 3. ... | u |
| 4. Kf2-g2 | |

And the draw is unavoidable.

D-391 Black threatens 1. ... Ra1# and 1. ... Kxf4. However, White has two ways of parrying these threats.

Solution 1:

1. Rf4-a4!

Decoying the Black Rook onto the fourth rank.

| 1. ... | Ra8xa4 |

Forced, for 2. Rh3# was threatened.

2. Rh1-h3 +

Now we have the position from Diagram 387.

| 2. ... | u |
| 3. Rh3-h4 + | |

White will remain a Rook up.

Solution 2:

This is possible only if the White King and the Rook on h1 have not moved so far in this game.

1. 0-0!

Saving the King from mate and at the same time defending the Rook on f4. Now White,

with an extra Rook, should win.

D-392

1. Qd3xd4 + !

A temporary Queen sacrifice.

1. ...	Ke5xd4
2. Ba3-b2 +	u
3. Bb2xh8	

As a result of his combination, White has won a Bishop and exchanged off Queens.

D-393

1. Rc1-c8!

A Rook sacrifice to decoy the Black Queen onto c8.

| 1. ... | Qd8xc8 |

Forced.

2. Qh5-h8 +

A check that wins the Black Queen. White gains a Queen for a Rook (9 − 5 = 4 points).

D-394

1. Rd1xd5!

With this Exchange sacrifice White decoys the Black Queen onto d5.

| 1. ... | Qd7xd5 |
| 2. Bf1-g2 | Qd5-d7 |

The Queen may move to other squares, too.

3. Bg2xa8

White has exchanged Rooks and won a Bishop.

D-395 Yes.

1. Rg7xf7!

A temporary Exchange sacrifice. 1. Ra8 + with the idea of winning the Rook on h8 doesn't work because of the reply 1. ... Nd8. So White first eliminates the Knight.

1. ...	Rf2xf7
2. Ra7-a8 +	u
3. Ra8xh8	

As a result of his combination, White has exchanged Rooks and won a Knight.

D-396 From the game Sanguinetti—Fischer, 1958.

| 1. ... | Nf4xd5! |

Fischer wins a pawn, since it turns out that White cannot play 2. Qxd5 because of 2. ... Rad8, winning a Rook.

D-397 From the game Ancigin—N. Guravlev, USSR 1952.

    1. Ke3-f2!

Locking the Black King in the corner. 1. Kxf3 would lose because of 1. ... Kg1 followed by the queening of the h-pawn.

    1. ...   **Kh2-h1**

Zugzwang. If it had been White's turn to move, Black would have won easily, *e.g.,* 2. Kf1 Kg3 3. Kg1 f2+ 4. Kf1 h2, etc.

    2. Kf2-f1!

Now the Black King cannot escape from the corner.

    2. ...   **f3-f2**

If 2. ... h2, then 3. Kf2 is stalemate.

    3. Kf1xf2   **Kh1-h2**

If now 3. ... h2, then 4. Kf1 is stalemate.

    4. Kf2-f1   **Kh2-g3**

    5. Kf1-g1!

The White King gets into the coveted corner, making the draw inevitable.

D-398 White to move draws after

    1. Kf2-g3!

Forcing Black to push the h-pawn, as otherwise both pawns would be lost.

    1. ...   **h3-h2**

    2. Kg3-f2!

Now the Black King is caught in the corner.

    2. ...   **f7-f5**

    3. Kf2-f1   **f5-f4**

    4. Kf1-f2   **f4-f3**

    5. Kf2-f1   **f3-f2**

    6. Kf1xf2   **Stalemate**

If Black moves first in Diagram 398, he wins easily after

    1. ...   **Kh1-h2!**

Putting White in Zugzwang: White must make some move and let the Black King out of the corner.

    2. Kf2-f1

2. Kf3 would not save White, because of 2. ... Kg1, winning.

    2. ...   **Kh2-g3**

Black, with two extra pawns, should win.

D-399 Yes!

    1. Kb3-b4!

Preventing the Black King from getting into the a8 corner.

    1. ...   **Kd4-d5**

    2. Kb4-b5!   **Kd5-d6**

    3. Kb5-b6!   **Kd6-d7**

    4. Kb6-b7!

Now the White pawn can queen.

    4. ...   **Kd7-d6**

    5. a2-a4   **Kd6-c5**

    6. a4-a5   **Kc5-b5**

    7. a5-a6

and so on.

D-400 Yes, Black can save himself, but only by means of the following Knight sacrifice:

    1. ...   **Nh4xg6!**

Otherwise White would queen his pawn after 2. g7+.

    2. Kh7xg6   **Kf8-g8**

and the draw is unavoidable.

D-401 It is theoretically possible for this position to occur but it wouldn't in practice. The Black pawns have made thirteen captures while fifteen White men have gone from the board. White draws with **1. Kg3-f2**, locking the Black King in the corner. After that, the White King shuttles back and forth between f1 and f2 until Black runs out of pawn moves and becomes stalemated. As you can see, it does not matter in this example how many extra pawns are on the f- and h-files.

D-402

    1. ...   **Kf2-e2!!**

Only thus can Black save himself. 1. ...Kg2 would lose because of 2. Kg4 Kf2 3. Kxh4 Kf3 4. Kg5, and the White King can occupy the critical square of g7 and escort the pawn to the queening square.

    2. Kf4-g4   **Ke2-e3**

    3. Kg4xh4   **Ke3-f4!**

The Black King heads for the h8 corner and at the same time restricts the White King to the h-file. When the Kings are placed like this, they are said to be **in opposition.**

    4. Kh4-h5   **Kf4-f5**

    5. Kh5-h6   **Kf5-f6**

    6. h3-h4   **Kf6-f7**

The Black King controls the critical square g7, making the draw inevitable.

SUPPLEMENTARY MATERIAL

for use at the teacher's discretion

The First Steps of the World Champions

The renowned champions began to play chess in the same way as you did. They made their very first chess moves when they were anywhere from 6 to 15 years old. They too "hung" their Queens and they too fell into "Scholar's Mates." Hard to believe? Well, let's start with Mikhail Tal, who was on the world chess throne from 1960 to 1961. Here is a game played by 9-year-old Mikhail and his brother.

Game 65
Mikhail Tal's Brother—Mikhail Tal
Riga 1945

1. e4-e4	e7-e5
2. Bf1-c4	Bf8-c5
3. Qd1-h5?	Nb8-a6??
4. Qh5xf7#	

See Diagram 403.

403

You of course know how to defend yourself against the Scholar's Mate, but Tal didn't until this game. However, he did not fall into such mates any more and fifteen years later he became the World Champion.

Boris Spassky was the World Champion from 1969 to 1972. When he was 11 years old, he played the following game:

Game 66
Boris Spassky—M. Podgaiskii, USSR 1948
Sicilian Defense

1. e2-e4	c7-c5
2. Ng1-f3	Nb8-c6
3. d2-d4	c5xd4
4. Nf3xd4	Ng8-f6
5. Nb1-c3	e7-e6
6. Bf1-e2	Bf8-b4

Pinning the Knight and threatening 7. ... Nxe4.

7. Be2-f3	Qd8-a5

Attacking the Knight on c3 a second time.

8. Nd4-b5??	

He had to defend with 8. Ne2.

8. ...	Qa5xb5

See Diagram 404.

404

The Knight on c3 is **absolutely** pinned by the Black Bishop. As Boris Spassky recalled later, he broke into tears after Black's move and resigned the game. It is, of course, painful to give away a piece just like that, for nothing. But in every game that a player loses, he has only himself to blame!

Now take a look at a game played in a schoolchildren's tournament between two future chess stars (although they didn't know that yet).

Game 67

Viktor Korchnoi	Boris Spassky
(17 years old)	(11 years old)

Leningrad, 1948
Sicilian Defense

1. e2-e4	c7-c5
2. Ng1-f3	d7-d6
3. d2-d4	c5xd4
4. Nf3xd4	Ng8-f6
5. Nb1-c3	g7-g6
6. f2-f4	Bc8-g4

Black has played the **Dragon Variation**, but his last move is a mistake. 6. ... Nc6 is better.

7. Bf1-b5 +	Nb8-d7
8. Bb5xd7 + !	

A strong move with the aim of exploiting the poor position of the Black Bishop on g4.

8. ...	Qd8xd7

8. ... Bxd7 would be met by the unpleasant 9. e5.

9. Qd1-d3	

Now 10. f5 is threatened, after which the Black Bishop might get trapped by 11. h3 and 12. g4.

9. ...	e7-e5
10. Nd4-f3	Bg4xf3
11. Qd3xf3	Qd7-g4?

Black's desire to bring about a draw by exchanging Queens leads to an immediate loss. Black could have put up resistance by 11. .. exf4 12. Bxf4 Bg7 and 13. ... 0-0

12. Nc3-d5!	

See Diagram 405.

405

```
   a b c d e f g h
```

Spassky resigned, thinking that he had to lose a piece. Indeed, 13. ... Qxf3 is no good because of White's in-between checks: 14. Nxf6 + Ke7 14. Nd5 + u 15. gxf3 and White remains a piece up. Nor would 12. ... Qh4 + save Black, because of the reply 13. g3.

However, Black can save the piece with the incredible move 12. ... Kd8!, although after 13. Qxg4 (if 13. Nxf6, then 13. ... Qh4 + followed by 14. ... Qxf6) 13. ... Nxg4 14. h3 Nh6 15. fxe5 dxe5 16. Bg5 + and 17. Bf6 White wins a pawn. As you can see, even in this line Black gets a difficult position.

World Champion Jose Raoul Capablanca reigned on the chess throne from 1921 to 1927. He learned chess at a very early age. Here is how it happened. One day, 4-year-old Jose Raoul went into his father's office and found him playing chess with a colonel. Little Capablanca's interest was aroused by the pieces moving on a board according to some rules that he did not yet know. The next day Jose Raoul again came and silently watched his father play. The third day, he suddenly saw that his father moved a Knight from a light square to another light square and that his opponent, also apparently a weak player, did not notice it. The little boy laughed and proceeded to accuse his father of cheating. The father became angry but the son immediately showed him on the board the mistake he had made. Finding it hard to believe that such a young boy could have mastered the rules of play by himself, Capablanca Senior asked his son whether he could set up the men in their starting positions. Jose Raoul not only passed this test without a mistake, but also won a game then and there against his father. A few days later, Capablanca Senior took the "Wunderkind"(child prodigy) to the chess club. One of the strongest club members agreed to play with the 4-year-old child, but insisted on giving him Queen odds. Here is what happened in that game:

Game 68
Iglesias—Capablanca (aged 4)
Havana, 1892
(White played without his Queen)

1. e2-e4	e7-e5
2. Ng1-f3	Ng8-f6
3. Nf3xe5	Nf6xe4
4. d2-d4	d7-d6
5. Ne5-f3	Bf8-e7
6. Bf1-d3	Ne4-f6

7. c2-c4	0-0
8. Nb1-c3	Nb8-c6
9. a2-a3	a7-a6
10. Bc1-d2	b7-b6
11. 0-0-0	Bc8-d7
12. Kc1-b1	

White is waiting for the child to start giving away pieces, but so far Black has been playing very well.

12. ...	Nc6-a5
13. Rd1-c1	Na5-b3
14. Rc1-c2	c7-c5
15. d4-d5	Rf8-e8
16. h2-h4	b6-b5!

Going over this game we get the impression that the players were modern experts and certainly older than four years.

17. g2-g4	Nb3-d4
18. Nf3xd4	c5xd4
19. Nc3-e4	b5xc4
20. Ne4xf6 +	Be7xf6
21. Bd3xc4	Bd7xg4
22. Bc4-d3	Bg4-f3
23. Rh1-h3	Bf3xd5
24. h4-h5	Bd5-e6
25. Rh3-g3	g7-g6
26. f2-f4	Bf6-h4
27. Rg3-g1	Kg8-h8
28. f4-f5	Be6xf5
29. Bd3xf5	g6xf5
30. Bd2-h6	Re8-g8
31. Rc2-g2	Rg8xg2
32. Rg1xg2	Qd8-f6
33. Bh6-g7 +	Qf6xg7
34. Rg2xg7 +	Kh8xg7
35. Kb1-c2	Kg7-f6
36. Kc2-d3	Kf6-e5
37. h5-h6	f5-f4
38. Kd3-e2	Ke5-e4

See Diagram 406.

406

Only here did the grown-up playing White acknowledge himself vanquished. Yes, Capablanca was not considered a Wunderkind for nothing!

The brilliant American Paul Morphy was undoubtedly the strongest chessplayer of his time. His splendid combinations even today thrill chess lovers. Here is a game that Morphy played blindfolded against his uncle. This game was played on Paul Morphy's birthday.

Game 69
P. Morphy (age 12)—E. Morphy,
New Orleans 1849
Giuoco Piano

1. e2-e4	e7-e5
2. Ng1-f3	Nb8-c6
3. Bf1-c4	Bf8-c5
4. c2-c3	d7-d6
5. 0-0	Ng8-f6

5. ... Bb6 or 5. ... Qe7 would be more prudent.

6. d2-d4	e5xd4
7. c3xd4	Bc5-b6
8. h2-h3	

8. Nc3 is a good move here, but Paul Morphy decides to prevent the Black Bishop from moving to g4.

8. ...	h7-h6
9. Nb1-c3	0-0
10. Bc1-e3	

Here White should retreat his other Bishop to b3.

10. ...	Rf8-e8

An unfortunate move. Black had a chance of equalizing by 10. ... Nxe4 11. Nxe4 d5.

| 11. d4-d5 | Bb6xe3? |

It was better to retreat the Knight to e7.

12. d5xc6	Be3-b6
13. e4-e5	d6xe5
14. Qd1-b3	

White could play 14. Qxd8 Rxd8 15. Nxe5, but Paul decides to keep his Queen for the attack.

| 14. ... | Re8-e7? |

He should have defended with 14. ... Be6.

15. Bc4xf7 + !

The young maestro immediately takes advantage of his opponent's hardly perceptible mistake.

15. ...	Re7xf7
16. Nf3xe5	Qd8-e8
17. c6xb7	Bc8xb7
18. Ra1-e1	Bb7-a6
19. Ne5-g6!	

Black loses because of the pin on the Rook at f7.

| 19. ... | Qe8-d8 |
| 20. Re1-e7 | |

See Diagram 407

407

Black resigns. 20. ... Nd5 will not save him, because of 21. Nxd5 Rxe7 22. Nf6#.

The onlookers' delight at this game was indescribable.

In 1978, a 17-year-old Soviet schoolgirl called Maia Chiburdanidze became the Women's World Champion. Never before in the history of chess had there been such a young world champion. The following game shows how strong a player Maia was even at the age of twelve.

Game 70
M. Chiburdanidze—O. Andreeva
(International Master), USSR 1973
Sicilian Defense

1. e2-e4	c7-c5
2. c2-c3	Ng8-f6
3. e4-e5	Nf6-d5
4. d2-d4	c5xd4
5. c3xd4	d7-d6
6. Ng1-f3	Nb8-c6
7. Nb1-c3	Nd5xc3
8. b2xc3	d6xe5?

It was better to play 8. ... d5 or 8. ... e6, with equal chances.

9. d4-d5! | e5-e4

Freeing e5 for the Knight.

10. Nf3-g5

10. dxc6 Qxd1 + 11. Kxd1 exf3 would be in Black's favor.

| 10. ... | Nc6-e5 |
| 11. Ng5xe4 | Qd8-c7 |

An inaccuracy. Better was 11. ... e6, undermining White's center.

12. Qd1-d4!

In this instance the Queen is splendidly placed in the center, for Black cannot attack it easily.

| 12. ... | Bc8-d7 |

Yet another inaccuracy. The development of the Kingside is urgently called for.

13. Bc1-a3!

Preparing the move 14. d6.

| 13. ... | f7-f6 |

Defending the Knight. 13. ... e6 would lose to 14. d6 Qa5 15. Bb4.

| 14. d5-d6 | Qc7-c6 |

14. ... exd6 would be inferior, because of 15. Nxd6 + Bxd6 16. Bxd6, and White has the advantage.

| 15. d6xe7 | Bf8xe7 |
| 16. Ba3xe7 | Ke8xe7 |

The Black King has lost her right to castle. White's task now is to organize an attack against the King stranded in the center.

17. Qd4-b4!

Forcing Black to determine the position of his King.

| 17. ... | Ke7-f7 |

The King had four squares, but none of them guaranteed it safety. It may be that 17. ... Kd8 was the best, but Black's desire to hide her

King on the Kingside is understandable.

18. f2-f4!

White's idea is to play Bc4+, but since the Black Knight controls c4 White tries to chase the Knight away with her pawn.

18. ...   Rh8-e8

18. .., Ng6 would lose after 19. Bc4+ Be6 20. Bxe6+ Qxe6 21. f5! Qxf5 22. Nd6+. Relatively best was 18. ... Ng4, although White would still maintain a very strong attack after 19. ... 0-0-0.

19. f4xe5   Re8xe5

Black sacrificed her Knight expecting that in return she would win the White Knight, which is now pinned. However, there is a surprise in store for her.

20. 0-0-0!

Excellently played! The King goes into hiding and at the same time the White Rook attacks the Bishop.

20. ...   Re5xe4
21. Rd1xd7+!   Kf7-e8?

21. ... Qxd7 was better, although Black would still have lost a piece after 22. Qxe4.

22. Rd7-e7+!!

See Diagram 408.

408

It's almost unbelievable that a 12-year-old girl could make such a move! Black resigns, since 22. ... Rxe7 would be followed by 23. Bb5, **pinning** and winning the Black Queen.

After looking at these games we can conclude that the champions possessed chess talent even in their childhood, but that they nevertheless made mistakes and were beatable. But what characterised the budding champions was above all this: even after the most unpleasant losses, they did not become disenchanted with chess or lose confidence in their abilitites. Rather, these children analyzed their mistakes and oversights with still greater energy, in order to avoid repeating them. That is what we too must learn to do!

Lesson Ten

A. Check Lesson 9 homework (as necessary).
B. *Review Questions*

Find the best continuation in Diagrams 409-420. Work directly from the diagrams, without setting up the men on a board.

411

White to play.

409

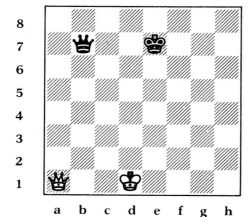

The player who moves first wins.

412

White to play.

410

White to play.

166

413

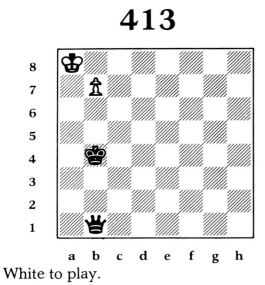

White to play.

414

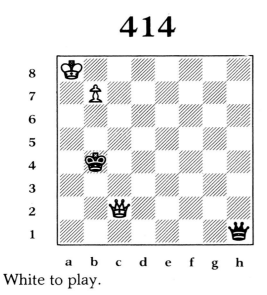

White to play.

415

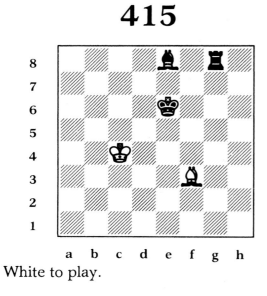

White to play.

416

White to play.

417

Black to play.

418

Black to play.

419

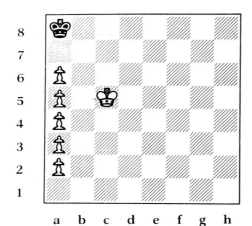

How should the game end with White to play? With Black to play?

420

How would you play if it was your turn with White? And if it was your turn with Black?

Answers to Review Questions

D-409 White to play: **1. Qa1-g7 +**
Black to play: **1. ... Qb7-h1 +**
D-410 1. Bd1-g4 +
D-411 1. Qe2xe6 + Kd7xe6 2. Bd1-g4 +
D-412 1. Qe2xe6 + Kd7xe6 2. Bd1-g4 +
D-413 1. b7-b8Q +
D-414 1. Qc2-b1 + Qh1xb1 2. b7-b8Q +
D-415 1. Bf3-d5 +
D-416 1. Re7xe6 +! Ke5xe6 2. Bf3-d5 +
D-417 1. ... Ra1-a2 +
D-418 1. ... Rh1-a1! (threatening 2. ... h1Q)
2. Rh7xh2 Ra1-a2 +
D-419 1. No matter who plays first, the game

should be a draw, as the Black King cannot be driven out of the corner.
D-420 White to play wins: **1. Kh7-g8 Kf6-g6 2. h6-h7** and the pawn will queen.
Black to play draws: **1. ... Kf6-f7 2. Kh7-h8 Kf7-f8.**

Typical Mating Combinations

The final aim of each of the players in a chess game is to checkmate his opponent's King. A combination which serves this aim is called a "mating combination." We can easily understand that a player will readily sacrifice any amount of material for a sound (correct) **mating combination.** Before playing the combination, the player must of course clearly visualize the **final mating position.**

There are many typical mating positions that often occur in games. A knowledge of these positions will help us to create typical mating combinations. However, they must be studied gradually.

The Back-Rank Mate

As you know, it is dangerous to waste time in the opening by making aimless pawn moves. But on the other hand, if you do not push up one of the pawns in front of the King after it has castled, you run the risk of getting mated on the back (1st or 8th) rank by your opponent's Rook or Queen. Pushing up one of the pawns in front of the castled King to avoid the danger of mate is known as "making an escape hatch" for the King. This should preferably be done in the middlegame, and the move should be tied in with the players's **plan of play.**

421

For example, let us look at Diagram 421, where it is White's turn to move. It would be advisable for White to make an escape hatch by playing 1. g2-g3. The g2 square is thereby freed for the King and at the same time the pawn on g3 controls f4 and h4, depriving the enemy Knight of these squares. Black can reply with 1. ... h7-h6, attacking the Knight and at the same time making an escape hatch for his King on h7. 1. ... f6?, on the other hand, would be bad because of 2. Ne6 Rd1 + (an in-between check) 3. Kg2 Rf7 4. Rb8 + Nf8 5. R1b7 Rdd7 6. Rxd7 Rxd7 7. Rxf8#, there being no escape hatch for the Black King on h7.

Sometimes a player pulls off a back-rank mate without having had to sacrifice anything, as a result of a gross blunder on the part of his opponent. Most of the time, however, the back-rank mate is the result of a combination.

Let us look at some examples. The patterns shown in Diagrams 422, 424 and 426 form the basis of the combinations in Diagrams 423, 425, and 427, respectively. Find these combinations. Solve the exercises directly from the diagrams, without setting up the men on a board. **Memorize the mating *patterns*, but not the positions of the various men in the combinations.**

423

White to play mates in two moves.

424

pattern

425

Black to play mates in two moves.

422

pattern

426

pattern

427

White to play mates in two moves.

Answers

D-423

    1. Qh4xd8 + !

The Queen is sacrificed in order to eliminate the piece guarding the eighth rank.

    1. ...   **Bc7xd8**

    2. Re2-e8#

D-425

    1. ...   **Qf4-c1 +**

This kind of combination is called an **x-ray attack**, because the Rook on c8 controls c1 **through** the enemy Rook on c2.

    2. Rc2xc1

Forced. But now the Black Rook can move to c1.

    2. ...   **Rc8xc1#**

D-427

    1. Qh7-h8 + !

An x-ray attack, with the Rook on h1 attacking h8 through the Black Rook on h6.

    1. ...   **Rh6xh8**

Forced, since the Knight is pinned. Now, however, the Rook on h1 enters the fray.

    2. Rh1xh8#

In some cases the Queen is able to mate the opposing King by simultaneously controlling both the back rank and the King's escape hatch. In Diagrams 429, 431, and 433 find the combinations using the patterns shown in Diagrams 428, 430 and 432, respectively. Solve the exercises directly from the diagrams, without setting up the men on a board.

428

pattern

429

White to play and mate in three moves.

430

pattern

431

White to play and mate in two moves.

432

pattern

433

White to play and mate in two moves.

setting up the men on a board), find the combinations in Diagrams 435, 437, and 439, using the patterns in Diagrams 434, 436, and 438, respectively.

434

pattern

435

White to play and mate in two moves.

Answers

D-429

    1. Rd4-d8 + !

The idea of this Rook sacrifice is to free the h5-e8 diagonal by deflecting the Knight.

    1. ...   **Ra8xd8**

If 1. ... Nxd8, then 2. Qe8#.

    2. Rd1xd8 +   **Nf7xd8**

Forced.

    3. Qh5-e8#

D-431

    1. Rf4-f8 + !

This move is possible because the White Queen controls f8 through the Bishop on g7 (x-ray attack).

    1. ...   **Bg7xf8**

    2. Qh6xf8#

D-433

    1. Rh1-h8 +   **Ng6xh8**

    2. Qd4xh8#

Working directly from the diagrams (without

436

pattern

437

a b c d e f g h

White to play and mate in two moves.

438

e f g h

pattern

439

a b c d e f g h

White to play and mate in three moves.

1. Re1-e8 + !	Bd7xe8
2. Rd1-d8#	

We achieved our goal by using the idea of **deflection**.

D-437

  1. Qb5-e8 + !

Again we make use of the x-ray attack idea. The e8 square is controlled not only by the Queen and the Bishop but also by the White Rook acting through the Black Rook on d8.

1. ...	Rd8xe8
2. Rc8xe8#	

D-439 This example makes use of two ideas: the deflection of the Black Rook from the eighth rank and the x-ray attack.

1. Qa2xf7 + !	Rf8xf7
2. Re2-e8 +	Rf7-f8
3. Re8xf8#	

Such combinations can occur even when the King has an escape hatch, provided that this escape square is controlled by an enemy man. Working directly from the diagrams (without setting up the men on a board), find the combinations in Diagrams 441, 443, and 446, using the patterns in Diagrams 440, 442, 444, and 445.

440

e f g h

pattern

<hr/>

Answers

D-435 Looking at the position, we get the idea of playing the move Rd8#, but the Rook cannot jump over the Black Bishop. How can we force the Black Bishop to abandon the d-file?

441

White to play and mate in three moves.

442

pattern

443

White to play and mate in two moves.

444

pattern

445

pattern

446

White to play and mate in two moves (two solutions).

Answers

D-441 Since the White Bishop controls the escape hatch on h7, White must break through to the eighth rank with his Rook or Queen.

    1. Qc3-c8 + !

We won't balk at sacrificing!

    1. ...   **Bb7xc8**

    2. Rc2xc8 +   **Nb6xc8**

    3. Rc1xc8#

D-443 We must first of all find the mating idea patterned in Diagram 442. Then we must decide how to **decoy** the Black King onto g8.

    1. Qh7-g8 + !   **Kf8xg8**

    2. Re1-e8#

D-446 Looking at the position, we must mentally visualize the patterns shown in Diagrams 444 and 445. We will realize then that the Black king must be **decoyed** onto h8 or f8.

Solution 1:
1. Rh1-h8 + !   Kg8xh8
2. Rf1-f8#

Solution 2:
1. Rf1-f8 + !   Kg8xf8
2. Rh1-h8#

Endgame With King and Non-Rook pawn vs. King

We shall examine positions with the pawn on any arbitrary non-Rook file (i.e., any file except the a-file and the h-file) since the results are the same for all non-Rook pawns.

A non-Rook pawn is easier to queen than a Rook pawn but here too you must have a sure knowledge of which positions are winning and which are not. Today we shall look at the positions in which the pawn can queen. You are recommended to memorize these positions.

447

White wins no matter who moves first.

448

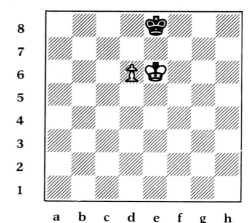

White wins only if it is Black's turn to play.

449

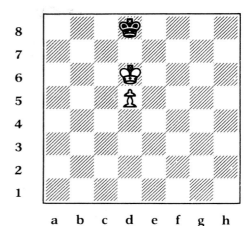

White wins no matter who moves first.

450

White to play wins.

174

451

a b c d e f g h

Black wins no matter who moves first.

452

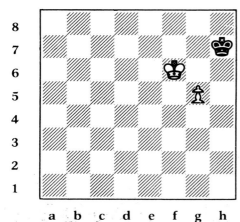

a b c d e f g h

White wins no matter who moves first.

D-447 The lone King can have chances of stopping the pawn only if it is in front of the pawn. A King that is beside the pawn cannot stop it.

White to play gains a decisive advantage by:

1. d5-d6	Ke5-e6
2. Kc5-c6	Ke6-f7
3. d6-d7	Kf7-e7
4. Kc6-c7	

White will get a new Queen on the next move.

Black to play:

| 1. 1. ... | Ke5-f6 |

Trying to stop the pawn from the front by playing Kf6-e7-d7.

2. Kc5-c6

The King hurries to the c7 square, from where it will control d6, d7, and d8, the pawn's queening route.

| 2. ... | Kf6-e7 |
| 3. Kc6-c7 | |

Protected by the King, the pawn will become a Queen in three moves.

Conclusion: If the two Kings and the pawn are all on the same rank, and the pawn is defended, then the side with the pawn wins no matter whose turn it is to play.

D-448 This extremely important position is encountered quite often in practice. Note the position of the Kings. You will remember that when the Kings are standing across from each other with one square between them, they are said to be in **opposition**. The King which has obtained such a position after making its move (so that it is the opposing side's turn to move) is said to have **taken the opposition**. In the present example, the outcome of the struggle depends on who has the opposition. If White has the opposition, so that it is Black's turn to play, then White wins:

| 1. ... | Ke8-d8 |

Trying to stop the pawn.

| 2. d6-d7 | Kd8-c7 |

Black had no other move — he was in zugzwang.

3. Ke6-e7

The pawn will queen next move.

If on the other hand Black has the opposition in Diagram 448, so that it is White's turn to move, then the game is a draw:

1. d6-d7 +

On any other move Black would reply 1. ... Kd7 and would again draw.

| 1. ... | Ke8-d8 |
| 2. Ke6-d6 | |

Stalemate. This time it was White who was in zugzwang. He could have avoided stalemate only by giving up his pawn, but that would of course be a draw anyway.

As you see, in this example the right to play first is advantageous neither for White nor for Black. Such a situation is known as **mutual zugzwang**.

Conclusion: If a protected pawn reaches the seventh rank **without check**, it will queen;

otherwise the game is a draw. (Of course, all the conclusions apply to Black as well, when it is Black who is trying to queen the pawn.)

D-449 When the King is in front of its own pawn, the chances of victory are considerably increased. If in addition, as in the present example, the King is on the sixth rank, then the pawn will queen by force no matter whose turn it is to move. The Kings are in opposition. This means that each King takes away three intervening squares (c7, d7, and e7 in the present case) from the other.

With Black to play, White's task is not complicated:

    1. ...   **Kd8-e8**

Because of Zugzwang, Black loses control of c7.

  2. Kd6-c7

Immediately occupying c7. Now the pawn will queen by force. The same thing would have happened after 1. ... Kc8, except that White would have played 2. Ke7 instead.

Let us see now what would happen with White to play:

  1. Kd6-e6   **Kd8-e8!**

The Black King takes the opposition. On any other move 2. Ke7 would be decisive.

  2. d5-d6!

This "reserve" tempo (move) forces Black to **yield the opposition.**

  2. ...   **Ke8-d8**

  3. d6-d7

The pawn has reached the seventh rank **without check!**

  3. ...   **Kd8-c7**

Zugzwang occurs very frequently in pawn endings.

  4. Ke6-e7

And White wins.

Conclusion: If the White King is on the sixth rank and in front of its own pawn, White is always assured of winning.

D-450

  1. Kc4-d5!

Only thus! The advantage of taking the opposition is that White puts Black into zug-

176

zwang, forcing him to move his King to one side, and thereby assures the penetration of his own King on the other side. 1. Kc5 would be a mistake since Black would draw by taking the opposition with 1. ... Kc7!. On any other White move, Black would save himself by 1. ... Kd6.

  1. ...   **Kd7-e7**

Forced to give up the opposition, Black loses control over c6. 1. ... Kc7 would be followed by 2. Ke6!.

  2. Kd5-c6!

The main idea of this outflanking maneuver with the King is to chase the enemy King away from the pawn, which is thereby enabled to advance to the queening square.

  2. ...   **Ke7-d8**

On 2. ... Ke6, 3. d5+ is decisive: 3. ... Ke7 4. Kc7 and the pawn queens.

  3. Kc6-d6!

As you already know, if the King is on the sixth rank and in front of its pawn, the win is assured.

  3. ...   **Kd8-e8**

  4. Kd6-c7!

The road has been cleared for the pawn, which will become a Queen in four more moves.

Conclusion: If the King is in front of its pawn and can take the opposition, the win is assured.

D-451 White to play has to give up the opposition immediately and lose the game. For example:

  1. Ke2-d2   **Ke4-f3**

Clearing the way for the pawn. 1. Kf2 would have been met by 1. ... Kd3.

  2. Kd2-d3   **e6-e5**

The pawn must be brought up.

  3. Kd3-d2   **e5-e4**

3. ... Kf2 would be bad because of 4. Kd3, forcing the Black King to retreat.

  4. Kd2-e1   **Kf3-e3!**

If Black gets his King on the third rank and in front of his pawn, he always wins! 4. ... e3 would be a mistake allowing White to draw by taking the opposition with 5. Kf1!. For example: 5. ... e2+ 6. Ke1 Ke3 stalemate.

  5. Ke1-d1   **Ke3-f2!**

On 5. Kf1 Black would have won by 5. ... Kd2. Now the pawn has obtained the green light and will queen in three moves.

With Black to move in Diagram 451, White has the opposition but must still lose, because Black can make it White's turn to play by pushing his pawn. After that, Black wins easily.

1. ...	e6-e5!

Regaining the opposition.

2. Ke2-f2	Ke4-d3
3. Kf2-f3	

3. Ke1 would also lose, because of 3. ... Ke3! 4. Kf1 Kd2! etc.

3. ...	e5-e4 +
4. Kf3-f2	Kd3-d2!

And the pawn cannot be stopped.

Conclusion: In positions where the King is in front of its pawn and there is at least one square between the King and the pawn, victory is always assured.

D-452 With Black to play, White wins easily:

1. ...	Kh7-g8

1. ... Kh8 would not save Black, as White wins after 2. g6 Kg8 3. g7 Kh7 4. Kf7.

2. Kf6-g6!	

Taking the opposition. 2. g6 would lead to a draw after 2. ... Kf8! 3. g7+ Kg8 4. Kg6 stalemate.

2. ...	Kg8-h8

If 2. ... Kf8, then the White pawn would be unstoppable after 3. Kh7.

3. Kg6-f7	Kh8-h7
4. g5-g6 +	Kh7-h8
5. g6-g7 +	Kh8-h7
6. g7-g8Q +	

And so on.

With White to play, a few complications arise as a result of the g-pawn being near the edge of the board.

1. Kf6-f7!	

Watch out for the trap! 1. g6 + ?? would be no good because of 1. ... Kh8! after which the draw is unavoidable in all variations:

(a) 2. Kf7 stalemate. This is possible only with a Knight (g or b) pawn.

(b) 2. g7+ Kg8 3. Kg6 is again stalemate.

(c) On any other move by the White King, Black draws with 2. ... Kg7.

1. ...	Kh7-h8
2. Kf7-g6!	

Again 2. g6? must be avoided because of stalemate.

2. ...	Kh8-g8
3. Kg6-h6!	

With the idea of controlling h7 in order to drive the Black King out of the corner.

3. ...	Kg8-h8

Or else 4. Kh7 would follow.

4. g5-g6	

Having completed the maneuvers with his King, White advances his pawn.

4. ...	Kh8-g8
5. g6-g7	Kg8-f7

Forced.

6. Kh6-h7	

And White wins.

Today we have looked at cases where the pawn has succeeded in forcing its way through to the queening square. The next lesson will acquaint you with examples where the pawn does not manage to do this and the game ends in a draw.

HOMEWORK
(Answers at the end)

Remember the pattern shown in each of the odd-numbered diagrams 453-463 and use it in solving the coresponding even-numbered diagrams 454-464.

453

pattern

454

White to play and mate in two moves.

455

pattern

456

Black to play and mate in two moves.

457

pattern

458

White to play and mate in two moves.

459

pattern

460

Black to play and mate in two moves.

461

pattern

462

White to play and mate in three moves.

	WHITE	BLACK
1.		
2.		

463

pattern

464

Black to play and mate in three moves.

	WHITE	BLACK
1.		
2.		

II. In Diagrams 465-476 find the strongest continuation. Use the tactical device of "back-rank mate."

465

White to play and mate in two moves.

	WHITE	BLACK
1.		
2.		

467

White to play and mate in three moves.

	WHITE	BLACK
1.		
2.		

466

White to play and mate in two moves.

	WHITE	BLACK
1.		
2.		

468

White to play and mate in three moves.

	WHITE	BLACK
1.		
2.		

469

White to play and mate in two moves.

	WHITE	BLACK
1.		
2.		

471

Black to play and mate in three moves.

	WHITE	BLACK
1.		
2.		

470

Black to play and mate in two moves.

	WHITE	BLACK
1.		
2.		

472

Black to play and mate in two moves.

	WHITE	BLACK
1.		
2.		

473

White to play and mate in four moves.

	WHITE	BLACK
1.		
2.		
3.		
4.		

474

White to play and win.

	WHITE	BLACK
1.		
2.		
3.		
4.		

475

White to play and win a piece.

	WHITE	BLACK
1.		
2.		

476

White to play and win.

	WHITE	BLACK
1.		
2.		

477

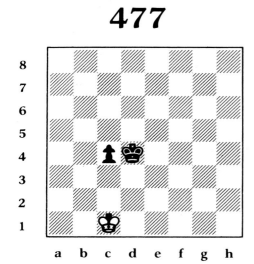

Black to play and queen the pawn (two solutions).

	WHITE	BLACK
1.		
2.		

	WHITE	BLACK
1.		
2.		

478

Either side to play. Queen the pawn.

	WHITE	BLACK
1.		
2.		

	WHITE	BLACK
1.		
2.		

479

White to play. Queen the pawn.

	WHITE	BLACK
1.		
2.		

480

Either side to play. Queen the pawn.

	WHITE	BLACK
1.		
2.		

	WHITE	BLACK
1.		
2.		

481

White to play. Queen the pawn.

	WHITE	BLACK
1.		
2.		

482

White to play. Queen the pawn.

	WHITE	BLACK
1.		
2.		

Answers

D-454
    1. g5-g6 + !
Forcing the King to retreat to the last rank.
    1. ...   **u**
    2. Re1-e8#

D-456
    1. ...   **Qe3-c1 + !**
By sacrificing his Queen, Black decoys the White King onto c1.
    2. Kb1xc1   **Ra8-a1#**

D-458 When you know the pattern, it's not hard to find the solution:
    1. Rf1xf8 + !   **Kg8xf8**
    2. Re1-e8#

D-460
    1. ...   **Qc6xc2 + !**
Deflecting the Rook from the defense of the first rank and **pinning** it at the same time.
    2. Rc1xc2   **Rd8-d1#**

D-462 How can the Black King be forced to retreat to the eighth rank?
    1. Qf4-f6 + !!

When we've found a mating idea, we can of course sacrifice any piece in order to make the idea a reality.

1. ...	e7xf6
2. e5xf6 +	any move
3. Rh2xh8#	

D-464   The idea of the combination is to entice (decoy) the White King onto h1. But the Black Queen cannot get to h1 so long as the Black Rook is in its way. So:

1. ...	Rf3-f1 + !!

Freeing the way for the Queen.

2. Re1xf1	Qe4-h1 + !
3. Kg1xh1	Rf7xf1#

D-465

1. Re1-e8 + !	

White makes use of the "x-ray attack" tactical device — the Rook on c8 controls e8 **through** the Black Rook on d8.

1. ...	Rd8xe8
2. Rc8xe8#	

D-466   We discover the idea of Re8#, but find that the Black Bishop is in the way. So:

1. Rc1-c8 + !	

White makes use of the tactical device of "line clearance."

1. ...	Be6xc8
2. Re1-e8#	

D-467   The White Rooks attack e8, but the square is defended by the Black Rook and Bishop. That is, there are apparently two attackers versus two defenders. Actually, however, the White Queen also attacks e8 (an x-ray attack), and so:

1. Re2-e8 +	Rd8xe8
2. Re1xe8 +	Bc6xe8

Clearing the way for the White Queen.

3. Qa4xe8#	

D-468   The White Rook and the pawn on c7 control the d8 square, but the two Black Rooks defend it. That is, there are two attackers against two defenders.

1. Qa6xc8 + !	

Eliminate one of the defenders **with check.** And not 1. Qxa8, allowing 1. ... Qh1#.

1. ...	Ra8xc8

2. Rd1-d8 +	Rc8xd8
3. c7xd8Q#	

D-469   We can't play 1. Rf8 + since the King would capture the Rook. So we make use of the "driving away" tactical device:

1. Be2-c4 +	Kg8-h8

Forced.

2. Rf1-f8#	

D-470

1. ...	Nc4-d2 +

The King is **driven away** from the White Rook.

2. Kb1-a1	Rc8xc1#

D-471   When you have the chance to capture your opponent's Queen, don't do it instantaneously. Always take a look first to see whether you don't have a better move. In the present case, for example, the White Queen is under attack, but more important is the fact that White's back rank (the first rank) is hopelessly weak:

1. ...	Rb8-d8!

A **quiet move.** White could well resign now.

2. Qb7xb5!	

The last chance. Maybe Black will hastily reply with 2. ... Rd1 + , when White would win by 3. Qf1.

2. ...	c6xb5
3. any move	Rd8-d1#

D-472

1. ...	Qa2-b1 + !!

The "decoy" theme.

2. Kc1xb1	Rd4-d1#

D-473   Looking at the e8 square, we see that it is attacked five times by White and defended only four times by Black. Therefore:

1. Qe4-e8 + !	

1. dxc8Q + would be no good because of 1. ... Qxc8!, when Black would maintain four defenders while White would also only have four attackers instead of five.

1. ...	Nf6xe8
2. d7xe8Q +	Rc8xe8
3. Re3xe8 +	Ra8xe8
4. Re1xe8#	

D-474   This is a position from a game between two outstanding grandmasters played in Margate, 1937. Paul Keres, playing White, defeated the world champion Alexander Alekhine as follows:

1. Qd3xd7 + !

Black resigned, 1. ... Rxd7 would have been met by 2. Re8 + Rd8 3. Rxd8#.

D-475   The Black Queen is **overloaded** with duties — it must defend both the eighth rank and the Bishop.

1. Qf3xb3!

The **deflection** theme. Black loses a Bishop, since he cannot reply 1. ... Qxb3, because of 2. Rd8 + Re8 3. Rxe8#.

D-476

1. Ra1-b1!

This move is possible because Black didn't make an escape hatch for his King in good time.

1. ...   **Ra8-f8**

1. ... Rxa7 would allow 2. Rb8#. Any other Black move would also let White win by 2. Rb8.

2. Rb1-b8   **g7-g6**

Creating an escape hatch.

3. a7-a8Q   **Rf8xb8**

4. Qa8xb8 +

With a Queen for four pawns (a five-point advantage), White should win.

D-477

a)   **1. ...**   **Kd4-c3**

2. Kc1-d1   **Kc3-b2**

And the pawn is unstoppable.

b)   **1. ...**   **Kd4-d3**

2. Kc1-d1   **c4-c3**

3. Kd1-c1   **c3-c2**

4. Kc1-b2   **Kd3-d2**

And so on.

D-478

a) Black to play:

1. ...   **Kc8-c7**

Taking the opposition.

2. Kc5-d5!

Forcing Black to yield the opposition.

2. ...   **Kc7-c8**

3. Kd5-c6!   **Kc8-d8**

4. Kc6-d6!   **Kd8-e8**

5. e6-e7

And the pawn will queen.

b) White to play:

1. Kc5-c6!

Achieving the familiar winning position.

D-479

1. Kd1-c2!

1. Kd2 would lead to a draw after 1. ... Ke7 2. Kc3 Kd6 3. Kc4 Kc6, with a theoretically drawn position.

1. ...   **Kf8-e7**

2. Kc2-b3!

Now 2. Kc3 would have led to a draw.

2. ...   **Ke7-d6**

3. Kb3-a4!

3. Kc4 would only draw.

3. ...   **Kd6-c6**

4. Ka4-a5!

Four strong moves have brought White to a theoretically won position. His King is in front of the pawn and he can capture the opposition.

4. ...   **Kc6-b7**

5. Ka5-b5!   **Kb7-a7**

6. Kb5-c6   **Ka7-a8**

7. Kc6-b6!   **Ka8-b8**

8. b4-b5   **Kb8-a8**

9. Kb6-c7

And the pawn will queen in three more moves.

D-480

a) Black to play:

1. ...   **Ka8-b7**

2. a7-a8Q + !

By sacrificing the pawn, White obtains a theoretically won position.

2. ...   **Kb7xa8**

3. Kb5-a6!

Taking the opposition.

3. ...   **Ka8-b8**

4. b6-b7

And White wins.

b) White to play:

1. Kb5-c5

Another way to win is 1. Ka5 Kb7 2. a8Q + Kxa8 3. Ka6, with a familiar position. But be careful — 1. Ka6 and 1. Kc6 lead to stalemate!

1. ...   **Ka8-b7**

2. a7-a8Q + !

This is the only way to win in this position — sacrifice the pawn and then take the opposition.

2. ...   **Kb7xa8**

3. Kc5-c6

White takes the **diagonal** opposition.

3. ...   Ka8-b8
4. b6-b7

And so on.

D-481

1. Bb1xd3!

White exchanges the last pair of pieces, knowing that the pawn ending is theoretically won for him.

1. ...   Ke3xd3
2. Kh1-h2!

2. g4 would lead to a draw since the Black King could enter the square of the pawn by 2. ... Ke4.

2. ...   Kd3-e4
3. Kh2-g3   Ke4-f5
4. Kg3-h4

And White should win (with correct play).

D-482

1. Ba8-d5!!

The only way to save the pawn.

1. ...   Kc5xd5
2. Ka6-b5!

The King manages to come to the pawn's aid in time.

2. ...   Kd5-d6
3. c3-c4   Kd6-c7
4. Kb5-c5!

Reaching a theoretically won ending. You already know how to play this position.

SUPPLEMENTARY MATERIAL

for use at the teacher's discretion

Defending the Back Rank

A back-rank mate is usually the result of the rank being **insufficiently defended** against invasion by the opponent's major pieces (Rooks and Queen.) Often a player falls into a back-rank mate because of **carelessness** on his part: he **moves instantly**, thinking only about his own aims and forgetting to take into consideration the **ideas of his opponent**. So, to begin with, you must pay **careful attention** to his back rank, both your own and your opponent's. And, of course, you have to know the

methods of defending the back rank. Let us now look at some examples.

483

Is this mate?

It's not, of course. Black has at his disposal the simplest method of defense — that of eliminating the enemy piece which has invaded the back rank:

1. ...   Bh1xa8

484

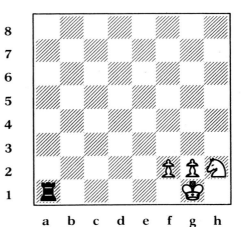

This only looks like mate, for White can play **1. Nh2-f1.** The Knight not only defends the King against the check but also creates an "escape hatch" for the King by vacating the square it was on (h2).

485

White to play. Can he checkmate Black?

No. White attacks e8 twice, butBlack has it defended an equal number of times. You can see that the **defence is sufficient** if the number of defenders is **not less** than the number of attackers.

487

White to play. Is Black's back rank sufficiently defended?

Yes, it is. Although White appears to have two attackers against only one defender, in actual fact his Rook on d1 is **pinned** and cannot leave the first rank.

486

Can White to play mate Black?

No. Black is saved by the **escape hatch**:

1. Qd2-d7 +   Kc8-b8
2. Qd7-d8 +   Rh8xd8
3. Rd1xd8 +   *Kb8-a7*

488

With which piece should Black capture the White Queen?

With the Rook, of course! Because otherwise:

1. ...   Kxf8
2. Rd8 +   Rxd8
3. Rxd8#

489

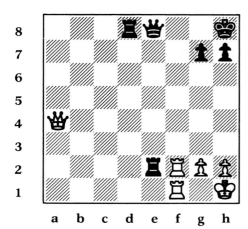

White played **1. Qa4xe8 +**. How should Black reply?

With **1. ... Re2xe8!** (maintaining two defenders on the back rank). Otherwise Black would be mated: **1. ... Rdxe8 2. Rf8 + Rxf8 3. Rxf8#.**

490

What to do? To take or not to take?

Not to take! Black wins by retreating his King into the corner, after which White cannot avoid getting mated by ... Qb2#. If, on the other hand, Black plays 1. ... Rxf7, **he** would be the one to get mated, after 2. Rd8 + Rxd8 3. Rxd8#.

491

Black threatens 1. ... Qg2#. Can White save himself?

No, he cannot. Black is able to defend his back rank because of an **x-ray attack**. Namely, his Bishop controls g8 **through** the Rook on e6. For example:

1. Qd4-d8 +	Re6-e8!
2. Qd8xe8 +	Ba2-g8

And White is defenseless.

492

White threatens 1. Rxg8 + Kxg8 2. Rd8#. Is Black in a position to defend himself?

Yes — Black can save himself by using the x-ray attack motif:

1. ...	Rb7-b8!

The Black Rooks defend each other **through** the White Rook on d8.

2. Rd8xb8	Rg8xb8

493

White to move. Who should win?
White loses.

    1. Rd4-d8 +

does not save him because Black can make use of the x-ray attack principle.

    1. ...   **Re6-e8!**

1. ... Rxd8 would lose to 2. Qxd8 + followed by mate next move.   Now, however, the Rook on c8 defends the Rook on e8 **through** the White Rook on d8.

    2. Rd8xe8 +

2. Rxc8 would not save White, because of 2. ... Qg2#.

    2. ...   **Rc8xe8**

White is defenseless against mate next move.

494

White threatens 1. Qxc8 + Kxc8 2. Rh8#. Can Black defend his back rank?

Yes, by

    1. ...   **Qd2-g5!**

The only move that save Black. It is obvious that Black cannot play 1. ... Rxh8, because of 2. Rxh8#, If now

    2. Qh8xc8 +   **Kb8xc8**
    3. Rh1-h8 +

then after

    3. ...   **Qg5-d8**
    4. Rh8xd8   **Kc8xd8**

White should lose, as Black is two pawns up in the pawn ending.

There are also other methods of defending the back rank. You will be introduced to them later on.

495

Black to move. Can he play **1. ... Qf6xb2?**
No. White wins material after:

    2. Qc5-e7!

Deflecting Black's Rook from the eighth rank.

    2. ...   **Re8-f8**

It doesn't help to play 2. ... Qe2 because of 3. Qxe2 Rxe2 4. Rd8 + Re8 5. Rxe8#.

    3. Rd1-d8   **Qb2-b1 +**
    4. Kg1-g2   **Qb1-e4 +**

Otherwise 4. ... h6 5. Rxf8 + and so on, or 4. ... Rxd8 5. Qxd8#.

    5. Qe7xe4   **Rf8xd8**

Black loses his Queen for a Rook and pawn. 9 − (5 + 1) = 3 points. Instead of capturing White's pawn, Black should make an escape hatch by playing 1. ... h6 or 1. ... g6.

Sample Games With a Back-Rank Mate

Game 71
(Schoolchildren's Tournament)
    1. d2-d4   **e7-e5?**

A very dubious opening, played with the intention of **surprising the opponent.**

2. d4xe5	Nb8-c6
3. Ng1-f3	Qd8-e7

Black tries to win back his pawn and at the same time sets a devious **trap** for his opponent.

4. Bc1-f4?

The pawn should be defended by 4. Qd5.

4. ...	Qe7-b4 +!

A triple attack! The King, Bishop, and the b-pawn are forked.

5. Bf4-d2	Qb4xb2
6. Bd2-c3?	

This Bishop is making too many moves in the opening. White has to play 6. Nc3, with an approximately equal game.

6. ...	Bf8-b4!

Black visualizes the back-rank mating pattern shown in Diagram 496.

496

7. Qd1-d2??

The White Queen helps the enemy to put his devious plans into effect. Instead, White had to play 7. Bxb4 Qxa1 8. Bc3 Qxa2, giving up the Exchange and a pawn but avoiding mate.

7. ...	Bb4xc3
8. Qd2xc3?	

It was at any rate better to give up the Rook and pawn by 8. Nxc3 Qxa1 + 9. Nd1 Qxa2.

8. ...	Qb2-c1#

497

Compare the final position in Diagram 497 with the pattern in Diagram 496. White's neglect of his development was the cause of his disastrous loss in this game.

Game 72
Danish Gambit (analysis)

1. e2-e4	e7-e5
2. d2-d4	e5xd4
3. c2-c3	

A pawn sacrifice for rapid piece development.

3. ...	d4xc3
4. Bf1-c4	

In order to gain a lead in development over his opponent, White sacrifices a second pawn.

4. ...	c3xb2
5. Bc1xb2	d7-d5!

By returning one pawn, Black gets a fine game.

6. Bc4xd5	Bf8-b4 +
7. Ke1-f1?	

7. Nc3 would be preferable, although even then Black would have the better position after 7. ... Bxc3 + 8. Bxc3 Nf6.

7. ...	Ng8-f6!

Black espies the possibility of the back-rank mating pattern shown in Diagram 498.

498

pattern

8. Bd5xf7 – ?

Nor does 8. Qa4 + work, because of 8. ... Nc6 9. Bxc6 + bxc6 10. Qxb4 Qd1 + 11. Qe1 Ba6 +! 12. Ne2 Bxe2 + 13. Kg1 Qxe1#.

(Compare with the pattern in Diagram 498.)

8. ...	Ke8xf7
9. Qd1-b3 +	

White has played a faulty combination, not having seen Black's mating counterattack.

9. ...	Bc8-e6
10. Qb3xb4	Qd8-d1 +
11. Qb4-e1	Be6-c4 +
12. Ng1-e2	Bc4xe2 +
13. Kf1-g1	Qd1xe1#

499

Compare the final position, shown in Diagram 499, with the back-rank mating pattern in Diagram 498.

After sacrificing a pawn in the opening, White was in too much of a hurry to get it back and miscalculated, underestimating Black's threats.

Game 73
Efimov–Bronstein, USSR 1942
King's Gambit

1. e2-e4		e7-e5
2. f2-f4		e5xf4

Black in this game was 17-year-old David Bronstein, who later went on to become one of the strongest players in the world.

3. Ng1-f3		Ng8-f6
4. e4-e5		Nf6-h5
5. Nb1-c3		d7-d6
6. Bf1-c4		d6xe5?

Better would be 6. ... Nc6 7. Qe2 Be6!, with an equal game.

7. Nf3xe5?

White could have gained an advantage by 7. Bxf7+! Kxf7 8. Nxe5+ and 9. Qxh5.

7. ...   Qd8-h4+

8. Ke1-f1

Not much better would be 8. Ke2, because of 8. ... f3+, when the White King would be in danger.

8. ...   Bc8-e6

500

Bronstein has seen the possibility of achieving the back-rank mating pattern shown in Diagram 500 and starts to put together a combination. To begin with, he decides to deflect White's Bishop.

9. Bc4xe6?

White had to play 9. d4 and sacrifice the Exchange with 9. ...Ng3+ 10. Kg1 Nxh1 11. Kxh1.

9. ...   Nh5-g3+

10. Kf1-g1?

The only way to offer resistance was with 10. hxg3 Qxh1+ 11. Kf2.

10. ...   Bf8-c5+!

Wins by force.

11. d2-d4   Bc5xd4+!

Deflecting the Queen from the first rank and at the same time **decoying** it onto the d4 square.

12. Qd1xd4   Ng3-e2+!

A fork! The Knight is sacrificed, but the road is cleared for the Queen.

13. Nc3xe2?

It is better to lose your Queen than to get mated.

13. ...   Qh4-e1#

501

Compare the final position, shown in Diagram 501, with the back-rank mating pattern in Diagram 500. Bronstein sacrificed three (!) pieces, but achieved his aim!

Game 74
Rudnev–Kopylev, USSR 1939
English Opening

1. c2-c4

The mid-19th century English masters used to open their games with this move, hence the opening's name.

1. ...	**Ng8-f6**
2. Nb1-c3	**d7-d5**

Attacking the center.

3. c4xd5	**Nf6xd5**
4. e2-e4	**Nd5-b4**

Black sets a pretty trap: 5. d4? would be followed by 5. ... Qxd4! 6. Qxd4 Nc2+ 7. ... Nxd4, and White would be a pawn down.

5. Qd1-a4 +

An unfortunate move that allows Black to develop his pieces. 5. d3 would have been a better move.

5. ...	**Nb8-c6**

6. d2-d4?

It would have been better to drive away the dangerous Knight by playing 6. a3.

6. ...	**Bc8-d7!**

White had hoped that Black would regale himself on a pawn by playing 6. ... Qxd4, when White would get a fine game after 7. Be3, 8. Rd1 or 8. a3, etc. After the move played in the game White is in considerable difficulties. No defense is visible against the threat of 7. ... Nxd4 8. Qxb4 Nc2+ 9. ... Nxb4.

7. Bf1-b5?

It would have been better to go home with the Queen and give up the pawn: 7. Qd1 Nxd4 8. Bd3, although even then White's position would have been difficult.

7. ...	**Nc6xd4!**

Again the Knight on b4 cannot be captured.

8. Ke1-f1?

The King is so frightened of the fork that it decides to run a bit farther away from the Black Knights. However, White would have done better to first exchange Bishops and Queens and then make a move; not with his King, but with his Rook. After the King move, the master playing Black **sensed a combination.** He **mentally** removed the White Queen and the Knight on c3 from the board and placed his own Queen on d1, and saw that White would be mated as in the back-rank mating pattern in Diagram 502.

But for the time being, all this was only a dream.

8. ...	**Nd4xb5**

Freeing the d-file for the Queen.

9. Qa4xb4

9. Nxb5 would not save White, because of 9. ... e5 followed by 10. ... a6, winning the pinned Knight.

9. ...	**e7-e5**

This pawn move opens up the diagonal for the Bishop, which now attacks the Queen. This type of tactical device is known as a "discovered attack."

10. Qb4-c4	**Nb5xc3**

Black's dreams are gradually starting to come true. The White Queen has lost control over d1 and the Knight on c3 has already been eliminated.

11. b2xc3	**a7-a6!**

A good move that at the same time sets a trap!

12. a2-a4?

Only 12. Ke1 could have saved White.

12. ...	**Bd7-b5!!**

White placed his pawn on a4 thinking that the Black Bishop would no longer dare to occupy b5, but . . . the Bishop sacrifices himself.

13. a4xb5

Alas! This is one of those positions in which even the World Champion could not help White!

13. ...	**Qd8-d1#**

503

Compare the final position, shown in Diagram 503, with the back-rank mating pattern in Diagram 502. As you can see, Black's dream has come true! The tragedy in this game occurred because the White Queen went travelling in the opening, leaving the King to the mercy of his fate.

Game 75
Caro-Kann Defense

This game was played in a simultaneous exhibition given by Grandmaster Igor Zaitsev in 1970. Zaitsev was White.

1. e2-e4	c7-c6
2. d2-d4	d7-d5
3. e4xd5	c6xd5
4. c2-c4	Ng8-f6
5. Nb1-c3	Nb8-c6
6. Bc1-g5	

So far everything is understandable. Both players have been rapidly bringing out their pieces and fighting for the center.

6. ...   **Qd8-b6?**

A more reliable move would have been 6. ... e6, with the idea of developing the dark-square Bishop and then castling.

7. c4xd5   **Nc6xd4**

If 7. ... Qxb2, then White obtains a considerably better position after 8. Rc1.

8. Ng1-f3

Even stronger would have been 8. Be3 e5 9. dxe6 Bc5 10. Qa4+ Qc6 11. 0-0-0!.

8. ...   **Nd4xf3+**
9. Qd1xf3   **Qb6xb2**

Finding himself in a difficult position, Black tries to complicate the struggle.

194

10. Ra1-c1

10. Rb1! would have been stronger. For example, 10. ... Qc2 11. Bb5+ Bd7 12. 0-0, with a huge advantage in development.

10. ...   **Bc8-d7**
11. d5-d6

It may well have been better to play 11. Be2 followed by 12. 0-0.

11. ...   **Ra8-c8?**

Black should have played 11. ... Bc6, with approximately equal chances.

After the move actually played, however, the Grandmaster espied a possibility of mating on the back rank and visualized the pattern shown in Diagram 504.

504

Foreseeing this mating position, White began to set up a combination.

12. Bf1-b5!

White needs the pawn on b7 but it is defended by the Black Queen. So White uses the tactical device of **interference**. The Bishop, by sacrificing itself, interferes with the Queen's action along the b-file.

12. ...   **Bd7xb5**

Allows a spectacular finish. However, on 12. ... Bc6 White could simply castle and remain in an overwhelming position.

13. Qf3xb7!

A double attack forking the Rook and the Bishop. While the Bishop cannot move because it is pinned, the Rook can capture the Knight that White is offering as a sacrifice.

13. ...   **Rc8xc3**

Black has a lost position even though he is up two pieces.

14. d6-d7+!!

As a preparation for carrying out the idea of a back-rank mate, White must first entice the Black Knight onto the d7 square.

14. ...   **Nf6xd7**

14. ... Bxd7 would be no better, because of 15. Qxb2, while 14. ... Kd8 would be followed by 15. Qc8+! Rxc8 16. dxc8 #.

15. Qb7-c8 + !	**Rc3xc8**
16. Rc1xc8#	

505

Compare the final position, shown in Diagram 505, with the back-rank mating pattern in Diagram 504.

Black played actively, but chose a faulty plan in the opening. He should have developed his Kingside and not his Queenside. The Grandmaster superbly exploited the weakness of the back rank and taught his opponent a good lesson.

Game 76
Richards–Locock, Correspondence 1975
Two Knights Defense

1. e2-e4	**e7-e5**
2. Ng1-f3	**Nb8-c6**
3. Bf1-c4	**Ng8-f6**

This is the starting position of the Two Knights Defense.

4. d2-d4	**e5xd4**
5. 0-0	

By sacrificing a pawn, White rapidly brings his pieces into the fray.

5. ...	**Bf8-c5**
6. e4-e5	**d7-d5**

A counterattack.

7. e5xf6	**d5xc4**
8. Rf1-e1 +	**Bc8-e6**
9. Nf3-g5	**Qd8-d5**

Not 9. ... Qxf6, because of 10. Nxe6 fxe6 11. Qh5 + 12. Qxc5.

10. Nb1-c3	**Qd5-f5**

Of course 10. ... dxc3 would be bad because of 11. Qxd5.

11. g2-g4	

An aggressive move.

11. ...	**Qf5-g6**

11. ... Qxf6 is considered to be weaker because of 12. Nce4 Qe7 13. Nxe6 fxe6 14. Bg5 Qf8 15. Qe2, with a strong attack.

12. Nc3-e4	

White would get nothing from 12. fxg7 Rg8 13. Nce4 Be7!.

12. ...	**Bc5-b6**
13. Ng5xe6	**f7xe6**
14. f6-f7 + !	

Decoying the King or the Queen onto the f7 square.

14. ...	**Qg6xf7**

Not 14. ... Kxf7, because of 15. Ng5 + and 16. Rxe6, catching the Queen.

15. Ne4-g5	**Qf7-d7**
16. Ng5xe6	**Nc6-e7?**

Black should have played 16. ... Kf7, removing the King from the e-file with the White Rook on it.

17. Bc1-g5	**Ke8-f7**
18. Qd1-f3 +	**Kf7-g8**
19. Bg5xe7	**Qd7xe7**

After this move White sensed a mating idea and came up with the back-rank mating patterns shown in Diagrams 506 and 507.

506

507

195

20. Qf3-d5   Qe7-f7?

A mistake. True, Black's position is bad anyway, but he could have offered more resistance with 20.... c6, although after 21. Qxc4 Qf7 22. Re4! White has a decisive attack.

21. Ne6-d8!

A spectacular stroke. 21. ... Qxd5 would be met by 22. Re8# as in Diagram 506.

21. ...   Ra8xd8
22. Qd5xd8 +   Qf7-f8
23. Qd8-d5 +   Qf8-f7
24. Re1-e8#

508

Compare the final position, shown in Diagram 508, with the back-rank mating pattern in Diagram 507.

Both sides played well in the opening, but in the middlegame Black committed an error which was brilliantly exploited by his opponent.

Game 77
Volchok–Kreslavskii, Kiev 1970
Ruy Lopez

1. e2-e4	e7-e5
2. Ng1-f3	Nb8-c6
3. Bf1-b5	a7-a6
4. Bb5xc6	d7xc6

A good move, opening up paths for the Bishop and the Queen. 4. ... bxc6 is not as good.

5. 0-0

5. Nxe5? would be unsatisfactory for White because of 5. ... Qd4 or 5. ...Qg5. In both cases Black would win back his pawn and obtain a good game.

5. ...   f7-f6

Now 6. Nxe5 was already a real threat.

6. d2-d4   Bc8-g4
7. c2-c3

White defends his center.

7. ...   e5xd4?

A risky continuation. 7. ... Bd6 would be better.

8. c3xd4   Bg4xf3?

Black continues his faulty plan. He should instead play 8. ... Qd7.

9. Qd1xf3!

White prefers to sacrifice the center pawn rather than expose his King by 9. gxf3.

9. ...   Qd8xd4?

Black's opening strategy of playing for material gain at the expense of development is fundamentally unsound.

10. Rf1-d1   Qd4-c4
11. Bc1-f4   Qc4-f7
12. Qf3-g3

Attacking the pawn on c7 a second time.

12. ...   Bf8-d6

In a difficult position, Black decides to return the pawn but complete his development.

13. Bf4xd6   0-0-0

Black counts on capturing the Bishop on his next move, as it is pinned and cannot move without allowing mate on the first rank. The master playing White thought for a long time here and came up with the pretty back-rank mating pattern shown in Diagram 509.

509

How did this idea arise? The starting point was the observation that if the Rook on d1 were **defended**, the Bishop would be unpinned. So the move 14. Qg4 +, defending the Rook on d1, was found. Then the reply 14. ... Qd7 was discovered. And only after that did White see the amazing variation 15. Be7!! Qxg4 16. Rxd8#, as in Diagram 509. However, the immediate 14. Qg4 + would achieve nothing if

Black replied 14. ... f5!. So White first tries to deflect the pawn from f6.

14. e4-e5!

A strong move that at the same time sets an original trap whose point is overlooked by Black.

14. ...   f6xe5?

Black had to play 14. ... cxd6, although after 15. exd6 White has the advantage because of his strong passed pawn and his chances for an attack on Black's King.

15. Qg3-g4 +   Qf7-d7

It is difficult to suggest anything better, as Black would anyway be a piece down.

16. Bd6-e7!

Here is the surprise! A very pretty move that could well be overlooked even by a strong player.

16. ...   Qd7xg4?

It would, of course, have been better to give up the Queen by playing 16. ... Nxe7, even though Black would have still stood to lose.

17. Rd1xd8#

510

Compare the final position, shown in Diagram 510, with the back-rank mating pattern in Diagram 509.

Black did not apprehend the threat of mate in time and was duly punished.

Game 78
Adams–Torre, New Orleans 1920
Philidor's Defense

1. e2-e4	e7-e5
2. Ng1-f3	d7-d6
3. d2-d4	e5xd4

An unfortunate move that leaves White with a free game. Instead, Black could with no risk have maintained the tension in the center by 3. ... Nf6 4. dxe5 Nxe4 or 3. ... Nbd7.

4. Qd1xd4

It is usually undesirable to bring the Queen out early, but here White plans to answer 4. ... Nc6 by 5. Bb5 and then exchange the Bishop for the Knight.

4. ...	Nb8-c6
5. Bf1-b5	Bc8-d7
6. Bb5xc6	Bd7xc6
7. Nb1-c3	Ng8-f6
8. 0-0	Bf8-e7
9. Nc3-d5	Bc6xd5
10. e4xd5	0-0
11. Bc1-g5	c7-c6?

A faulty plan. Black's position is somewhat cramped, and in such situations a player should not open lines but rather try to exchange some pieces in order to increase the activity of the remaining ones. Consequently, it would have been useful here to make the move 11. ... h6, to be followed by 12. ... Nd7. Although the position then would be favorable for White, Black would nevertheless have every chance of equalizing the game.

12. c2-c4	c6xd5
13. c4xd5	Rf8-e8
14. Rf1-e1	a7-a5
15. Re1-e2	

Vacating e1 for the other Rook.

15. ...   Ra8-c8?

For many moves Black has had the opportunity of playing ... h6, attacking the Bishop and at the same time creating an escape hatch for his King. He will have occasion to regret ignoring this possibility.

16. Ra1-e1!

Now 16. ... h6 would already be too late, because of 17. Bxf6 Bxf6 18. Rxe8, winning the Queen.

16. ...   Qd8-d7

Connecting the Rooks and intending 17. ... h6 after all.

17. Bg5xf6!!

White has discovered the possibility of a back-rank mate according to the pattern shown in Diagram 511, and starts a deeply thought-out combination.

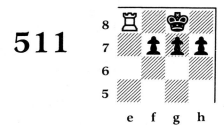

511

17. ...   Be7xf6?

Of course if Black had foreseen the further course of events, he would have played 17. ... gxf6, although even then he would have had a difficult position after 18. h3, threatening 19. Rxe7 Rxe7 20. Rxe7 Qxe7 21. Qg4+ and 22. Qxc8+, remaining a piece up. The immediate 18. Rxe7 would not work because of 18. ... Qxe7! 19. Rxe7 Rc1+ 20. Re1 Rcxe1+ 21. Nxe1 Rxe1# (compare with the back-rank mating pattern in Diagram 512.)

512

18. Qd4-g4!!

The start of a forcing maneuver that will result in one of the Black pieces (the Queen or the Rook on c8) being deflected from the defense of the Rook on e8.

18. ...   Qd7-b5

Declining the present, since if 18. ... Qxg4, then 19. Rxe8+ Rxe8 20. Rxe8#. Now Black is threatening to mate White according to the pattern of Diagram 512: 19. ... Qxe2 20. Rxe2 Rc1+ 21. Re1 Rcxe1+ 22. Nxe1 Rxe1#.

19. Qg4-c4!

Take me, please!

19. ...   Qb5-d7

20. Qc4-c7!

Take, me please! A most interesting situation! The undefended White Queen pursues the Black Queen, depriving it move by move of all the squares on the a4-e8 diagonal.

20. ...   Qd7-b5

21. a2-a4!

Not 21. Qxb7? Qxe2! and it's Black who now

wins: after 22. Qxc8 Qxe1+ 23. Ne1 Rxc8 he is up a Rook (or 22. Rxe2 Rc1+ 23. Ne1+ Rxe1+ 24. Rxe1 Rxe1#, as in the mating pattern of Diagram 512).

21. ...   Qb5xa4

The other variations also lose:

a) 21. ... Rxc7 22. Rxe8+ Qxe8 23. Rxe8# (pattern of Diagram 511);

b) 21. ... Qxe2 22. Rxe2 Rxe2 23. Qxc8+ Re8 24. Qxe8# (pattern of Diagram 511.);

c) 21. ... Rxe2 22. Qxc8+ Qe8 23. Qxe8+ Rxe8 24. Rxe8# (pattern of Diagram 511)

22. Re2-e4!

The chase continues!

22. ...   Qa4-b5

On 22. ... Kf8, 23. Qxd6+ etc. would be decisive, while other moves would lose because of the variations given above.

23. Qc7-b7!

The pursuit has ended. The Black Queen has nowhere left to go, and so Black resigned. The final position is shown in Diagram 513.

513

In this game you saw a complicated but undoubtedly one of the most beautiful combinations on the theme of back-rank mate. However, if Black had taken care in good time to make an **escape hatch** for his King, we would have been deprived of the opportunity of seeing this chef d'oeuvre.

Game 79
Alekhine (aged 16)—Kenlein,
Moscow 1908
Colle System

1. d2-d4   d7-d5

2. Ng1-f3	Ng8-f6
3. e2-e3	e7-e6
4. Bf1-d3	Nb8-d7
5. Nb1-d2	Bf8-d6

This opening is named after the Belgian master Edgar Colle.

6. e3-e4

Attacking the center and opening a pathway for the dark-square Bishop.

6. ...	d5xe4

White was threatening the fork 7. e5.

7. Nd2xe4	Nf6xe4
8. Bd3xe4	0-0
9. 0-0	

The player of the White pieces later went on to become the world champion, but at the time of this game he was only sixteen years old.

9. ...	f7-f5?

Black attempts to develop an attack even before completing the development of his Queenside. The pawn on f7 defended the King and the pawn on e6. After Black's move, both e6 and the a2-g8 diagonal have become weak. 9. ... e5 would also have been bad, because of 10. dxe5 Bxe5 11. Nxe5 Nxe5 12. Bxh7+ Kxh7 13. Qh5+ followed by 14. Qxe5, and White is a pawn up. The correct move for Black was 9. ... Nf6, bringing the Knight closer to the King.

10. Be4-d3	e6-e5?

Here again 10. ... Nf6 would have been better.

11. Bc1-g5!

Decoying the Queen onto the e-file.

11. ...	Qd8-e8

Even worse would be 11. ... Be7, because of 12. Bxe7 Qxe7 13. Nxe5 Nxe5 14. Re1, with advantage to White.

12. d4xe5	Nd7xe5
13. Rf1-e1	

Pinning the Knight and threatening to win a piece by 14. Nxe5 Bxe5 15. Bf4. At this point Alekhine sensed the possibility of the back-rank mating pattern shown in Diagram 514.

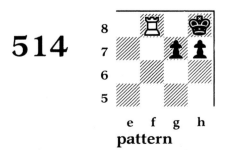

pattern

However, to turn this possibility into reality, Black's **help** is needed.

13. ...	Qe8-h5??

By abandoning the eighth rank, the Queen helps White to turn his plans into reality. Instead, Black must play 13. ... Nxf3+, although White will have a big advantage in development after 14. Qxf3.

14. Nf3xe5!

Preparing a combination.

14. ...	Qh5xg5

Or else Black would lose a piece.

15. Bd3-c4+

Chasing the King into the corner and clearing the d-file for the Queen.

15. ...	Kg8-h8
16. Qd1xd6!!	

Alekhine could have won the exchange by 16. Nf7+ Rxf7 17. Bxf7 (17. Re8+ does not work because of 17. ... Rf8, the Rook on f8 being defended by the Bishop on d6). However, the weakness of Black's back rank allows White to win more than just the exchange. See Diagram 515 for the final position, after 16. Qd1xd6.

515

Black resigned, since after 16. ... cxd6 there would have followed 17. Nf7+, and if 17. ... Rxf7, then 18. Re8+ Rf8 19. Rxf8# — the back-rank mating pattern illustrated in Diagram 514. If instead of 17. ... Rxf7, Black plays 17. ... Kg8, he would end up a piece and a pawn down after 18. Nxg5+ (discovered check) 18. ... Kh8 19. Nf7+ Kg8 20. Nxd6+. Playing 13. ... Qh5?, Black did not notice White's combination and lost by force.

Game 80
Martinik–Dobosz, Poland 1973
Sicilian Defense

1. e2-e4	c7-c5
2. f2-f4	e7-e6
3. Ng1-f3	d7-d5
4. Bf1-b5 +	Bc8-d7
5. Bb5xd7 +	Qd8xd7
6. e4xd5	e6xd5
7. 0-0	Nb8-c6
8. d2-d4	Ng8-f6

So far both sides have played well, rapidly bringing out their pieces.

9. b2-b3?

A faulty plan. The Bishop should not abandon the important c1-h6 diagonal. Better would be 9. Ne5 Nxe5 10. fxe5, opening lines for the Bishop and the Rook.

9. ...	c5xd4
10. Bc1-b2	Bf8-c5
11. Kg1-h1	0-0
12. Nf3xd4	Nf6-g4

Threatening a fork with 13. ...Ne3.

13. Nd4xc6

White's position would be bad after 13. Qd2 too: 13. ... Rae8 14. c3 Re4, with the idea of 15. ... Rfe8.

13. ...	b7xc6
14. Qd1-f3?	

Black's Bishop is very dangerous and White should have tried to exchange it off by playing 14. Bd4. Instead White plays a move that is based on the hope that Black will not notice the **trap** 15. Qc3, with the double threat of 16. Qxg7# and 16. Qxc5.

14. ...	Rf8-e8!

Black of course sees through White's trap and makes a good developing move that at the same time sets a counter-trap based on the weakness of the first rank.

15. Qf3-c3?

Expecting only 15. ... Bf8.

15. ...	Ng4-f2 +!

The Rook is deflected from the first rank.

16. Rf1xf2

If 16. Kg1, then the White Queen is lost after 16. ... Ne4 + (discovered check).

16. ...	Bc5-d4!!

A quiet move after which White resigned. See Diagram 516 for the final position.

516

If 17. Qxd4, then after 17. ... Re1 + 18. Rf1 Rxf1 + 19. Qg1 Rxg1 + 20. Kxg1 Black has a Queen for two minor pieces, while if 17. Qd2, Black wins by 17. ... Bxb2 followed by 18. ... Bxa1, finishing a Rook ahead.

Although White managed to avoid mate in this game, the weakness of his back rank cost him a considerable amount of material.

Lesson Eleven

A. Check Lesson 10 Homework (as necessary).

B. *Review Questions*

Find the solutions to Positions 517–522 directly from the diagrams — do not set up the men on a board.

517

How should the game end?

518

White to move. What would you play?

519

Whoever moves first wins. How?

520

White to move. How should the game end?

521

White to move. What would you play?

522

White to move. Find the strongest continuation.

Solve positions 523–526 directly from the diagrams, without setting up and moving the men. Positions 527 and 528 you can set up on a chessboard.

523

White to play. How should the game end?

524

White to play. Who should win?

525

White to play and mate in two moves.

526

White to play and mate in three moves.

527

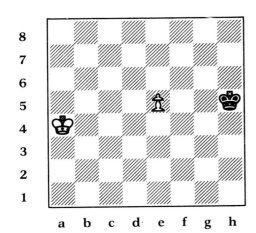

White to play. Can he win?

528

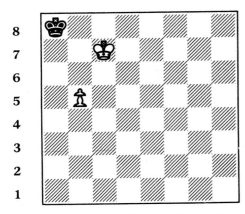

White to play and win.

D-517 White will be mated on the fourth move at the latest:

1. Bf5-b1	Ra1xb1 +
2. Rc3-c1	Rb1xc1 +
3. Rd2-d1	Rc1xd1 +
4. Qe6-e1	Rd1xe1#

A back-rank mate.

D-518 1. Qa3-f8#

1. Qa8 + would not work because of 1. ... Rc8, parrying the check while continuing to threaten 2. ... Qg2#.

D-519 White to play wins by

1. Qd4xe5	Re8xe5
2. Rd1-d8 +	Re5-e8
3. Rd8xe8#	

A back-rank mate.

Black to play wins by

1. ...	Qe5-e1 +
2. Rd1xe1	Re8xe1#

A back-rank mate.

D-520 White attains victory by sacrificing his Queen:

1. Qc3-c8 + !	Ba6xc8
2. Rc2xc8 +	Nb6xc8
3. Rc1xc8#	

A back-rank mate.

D-521

1. Re2-e8 + !	Bf7xe8
2. Re1xe8#	

A back-rank mate.

D-522

1. Qa5xd8 + !	

1. Qxa8 does not work because of 1. ... Qg2#.

1. ...	Ra8xd8
2. Re2-e8 +	Rd8xe8
3. Re1xe8#	

A back-rank mate.

D-523 White should lose, even if he moves first. 1. Qa4xe8 + does not save him, because of 1. ... Qh5xe8!, defending the last rank against mate. Nor is there any other satisfactory defense against the threat of 1. ... Qh1#.

D-524 Black wins, since White cannot defend himself against the threat of 1. ... Qg2#. If 1. Qb4-b8 +, then 1. ... Rd7-d8! (but not 1. ... Rxb8, because of 2. Rxb8 + Rd8 3. Rxd8# — a back-rank mate) 2. Qb8xd8 + (any other move would be followed by 2. ... Qg2#) 2. ... Ra8xd8 3. any move Qh3-g2#.

D-525 1. Rc1-g1 any; 2. Rc6-c8#.

D-526
    1. Re1-e8 +   Bg7-f8
    2. Rd1-g1 +   Kg8-h8
    3. Re8-f8#

D-527 White wins:
    1. Ka4-b5   Kh5-g6
    2. Kb5-c6   Kg6-f7
    3. Kc6-d7
and White will queen his pawn by force in three moves.

D-528
    1. Kc7-b6!
Careful! After 1. b6 it's stalemate!
    1. ...   Ka8-b8
    2. Kb6-a6   Kb8-a8
    3. b5-b6   Ka8-b8
    4. b6-b7   Kb8-c7
    5. Ka6-a7
and White gets a Queen next move.

Typical Mating Combinations
Mate by a Major Piece (Queen or Rook) Helped by Other Men

There are many typical mating patterns, and they often serve as the basis of beautiful combinations. Let us examine the mechanisms involved in such combinations.

To begin with, look at the mating pattern shown in Diagram 529.

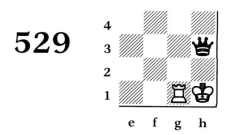

Now find the solutions to Positions 530–533.

530

Black to play and mate on his first move.

531

Black to play and mate in two moves.

532

Black to play and mate in three moves.

533

Black to play and mate in four moves.

This position occurred in a game played by Adolph Anderssen, the strongest player of the mid-19th century.

Solutions to D-530 to D-533

D-530   1. ... Qf1-h3#

D-531
1. ...	Nf5-g3 +

Exposing *the White King.*
2. h2xg3	Qf1-h3#

D-532
1. ...	Qf2-f1 +

With the idea of blocking g1 with the Rook and **opening** the f1-h3 line.
2. Rg2-g1	Nf5-g3 +
3. h2xg3	Qf1-h3#

D-533
1. ...	Bh3-g2 +

Deflecting the Rook from the first rank and **freeing** h3 for the Queen.
2. Rg1xg2	Qf2-f1 +
3. Rg2-g1	Nf5-g3 +
4. h2xg3	Qf1-h3#

Thus, Black in Position 533 made a complex combination based on mating pattern 529 and using five different tactical motifs.

Let us look at some other commonly encountered mating patterns and combinations based on them.

Solve positions 535–539 by making use of the mating pattern shown in Diagram 534.

534

pattern

535

White to play and mate on his first move.

536

White to play and mate in two moves.

205

537

White to play and mate in three moves.

538

White to play and mate in four moves.

539

White to play and mate in five moves.

This position is based on a problem published in the year 1512 by P. Damiano, and the type of mating pattern it illustrates is known as Damiano's mate.

Solutions to D-535 to D-539

D-535   1. Qh1-h7# Damiano's mate.

D-536   1. Qd1-h1+ Kh8-g8 2. Qh1-h7# Damiano's mate.

D-537
    1. Rh1-h8 +
Deflecting the King to a square where it can be checked by the Queen, and **clearing the square** h1 for the Queen.

1. ...	Kg8xh8
2. Qd1-h1 +	Kh8-g8
3. Qh1-h7#	

Damiano's mate.

D-538
    1. Re1-h1 +.
Clearing the line for the Queen.

1. ...	Kh8-g8
2. Rh1-h8 +	Kg8xh8
3. Qd1-h1 +	Kh8-g8
4. Qh1-h7#	

Damiano's mate.

D-539
    1. Rh1-h8 +
Deflecting the King to a square where it can be checked and **clearing the square** h1 for the other Rook.

1. ...	Kg8xh8
2. Re1-h1 +	Kh8-g8
3. Rh1-h8 +	Kg8xh8
4. Qd1-h1 +	Kh8-g8
5. Qh1-h7#	

Damiano's mate.

Thus, White in the position of Diagram 539 carries out a complex combination involving three tactical motifs.

Solve positions 541–544 by making use of the mating pattern shown in Diagram 540.

540

pattern

541

Black to play and mate on his first move.

542

Black to play and mate in two moves.

543

Black to play and mate in three moves.

544

Black to play and mate in four moves.

Solutions to D-541 through D-544.

D-541   1. ... **Qh2xf2#**

D-542   1. ... **Qh3-h2 + 2. Kg1-f1 Qh2xf2#**

D-543
| 1. ... | **Bh2-g3 +** |
Discovered check.
| **2. Kh1-g1** | **Qh3-h2 +** |
| **3. Kg1-f1** | **Qh2xf2#** |

D-544
1. ...	**Bd6xh2 +**
2. Kg1-h1	**Bh2-g3 +**
3. Kh1-g1	**Qh3-h2 +**
4. Kg1-f1	**Qh2xf2#**

The combination in Position 544 is based on the tactical motif of discovered check.

Solve positions 546–549 using the mating pattern shown in Diagram 545.

Black to play and mate in three moves.

Black to play and mate on his first move.

Black to play and mate in four moves.

Black to play and mate in two moves.

Solutions to D-546 through D-549

D-546   1. ... Ra4xh4#

D-547

1. ...	Qb4xh4 + !
2. Rh7xh4	Ra4xh4#

D-548

1. ...	Rf4-h4 + !
2. g3xh4	Qb4xh4 + !
3. Rh7xh4	Ra4xh4#

D-549

1. ...   Nf1-g3! +

Exposing the White King.

2. h2xg3	Rf4-h4 + !
3. g3xh4	Qb4xh4 + !
4. Rh7xh4	Ra4xh4#

The combination in Position 549 works with the help of the tactical motif of **exposing the King.**

Solve Positions 551–554 using the mating pattern shown in Diagram 550.

550

pattern

551

White to play and mate on his first move.

552

White to play and mate in two moves.

553

White to play and mate in three moves.

554

White to play and mate in four moves.

The position in Diagram 554 is from a game won by the outstanding grandmaster Rudolf Spielmann against Henschtscher in Vienna in 1929.

Solutions to D-551 through D-554
D-551   1. Rh5-h8#
D-552
     1. Re5-h5 +
Exploiting the **pin** on the g6 pawn.
     1. ...   Kh7-g8
     2. Rh5-h8#

D-553
     1. Qh6xh7 +!
Exposing the King and **decoying** it to a square where it will be checked.

```
    1. ...                          Kg8xh7
    2. Re5-h5 +                      Kh7-g8
    3. Rh5-h8#
```

D-554
```
    1. Nf5-e7 + !
```
Clearing a line for the Rook.
```
    1. ...                          Qc5xe7
    2. Qh6xh7 + !                    Kg8xh7
    3. Re5-h5 +                      Kh7-g8
    4. Rh5-h8#
```

Grandmaster Spielmann made use of four tactical motifs in his fine combination.

Solve positions 556–559 using the mating pattern shown in Diagram 555.

555

pattern

556

Black to play and mate on his first move.

557

Black to play and mate in two moves.

558

Black to play and either win a piece or mate in three moves.

559

Black to play and either win a piece or mate in four moves.

Position 559 occurred in the game Giuli–Henneberger played in Zurich in 1941. The mating pattern illustrated there is known as "Anastasia's mate" because the idea was first published in the novel *Anastasia and Chess* printed in 1803.

Solutions to D-556 through D-559

D-556

    1. ...   **Re4-h4#**
Anastasia's mate.

D-557

    1. ...   **Re5-h5 + !**
Clearing the line for the other Rook.

    2. g4xh5   **Re4-h4#**

D-558

    1. ...   **Qf4xg4!**
Exposing the King.

    2. h3xg4

2. f3 does not save White, because of 2. ... Ng3+ 3. Kg1 Nxf1 4. fxg4 Nxd2.

    2. ...   **Re5-h5 + !**
    3. g4xh5   **Re4-h4#**

D-559

    1. ...   **Nd4-e2 +**
Decoying the Black King onto the h-file.

    2. Kg1-h1   **Qf4xg4!**
    3. h3xg4

Or else White loses a piece.

    3. ...   **Re5-h5 + !**
    4. g4xh5   **Re4-h4#**

Black exploited three tactical motifs in this combination.

Endgames with King and non-Rook Pawn vs. King

(Continuation. For beginning, see Lesson 10)

In this lesson we shall study examples in which the pawn is unable to queen and the game ends in a draw.

560

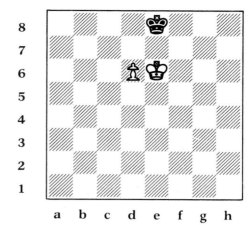

Drawn only if it is White's turn.

561

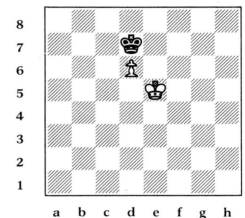

Drawn no matter who moves first.

562

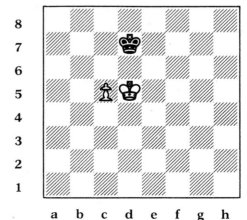

Drawn no matter who moves first.

563

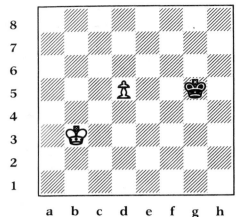

Drawn only if it is Black's turn.

564

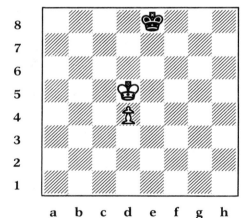

Drawn only if it is Black's turn.

565

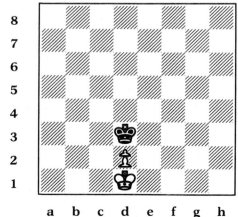

Drawn no matter who moves first.

D-560 The Kings are in opposition and the position is one of mutual Zugzwang: it is disadvantageous both for White and for Black to make the first move. If Black begins, he loses, since the White pawn will reach the seventh rank **without checking**:

1. ...	Ke8-d8
2. d6-d7	Kd8-c7

There is no other move. Black is thus forced to give up control over e7.

3. Ke6-e7

and White wins.

With White to play, the position is drawn, since the pawn reaches the seventh rank **with check**:

1. d6-d7 +

Or else Black will draw with 1. ... Kd7 (see the next example).

1. ...	Ke8-d8
2. Ke6-d6	stalemate

Conclusion: If the pawn, defended by its King, reaches the seventh rank with check, the game is drawn; otherwise, it will be able to queen.

D-561 This is a theoretically drawn position. However, Black has to know how to maneuver correctly with his King, since the slightest mistake will lead to a loss. The Black King should shuttle back and forth between d7 and d8 and occupy c8 or e8 **only** when by doing so it takes the opposition. For example:

1. Ke5-d5   Kd7-d8!

Waiting for White's next move. Otherwise Black would lose the opposition and the game: **a)** 1. ... Ke8 2. Ke6! Kd8 3. d7 Kc7 4. Ke7 etc.; or **b)** 1. Kc8 2. Kc6!, winning.

2. Kd5-c5

Trying to confuse the opponent.

2. ...   Kd8-d7!

Again the only move.

3. Kc5-d5   Kd7-d8!

The only way.

4. Kd5-c6   Kd8-c8!

Taking the opposition.

5. d6-d7 +	Kc8-d8
6. Kc6-d6	stalemate

If he moves first in the above example (Diagram 561), Black defends in the same way:

| 1. ... | Kd7-d8! |
| 2. Ke5-d5 | Kd8-d7! |

and so on.

Conclusion: If the lone King can take the opposition on the eighth rank when the enemy King and pawn are on the sixth rank, the game is always drawn.

D-562 Having the opposition is not of decisive importance in this position since Black will have the opportunity of taking the opposition on the last rank, as in the previous example.

| 1. c5-c6 + | Kd7-c7! |

1. ... Kc8 2. Kd6 Kd8!, taking the opposition, also leads to a draw. All other moves lose, since they allow White to take the opposition with the Black King on the last rank:

a) 1. ... Kd8 2. Kd6! Kc8 3. c7 Kb7 4. Kd7 any 5. c8Q;

b) 1. ... Ke8 2. Ke6! Kd8 3. Kd6!, etc.;

c) 1. ... Ke7 2. Ke5! Ke8 3. Ke6! Kd8 4. Kd6!, with a familiar position.

2. Kd5-c5	Kc7-c8!
3. Kc5-b5	Kc8-c7!
4. Kb5-c5	Kc7-c8!
5. Kc5-d6	Kc8-d8!
6. c6-c7 +	Kd8-c8
7. Kd6-c6	stalemate

Black to move draws in the following manner:

| 1. ... | Kd7-c7! |

The only move to draw. All other moves lose:

a) 1. ... Kc8 2. Kc6! Kb8 3. Kd7 and the pawn cannot be stopped;

b) 1. ... Kd8 2. Kd6! Kc8 3. Kc6 etc.;

c) 1. ... Ke8 (or 1. ... Ke7) 2. Kc6! Kd8 3. Kb7 and the pawn will queen.

2. c5-c6	Kc7-c8!
3. Kd5-d6	Kc8-d8!
4. c6-c7 +	Kd8-c8

with a draw.

Conclusion: If the pawn is no further than the fifth rank, then the lone King draws whether it has the first move or not, provided that it is in front of the pawn and there is no more than one square separating it from the pawn.

D-563 We already know that a King can hold back an enemy pawn if it can get in **front** of the pawn, but **not from the side.** So the Black King here must try to go round to the front of the pawn:

| 1. ... | Kg5-f6! |

1. ... Kf5 loses because of 2. Kc4 Ke5 3. Kc5, when the pawn will queen easily.

| 2. Kb3-c4 | Kf6-e7 |
| 3. Kc4-c5 | Ke7-d7! |

Just in time! Now it's a draw.

4. d5-d6	Kd7-d8!
5. Kc5-c6	Kd8-c8!
6. d6-d7 +	Kc8-d8
7. Kc6-d6	stalemate

If White has the first move, he wins as follows:

1. Kb3-c4	Kg5-f6
2. Kc4-c5	Kf6-e7
3. Kc5-c6!	

The King has reached the sixth rank ahead of the pawn. This is always a win.

3. ...	Ke7-d8
4. Kc6-d6!	Kd8-c8
5. Kd6-e7	

and the pawn will queen in three more moves.

D-564 It goes without saying that White to move can win easily in a number of ways, e.g.:

1. Kd5-e6	Ke8-d8
2. Ke6-d6	Kd8-e8
3. Kd6-c7	

and the pawn will advance unhindered to its queening square.

However, Black can draw if he has the first move:

| 1. ... | Ke8-d7! |

The saving move! Black seizes the opposition.

| 2. Kd5-e5 | Kd7-e7! |

Keeping the opposition. All other moves would lose:

a) 2. ... Kc6 3. Ke6 Kc7 4. d5 Kd8 5. Kd6! etc.;

b) 2. ... Kc7 3. Ke6 Kc6 4. d5 + Kc7 5. Ke7 and the pawn will queen;

c) on any other second move by Black, White wins easily by 3. Kd6.

| 3. d4-d5 | |

White cannot break through with his King and has to push his pawn. If 3. Kf5, Black draws by 3. ... Kf7 or 3. ... Kd6.

3. ...	**Ke7-d7!**

Again the only move. Any other move would lose to 4. Kd6.

4. d5-d6	**Kd7-d8!**

Once again the only drawing move. Black fights for the opposition. Any other move would allow White to win by 5. Ke6.

5. Ke5-d5

White tries to confuse his opponent. On 5. Ke6 Black would take the opposition by 5. ... Ke8, after which the draw is inevitable.

5. ...	**Kd8-d7!**

The only way!

6. Kd5-c5

Maybe Black will blunder?

6. ...	**Kd7-d8!**

Black maneuvers his King correctly and gets the draw.

7. Kc5-c6	**Kd8-c8!**

Black has won the opposition.

8. d6-d7 +	**Kc8-d8**
9. Kc6-d6	**stalemate**

Conclusion: If the lone King is in front of the pawn, but not on the last rank, and gets the opposition against the enemy King, the game is drawn provided that the pawn does not have any spare moves, i.e., if the enemy King is on the square directly in front of its pawn.

D-565 Finally, let us see how to fight against a pawn that is on its starting square. In Diagram 565, the Black King has occupied the square in front of the White pawn and prevents the latter from moving. However, the King cannot remain on this square forever since it will have to retreat when it is Black's turn to move. Then the pawn will be able to advance, supported by the White King, but if Black maneuvers correctly with his King, he should draw. Otherwise, he will lose. It does not matter whose turn it is in Diagram 565; let us suppose that it is White's turn:

1. Kd1-c1

A waiting move that transfers the obligation to move to Black. 1. Ke1 would also be possible.

1. ...	**Kd3-d4!**

Although in the present position it is not of crucial importance where the King moves to (except of course 1. ... Ke2, when the reply 2. d4 puts the pawn out of reach), **you should develop the habit of retreating along the file on which the pawn stands.**

2. Kc1-c2

Controlling d3.

2. ...	**Kd4-c4!**

Taking the opposition and hindering the advance of the White King. All other moves would lose, since the White King would **get the opposition in front of its pawn.**

3. d2-d3 +	**Kc4-d4**
4. Kc2-d2	**Kd4-d5**
5. Kd2-e3	**Kd5-e5!**
6. d3-d4 +	**Ke5-d5**
7. Ke3-d3	**Kd5-d6**
8. Kd3-c4	**Kd6-c6!**
9. d4-d5 +	**Kc6-d6**
10. Kc4-d4	**Kd6-d7**
11. Kd4-e5	**Kd7-e7!**
12. d5-d6 +	**Ke7-d7!**
13. Ke5-d5	**Kd7-d8!**
14. Kd5-c6	**Kd8-c8!**
15. d6-d7 +	**Kc8-d8**
16. Kc6-d6	**stalemate**

As you can see, in order to play pawn endgames well you have to know how to make use of **tactical devices** such as the **opposition, waiting move, Zugzwang,** etc. You also have to know inside out (like a multiplication table) which positions are won and which are drawn.

You have now worked through Level II (Intermediate I) of our chess training program. The next, and last, lesson will be a test. Twenty tests of equal difficulty, each containing six questions, have been prepared. Each student will pick one at random and answer all six questions on it. The test will show how well you have mastered the contents of the course.

HOMEWORK

1. Review the homework assignments of previous lessons.
2. Play often, but not more than one and a half hours a day.
3. Familiarize yourself with the typical mating patterns shown in Diagrams 566–601. These involve a major piece (Queen or Rook) assisted by other pieces and pawns.
4. Make up positions in which White (or Black) can make a two-move combination leading to these typical mating patterns.

566

571

567

572

568

573

569

574

570

575

576

581

577

582

578

583

579

584

580

585

586

591

587

592

588

593

589

594

590

595

596

601

597

SUPPLEMENTARY MATERIAL

for use at the teacher's discretion

Sample Games Illustrating
Typical Major Piece (Queen or Rook)
Mating Patterns

598

Game 81
Ruy Lopez

In 1895 Emanuel Lasker, who was just beginning his 27-year reign as World Champion, published his *Common Sense in Chess*, a book that acquired great fame. Let us look at an interesting game from that book.

1. e2-e4	e7-e5
2. Ng1-f3	Nb8-c6
3. Bf1-b5	Ng8-f6
4. 0-0!	Nf6xe4
5. Rf1-e1	

Stronger would be 5. d4 Be7 6. Qe2, with a complicated position.

| 5. ... | Ne4-d6 |

5. ... Nf6 6. Nxe5 Be7 7. d4 0-0 8. Nc3 would be to White's advantage.

599

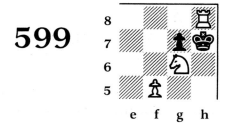

6. Nb1-c3

Since Black cannot defend the pawn on e5, White is in no rush to capture it and instead develops a piece.

| 6. ... | Nd6xb5 |

It was more important to block the e-file by playing 6. ... Be7.

7. Nf3xe5!

600

Luring Black into a clever trap. White does not hurry to capture the Knight on b5 since Black does not have time to save it. The threat is to win Black's Queen by means of the **discovered check** 8. Nxc6 + .

7. ...   **Nc6xe5?**

It was still not too late to play 7. ... Be7, preventing the discovered check and preparing to castle. 7. ...Nxc3 would lose after 8. Nxc6 + Be7 9. Nxe7 Nxd1 10. Ng6 + (another discovered check) 10. ... Qe7 11. Nxe7, when White remains a piece up.

8. Re1xe5 +   **Bf8-e7**
9. Nc3-d5!

White could capture the Knight with his Rook or his Knight but prefers to pile up on the pinned Bishop, which cannot be defended.

9. ...   **0-0**

Trying to get his King out of danger.

10. Nd5xe7 +   **Kg8-h8**

If White looks at the position closely, he can see five possible mating patterns (see Diagrams 602–606).

602

603

604

605

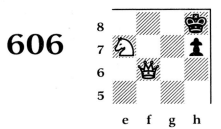

606

11. Qd1-h5!

Threatening 12. Qxh7 + Kxh7 13. Rh5# (Anastasia's mate, Diagram 602). White could also win with 11. Nxc8 Nd4 12. Ne7 Re8 13. c3, remaining a piece up.

11. ...   **g7-g6**

A pretty variation is 11. ... h6 12. d3! d6 13. Bxh6 gxh6 14. Qxh6# (Diagram 604). If instead of 13. ... gxh6, Black replied to 13. Bxh6 with 13. ... g6, then 14. Bxf8 +! gxh5 15. Rxh5# (Diagram 605). White's attack is irresistible in other variations as well.

12. Qh5-h6   **d7-d6**

There is already no satisfactory defense for Black.

13. Re5-h5!

Threatening 14. Qxh7# (Diagram 603).

13. ...   **g6xh5**
14. Qh6-f6#

The mating pattern shown in Diagram 606. See Diagram 607 for the final position.

607

A beautiful game, made up by World Champion Lasker especially for instructional purposes.

Game 82
Giuoco Piano

Gioachino Greco, an early 17th century Italian chessplayer, left behind a manuscript containing analyses of many opening variations used in his time. This game is one of the analyses.

1. e2-e4	e7-e5
2. Ng1-f3	Nb8-c6
3. Bf1-c4	Bf8-c5
4. c2-c3	Ng8-f6

All these moves are encountered even today in the games of chessplayers of all levels.

5. Nf3-g5?

The best move is 5. d4, but 5. d3 is also possible. As you can see, 350 years ago players sometimes ignored the main principles of opening play and moved the same piece twice in the opening.

5. ...	0-0
6. d2-d3	h7-h6?

Black was not faced with any threat and should have continued his development by means of the move 6. ... d6.

7. h2-h4   **h6xg5??**

There is no rule in chess that says that capturing is obligatory! With this capture Black only furthers White's aggressive designs. 7. ... d6 should still have been played.

8. h4xg5   **Nf6-h7?**

We like to capture pieces but are not so eager to give them back! Black had to play 8. ... g6,

maintaining control over h5.

9. Qd1-h5

Various mating patterns are in the air (see Diagrams 608-610).

9. ...   **Rf8-e8**

Planning to answer 10. Qxh7+ with 10. ... Kf8. 9. ... Nxg5 would not save Black, because of 10. Qh8# (back-rank mate, Diagram 609), while any other move would run up against 10. Qxh7# (Diagram 608).

608

609

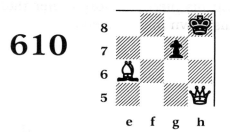

610

10. Qh5xf7+	Kg8-h8
11. Rh1xh7+!	Kh8xh7
12. Qf7-h5#	

The mating pattern of Diagram 610. The final position is shown in Diagram 611.

611

This is the famous Greco's Mate. This analysis shows the great danger of a coordinated attack by the Queen and a Rook along the open h-file.

Game 83
Reiner–Steinitz, Vienna 1860
Scotch Gambit

1. e2-e4	e7-e5
2. Ng1-f3	Nb8-c6

The Black pieces were conducted by a great player who in 1886 became the first official World Champion in chess history.

3. d2-d4	e5xd4
4. Bf1-c4	

This opening is a gambit as White strives to develop his pieces rapidly rather than recapture his pawn immediately.

4. ...	Bf8-c5

Black develops and defends the pawn at the same time. 4. ... Bb4+ would be risky due to 5. c3 dxc3 6. 0-0 cxb2 7. Bxb2, with a considerable advantage in development for White.

5. 0-0	d7-d6

5. ... Nge7 would be a mistake because of 6. Ng5 Ne5 7. Bb3 h6 8. f4 hxg5 9. fxe5, with an irresistible attack for White. Downright bad after 6. Ng5 would be 6. ... 0-0, because of 7. Qh5 h6 8. Nxf7, with a quick victory in sight.

6. c2-c3	Bc8-g4!

Black aims for a counter-attack. 6. ... dxc3 7. Nxc3 would give White good play.

7. Qd1-b3	

A fork: both the b7 pawn and the f7 pawn are attacked. This would be fine if it didn't lead to White's own King becoming exposed.

7. ...	Bg4xf3!

Ignoring White's threats.

8. Bc4xf7 +	Ke8-f8
9. Bf7xg8	Rh8xg8
10. g2xf3	

Let us evaluate the position that has arisen. By giving back the pawn, Black has achieved excellent development and has good chances for an attack against White's weakened King.

10. ...	g7-g5!

Energetically played! There is no time to protect the pawn on b7.

11. Qb3-e6	

After 11. Qxb7 Ne5 White would find it very difficult to defend his King.

11. ...	Nc6-e5
12. Qe6-f5 + ?	

Weak players love to check. But it is better to checkmate once than to check 1000 times. Here White should have played 12. Kh1 and then tried to develop his Queenside.

12. ...	Kf8-g7!

A clever move! 13. Bxg5 is to be met by 13. ... Kh8!, when the White Bishop would be caught in a dangerous pin.

13. Kg1-h1	Kg7-h8
14. Rf1-g1	

White will pay a heavy price for forgetting about his Queenside. He had to play 14. cxd4 Bxd4 15. Nc3 g4 16. Bf4, bringing out his pieces at the cost of a pawn.

14. ...	g5-g4!

Clearing the way for the Queen and anticipating the mating patterns shown in Diagrams 612 and 613.

15. f3-f4?	

The best chance was 15. Bf4. 15. fxg4 would have been met by 15. ... Qh4, threatening 16. ... Raf8.

15. ...	Ne5-f3
16. Rg1xg4	

White does not sense the danger.

16. ...	Qd8-h4!!

Take me, please! The threat is 17. ... Qxh2 mate (Diagram 612).

612

17. Rg4-g2

613

White doesn't like the idea of getting mated 17. Rxh4 Rg1# (Diagram 613).

17. ...	Qh4xh2 + !

Forcing White to accept the Queen sacrifice!

18. Rg2xh2	Rg8-g1#

614

A beautifully played game by the World Champion. As for White, he got mated before he got around to making a single move with his Queenside pieces.

Game 84
Koshtenko–Lerner, Soviet Union 1962
French Defense

1. e2-e4	e7-e6
2. d2-d4	d7-d5

These moves constitute the French Defense.

3. Nb1-c3	Bf8-b4
4. Ng1-e2	

White sacrifices the pawn on e4. Former World Champion Alexander Alekhine sometimes utilized this idea with success.

4. ...	d5xe4
5. a2-a3	Bb4xc3 +

Or else White would win back the pawn on e4 and Black's 3. ... Bb4 would turn out to have been pointless.

6. Ne2xc3	Ng8-f6?

Black could hold onto the pawn with 6. ... f5, but that would allow White to whip up a strong attack after 7. f3! exf3 8. Qxf3 Qxd4 9. Qg3!. It is better to give back such pawns and instead concentrate on developing your pieces quickly. Here, for example, after 6. ... Nc6 7. Bb5 Ne7 8. Nxe4 0-0 9. c3 e5! the game is equal.

7. Bc1-g5!

White not only wins back his pawn but also pins the Knight on f6, a pin which will be very unpleasant for Black as he has already exchanged off his dark-square Bishop.

7. ...	Nb8-c6
8. Bf1-b5	

Pinning the other Knight.

8. ...	0-0

If 8. ... Bd7, then 9. Nxe4, which cannot be met by 9. ... Nxd4 because of 10. Bxf6 gxf6 11. Bxd7 + Qxd7 12. Nxf6 +, winning the Queen.

9. Bb5xc6	b7xc6
10. Nc3xe4	

White has won back his pawn and it is not obvious how Black can unpin his Knight.

10. ...	Qd8-d5

It is on this move that Black had placed his hopes. Realizing that his position is difficult, he decides to take a risk.

11. Ne4xf6 +

White sees that the Pillsbury mating pattern (Diagram 615) is a possibility and begins to prepare a combination.

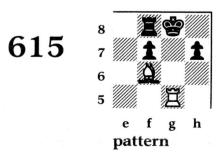

615

pattern

11. ...   **g7xf6**

Forced.

12. Bg5xf6   **Qd5xg2?**

A fatal mistake! Black has to play 12. ... Qf5, trying to chase away White's dangerous Bishop. However, he thinks that White will save his Rook with 13. Rf1, whereupon after 13. ... Ba6 it would be White who is in trouble.

13. Qd1-f3!!

Now there's a move for you! Black resigned right away. The Queen cannot be taken because of Pillsbury's mate (Diagram 615): 13. ... Qxf3 14. Rg1+ Qg4 15. Rxg4#. And after 13. ... Qg6 14. 0-0-0 Qh6+ 15. Kb1 White wins easily too. See Diagram 616 for the final position.

616

Black lost because of the dangerous pin on the f6 Knight, while the final catastrophe occurred because he did not notice Pillsbury's mate.

Game 85
(from under-13 tournament)

1. d2-d4   **Ng8-f6**

The Knight controls e4, preventing the White e-pawn from moving there.

2. Nb1-d2?

An unfortunate move that blocks the Bishop and Queen. 2. c4 or 2. Nf3 are better.

2. ...   **e7-e5**

Black sacrifices a pawn in the hopes of rapidly bringing out his pieces.

3. d4xe5   **Nf6-g4**

4. Ng1-f3   **Bf8-e7**

4. ... Nc6 would be more accurate, but Black

was tempted by the trap from the game Gibeau–Lazard (Game 6), and plays 4. ... Be7 in anticipation of the mating pattern shown in Diagram 617.

617

5. h2-h3??

It was this "natural" move that Black was counting on. Instead of hurrying to chase away the Knight, White could have got a good game after 5. e3 Nc6 6. Nc4 b5 7. Ncd2 a6 8. a4.

5. ...   **Ng4-e3!**

White resigned. He had not taken Black's last move into account in his earlier calculations. If 6. fxe3 (otherwise the Queen is lost), then 6. ... Bh4+ 7. Nxh4 Qxh4+ 8. g3 Qxg3# (see the mating pattern of Diagram 617). The final position is shown in Diagram 618.

618

White was routed because of his carelessness.

Game 86
Mayet–Anderssen, Berlin 1851
Ruy Lopez

1. e2-e4   **e7-e5**

2. Ng1-f3   **Nb8-c6**

Black was Adolph Anderssen, a German

master who was the strongest player in the world in the middle of the nineteenth century.

3. Bf1-b5	**Bf8-c5**
4. c2-c3	**Ng8-f6**
5. Bb5xc6?	

This exchange only helps Black to bring out his Bishop. 5. d4 is better.

5. ...	**d7xc6**
6. 0-0	**Bc8-g4**
7. h2-h3	

It would be safer to play 7. d3 followed by 8. Be3, trying to exchange off the dark-square Bishops.

7. ...	**h7-h5**

Anderssen sacrifices the Bishop in order to open the h-file. Feeling more at home in complications than his opponents, Anderssen often took risks.

8. h3xg4	**h5xg4**
9. Nf3xe5?	

When you have a material advantage you should try to exchange pieces. It was better therefore to play 9. d4 exd4 10. Nxd4.

9. ...	**g4-g3**

It is easy to make a mistake in such sharp positions. 9. ... Nxe4! is stronger. This cannot be met by 10. Qxg4 since after 10. ... Bxf2+! 11. Rxf2 Rh1+!! 12. Kxh1 Nxf2+ 13. Kg1 Nxg4 14. Nxg4 Qd3 it would be difficult for White to develop his Queenside pieces. Even worse would be 10. Nxg4 because of 10. ... Qh4 with an unstoppable mate.

10. d2-d4	**Nf6xe4**
11. Qd1-g4?	

White sees that the mating pattern of Diagram 619 is a possibility: the move 11. Qd1-g4 is directed against the threat of 11. ...Rh1+! 12. Kxh1 Qh4+ 13. Kg1 Qh2#. However, a better defense was 11. fxg3! Nxg3 12. Re1, eliminating all of Black's threats.

11. ...	**Bc5xd4?**

Both adversaries have overlooked a typical tactical device: 11. ... gxf2+ 12. Rxf2 Rh1+! 13. Kxh1 Nxf2+ followed by 14. ... Nxg4, when White has only two minor pieces for his Queen. Anderssen was tempted by the mating pattern shown in diagram 620.

12. Qg4xe4?	

The last mistake. It was necessary to play 12. cxd4, intending to reply to 12. ... Qxd4 with 13. Qd7+, with complicated play. Black would do better to instead play 12. ... gxf2+ 13. Rxf2 Rh1+ 14. Kxh1 Nxf2+ 15. Kg1 Nxg4, winning the Queen, although now he has had to give up three minor pieces for it instead of only two.

12. ...	**Bd4xf2+!**

White resigned, since mate is unavoidable: 13. Rxf2 Qd1+ 14. Rf1 Rh1+! 15. Kxh1 Qxf1# (mating pattern shown in Diagram 620). The final game position is shown in Diagram 621.

Both players made mistakes in this game, but it was White who made the last mistake and as a result fell victim to a beautiful mate.

Game 87
Rieman–Anderssen, Germany 1876
King's Gambit

1. e2-e4	**e7-e5**

Black was played by the strongest chess-player of the mid-19th century.

2. f2-f4

This gambit was very popular in those times.

2. ...	**e5xf4**
3. Bf1-c4	**Qd8-h4 +**
4. Ke1-f1	

White has lost his right to castle but in compensation he has gained the center and can develop his pieces more quickly. The game is equal.

4. ...	**d7-d5!**

Black is willing to give back the pawn in order to gain a **tempo** for developing his pieces.

5. Bc4xd5	**Ng8-f6**
6. Nb1-c3	**Bf8-b4**
7. e4-e5	

The idea of this pawn sacrifice is to keep the Black King in the center and whip up an attack.

7. ...	**Bb4xc3**
8. e5xf6	**Bc3xf6**
9. Ng1-f3	**Qh4-h5**
10. Qd1-e2 +	

It was for the sake of this check that White sacrificed a pawn on the seventh move.

10. ...	**Ke8-d8!**

622

pattern

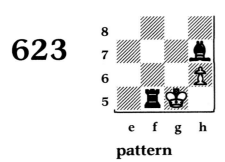

623

pattern

Anderssen visualizes several potential mating patterns (Diagrams 622 and 623) and begins to set up a combination. That is why he frees e8 for his Rook.

11. Qe2-c4	**Rh8-e8**

A trap! In order to see it, you don't necessarily have to be a very strong player, but all the same it is Queen sacrifices that are the most often overlooked.

12. Bd5xf7?

White had to play 12. d3, with a good game. Instead, he gets mated in five moves.

12. ...	**Qh5xf3 + !**

Exposing the King and **deflecting** the pawn on g2 from control of h3. At the same time, the Knight controlling e1 is eliminated — this tactical motif is known as "eliminating the defense." Anderssen thus makes use of three tactical motifs in one move.

13. g2xf3	**Bc8-h3 +**
14. Kf1-f2	

Or 14. Kg1 Re1 + 15. Kf2 Bh4# (Mating pattern of Diagram 622).

14. ...	**Bf6-h4 +**
15. Kf2-g1	**Re8-e1 +**
16. Qc4-f1	**Re1xf1#**

The mating pattern of Diagram 623. The final position is shown in Diagram 624.

624

White lost because he "fell into" Black's combination.

Game 88
Sanchez–Sotolareya, Mexico 1948
Veresov's Opening

1. d2-d4	Ng8-f6
2. Bc1-g5	d7-d5
3. Nb1-c3	

These moves constitute Veresov's Opening, named after a Soviet master.

3. ...	c7-c5
4. d4xc5	

A risky move. It would be better to play 4. e3 and develop the Kingside as soon as possible.

4. ...	d5-d4
5. Bg5xf6	e7xf6

Opening a diagonal for the Bishop.

6. Nc3-e4	Bc8-f5

The opening has given Black the upper hand — he can bring out his pieces quickly.

7. Ne4-d6 +	

White decides to return the pawn in order to exchange off the dark-square Bishops.

7. ...	Bf8xd6
8. c5xd6	Qd8xd6
9. Ng1-f3	Nb8-c6

Black has completed his development and is ready to castle on either side, while the White King, on the other hand, will be stuck in the center for a long time.

10. c2-c3	

It would be better to play 10. a3, controlling the b4 square. **Opening up the position is advantageous only to the better-developed side** (in this case, Black).

10. ...	0-0-0

By castling, Black automatically brings his Rook into the attack along the d-file.

11. c3xd4?	

It would be better to play 11. Nxd4 and try to exchange Queens.

11. ...	Qd6-b4 + !

This **in-between** check was underestimated by White. Black on the other hand visualizes two mating patterns (Diagrams 625 and 626).

625

626

12. Qd1-d2	Nc6xd4!

Now White cannot play 13. Qxb4 because of 13. ... Nc2# (mating pattern of Diagram 625).

13. Ra1-c1 + ??	

White had to play 13. Nxd4 and exchange Queens.

13. ...	Nd4-c2 + !!
14. Rc1xc2 +	Bf5xc2
15. Qd2xb4	Rd8-d1#

The mating pattern of Diagram 626. The final position is shown in Diagram 627.

627

White was severely punished for not getting around to developing his Knights.

Game 89
Ezerskii–Lel'chuk, Soviet Union 1950
King's Gambit

1. e2-e4	e7-e5
2. f2-f4	

The aim of this pawn sacrifice is to develop as speedily as possible and open up the f-file for the Rook.

2. ...	Nb8-c6
3. Ng1-f3	d7-d6
4. f4xe5?	

4. d4, attacking the central pawn on e5, is better.

4. ...	Nc6xe5?

Why give up the center? After 4. ... dxe5, opening lines for the dark-square Bishop and the Queen, Black would have a fine game.

5. d2-d4	

White now has a strong pawn center.

5. ...	Ne5-g6?

Black should not lose time by retreating the Knight. It would be better to play 5. ... Nxf3+ 6. Qxf3 Qf6, trying to exchange Queens, although even then White would undoubtedly have the better position.

6. Bf1-c4	Bf8-e7
7. 0-0	Ng8-f6
8. Nb1-c3	0-0
9. Qd1-e1!	

Black was threatening 9. ... Nxe4 10. Nxe4 d5, breaking up White's pawn center. The White Queen therefore defends the pawn on e4 while at the same time trying to penetrate into the Kingside.

9. ...	Rf8-e8?

Black's desire to place his Rook on the same file as the White Queen is understandable, but the move weakens the f7 pawn. Since Black's position is cramped, a better move would be 9. ... Be6, trying to exchange Bishops. 10. d5 in reply would not be dangerous for Black, since the move would block the diagonal of White's Bishop.

10. Nf3-g5	

White immediately exploits the weakness of the f7 pawn by attacking it.

10. ...	d6-d5?

Black should admit his mistake and return his Rook to f8. He could also play 10. ... Nh8. The text move leads to an opening of lines that is favorable for White, since his pieces are the more active.

11. Nc3xd5	Nf6xd5?

Black rushes to his doom. It is better to give up a pawn than to lose the game right away. He had to defend the f7 pawn by 11. ... Be6, 11. ... Rf8, or 11. Nh8.

12. Bc4xd5	

Even simpler was 12. Nxf7

12. ...	Be7xg5
13. Bd5xf7 +	Kg8-h8
14. Bf7xe8	Bg5xc1

Around now, White started to visualize the following potential mating patterns (see Diagrams 628–631). But they can become reality only if Black plays poorly.

628

629

pattern

630

pattern

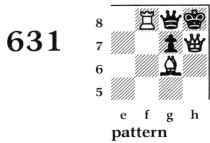

631

pattern

15. Be8xg6

Eliminating the Knight that was defending the important f8 square.

    15. ...   **Bc1xb2?**

The last mistake. Better is 15. ... Bg5 followed by 16. ... Qxd4+, with some counter-play for the lost exchange. 16. Qb4 would not work for White because of 16. ... Be7, winning a Bishop.

    16. Qe1-h4!!   **Qd8-g8**

16. ... Qxd4+ (or 16. ... Bxd4+) would not save Black since White can reply 17. Kh1, with a mating attack. After 16. ... Qxh4?, the mating pattern of Diagram 629 would become reality: 17. Rf8#.

    17. Rf1-f8!

The Rook attacks the Queen and says, "Take me, please!" Such effrontery turned out to be too much for Black, and he resigned. The fact is that he gets mated in all variations:

a)   17. ... Qxf8 18. Qxh7# (pattern of Diagram 630);

b)   17. ... h6 18. Rxg8+ Kxg8 19. Qd8# (pattern of Diagram 628 — a back-rank mate);

c)   17. ... Bxd4+ 18. Kh1 Be6 19. Qxh7# (pattern of Diagram 631).

The final position is shown in Diagram 632.

632

Black played actively . . . , but badly! The safety of his King should have been his primary concern.

Game 90
Gruenfeld–Torre, Baden-Baden 1925

Dutch Defense
    1. d2-d4

White was an outstanding Austrian grandmaster after whom one of the most popular modern openings, the Gruenfeld Defense, is named. His opponent was a talented Mexican master.

    1. ...   **e7-e6**
    2. Ng1-f3   **f7-f5**

This move introduces the Dutch Defense.

    3. g2-g3

This move, recommended by Gruenfeld, is often played in such positions even today.

    3. ...   **Ng8-f6**
    4. Bf1-g2   **d7-d5**

This variation is called the "stonewall" variation.

    5. 0-0   **Bf8-d6**
    6. c2-c4   **c7-c6**

If 6. ... dxc4, then White plays 7. Qa4, winning back the pawn with a good position.

    7. Qd1-c2   **0-0**
    8. b2-b3   **Nf6-e4**
    9. Bc1-b2   **Nb8-d7**

Both players are developing rapidly. The position is about even.

    10. Nf3-e5   **Qd8-f6**
    11. f2-f3

After this move, Torre noticed an interesting potential mating pattern (Diagram 633) that was overlooked by White.

633

pattern

    11. ...   **Nd7xe5**
    12. d4xe5??

Gruenfeld could have obtained the better game by means of the **in-between** move 12.

c5!. E.g., 12. ... Bc7 13. dxe5 Bxe5 14. Bxe5 Qxe5 15. fxe5, and 15. ... Qxa1 doesn't work, because of 16. Nc3, netting the Queen. However, Gruenfeld overlooked Black's **in-between** check which immediately decides the outcome of the struggle.

| 12. ... | **Bd6-c5 + !** |

The Bishop escapes from the pawn with check! 12. ... Bxe5 would not work, because of 13. Bxe5 Qxe5 14. fxe4 Qxa1 15. Nc3, and Black must lose material.

| **13. Kg1-h1** | **Ne4xg3 + !** |

White resigned, since he will be mated by force: 14. hxg3 Qh6 + 15. Bh3 Qxh3# (mating pattern of Diagram 633). The final game position is shown in Diagram 634.

634

Grandmaster Gruenfeld was caught in his opponent's trap and, it goes without saying, he remembered this game for the rest of his life.

Game 91
Alekhine–Mindeno, Holland 1933

Ruy Lopez

1. e2-e4	e7-e5
2. Ng1-f3	Nb8-c6
3. Bf1-b5	

White was the reigning World Champion. This game was played during a simultaneous exhibition where Alekhine was playing many games against different opponents at the same time.

3. ...	d7-d6
4. d2-d4	e5xd4
5. Qd1xd4	

The idea behind this move is to prepare Queenside castling.

5. ...	**Bc8-d7**
6. **Bb5xc6**	**Bd7xc6**
7. **Nb1-c3**	

7. Bg5 would be premature because of 7. ... Be7! 8. Qxg7 Bf6, with a good game for Black.

7. ...	**Ng8-f6**
8. **Bc1-g5**	**Bf8-e7**
9. **0-0-0**	**0-0**

Both sides have brought out all their minor pieces. They have both castled, but on different sides. White's position is preferable, as Black is cramped

10. h2-h4

Preparing 11. Nd5 by protecting the Bishop, since 10. Nd5 would lose a piece after 10. ... Nxd5. Another possible plan for White was to play 10. Rhe1, threatening 11. e5, but Alekhine always preferred to attack the King.

| 10. ... | **h7-h6** |
| 11. **Nc3-d5!** | **h6xg5?** |

Accepting the sacrifice leads to defeat. Black should have played 11. ... Nxd5 12. exd5 Bd7.

12. Nd5xe7 + !

12. hxg5 would be followed by 12. .. Nxd5 13. exd5 Bxg5 + .

12. ...	**Qd8xe7**
13. **h4xg5**	**Nf6xe4**
14. **Rh1-h5**	

Black has an extra Bishop but his position is lost, since White's attack along the h-file cannot be parried. The World Champion visualized five potential mating patterns at this point (see Diagrams 635–639) and began to set up a brilliant combination.

635

pattern

229

636

pattern

637

pattern

638

pattern

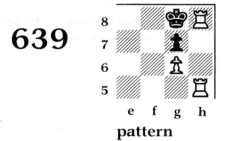

639

pattern

14. ...   **Qe7-e6**
15. Rd1-h1

Threatens 16. Rh8# (the pattern of Diagram 637 — a back-rank mate).

15. ...   **f7-f5**

Making a hole for the King on f7. White's task is to keep the Black King in the mating net by maintaining control over f7 at any cost.

16. Nf3-e5!!

An astoundingly beautiful and strong move! The threat is 16. Rh8# (the mating pattern of Diagram 635 — a back-rank mate). 16. ... g6

does not save Black, because of 17. Rh8+ Kh7 18. R1h7# (mating pattern of Diagram 636). If the White pawn manages to reach g6 unpunished, Black will not be able to avoid mate. It is for that reason that Alekhine tries to **deflect** either the Black Queen from controlling g6 or the d6 pawn from being able to interpose on the a2-g8 diagonal.

16. ...   **d6xe5**

On 16. ... Qxe5 White wins by 17. Qxe5 dxe5 18. g6 any 19. Rh8# (mating pattern of Diagram 639 — a back-rank mate).

17. g5-g6!

Only now did Black understand the World Champion's brilliant idea. He immediately resigned, since the threat of 18. Rh8# is deadly. The only defense, 17. ... Qxg6, abandons the a2-g8 diagonal and allows the White Queen to deliver a fatal check: 18. Qc4+ Rf7 19. Rh8# (mating pattern of Diagram 638 — a back-rank mate). The final game position is shown in Diagram 640.

640

This game shows the importance of open lines in attacking the enemy King.

Game 92
Fink–Alekhine, Pasadena 1932
Ponziani's Opening

1. e2-e4	e7-e5
2. Ng1-f3	Nb8-c6
3. c2-c3	

This move introduces the opening worked out more than two hundred years ago by the great Italian chessplayer Domenico Ponziani.

| 3. ... | d7-d5 |

Black, the reigning World Champion, immediately counterattacks in the center.

| 4. Qd1-a4 | Ng8-f6 |

Alekhine plays a gambit variation, sacrificing a pawn but developing rapidly.

5. Nf3xe5	Bf8-d6
6. Ne5xc6	b7xc6
7. e4-e5	

The first mistake. White could have maintained the equilibrium by 7. d3 0-0 8. Be2, with the idea of 9. Nd2 and 10. 0-0. 7. Qxc6 + Bd7 8. Qa6 would be bad for White because of 8. ... dxe4, with the better game for Black. White decides to return the pawn to gain time for developing his pieces.

7. ...	Bd6xe5
8. d2-d4	Be5-d6
9. Qa4xc6 + ?	

White should have resisted this temptation and instead thought about developing his pieces!

| 9. ... | Bc8-d7 |
| 10. Qc6-a6 | 0-0 |

Black has finished his development while his opponent has in effect been moving only his Queen. White has a lost position in spite of his extra pawn.

| 11. Bf1-e2 | Rf8-e8 |
| 12. Nb1-d2 | |

White was afraid to castle, what with the Black pieces looking straight at the Kingside.

| 12. ... | Ra8-b8 |
| 13. a2-a4 | |

Parrying the threat of 13. ... Bb5, winning the pinned Bishop. 13. 0-0 would not help, because of 13. ... Rb6 14. Qd3 Bb5, winning a piece.

| 13. ... | Qd8-e7 |

The World Champion prepares the mating pattern shown in Diagram 641.

641

14. Nd2-f1?
White can save himself only by playing

14. Kd1, unpinning the bishop, although he would still be in a bad state because of his hopelessly retarded development.

| 14. ... | Bd7-b5! |

The tactical motif of **interference.** Now the White Queen can no longer defend the Bishop.

| 15. a4xb5 | Qe7xe2# |

The mating pattern of Diagram 641. The final game position is shown in Diagram 642.

642

White received a good lesson! You must play with **all** your pieces, and not just your Queen.

Game 93
Alekhine–DeCassio, 1944
Vienna Game

| 1. e2-e4 | e7-e5 |
| 2. Nb1-c3 | |

This introduces an opening worked out by a group of Viennese chessplayers in the 19th century.

| 2. ... | Bf8-c5 |
| 3. Bf1-c4 | Ng8-e7? |

The Knight is passively placed here. You should generally try to place it on f6, from where it controls many important squares.

| 4. d2-d3 | |

World Champion Alekhine was playing this game blindfolded.

| 4. ... | Nb8-c6 |
| 5. Qd1-h5! | |

Threatens 6. Qxf7#. This is the "Scholar's Mate" pattern shown in Diagram 643.

643

Why can the World Champion bring his Queen out early in the game while we are advised not to do so? The reason is that in this case Black made a poor move, 3. ... Ne7, and only after that did Alekhine allow himself to bring out his Queen. Moreover, the World Champion foresaw a mating attack many moves ahead. And the fact is that it is not so easy for Black to gain time by attacking the Queen. For example, 5. ... g6 is met by 6. Qh6, preventing Black from castling.

5. ...	**0-0**
6. Bc1-g5	

Pinning the Knight.

6. ...	**Qd8-e8?**

Black of course knows **how** the pieces move, but he doesn't know **where** they should go. He had to pin the **dangerous** White Knight by 6. ... Bb4, and then neutralize White's **dangerous** light-square Bishop by 7. ... d6 and 8. ... Be6.

7. Ng1-f3	**Ne7-g6?**

It was still not too late to play 7. ... Bb4.

8. Nc3-d5!

Though blindfolded, the Grandmaster sees several potential mating patterns (Diagrams 644 and 645) and begins to set up a combination.

644

645

---

8. ...	**Bc5-b6**

All of White's minor pieces as well as his Queen are taking part in his attack, while the Black pieces are placed passively and are unable to help their King.

9. Nd5-f6 + !   **g7xf6**

Forced. 10. Qxh7# (mating pattern of Diagram 644) was threatened.

10. Bg5xf6

White has the double threat of 11. Ng5 followed by 12. Qxh7# (mating pattern of Diagram 644) and 11. Qh6 followed by 12. **Qg7#** (mating pattern of Diagram 645). Since Black cannot defend against both threats, he resigned. The final game position is shown in Diagram 646.

646

The World Champion's opponent played aimlessly and was routed right at the start of the game.

Game 94
Mardle–Gaprindashvili, Hastings 1965
Sicilian Defense

1. e2-e4	**c7-c5**
2. Ng1-f3	**Nb8-c6**

The Women's World Champion Nona Gaprindashvili played this game in a men's tournament.

2. d2-d4	**c5xd4**
3. Nf3xd4	**e7-e6**
4. Bc1-e3	**Ng8-f6**
5. Nb1-d2	

A passive move! 6. Bd3 is stronger. Also possible is 6. Nc3, but White didn t like the pin arising after 6. ... Bb4.

6. ...	**e6-e5**

Black can allow herself to make two moves with the e-pawn in the opening because White's last move was weak.

7. Nd4xc6   **d7xc6**

Opening a diagonal for the Bishop.

8. f2-f3

Preventing Black from playing her Knight to g4.

8. ...   **Bf8-e7**
9. Bf1-c4   **0-0**
10. 0-0   **Nf6-h5**

With the idea of exchanging Bishops after 11. ... Bg5.

11. Nd2-b3

Safer is 11. g3, controlling f4.

11. ...   **Be7-g5**
12. Be3-c5

12. Qxd8 is of course bad because of the **in-between** check 12. ... Bxe3 +, winning a piece.

12. ...   **Qd8-f6**

The Women's World Champion sees a possibility of creating a ''Greco's Mate'' pattern (Diagram 647), and so she leaves her Rook en prise.

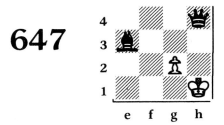

647

13. Bc5xf8?

White does not notice the trap. He had to play 13. f4 Nxf4 14. Bxf8, with a double-edged position.

13. ...   **Bg5-e3 +**
14. Kg1-h1??

Mate could have been prevented only by 14. Rf2.

14. ...   **Nh5-g3 +!**

White resigns. 15. hxg3 Qh6# is a ''Greco's mate'' (pattern of Diagram 647). The final game position is shown in Diagram 648.

648

The Women's World Champion wasn't playing specially to catch her opponent in a trap, and it wasn't her fault if he voluntarily fell into the trap and got mated!

Game 95
Gaprindashvili–Servati, Germany 1974
Sicilian Defense

1. e2-e4   **c7-c5**
2. Ng1-f3   **Nb8-c6**
3. d2-d4

White was Nona Gaprindashvili, Women's World Champion from 1962 to 1978.

3. ...   **c5xd4**
4. Nf3xd4   **g7-g6**

The Dragon Variation.

5. c2-c4

Controlling d5.

5. ...   **Bf8-g7**
6. Bc1-e3   **Ng8-f6**
7. Nb1-c3   **Nf6-g4**
8. Qd1xg4

8. Nxc6 is unsatisfactory because of 8. ... Nxe3 9. Nxd8 Nxd1 10. Nxd1 Kxd8, with the better game for Black.

8. ...   **Nc6xd4**
9. Qg4-d1   **e7-e5**

9. ... Ne6 would give better chances of equalizing.

10. Nc3-b5   **0-0**
11. Bf1-e2   **Qd8-h4?**

Black had to play 11. ... Nxb5 12. cxb5 d6 13. Bc4 Be6, with an approximately equal game.

12. Nb5xd4   **e5xd4**
13. Be3xd4   **Qh4xe4**

14. Bd4xg7   Qe4xg2?

No good can come out of greediness. Black should have played 14. ... Kxg7, although even then White has the freer game after 15. 0-0.

15. Qd1-d4!

A pretty double-Rook sacrifice! The Women's World Champion sees the potential mating pattern shown in Diagram 649.

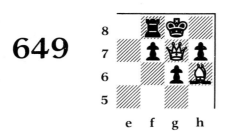

649

15. ...   Qg2xh1+
16. Ke1-d2   Qh1xa1?

Again Black is greedy. He still had some chances of saving his game by playing 16. ... Qxh2, controlling h6.

17. Qd4-f6!

Black only now realized that he was in a trap, and capitulated. There is no defense to be seen against White's threat of 18. Bh6 followed by 19. Qg7# (mating pattern of Diagram 649). The immediate 17. Bh6 would not have worked, because of 17. ... f6, defending against the mate. The final game position is shown in Diagram 650.

650

Black made a mistake in his calculation of the variations. He overlooked the Women's World Champion's last move, which made it impossible for Black to save himself.

Game 96
Shamkovich–Ivashin, 1946
Ruy Lopez

1. e2-e4	**e7-e5**
2. Ng1-f3	**Nb8-c6**
3. Bf1-b5	**a7-a6**
4. Bb5-a4	**d7-d6**
5. c2-c4	

With the idea of strengthening his control over b5 and d5.

5. ...	**Ng8-e7**
6. Nb1-c3	**Bc8-g4**

Pinning the Knight.

7. d2-d4

White sacrifices a pawn with the aim of developing his pieces as rapidly as possible.

7. ...	**e5xd4**
8. Nc3-d5	

The well-known Grandmaster playing White anticipated several possible mating patterns at this point (see Diagrams 651–656).

651

652

234

653

654

655

656

| 8. ... | Ra8-b8 |

Black prepares the move ... b5 to try and free his Knight from the pin. 8. ... g6 was not possible, because of 9. Nf6# (pattern of Diagram 651 — a smothered mate).

9. Bc1-g5	b7-b5
10. c4xb5	a6xb5
11. Ba4-b3	Nc6-e5?

Delighted at being unpinned, the Black Knight rushes to attack the pinned White Knight. However, Black should have instead been thinking of how to unpin his other Knight (the one on e7) and prepare for castling. 11. ... f6 immediately, though, would not work, because of 12. Bxf6 gxf6 13. Nxf6# (mating pattern of Diagram 652).

12. Nf3xe5!

This move had been overlooked by Black.

| 12. ... | Ne7xd5 |

A pretty mate would have resulted after 12. ... Bxd1 13. Nf6 +! gxf6 14. Bxf7# (mating pattern of Diagram 653). If instead Black plays 12. ... dxe5, he will remain a piece down after 13. Qxg4.

| 13. Qd1xg4 | f7-f6 |
| 14. Bg5xf6!! | |

Black can take the Bishop in any one of three ways, but in each case he gets mated.

If he takes with the pawn by 14. ... gxf6, then 15. Qh5 + Ke7 16. Qf7# (pattern of Diagram 654 — an epaulette mate).

If he takes with the Knight by 14. ... Nxf6, then 15. Bf7 + Ke7 16. Qe6# (pattern of Diagram 655 — an epaulette mate).

Finally, if he takes with the Queen by 14. ... Qxf6, then 15. Qd7# (pattern of Diagram 656).

So **Black resigned.** The final game position is shown in Diagram 657.

657

Black started active operations before completing his development and underestimated his opponent's threats. As a result, he deservedly lost.

Game 97
Marshall–Burn, Paris 1900
Queen's Gambit Declined

This pretty game, which we take from Frank Marshall's book *Marshall's Best Games of Chess*, is annotated by the grandmaster in an original and amusing way: "I attribute the win largely to the fact that my opponent never had time to get his pipe lit! . . . Britisher Amos Burn was a very conservative player and liked to settle down for a long session of close, defensive chess. He loved to smoke his pipe while he studied the board. As I made my second move, Burn began hunting through his pockets for his pipe and tobacco."

1. d2-d4		d7-d5
2. c2-c4		e7-e6
3. Nb1-c3		Ng8-f6
4. Bc1-g5		Bf8-e7

"Not much thought needed on these moves, but Burn had his pipe out and was looking for a pipe cleaner."

5. e2-e3		0-0
6. Ng1-f3		b7-b6
7. Bf1-d3		Bc8-b7
8. c4xd5		e6xd5

"He began filling up his pipe. I speeded up my moves."

9. Bg5xf6		Be7xf6
10. h2-h4		

"Made him think on that one — and he still didn't have the pipe going. The threat is 11. Bxh7+ Kxh7 12. Ng5+, known as the Pillsbury attack."

10. ...		g7-g6

(A mistake. 10. ... c5 is better —Pelts).

11. h4-h5		Rf8-e8

(A loss of time. He had to play 11. ... Qe7 and answer 12. hxg6 with 12. ... fxg6, allowing the Queen to take part in the defense of the King —Pelts).

12. hxg6		hxg6

"Now he was looking for matches."

13. Qd1-c2		Bf6-g7

(A serious mistake, for now the Bishop no longer controls the important g5 square. It was necessary to play 13. ... Kg7 14. 0-0-0 Nd7, when Black would have good defensive chances —Pelts).

14. Bxg6

(Marshall sees several potential mating patterns [Diagrams 658–660] and makes an absolutely

sound sacrifice of a Bishop for two pawns —Pelts).

658

659

660

14. ...		f7xg6

"He struck a match, appeared nervous. The match burned his fingers and went out."

15. Qc2xg6		Nb8-d7

"Another match was on its way." *(15. ... Re7 would not save Black, because of 16. Ng5 [threatening 17. Rh8+! followed by 18. Qh7# — the mating pattern of Diagram 660], and 16. ... Kf8 would be met by 17. Nh7+ Kg8 18. Nf6+ Kf8 19. Rh8+ Bxh8 20. Qg8# — the mating pattern of Diagram 658 —Pelts.)*

16. Nf3-g5

(Threatens 17. Qf7# — the mating pattern of Diagram 659 —Pelts).

16. ...		Qd8-f6

"He was puffing away and lighting up at last. No time left."

17. Rh1-h8+		Resigns

"For if 17. ... Kxh8, 18. Qh7#." *(Mating pattern of Diagram 660. The final game position is shown in Diagram 661. —Pelts).*

661

"Poor Burn. I think I swindled him out of that one. If he could only have got that pipe going, it might have been a different story. He took it good-naturedly and we shook hands. Then his pipe went out."

To these comments by the great Marshall we can only add that he played the game brilliantly, while his opponent helped him by underestimating White's attack.

Game 98
Keres–Meeke, Correspondence, 1933
King's Gambit

1. e2-e4	e7-e5
2. f2-f4	

White was a sixteen-year-old Estonian chess-player who later became one of the top players in the world.

2. ...	e5xf4
3. Nb1-c3	Qd8-h4 +
4. Ke1-e2	d7-d5!

The opponents are playing a very sharp opening variation that gives chances to win to both sides. With his last move, Black returns the pawn in order to gain time.

5. Nc3xd5	Bc8-g4 +
6. Ng1-f3	Nb8-c6

Sacrificing a Rook to launch a dangerous attack against the White King, which is stranded in the center. In such sharp positions, a single mistake can lead to a catastrophe.

7. Nd5xc7 +	Ke8-d8
8. Nc7xa8	Nc6-e5

This sets up the possibility of 9. ... Nxf3 10. gxf3 Bxf3 +! 11. Kxf3 Qh5 + 12. any Qxd1.

9. h2-h3!

White is prepared to return some material in order to weaken Black's attack. Now 9. ... Nxf3 can be met by 10. hxg4 Nd4 + 11. Kd3 Qxh1 12. Kxd4, and White's position is better, since he can later hide his King on c2 after the preliminary move c2-c3.

9. ...	Bg4-h5

Also possible was 9. ... Bxf3 + 10. gxf3 Qg3 11. d3, with unclear play.

Black, however, has in mind the mating pattern shown in Diagram 662 and so decides to keep his Bishop.

662

10. Rh1-g1?

The decisive mistake! A loss of valuable time! White must instead sacrifice his Queen to maintain approximate equality: 10. d4! Nxf3 11. gxf3 Bxf3 + 12. Kxf3 Qh5 + 13. Kg2 Qxd1 14. Bd3.

10. ...	Qh4-g3

Now the Knight on f3 cannot be defended.

11. Qd1-e1

Only 11. d3 would prevent mate, but after 11. ... Nxf3 12. gxf3 Qxf3 + White would suffer huge material losses.

11. ...	Bh5xf3 +
12. g2xf3	Qg3xf3#

The mating pattern of Diagram 662. The final game position is shown in Diagram 663.

663

White lost even though he just made one mistake!

Game 99
Johner–Tartakower, 1928
Sicilian Defense

1. e2-e4	**c7-c5**

Black was a famous grandmaster.

2. Ng1-f3	**Ng8-f6**

A rare move.

3. Nb1-c3

3. e5 would be met by 3. ... Nd5, with chances for both sides.

3. ...	**d7-d5**
4. e4xd5	

4. e5 is not dangerous for Black in view of 4. ... d4 5. exf6 dxc3 6. fxg7 cxd2 +, with an even game.

4. ...	**Nf6xd5**
5. Nc3-e4	

It would be better to bring fresh forces into play. For example, 5. Bb5 + Bd7 6. Ne5 Bxb5 7. Qf3 f6 8. Nxb5 fxe5 9. Qxd5 Qxd5 10. Nc7 + with advantage to White.

5. ...	**e7-e6**
6. d2-d4	**c5xd4**
7. Nf3xd4	**Bf8-e7**
8. Bf1-b5 +	**Bc8-d7**
9. c2-c4	**Nd5-f6**
10. Ne4-c3	**0-0**
11. 0-0	**Qd8-c7**

The position is even. Both sides have finished their development without difficulty.

12. Qd1-e2	**Nb8-c6**
13. Nd4-f3	

It would be more logical to exchange Knights instead of losing time by retreating.

13. ...	**Rf8-e8**

Preparing to push the e-pawn.

14. Bc1-g5

Safer would be 14. h3, controlling g4.

14. ...	**Nf6-g4!**

Preparing the mating pattern shown in Diagram 664.

664

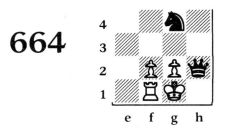

15. Bg5xe7?

Johner does not suspect anything and decides to exchange Bishops. If he had discovered White's threat, he would have replied 15. g3.

15. ...	**Nc6-d4!**

An **in-between** move! Instead of capturing the Bishop, Black makes use of the tactical motif of **deflection. White resigned** since 16. Nxd4 would be met by 16. ... Qxh2# (pattern of Diagram 664) and 16. Qd3 would fail to 16. ... Nxf3 + 17. ... Qxh2# (pattern of Diagram 664). The final game position is shown in Diagram 665.

665

White lost because he did not see Black's threat in time.

667

668

669

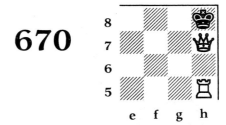

670

Game 100
Serebryanskii–van Gompel
Correspondence, 1973
Queen's Pawn Game

1. d2-d4	d7-d5
2. Ng1-f3	Ng8-f6
3. e2-e3	e7-e6
4. Bf1-d3	c7-c5
5. 0-0	Nb8-c6
6. b2-b3	Bf8-d6
7. Bc1-b2	0-0
8. Nf3-e5	

This quiet opening is known as the Queen's Pawn Game. Sometimes White plays 8. a3 here, depriving the Black Knight of the b4 square.

8. ...	Qd8-c7
9. f2-f4	

With the idea of transferring the Rook to the Kingside via f3.

9. ...	c5xd4
10. e3xd4	Nc6-b4
11. Nb1-c3	Nb4xd3

Eliminating the dangerous Bishop that was pointed at Black's Kingside.

12. Qd1xd3	a7-a6

Depriving the White Knight of the b5 square.

13. Rf1-f3!

White has completed his development and is ready to attack the enemy King.

13. ...	b7-b5

Black's desire to bring out his light-square Bishop is understandable, but it was more important to see to the safety of his King by playing 13. ... g6, with the idea of 14. ... Ne8 and 15. ... f5.

14. Rf3-h3	Bc8-b7??

Black suspects nothing. 14. ... g6 was obligatory. The position is now ripe for combinational play and White visualizes several potential mating patterns (Diagrams 666–670).

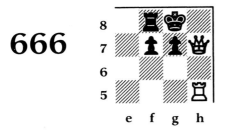

666

15. Ne5-g4!

To **deflect** the Knight from the defense of h7.

15. ...	Nf6-e4

Blocking the Queen's path. 15. ... Nxg4 would of course allow 16. Qxh7# (pattern of Diagram 666).

16. Nc3xe4!

Eliminating the Knight, which was controlling f6.

16. ...	d5xe4
17. Ng4-f6 + !	

Exposing the King.

17. ...	g7xf6

Else 18. Rxh7# (pattern of Diagram 667 — an Arabian mate).

| 18. Qd3-g3 + | Kg8-h8 |
| 19. Qg3-h4 | Resigns |

For there is no satisfactory defense against the threat of 20. Qxh7# (if 20. ... h6 or ... h5, then 21. Qxh6(5)+ and 22. Qh7#). Black must succumb to one of the mating patterns shown in Diagrams 668 (epaulette mate), 669, and 670. The final position is shown in Diagram 671.

671

Black lost this game because he underestimated White's attack.

Lesson Twelve

672

White to play and draw.

_____

_____

_____

674

White to play and mate in two moves.

_____

_____

_____

673

Black to play. Can he avoid losing a piece?

_____

_____

_____

675

Black to play resigned. Why?

_____

_____

_____

676

White to play. Find his strongest continuation.

_____

_____

_____

677

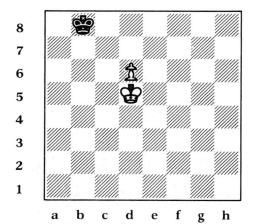

How does White queen his pawn if it is his turn to play? And if it is Black's turn?

_____

_____

_____

678

White to play and draw.

_____

_____

_____

680

Black to play and win a piece.

_____

_____

_____

679

White to play. Why did he resign?

_____

_____

_____

681

White to play. Find the strongest continuation.

_____

_____

_____

682

White to play and win a piece.

_____

_____

_____

683

White to play and queen his pawn. Can Black save himself if it is his move?

_____

_____

_____

684

Black to play. Can he win the pawn on e4?

686

White to play and win a piece.

685

Black to play and win a piece.

687

White to play and mate in three moves.

688

Is 1. ... Bg7xd4 a good move?

_____

_____

_____

689

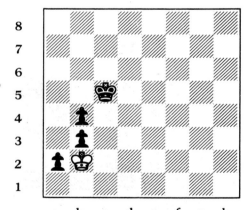

Black to play and queen a pawn.

_____

_____

_____

690

White to play and win a piece.

_____

_____

_____

691

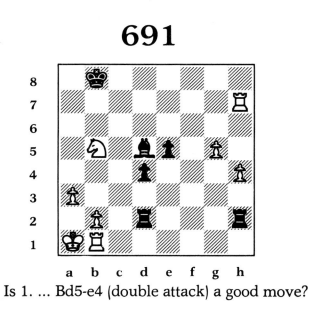

Is 1. ... Bd5-e4 (double attack) a good move?

_____

_____

_____

692

White to play and win a piece.

_____

_____

_____

693

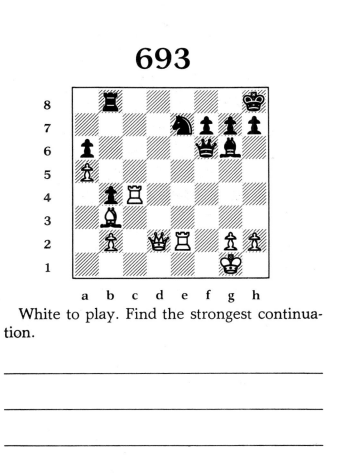

White to play. Find the strongest continuation.

_____

_____

_____

694

White to play and mate in three moves.

_____

_____

_____

695

White to play and queen his pawn. Can Black save himself if it is his turn to play?

_____

_____

_____

Test Five
Write your answers below.

696

White to play and mate in two moves. (The White King and Rook have not moved in the game so far.)

_____

_____

_____

697

Black to play and win a piece.

_____

_____

_____

698

White to play and win a piece.

_____

_____

699

Black to play and win a piece.

_____

_____

_____

700

a b c d e f g h

White to play and mate in three moves.

_____

_____

_____

701

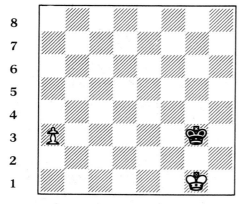

a b c d e f g h

White to play. Can he queen his pawn? Can Black stop the pawn if it is his turn to play?

_____

_____

_____

702

Black to play. What is his strongest continuation?

_____

_____

_____

703

Black to play. Why did he resign?

_____

_____

_____

704

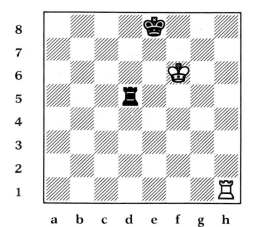

Black to play and win a pawn.

_____

_____

_____

705

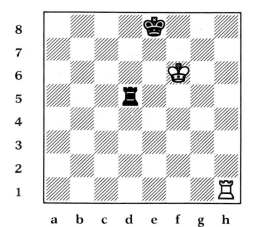

White to play and win a Rook.

_____

_____

_____

706

White to play and mate in two moves.

_____

_____

_____

707

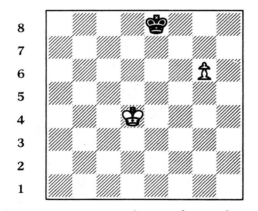

White to play and queen his pawn.

_____

_____

_____

708

710

White to play and draw.

White to play. How can he avoid losing a piece?

_____

_____

_____

709

711

White to play and win a piece.

Black to play and mate in three moves.

_____

_____

_____

712

White to play and mate in three moves.

_____

_____

_____

713

White to play and queen his pawn. Black to play and draw.

_____

_____

_____

Test Eight
Write your answer below.

714

White to play and draw.

_____

_____

_____

716

White to play and draw.

Black to play and win a piece.

_____

_____

_____

715

Is 1. Rf1-e1 a good move?

_____

_____

_____

717

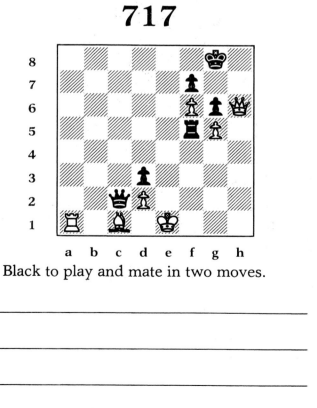

Black to play and mate in two moves.

_____

_____

_____

718

White to play and mate in four moves.

_____

_____

_____

719

Show that the result should be a draw no matter who moves first.

_____

_____

_____

720

Black to play. How should the game end?

_____

_____

_____

722

White to play and win a pawn.

_____

_____

_____

721

White to play and win a piece.

_____

_____

_____

723

Black to play and mate in two moves.

_____

_____

_____

724

White to play. Find his strongest continuation.

_____

_____

_____

725

White to play and queen his pawn.

_____

_____

_____

726

White to play and draw.

_____

_____

_____

728

Black to play. Can he save his Queen?

_____

_____

_____

727

White to play and win a piece.

_____

_____

_____

729

Black to play and mate in two moves.

_____

_____

_____

730

White to play and mate in three moves.

_____

_____

_____

731

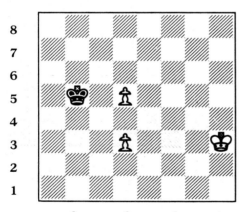

White to play and queen a pawn.

_____

_____

_____

732

Black to play and draw.

_____

_____

_____

734

White to play and win material.

_____

_____

_____

733

Black to play. Can he save his Bishop?

_____

_____

_____

735

White to play and win material.

_____

_____

_____

736

White to play and mate in two moves.

_____

_____

_____

737

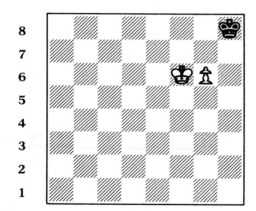

How should the game end if it is White's turn to play? And if it is Black's turn?

_____

_____

_____

738

Black to play. Show how White mates Black in one move after each of Black's possible moves.

_____

_____

_____

739

Black to play. Find his strongest continuation.

_____

_____

_____

740

White to play and mate in two moves.

_____

_____

_____

741

Is 1. Ng3xh5 a good move?

_____

_____

_____

742

The player whose turn it is to move wins.

_____

_____

_____

743

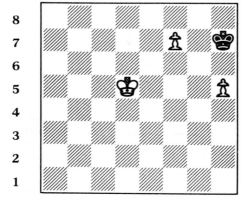

White to play and queen a pawn. Can Black save himself if it is his move?

_____

_____

_____

744

White to play and win Black's Queen.

_____

_____

_____

746

White to play. Find his strongest continuation.

_____

_____

_____

745

Black to play and win White's Queen.

_____

_____

_____

747

White to play and mate in two moves.

_____

_____

_____

748

Is 1. ... Bb7xg2 a good move?

_____

_____

_____

749

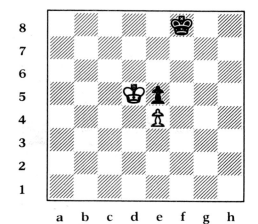

White to play. Can Black save himself?

_____

_____

_____

750

White to play. How should the game end?

_____

_____

_____

752

Black to play and mate in two moves.

_____

_____

_____

751

White to play. Find his strongest continuation.

_____

_____

_____

753

White to play and mate in two moves.

_____

_____

_____

754

White to play and mate in two moves.

_____

_____

_____

755

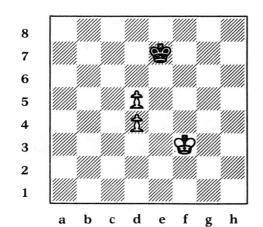

White to play and queen a pawn.

_____

_____

_____

756

White to play and win material.

_____

_____

_____

758

White to play and mate in two moves.

_____

_____

_____

757

White to play and win Black's Queen.

_____

_____

_____

759

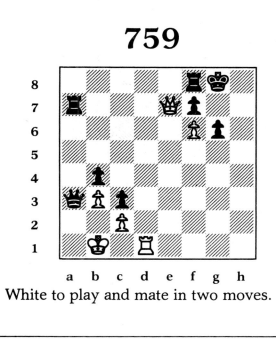

White to play and mate in two moves.

_____

_____

_____

760

White to play. Find his strongest continuation.

_____

_____

_____

761

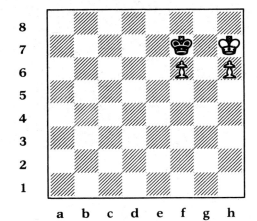

Can White win if it is his turn to play? What would happen if it were Black's turn?

_____

_____

_____

762

White to play. Can he win a piece?

_____

_____

_____

764

White to play. Can White to play avoid losing a piece?

Can White to play avoid losing a piece?

_____

_____

_____

763

White to play and win material.

_____

_____

_____

765

Black to play and mate in two moves.

_____

_____

_____

766

a b c d e f g h

Black to play. Find a winning combination for him.

_____

_____

_____

767

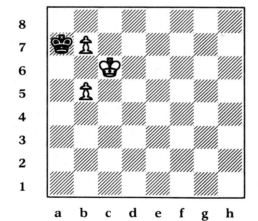

a b c d e f g h

White to play and queen a pawn. Can Black save himself if it is his turn to play?

_____

_____

_____

768

White to play. Find his strongest continuation.

_____

_____

_____

770

White to play and win a piece.

_____

_____

_____

769

White to play and win Black's Queen.

_____

_____

_____

771

White to play and mate in two moves.

_____

_____

_____

772

White to play. Find a winning combination for him.

_____

_____

_____

773

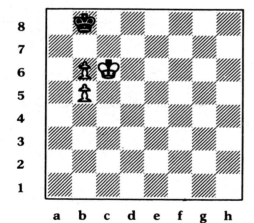

White to play and queen a pawn. Could Black save himself if it were his turn to play?

_____

_____

_____

774

White to play and win material.

_____

_____

_____

776

White to play. Can he avoid losing a piece?

_____

_____

_____

775

White to play. Find a winning combination for him.

_____

_____

_____

777

Can Black avoid getting mated on the back rank?

_____

_____

_____

778

Show how the player whose turn it is to play wins.

_____

_____

_____

779

Show how the game is drawn no matter who moves first.

_____

_____

_____

780

White to play and win material.

_____

_____

_____

782

White to play and mate in two moves.

_____

_____

_____

781

White to play. Find his strongest continuation.

_____

_____

_____

783

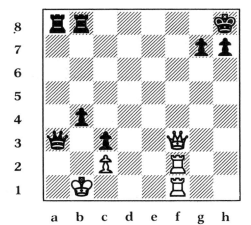

White to play and mate in three moves.

_____

_____

_____

784

Black to play and mate in three moves (two solutions.)

_____

_____

_____

785

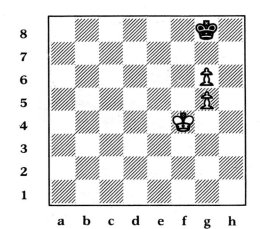

Show that the game should be drawn no matter who moves first.

_____

_____

_____

786

Black to play and win material.

_____

_____

_____

788

White to play. Can he avoid losing a piece?

_____

_____

_____

787

White to play. Find his strongest continuation.

_____

_____

_____

789

White to play and mate in two moves.

_____

_____

_____

790

Black to play. Find a winning combination for him.

_____

_____

_____

791

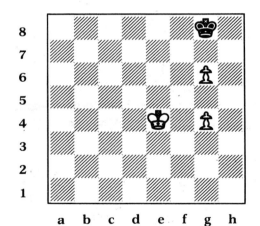

Show that White wins no matter who moves first.

_____

_____

_____

Test One Answers

Diagram 672 **1. Bd1-c2 +!** (Double attack) **1. ... Qb1xc2; 2. Nf1-e3 +** (fork) **2. ... Bf4xe3** stalemate.

Diagram 673 Ilyin-Zhenevsky–Levenfish, Moscow 1936. Black avoids losing a piece as follows: **1. ... Qd7-d4! 2. Bb5xc6 + b7xc6 3. Qe4xd4** (if 3. Qxc6 +, then 3. ... Kf7) **3. ... Ne3-c2 +** (fork) **4. any Nc2xd4.**

Diagram 674 **1. Qf1-f8 + Re8xf8 2. Rc8xf8#** (a back-rank mate).

Diagram 675 Pelts–Fauzi, Chess Olympics, Lucerne 1982. White is threatening 1. Qf8 + Rxf8 2. Rxf8#. If **1. ...Kh8**, then **2. R1d7** (threatening 3. Qf8 + Rxf8 4. Rxf8 + Bg8 5. Bg7#) **2. ... Rxd8 3. Rxd8 + Bg8 4. Qf8** and Black cannot avoid mate.

Diagram 676 Reti–Bogoljubow, New York 1924. **1. Bf7-e8!** Black resigned.

If 1. ... Rxe8, then 2. Qxf8 + Rxf8 3. Rxf8# (back-rank mate);

if 1. ... Be7, then 2. Qf8 Bxf8 3. Rxf8# (back-rank mate);

if 1. ... h6, then 2. Qxf8 + Kh7 3. Bg6 + Kxg6 4. Qf5#;

if 1. ... h5, then 2. Qxf8 +, and White is up a Bishop.

Diagram 677 White to play: **1. Kd5-e6 Kb8-c8 2. Ke6-e7** and the pawn queens by force.

Black to play: **1. ...Kb8-c8 2. Kd5-c6** (or 2. Ke6) **2. ... Kc8-d8 3. d6-d7** etc.

Test Two Answers

Diagram 678 **1. Nf4-g6 +! Bf5xg6** (or else 2. Kxh7 follows) **stalemate.**

Diagram 679 Leonhardt–Englund, Stockholm 1908. Black threatens 1. ...Rxh2 + Kxh2 Rh8 + 3. Bh6 Rxh6# (Anastasia's mate). If 1. h3, then **1. ...Rxh3#**, while on 1. Bf4 the reply **1. ... Nxf4** is decisive.

Diagram 680 Bogoljubow–Capablanca, New York 1924. **1. ... Rc8xc5!** White re-signed. If 2. Rxc4, then 2. ... Rxc4, while 2. dxc5 is followed by 2. ... Qxc5 + (double attack) 3. any Rxc1.

Diagram 681 **1. Ra1-f1** (or 1. Rh1-f1) *a pin.* If now 1. ... Rxg2 +, then 2. Qxg2 Bxg2 3. Rxf8# is a back-rank mate.

Diagram 682 Capablanca–Tanarov, New York 1910. **1. Qg3xe5! Qc7xe5 2. Nh6xf7 +** (double attack) **2. ... Kh8-g8** (if 2. ... Rxf7, then 3. Rd8 + Qe8 4. Rxe8 + Rf8 5. Rxf8# is a a back-rank mate). **3. Nf7xe5** and Black resigned.

Diagram 683 White to play wins as follows: **1. Kg5-f6 Kg8-f8 2. f4-f5 Kf8-e8** (if 2. ... Kg8, then 3. Ke7) **3. Kf6-g7** and the pawn will queen by force.

Black to play draws: **1. ... Kg8-g7!** (taking the opposition) **2. Kg5-f5 Kg7-f7** (again the opposition) **3. Kf5-e5 Kf7-e7** (still keeping the opposition) **4. f4-f5 Ke7-f7 5. f5-f6 Kf7-f8 6. Ke5-e6 Kf8-e8** (the opposition) **7. f6-f7 + Ke8-f8 8. Ke6-f6 stalemate.**

Test Three Answers

Diagram 684 No, Black cannot win the pawn on e4; if **1. ... Nf6xe4**, then **2. Rd6xc6! Rc8xc6 3. Re1xe4** (an equal trade); if **1. ... Bc6xe4**, then **2. Rd6xf6! g7xf6 3. Re1xe4**, and again the trade has been equal, each side having lost six points forth of material.

Diagram 685 Hasenfus–Flohr, Latvia 1937. **1. ... Qf6-g5 + 2. Kg2-h1** (if 2. Kh3, then 2. ... Qg4#) **2. ... Qg5xd2** (the N on f3 is pinned; White resigned).

Diagram 686 Stahlberg–Saemisch. **1. Qh5-g6 +!** Black resigned, since if 1. ... Qxg6 (or else 2. Qxh6 + follows), then 2. f5xg6 + (fork) 2. ... any 3. g6xf7.

Diagram 687 **1. Qf1-f6 +! e7xf6 2. e5xf6 +** (or 2. gxf6 +) **2. ... Kg7-g8 3. Rh2xh8#.**

Diagram 688 Eve–Loman, Rotterdam 1923. **1. ... Bg7xd4?? 2. Qh3-h8 + Bd4xh8 3. Rh1xh8#.**

Diagram 689 1. ... Kc5-c4 (putting White in Zugzwang) 2. Kb2-a1 b3-b2+!! 3. Ka1xa2 (if 3. Kxb2, then 3. ... a1Q+ 4. Kxa1 Kb3 5. Kb1 — taking the opposition — 5. ... Ka3 6. Ka1 — keeping the opposition — 6. ... b3 7. Kb1 b2 8. Kc2 Ka2 and Black wins) 3. ... b2-b1Q+! 4. Ka2xb1 Kc4-b3 (taking the opposition) 5. Kb1-c1 (if 5. Ka1, then 5. ... Kc2) 5. ... Kb3-a2 and the pawn will queen by force.

Test Four Answers

Diagram 690 1. Qd6xd4! (if 1. Qxd8, then 1. ... Qxd8; if 1. cxb6, then 1. ... Rxd6) 1. ... Rd8xd4 2. c5xb6.

Diagram 691 1. ... Bd5-e4? (double attack) 2. Rh7-h8+ (an in-between check) 2. ... Kb8-b7 3. Nb5-d6+ (fork) any 4. Nd6xe4.

Diagram 692 Pirc–Stolz, Prague 1931. 1. ... Qa3-a1+ (a skewer) **White resigned.**
   If 2. Ke2, then 2. ... Qxh1;
   if 2. Qd1, then 2. ... Qxc3+;
   if 2. Nd1, then 2. ... Qxd4 (the pawn on e3 is pinned).

Diagram 693 Keres–Levenfish, Moscow 1949. 1. Qd2xb4! **Black resigned.**
   If 1. ... Rxb4, then 2. Rc8+ Ng8 (or 2. ... Nxc8 3. Re8# — a back rank mate) 3. Re8xg8+! Kh8xg8 4. Re2-e8# (a back-rank mate).
   If 1. ... Re8, then 2. Qxe7 Rxe7 3. Rc8+ Re8 4. Rxe8#

Diagram 694 Morphy–Amateur, New York 1857. 1. Rf3-f8+! Qe8xf8 2. Rf1xf8+ Ra8xf8 3. Qh6xg6# (an epaulette mate).

Diagram 695 White to play: 1. Ke5-e6! (taking the opposition) 1. ... Ke8-d8 (if 1. ... Kf8, then 2. Kd7 Kf7 3. Kc7) 2. Ke6-d6 (opposition) 2. ... Kd8-c8 (if 2. ... Ke8, then 3. Kc7) 3. Kd6-e7 and the pawn queens by force.
   Black to move draws: 1. ... Ke8-e7! (taking the opposition) 2. d5-d6+ Ke7-d7 3. Ke5-d5 Kd7-d8! 4. Kd5-e6 (if 4. Kc6, then 4. ...Kc8!, keeping the opposition) 4. ... Kd8-e8! (opposition) 5. d6-d7+ Ke8-d8 6. Ke6-d6 stalemate.

Test Five Answers

Diagram 696 1. 0-0 Kh3-g3 2. Rf1-f3#

Diagram 697 Makogonov–Chehover. 1. ... Qg4-h4+! (a double attack; the White Queen is pinned). White resigned, since after 2. any there follows 2. ... Qxf6.

Diagram 698 Morphy–Mongredien, Paris 1859. 1. Qc4-b4! (a double attack). Black resigned, since if 1. ... Nd7 (1. ... Qxb4 leads to a back-rank mate: 2. Re8+ Qf8 3. Rxf8#), then 2. Qxb7.

Diagram 699 Alekhine–Bogoljubow, Match, Berlin 1929. 1. ... Qd3-e4! (a double attack). White resigned, since if 2. Rxe4, then 2. ... Rc1+ 3. Re1 Rxe1# is a back-rank mate, while 2. Qb1 is met by 2. ... Qxa4.

Diagram 700 Vladimirov–Bobotsov, 1966. 1. Qh4-h8+!. Black resigned, since if 1. ... Bxh8 (if 1. ... Ke7, then 2. Qe8#), then 2. Rg8+ Ke7 3. Re8#.

Diagram 701 White to play wins by 1. a3-a4, since the Black King cannot enter the square of the pawn: 1. ... Kg3-f4 2. a4-a5 Kf4-e5 3. a5-a6 Ke5-d5 4. a6-a7 Kd5-c6 5. a7-a8Q+.
   Black to play will stop the pawn since his King can enter the square of the pawn by 1. ... Kg3-f3, e.g.: 2. a3-a4 Kf3-e4 3. a4-a5 Ke4-d5 4. a5-a6 Kd5-c6 5. a6-a7 Kc6-b7 6. a7-a8Q+ Kb7xa8.

Test Six Answers

Diagram 702 Keres–Holmov, Moscow 1948. 1. ... Qh3-g4+! (double attack) 2. f3xg4 stalemate (or else Black plays 2. ... Qxa4, winning back his pawn, after which the game should be a draw).

Diagram 703 Morphy–Bogier, Paris 1858. Black is faced with a double attack on the Bishop on d7 and the pawn on h6; if he saves the Bishop by 1. ... Bxe6, then 2. Rxh6+ gxh6 3. Qxh6#.

Diagram 704 Chekhover–Kasparyan, Moscow 1936. **1. ... Nf6xe4!** The pawn on f3 is pinned: if 2. fxe4, then 2. ... Bxe2. If 2. Qxe4, then 2. ... Bg6 pins and wins the White Queen.

Diagram 705 **1. Kf6-e6!** (a double attack! The Rook is attacked and 2. Rh8# is threatened at the same time!) **1. ... Ke8-f8 2. Ke6xd5.**

Diagram 706 Romanovski–Rohlin, Moscow 1927. **1. Qh5-g6!** (threatening 2. Qh7#). Black resigned.
If 1. ... hxg5, then 2. Qh5#;
if 1. ... Qd3, then 2. Nf7#.

Diagram 707 **1. Kd4-e5 Ke8-e7** (opposition: if 1. ... Kf8, then 2. Kf6 with the opposition) **2. Ke5-f5 Ke7-e8 3. Kf5-e6** (opposition) **3. ... Ke8-f8 4. Ke6-f6** (opposition) **4. ... Kf8-g8 5. g6-g7 Kg8-h7 6. Kf6-f7** and the pawn will queen by force.

Test Seven Answers

Diagram 708 Gurgenidze–Suetin, Moscow 1961. **1. Rf7xh7+! Kh6xh7 2. Qe8-h8+! Kh7xh8 stalemate.**

Diagram 709 Chigorin–Janowski, Paris 1900. **1. Qc3-c5!** Black resigned because of the double threat of capturing the Bishop on f5 and 2. Qf8#.

Diagram 710 **1. Rc5-d5!** 1. Rc4 would not save the piece, because of 1. ... c5 2. Rxc5 Rxd4+) **1. ... c6xd5 2. Bd4xf6+** (the unpinned Bishop makes a double attack) **2. ... any 3. Bf6xd8.**

Diagram 711 **1. ... Rd7-d1+! 2. Rb1xd1** (if 2. Nxd1, then 2. ... Qe1# — a back-rank mate) **2. ... Rd8xd1+ 3. Nc3xd1 Qa5-e1#** (a back-rank mate).

Diagram 712 Johanson–Rey, 1935. **1. Rh3-h8+! Kg8xh8 2. Qe8xf8+ Rg7-g8 3. Qf8-h6#.**

Diagram 713 White to play wins as follows: **1. Kc5-c6** (opposition) **1. ... Ke6-e7 2. Kc6-b7 Ke7-d6 3. a2-a4** and the pawn will queen by force.

Black to play draws as follows: **1. ...Ke6-d7 2. Kc5-b6 Kd7-c8 3. Kb6-a7** (if 3. a4, then 3. ... Kb8 [opposition] 4. a5 Ka8 5. a6 Kb8 [opposition] 6. a7+ Ka8 7. Ka6 stalemate) **3. ... Kc8-c7** (opposition) **4. a2-a4 Kc7-c8 5. a4-a5 Kc8-c7** (opposition) **6. a5-a6 Kc7-c8 7. Ka7-a8** (opposition) **7. ... Kc8-c7 8. a6-a7 Kc7-c8 stalemate.**

Test Eight Answers

Diagram 714 Troitzky–Foht, 1896. **1. Qc2-d1+!!** (double attack) **1. ... Qf3xd1 stalemate** (or else 2. Qxf3).

Diagram 715 **1. Rf1-e1?** (pin) **1. ... Ne5-f3+** (double attack) **2. g2xf3 Qe8xe1+.**

Diagram 716 Stolyar–Averbakh, Leningrad 1938. **1. ... Rd8xd1! 2. Re1xd1** (if 2. Qxc6, then 2. ... Rxe1+ 3. Kg2 Rxc6) **2. ... Qc6xg2+ 3. Kh1xg2 Ng4-e3+** (fork) **4. any Ne3xd1.**

Diagram 717 **1. ... Qc2-d1+! 2. Ke1xd1 Rf5-f1#** (back-rank mate).

Diagram 718 **1. Qh2xh7+! Nf8xh7 2. Re1-e8+ Nh7-f8 3. Re8xf8+ Kg8xf8 4. Rh1-h8#** (a back-rank mate).

Diagram 719 White to play: **1. Kd5-e5 Kd7-d8! 2. Ke5-e6 Kd8-e8!** (opposition) **3. d6-d7+ Ke8-d8 4. Ke6-d6 stalemate.**
Black to play: **1. ... Kd7-d8! 2. Kd5-c6 Kd8-c8** (opposition) **3. d6-d7+ Kc8-d8 4. Kc6-d6 stalemate.**

Test Nine Answers

Diagram 720 Emanuel Lasker–Lisitsyn, Moscow 1935. Black draws by perpetual check: **1. ... Qf4xf2+ 2. Kg1-h1 Qf2-h4+ 3. Kh1-g1 Qh4-e1+ 4. Kg1-h2 Qe1-h4+** (if Black doesn't take the perpetual check, White will queen his pawn on d7.)

Diagram 721 **1. g2-g4** A double attack. The Rook is attacked and at the same time the fork 2. g5+ is threatened.

283

Diagram 722 1. Bc4xf7 + ! Kg8xf7 2. Nf3-e5 + (the Knight escapes from the pin and forks the White King and Bishop) 2. ... any 3. Ne5xg4 Nf6xg4 4. Qd1xg4.

Diagram 723 1. ... Bb3-a2 + 2. Kb1-a1 Rg1xc1# (A back-rank mate.)

Diagram 724 Bronstein–Keres, Budapest 1950. 1. Qg5-h6!. Black resigned. 2. Qg7# is threatened, and 1. ... Qxb1 + would be met by 2. Kh2 Rg8 3. Qxh7 + ! Kxh7 4. Rh4#.

Diagram 725 1. Na6-b4!! (Black was threatening a double attack by 1. ...Kb5. If 1. Nb8, then 1. ... Kb5 2. a6 Kb6 3. Ke5 Ka7 — again a double attack. If 1. Nc7, then 1. ... Kc5 2. Ke5 Kc6 3. N-any Kb5 and the pawn is lost.) 1. ... Kc4-b5 (If 1. ... Kxb4, then 2. a6 and the pawn will queen.) 2. a5-a6 Kb5-b6 3. Kf4-e5 Kb6-a7 4. Ke5-d6 Ka7-b6 (opposition) 5. Kd6-d7 Kb6-a7 6. Kd7-c6 Ka7-a8 (opposition) 7. Kc6-b6 Ka8-b8 (opposition) 8. Nb4-d5 Kb8-a8 9. Nd5-c7 + Ka8-b8 (opposition) 10. a6-a7 + and the pawn will queen.

Test Ten Answers

Diagram 726 1. Kg3-h4! any 2. g2-g3! any stalemate.

Diagram 727 1. Ng5xe6 f7xe6 2. Qd1-h5 + (double attack) 2. ... any 3. Qh5xc5.

Diagram 728 Black can save his Queen after 1. ... Nf8-e6 + (an in-between check).

Diagram 729 1. ... Qf1xb1 + ! 2. Ka1xb1 (the Rook on b2 is pinned) 2. ... Rd8-d1# (a back-rank mate).

Diagram 730 Verlinski–Yuhtman, USSR 1949. 1. Rg5-g7! Black resigned. The threat is 2. Rxh7# (Arab mate). 1. ... Qb1 would be met by 2. Rg8 + Rxg8 3. Rxg8# (Arab mate), while if 1. ... Ra7, then 2. Rg8 + Qxg8 3. Rxg8#, again with an Arab mate.

Diagram 731 1. d3-d4! (If 1. Kg4, then 1. ... Kc5 2. Kf5 Kxd5 and Black should draw with

284

correct play) 1. ... Kb5-b6 2. Kh3-g4 Kb6-c7 3. Kg4-f5 Kc7-d6 4. Kf5-e4 Kd6-d7 5. Ke4-e5 Kd7-e7 (opposition) 6. d5-d6 + Ke7-d7 7. Ke5-d5 (opposition) 7. ... Kd7-d8 8. Kd5-c6 Kd8-c8 9. d6-d7 + Kc8-d8 10. d4-d5! Kd8-e7 11. Kc6-c7 and the pawn will queen.

Test Eleven Answers

Diagram 732 1. ... Rf1xf6 + (double attack) 2. Qf8xf6 stalemate (or else 2. ... Rxf8 would follow).

Diagram 733 Black loses in Bishop in all variations:

1. ... Ba2 (or 1. ... Ba4) 2. Ra6 + (double attack);

1. ... Bf7 2. Rd8 + any 3. Rd7 + (double attack);

1. ... Bg8 2. Rd8 + (double attack).

Diagram 734 1. Rc4-c5 + (a double attack; the Bishop on b6 is pinned) 1. ... Rd5xc5 (or else 2. Qxd5) 2. Qd8xd3 (the Rook on d5 was also pinned. Black has lost a Queen for a Rook).

Diagram 735 1. Re3xe6! Rf7-f8! (if 1. ... Rxe6, then 2. Qd8 + Qe8 3. Qxe8 + Rxe8 4. Rxe8 + Rf8 5. Rxf8# [a back-rank mate]) 2. Qd4-e5 and White has won a pawn. But White must not play 2. Rxc6, for Black would then win a Rook by 2. ... Rxe1 + 3. Qg1 Rxg1 + 4. Kxg1 bxc6.

Diagram 736 Kramstov–Vaisberg, USSR 1938. 1. Rd7xb7 + ! Kb8xb7 (the Bishop on c8 was pinned) 2. Qd8-b6# (an epaulette mate).

Diagram 737 With White to play, the game should be drawn: 1. Kf6-g5 (or 1. g7 + Kg8 2. Kg6 stalemate; or 1. Kf7 stalemate) 1. ... Kh8-g7 2. Kg5-h5 Kg7-g8 3. Kh5-h6 Kg8-h8 (opposition) 4. g6-g7 + Kh8-g8 5. Kh6-g6 stalemate.

With Black to play, White wins: 1. ... Kh8-g8 2. g6-g7 Kg8-h7 3. Kf6-f7 and the pawn will queen.

Test Twelve Answers

Diagram 738 This is a problem by Sam

Loyd. Black is in Zugzwang — every move of his allows White to mate him immediately:

1. 1. ... Bb7 2. Nf5#;
2. 1. ... Bd7 2. Qd5#;
3. 1. ... Be6 1. Qe5#;
4. 1. ... Bf5 2. Nxf5#;
5. 1. ... Rd7 2. Nf5#;
6. 1. ... Rd6 2. Qxb4#;
7. 1. ... Rd5 2. Qxd5#;
8. 1. ... Re7 2. Qxb4#;
9. 1. ... Re6 2. Nf5#;
10. 1. ... Re5 2. Qxe5#;
11. 1. ... Bc5 2. Qa1#;
12. 1. ... Bd6 2. Qd5#;
13. 1. ... Be7 2. Qe5#;
14. 1. ... Bg7 2. Qb6#;
15. 1. ... Bh6 2. Qb6#.

Diagram 739 Mikenas—Pelts, Leningrad 1969. **1. ... Qd8xd4!** (double attack on the Bishop and the pawn on b2) **2. Qd3xd4 Ne3xc2 +** (fork) **3. any Nc2xd4.**

Diagram 740 **1. Rg6xg7!** (the Black Queen and the Rook on g8 are pinned) **1. ... Rg8xh8** (or else 2. Rhxg8#) **2. Qf6xf7#.**

Diagram 741 Taimanov–Kotov, Moscow 1948. **1. Ng3xh5?? Bf4-e3 +** White resigned. (2. any Rg1#).

Diagram 742 White to play: **1. Qc1-g5! g7-g6 2. Qg5-h6 Ra8-a1 + 3. Kb1xa1 Qe8-a8 + 4. Ka1-b1 Qa8-a2 + 5. Kb1-c1 Qa2-a1 + 6. Kc1-d2 Qa1-a5 + 7. c2-c3 Qa5xc3 + 8. b2xc3 any 9. Qh6-g7#.**
Black to play: **1. ... Ra8-a1 +! 2. Kb1xa1 Qe8-a8 + 3. Ka1-b1 Qa8-a2#.**

Diagram 743 White to play: **1. Kd5-e6 Kh7-g7 2. Ke6-e7 Kg7-h7 3. Ke7-f6** (3. f8Q?? is stalemate) **3. ... Kh7-h6 4. f7-f8Q +** etc.
Black to play draws: **1. ... Kh7-g7 2. Kd5-e6 Kg7-f8** (White is now in Zugzwang) **3. Ke6-f5** (3. Kf6 or 3. h6 is stalemate) **3. ... Kf8xf7** (opposition) **4. h5-h6 Kf7-g8 5. Kf5-g6** (opposition) **5. ... Kg8-h8 6. h6-h7** stalemate.

Test Thirteen Answers

Diagram 744 **1. Nb7-c5 +** (or 1. Nd6 +) **1. ...**

Ke4-d5 2. Qc3-f3 +! (skewer) **2. ... any 3. Qf3xa8.**

Diagram 745 Amateur-Leonhardt, Leipzig 1903. **1. ... Bc5xf2 +! 2. Qg3xf2** (if 2. Kxf2, then 2. ... Nxe4 + [fork] 3. any Nxg3) **2. ... Ne5-d3 +** (fork) **3. any Nd3xf2.**

Diagram 746 **1. Kh3-g4! Rh8xh6 3. Kg4-g5!** (double attack) **2. ... Rh6-h2 3. Kg5xg6.**

Diagram 747 **1. Bf1-c4 + Kf7-f8 2. Rd1-d8#.**

Diagram 748 Kan–Alatortsev, Leningrad 1951. If **1. ... Bxg2??**, then **2. Ne7 +! Kh8 3. Qxh7 +! Kxh7 4. Rh4 + Qh5 5. Rxh5#** (Anastasia's mate).

Diagram 749 The position is drawn no matter who plays first. **1. Kd5xe5 Kf8-e7!** (opposition) **2. Ke5-d5 Ke7-d7** (opposition) **3. e4-e5 Kd7-e7 4. e5-e6 Ke7-e8 5. Kd5-d6 Ke8-d8** (opposition) **6. e6-e7 + Kd8-e8 7. Kd6-e6** stalemate.

Test Fourteen Answers

Diagram 750 White draws by perpetual check:

1. Qh3-c8 +	Rb7-b8
2. Qc8-c6 +	Rb8-b7
3. Qc6-c8 +	Rb7-b8
4. Qc8-c6	Rb8-b7
5. Qc6-c8 +	

Diagram 751 **1. Re1xe5 +** (double attack) **1. ... Rd5xe5 2. f2-f4 +!** (fork) **2. ... Kg5-f5 3. f4xe5 Kf5xe5 4. Kg2-h3! Ke5-f5** (opposition) **5. Kh3-h4! Kf5-g6 6. Kh4-g4!** and with correct play White should win, since his King has the opposition in front of his pawn.

Diagram 752 **1. ... Qc7-c1 +! 2. Rh1xc1** (the Knight and Rook on b2 are pinned) **2. ...Rc8xc1#** (a back-rank mate).

Diagram 753 **1. Re4-e8 +! Kf8xe8 2. Rg2-g8#** (a back-rank mate).

Diagram 754 Duras–Olland, Karlsbad 1907. **1. Qh4xh5 +! g6xh5 2. Rd6-h6#.**

Diagram 755   1. Kf3-f4! (if 1. Ke4, then 1. ... Kd6 puts White in Zugzwang: 2. any Kxd5 and Black should draw with correct play.) 1. ... Ke7-d6 (opposition) 2. Kf4-e4 (now it is Black who is in Zugzwang) 2. ... Kd6-d7 3. Ke4-e5 Kd7-e7 (opposition) 4. d5-d6+ Ke7-d7 5. Ke5-d5 Kd7-d8 6. Kd5-e6 Kd8-e8 (opposition) 7. d6-d7+ Ke8-d8 8. d4-d5! (a waiting move) 8. ...Kd8-c7 9. Ke6-e7 and the pawn will queen by force.

Test Fifteen Answers

Diagram 756   1. Ra1-a8! (threatening 2. g8Q) 1. ... Rg2xg7 2. Ra8-a7+ (skewer) 2. ... any 3. Ra7xg7.

Diagram 757   1. e4-e5+ (a fork) 1. ... Qd6xe5 (or 1. ... Kxe5 2. Nc4+ [fork] 2. ... any 3. Nxd6) 2. Ne3-g4+ (fork) 2. ... any 3. Ng4xe5.

Diagram 758   1. Qh5-g6! (the pawn on f7 is pinned) 1. ... any 2. Qg6-h7#.

Diagram 759   1. Qe7xf8+! Kg8xf8 (or else 2. Qg7# would follow) 2. Rd1-d8# (a back-rank mate).

Diagram 760   Kolisch–Loyd, Paris 1867. 1. Qg3xg6!! h7xg6? 2. Rf1-f3 Black resigned, since 3. Rh3# (Greco's mate) is threatened and if 2. ... Re6, then 3. Bxe6 Qf7 4. Bxf7 any 5. Rh3# (Greco's mate).

Diagram 761   This is a position of mutual Zugzwang. If White starts, Black draws, while if Black moves first, White queens his pawn and wins.

With White to move: 1. Kh7-h8 Kf7-f8! (opposition) 2. f6-f7 (or 2. h7 Kf7 stalemate) 2. ... Kf8xf7 3. Kh8-h7 (opposition; if 3. h7, then 3. ... Kf8 stalemate) 3. ... Kf7-f8 4. Kh7-g6 Kf8-g8 (opposition) 5. h6-h7+ Kg8-h8 6. Kg6-h6 stalemate.

With Black to move: 1. ... Kf7-f8 (or 1. ... Kxf6 2. Kg8) 2. Kh7-g6 Kf8-g8 (opposition) 3. f6-f7+ Kg8-f8 4. h6-h7 and the h-pawn will queen.

Test Sixteen Answers

Diagram 762   No, White cannot win a piece. If 1. Rf2? (skewer), then 1. ... Bh4 (counter skewer) 2. Rxf3 Bxe1 and White has lost an Exchange.

Diagram 763   1. Rb6xc6! Rc7-d7 (the Bishop on d5 is pinned, while 1. ... Rxc6 is met by the fork 2. Bxd5+ winning a Bishop and a Rook. If 1. ... Bxa2, then 2. Rxc7) 2. Rc6-c8+ (White has won a pawn by his combination).

Diagram 764   1. Re1-e6! (a counter pin) saves the piece.

Diagram 765   1. Qb7-b1+! Kc1xb1 Rd8-d1# (a back-rank mate).

Diagram 766   Delva–Pelts, Ottawa 1981. 1. ... Rf8-f3!! White resigned. 2. Bxf3 is met by 2. ... Qxh4# and 2. Rxf3 by 2. ... Qg2#.

Diagram 767   White to play: 1. b7-b8Q+! (not 1. Kc7 stalemate or 1. b6+ Kb8 2. Kc5 Kxb7 3. Kb5 Kb8 4. Kc6 Kc8 [opposition] 5. b7+ Kb8 6. Kb6 stalemate) 1. ... Kxb8 2. Kc6-b6! (opposition) 2. ... Kb8-a8 (or 2. ...Kc8 3. Ka7) 3. Kb6-c7 and the pawn queens by force.

Black to play draws: 1. ... Ka7-b8 (White is now in Zugzwang) 2. Kc6-c5 (if 2. Kb6 or 2. b6 it is stalemate) 2. ... Kb8xb7 3. b5-b6 Kb7-b8 4. Kc5-c6 Kb8-c8 (opposition) 5. b6-b7+ Kc8-b8 6. Kc6-b6 stalemate.

Test Seventeen Answers

Diagram 768   1. Qd1-h5+ Kf7xf6 2. Qh5-h4+! (skewer) 2. ... any 3. Qh4xd8.

Diagram 769   1. Bf1-b5! (pin) 1. ... Qc6xb5 2. Nd5-c7+ (fork) 2. ... any 3. Nc7xb5.

Diagram 770   1. Rd3xd6! Re6xd6 (now the Rook is pinned) 2. e4-e5 any 3. Ba3xd6.

Diagram 771   1. Nd5-c7+! Ne6xc7 2. Rd3-d8# (back-rank mate).

Diagram 772 1. Qh3-b3 +!! Qb8xb3 (or 1. ... Kh7 2. Qxb8 Rh2 + 3. Qxh2 Rxh2 + 4. Kxh2) 2. Re1-e8 + Kg8-f7 (or 2. ... Kh7 3. Rh8#) 3. Re8-f8#.

Diagram 773 White to play: 1. b6-b7 Kb8-a7 2. b7-b8Q +! (not 2. Kc7 stalemate or 2. b6 + Kb8 3. Kc5 Kxb7 4. Kb5 Kb8 5. Kc6 Kc8 [opposition] 6. b7 + Kb8 7. Kb6 stalemate) 2. ... Ka7xb8 3. Kc6-b6! (opposition) 3. ... Kb8-a8 (or 3. ... Kc8 4. Ka7) 4. Kb6-c7 and the pawn will queen by force.

Black to play draws: 1. ... Kb8-a8 (or 1. ... Kc8) 2. b6-b7 + (2. Kc7 gives a stalemate) 2. ... Ka8-b8 (White is now in Zugzwang) 3. Kc6-c5 (after 3. Kb6 or 3. b6 it is stalemate) 3. ... Kb8xb7 4. b5-b6 Kb7-b8 5. Kc5-c6 Kb8-c8 (opposition) 6. b6-b7 + Kc8-b8 7. Kc6-b6 stalemate.

Test Eighteen Answers

Diagram 774 1. h6-h7 Qg3-h2 2. h7-h8Q +! Qh2xh8 3. Ra7-a8 + (skewer) 3. ... any 4. Ra8xh8.

Diagram 775 1. Qc4xe6! Qd7xe6 (or else 2 Qe8 followed by 3. f8Q) 2. f7-f8N +! any 3. Nf8xe6.

Diagram 776 White saves the piece by playing 1. Nd4-f5!. Then 1. ... Bxb2 is met by 2. Nxh6 (an even trade) while 1. ...Nxf5 is met by 2. Bxf6 + (also an even trade).

Diagram 777 Black can defend his back rank by playing 1. ... Rd7-d8! and now 2. Rc8xa8 can be met by 2. ... Rd8xa8 while if 2. Rc8xd8, then 2. ... Ra8xd8. But 1. ... Rxc8 would lose to 2. Rxc8 + Rd8 3. Rxd8# (back-rank mate).

Diagram 778 Composed by Kubbel. White to play: 1. Rh3xh7 +! Kh8xh7 2. Qe6-h3 + Bf6-h4 3. Qh3xh4 + Qc5-h5 4. Qh4xh5# (Greco's mate).

Black to play: 1. ... Qc5xf2 +!! 2. Rf1xf2 (or else 2. ... Qxf1# [back-rank mate]) 2. ... Rb2-b1 + 3. Rf2-f1 Bf6-d4 + 4. Rh3-e3 Bd4xe3 + 5. Kg1-h1 Rb1xf1# (back-rank mate).

Diagram 779 White to play: 1. Ka7-a6 (opposition; if 1. Ka8 or 1. Kb8, then 1. ...Kb5, while if 1. a6, then 1. ... Kc7 [opposition] 2. Ka8 Kc8 [opposition] 3. a7 Kc7 stalemate) 1. ... Kc6-c7 2. Ka6-b5 2. ... Kc7-b7 (opposition) 3. a5-a6 + Kb7-a7 4. Kb5-a5 Ka7-b8 5. Ka5-b6 (opposition) 5. ... Kb8-a8 6. a6-a7 stalemate.

Black to play: 1. ... Kc6-c7 (opposition) 2. a5-a6 (if 2. Ka8, then 2. ...Kc8 [opposition]; if 2. Ka6, then 2. ...Kc6 [opposition]) 2. ... Kc7-c8 3. Ka7-b6 (if 3. Ka8 [opposition], then 3. ...Kc7 4. a7 Kc8 stalemate) 3. ... Kc8-b8 (opposition) 4. a6-a7 + Kb8-a8 5. Kb6-a6 stalemate.

Test Nineteen Answers

Diagram 780 1. Bc1-g5 + (skewer) 1. ... f7-f6 (or else 2. Rxd8#) 2. e5xf6 + g7xf6 (if 2. ... Ke8, then 3. f7 + [in-between check] followed by 4. Rxd8) 3. Bg5xf6 +! Ke7xf6 4. Rd1xd8 and White has won the Exchange and a pawn.

Diagram 781 1. Nh4-g6 + Kh8-h7 2. Ng6-f8 + (fork) 2. ... Kh7-h8 3. Nf8xe6 (fork).

Diagram 782 1. Qd1xh5 + (the pawn on g6 is pinned) 1. ... Kh7-g8 2. Qh5-h8#.

Diagram 783 1. Qf3-f8 +! Rb8xf8 2. Rf2xf8 + Ra8xf8 3. Rf1xf8# (back-rank mate).

Diagram 784

solution a): 1. ... Qb6-b1 + 2. Rg1xb1 Rb7xb1 + 3. Rh1xb1 Rb8xb1#.

solution b): 1. ... Qb6xg1 +! 2. Rh1xg1 Rb7-b1 + 3. Rg1xb1 Rb8xb1#.

Diagram 785 White to play: 1. Kf4-e5 (or 1. Kf5 Kg7 and White is in Zugzwang: 2. any Kxg6 and Black should draw with correct play) 1. ... Kg8-g7 2. Ke5-f5 Kg7-g8! 3. Kf5-f6 Kg8-h8 (or 3. ...Kf8 [opposition]) 4. g6-g7 + (or 4. Kf7 stalemate) 4. ... Kh8-g8 5. Kf6-f5 (after 5. g6 or 5. Kg6 it is stalemate) 5. ... Kg8xg7 6. g5-g6 Kg7-g8 7. Kf5-f6 Kg8-h8 (or 7. ... Kf8 [opposition]) 8. g6-g7 + (or 8. Kf7 stalemate) 8. ... Kh8-g8 9. Kf6-g6 stalemate. Black to play draws in an analogous manner.

Test Twenty Answers

Diagram 786 1. ...Rc7-c2! (pin) 2. Qd2xc2 Qb8-h2 + (skewer) 3. any Qh2xc2.

Diagram 787 1. Qe2-e4! (with the double threat of 2. Qh7# and 2. Qxa8) 1. ... g7-g6 2. Qe4xa8.

Diagram 788 White saves his pinned Knight as follows: 1. Nd4-e6! Rd7xd3 (or 1. ... fxe6 2. Rxd7) 2. Ne6xc5 + (fork) 2. ... any 3. Nc5xd3.

Diagram 789 1. Rc8-h8 + Bg7xh8 2. Qe5xh8#.

Diagram 790 Gutop–Roshal, Moscow 1963. 1. ... Qd6xd5!! (threatening 2. ... Qxg2#) 2. Bg2xd5 Bb7xd5 (the pawn on f2 is pinned and so White has no defense against 3. ... Rh1#). White resigned.

Diagram 791 White to play: 1. Ke4-f5 Kg8-g7 2. Kf5-g5 (2. g5? leads to a draw) 2. ... Kg7-g8 3. Kg5-h6 Kg8-h8 (opposition) 4. g6-g7 + Kh8-g8 5. g4-g5! (a waiting move: the immediate 5. Kg6 gives stalemate) 5. ... Kg8-f7 6. Kh6-h7 and the pawn will queen by force.

Black to play: 1. ... Kg8-g7 2. Ke4-f5 Kg7-h6! 3. g6-g7! (3. Kf6 gives stalemate; 3. g5? leads to a drawn position after 3. ... Kg7) 3. ... Kh6xg7 4. Kf5-g5 (opposition) 4. ... Kg7-f7 (or 4. ... Kh7 5. Kf6) 5. Kg5-h6 Kf7-g8 6. g4-g5 Kg8-h8 (opposition) 7. g5-g6 Kh8-g8 8. g6-g7 Kg8-f7 9. Kh6-h7 and the pawn queens by force.

Solution to the diagrammed position on the back cover:
a) White to play draws by playing 1. f4 Ke4 2. Kg2 Kxf4 3. Kf2 (see p. 176, notes to D-450).
b) Black to play wins: 1. ... f4! (Natural looking 1. ... Ke3 misses the win because of 2. f4, and later, as above), and Black eventually wins the pawn on f3 and then the game (D-449, pages 174 and 176).